Ius Gentium: Comparative Perspectives on Law and Justice

Volume 97

Ius Gentium is a book series which discusses the central questions of law and justice from a comparative perspective. The books in this series collect the contrasting and overlapping perspectives of lawyers, judges, philosophers and scholars of law from the world's many different jurisdictions for the purposes of comparison, harmonisation, and the progressive development of law and legal institutions. Each volume makes a new comparative study of an important area of law. This book series continues the work of the well-known journal of the same name and provides the basis for a better understanding of all areas of legal science.

The *Ius Gentium* series provides a valuable resource for lawyers, judges, legislators, scholars, and both graduate students and researchers in globalisation, comparative law, legal theory and legal practice. The series has a special focus on the development of international legal standards and transnational legal cooperation.

Ricardo Lillo Lobos

Understanding Due Process in Non-Criminal Matters

How to Harmonize Procedural Guarantees with the Right to Access to Justice

Springer

Ricardo Lillo Lobos
School of Law
Universidad Adolfo Ibañez
Santiago, Chile

ISSN 1534-6781 ISSN 2214-9902 (electronic)
Ius Gentium: Comparative Perspectives on Law and Justice
ISBN 978-3-030-95533-5 ISBN 978-3-030-95534-2 (eBook)
https://doi.org/10.1007/978-3-030-95534-2

This Springer imprint is published by the registered company Springer Nature Switzerland AG
The registered company address is: Gewerbestrasse 11, 6330 Cham, Switzerland

To Shantal.
The love of my life.
For Domingo, Isidora, and Raimundo.
My whole life.

Foreword

Due process is one of the most fundamental and cherished legal concepts and values of our time. Yet, courts and commentators have underexplored and untheorized what due process requires in civil cases. This important and original book contributes to fill this vacuum.

The central argument of this book is that due process should be thought of not in parallel to, but in conjunction with, access to justice—another fundamental and cherished legal concept and value. Legal systems do not have unlimited resources and deal with various and very different types of legal cases—e.g., small-and-big-claim, low-and-high-complexity, and criminal-and-noncriminal cases. The argument of this book is that if wrongly conceptualized and defined, due process requirements may make impossible in many cases that people who need the courts or other mechanisms to protect their rights, interests, and well-being get access to these bodies and the justice they provide. This book then offers a framework within which both due process and access to justice can be properly integrated with each other and advanced. In this regard, this book speaks not only to academics, but also to policy makers who design, regulate, and administer the legal process—particularly, noncriminal proceedings.

To flesh out and substantiate this argument, this book uses a wide and sophisticated set of tools and makes various analytical, comparative, and empirical contributions, each of them insightful and important on their own right. Analytically, the book articulates two conceptions of due process. The first is the checklist model under which due process is a legal rule that requires a strict minimum specific set of conditions that are decided ex ante by a rule-making authority and that apply to broad categories of legal cases. The second conception is the flexible model under which due process is a legal principle whose content is defined on a case-by-case basis depending on the details of each case. The book conceives of these two models as ideal types that create a continuum that the book then uses to classify conceptions of due process in jurisdictions and adjudicative bodies in Europe, Latin America, and the USA. But these powerful analytical tools could be applied and shed light on other jurisdictions and due process regulations beyond the ones this book covers.

Using this combination of analytical, comparative, and empirical approaches, the book discusses noncriminal/nonpunitive conceptions of due process in Latin America, in Chile and California, in the European and the Inter-American systems of human rights, and in the USA. Each of these specific comparisons, empirical studies, and conceptual and legal analyses is enlightening not only to advance this book's central argument, but to understand these jurisdictions.

Regarding Latin America, one of the book's chapters describes the features of traditional Latin American civil procedure, how they have differed from civil procedure in Europe, recent civil procedure reforms and reform attempts in the region—including those prompted by the Iberian-American Model Code of Civil Procedure, and how they relate to what has been called the crisis of civil justice and to the access-to-justice movement around the world. In relation to its main argument, the book also explains that the Model Code has been criticized, among other reasons because it establishes a common procedural regulation for all noncriminal cases that include only three types of proceedings: ordinary, extraordinary, and the order for payment procedure, without leaving room for special courts or venues to deal with certain cases and to address certain problems of social justice.

Another chapter of the book also includes a fascinating and illuminating comparison between civil justice in California and Chile, showing how each of these jurisdictions would deal differently with a concrete hypothetical case. This comparative examination includes not only legal analysis but also two empirical studies that Ricardo Lillo made of the Small Claims Court of Los Angeles, California, and the Civil Courts of Santiago, Chile. His data show they are mostly corporations the ones that use civil procedure in Santiago against individual defendants. Through such a legal and empirical comparison, Ricardo Lillo shows how different conceptions of fair trial can have a substantial impact on civil procedure design and on to what extent human beings with actual legal needs may or may not access justice. The chapter in question is a model that future studies could follow on how the comparative legal analysis of a hypothetical case can be integrated with a comparative empirical analysis of two jurisdictions.

With an impressive analytical and empirical study, the book also examines and compares how the case law of the European Court of Human Rights and that of the Inter-American Court of Human Rights understand fair trial requirements in civil cases in their respective human rights systems. To that effect, Ricardo Lillo created a database from scratch for each of these courts, using his own operational definition of civil justice and of noncriminal and nonpunitive cases, and coded various variables on the characteristics of each case, the main legal issue under discussion, on many dimensions of the right to a fair trial—e.g., effective remedy, equality of arms, independent and impartial, and opportunity to be heard—and on the specific procedural elements analyzed by the court. Ricardo Lillo also originally created and coded various variables to operationalize the checklist and flexible due process models articulated earlier in the book. These variables included, among others, whether the court applies a procedural guarantee from the criminal prong of the clause over noncriminal cases versus whether the court considers the complexity of the case or its particular circumstances as a factor to determine whether a procedural guarantee is required, whether the court interprets the procedural element or dimension as a clear-cut rule versus whether the court considers that a less formalistic approach is required, etc.

His analysis shows that despite the similarities in the texts of the American Convention of Human Rights and the European Convention of Human Rights in their regulation of the right to a fair trial, there are important differences in the case law of the two courts. The case law of the Inter-American Court of Human Rights is located somewhere in between the checklist and the flexible models, but with an important retention of the checklist model. In contrast, the case law of the European Court of Human Rights in civil cases has followed what the book calls a concrete analysis of effectiveness as its main approach, placing its case law closer to the flexible model. The book suggests as possible explanations for these differences the type of cases filed in each system—given that authoritarian governments have been more widespread and lasted longer in Latin America than in Europe after World War II; the larger influence of common law in the European system through the UK cases; and the *margin of appreciation* doctrine by the European Court of Human Rights.

The last case study of the book consists of an analysis of the evolution of procedural due process in noncriminal cases in the USA from its British origins until our day, using the checklist and the flexible models of due process as analytical tools. The analysis also explores why there has not been more case law by the US Supreme Court on what due process requires in noncriminal law cases other than in administrative law ones. The book suggests that the State action doctrine and the lack of a horizontal rights conception theory in the American legal system may help explain the relative paucity of such case law.

The book ends by articulating a theory of due process for noncriminal cases. The first step in this regard is that civil justice needs to escape the shadow of criminal justice regarding due process since these two fields of justice differ in important respects. The differences go beyond the different level of seriousness of the potential consequences of an adverse decision in each of these settings—e.g., deprivation of liberty in criminal justice versus economic consequences in civil justice. The book argues that in civil cases procedural fairness requires not only procedural rights that advance the accuracy of the verdict, but also a basic right to be able to use a legal procedure so that a legal need is satisfied, a dispute is solved, and a right is protected. In that regard, an accurate procedure would still be unfair if it were too costly or ineffective to be useful.

The book further distinguishes between legal processes based on two dimensions. The first is whether the goal of the legal process is dispute resolution or the imposition of a sanction. The second is whether there is high or low imbalance between the parties of the legal process. Using the two continuums created by these two opposing pairs, the book argues that in the criminal realm in which the goal is the imposition of a sanction and there is a high imbalance between public prosecution and defense, due process requires focusing on procedural protections for defendants. In contrast, in nonpunitive legal proceedings in which there is not such a high imbalance, due process requires the right to a court/to access justice as its core requirement. The book argues that such an understanding of procedural due process is consistent with the conception of due process in the national and international jurisdictions discussed in the prior chapters.

Finally, the book argues that to make the right to a court/to access justice a central component of due process in noncriminal cases, the flexible conception of due process should be used to determine what due process requires in specific cases. However, the checklist approach should provide a "minimum floor" that would include, among others, the right to prior notice, to a hearing, and to an independent and impartial tribunal.

As the reader can tell from my short description of the book, this is an ambitious work at multiple levels. It uses various analytical, comparative, empirical, and normative methodologies and arguments in innovative and insightful ways. It covers a remarkable range of jurisdictions in at least three continents, thus providing a picture of how due process is understood in noncriminal matters in substantial portions of the world. The book also makes a crucial theoretical and policy contribution by articulating a theory on what due process requires in noncriminal cases. Like the best theories, the one from this book is consistent with many of the regulations and case law of many of the jurisdictions covered in it, but also enables a critique of them. Finally, the book is not only a crucial contribution to the academic literature, but also provides a framework and roadmap for policy makers.

This book is based on the dissertation that Ricardo Lillo completed as part of the requirements for his Doctor of Juridical Science (S.J.D.) degree at the School of Law of the University of California, Los Angeles, and his joint Ph.D. degree at the School of Law of University Diego Portales, Chile. I had the honor to supervise this dissertation. But the credit for it is Ricardo Lillo's. The book reflects the outstanding quality of his work, his exceptional work ethics and capacity to get things done, his maturity as a scholar despite his youth, and his strong commitment to improving the administration of justice, democracy, and rule of law in Chile, Latin America, and elsewhere.

David G. Price and Dallas P. Price Professor of Law, UCLA School of Law, Los Angeles, CA, USA

President of the American Society of Comparative Law, Los Angeles, CA, USA

Máximo Langer

Preface

How to understand what procedure is due as a fundamental or constitutional right may have a critical impact on designing a civil procedure. Using comparative law and empirically oriented methodologies, I study how procedural due process is understood in national and international jurisdictions. Based on those findings, I argue that non-criminal matters in general, and civil adjudication in particular, require a theoretical basis on which to address the question: what are the basic requirements of due process, as distinct from conceptions that originate in criminal justice?

To propose a theoretical framework, I pursue two types of argument. First, I will use an ideal type approach to explain different conceptions of how due process is understood in different jurisdictions from a practical perspective. Based on my study of national and international notions of due process, I will construct an analytical framework to analyze the concept according to two basic models which I have called the checklist model and the flexible model. After constructing this analytical tool, I will move to a second level analysis, this time normative in character. I will advocate for a theory of procedural due process that is specially designed for legal procedures of a non-punitive nature. The main purpose of this framework is, on the one hand, to reconcile the requirements of procedural fairness with social demands for justice, as expressed by the access to justice movement, and, on the other hand, with the need to distribute the limited resources of the State.

Santiago, Chile
December 2021

Ricardo Lillo Lobos

Acknowledgments

I would like to thank Maximo Langer, who has truly been a mentor since 2013 for his continuous support and for encouraging me into the world of academia. I am very glad that today I can also call him a friend. I would like to express my gratitude to Javier Couso for accepting to be my co-advisor during the long journey that has been my doctorate. I am thankful as well to Joanna Schwartz and Bryant Garth, for their kind and useful comments on my work. I am very thankful to the Office of Graduate Studies and International Programs and the Hugh & Hazel Darling Law Library at UCLA School of Law, and also to the Doctoral Program of Universidad Diego Portales (UDP) Law School staff. I would as well like to thank Carlos Peña and Judith Schönsteiner for serving as committee members at my presentation of research proposals, whose comments were really appreciated for this book. To my mentors and friends at the Procedural Reform and Litigation Program at UDP School of Law: Eduardo Alcaíno, Mauricio Duce, Claudio Fuentes, Alejandra Mera, Cristian Riego, Juan Enrique Vargas, and Macarena Vargas. I would as well like to thank Lidia Casas, Juan Ignacio Contardo, Jaime Couso, Matías Güilloff, Héctor Hernández, Fernando Londoño, Domingo Lovera, Judith Schönsteiner, and all my friends and colleagues who had an opportunity to comment on previous versions or chapters. I would like to express my gratitude to the Dean's Fellowship at UCLA School of Law, to the Doctoral Scholarship provided by UDP, and to Becas Chile for their financial support. Last but not least, to my parents and family for all their support during the years.

Contents

Chapter 1
Introduction

The right to a due process of law is a complex concept for jurisprudence theory. Today, as a legal institution that crosses national boundaries it is considered an element that is inherent in our Western legal tradition. Legally binding in many national constitutions and international instruments, called by different names or shaped by normative provisions when applied to legal procedures, it might be characterized as an attribute of the rule of law, rooted in basic conceptions of justice and fairness.[1] Its complexity comes from the profound philosophical ideas from which it is derived, which in turn originate in different historical and political traditions concerning the relationship between individuals and the State, and specifically the protection of individuals against arbitrary actions by State authorities.[2]

Due process is a complex concept also because it addresses different types of public authority that are mandated to follow its requirements in their relationships with citizens. As such, it applies to legal institutions of adjudicative and legislative capabilities. In this regard, due process and its requirement of a fair legal procedure—two concepts that I will use as synonyms in this book—applies to courts as to other legal institutions. While courts decide cases following a legally established procedure, fair trial standards are mandates directed as much to judges as to legislators. Nevertheless, courts in their adjudicative capacities are important to analyze,[3] and this book might be useful in that regard, its main application is intended to be in the field of legal procedure design.

For this purpose, as an underlying assumption of my work is that during the design of legal proceedings, those in charge of enacting such regulation are mandated to establish and provide safeguards for the requirements of fairness. Such

[1] See, e.g.: Raz (1995), pp. 373–374; Waldron (2011), pp. 3–31, p. 6; Sampford (2005), p. 11.

[2] Miller (1977), p. 3. See also: Galligan (1996), p. 166.

[3] For example, because they are supposed to be impartial and independent third parties that are empowered to review whether another public authority's decision against an individual was arbitrary from a procedural or a substantive perspective. See: Scanlon (1977), pp. 94–106.

R. Lillo Lobos, *Understanding Due Process in Non-Criminal Matters*, Ius Gentium: Comparative Perspectives on Law and Justice 97,
https://doi.org/10.1007/978-3-030-95534-2_1

requirements, as a normative demand on how the State must treat individuals, are expressed not just in the question of which procedural guarantees should be afforded them, but also on the question of the access they should have. This is the key idea that it is intended to be further developed with this book.

Civil justice should be accessible to solve different types of legal needs or disputes, big and small claims, of high or low complexity. And in this regard, how to understand due process and its requirements in civil matters has a critical impact on the design of a civil procedure that provides access to civil justice. The point is that no matter how many procedural guarantees are legally provided, people would use other non-judicial mechanisms or no mechanisms at all to satisfy their legal needs if they believe the proceeding would take too much time or money, or in general if a procedure is perceived to be ineffective.

The contribution intended in this book is to provide a normative theory based on empirical considerations. As such, I provide a theoretical framework that allows procedural fairness requirements to be reconciled with social demands for justice and the need to distribute limited resources, without detracting from the goal of accuracy inherent to any legal procedure. This framework is relevant because in the literature that calls for an improvement of access to civil justice it is not clear what might be sacrificed to successfully meet this goal without compromising the right to a fair legal procedure. In other words, to provide an answer to the question of which procedural guarantees should be afforded as a matter of basic protection, and how this should be decided.

Suggesting answers to this question may be useful for judicial reform and policy decisions. At the very least, it may clarify our thinking about what we may be sacrificing by fulfilling the goal of providing a more flexible, speedy, and in general accessible, civil procedure. As a former researcher at an international organization working on judicial reform and access to justice, I have found that while the literature on this subject calls for simpler legal proceedings, there is a common resistance in terms that this type of mechanisms would be against the right to a fair trial. For many former or current practitioners working on academia or government I met along the way, due process would serve as a wall against this type of arguments. As such, while access to justice problems might be caused by several factors, from a legal theory perspective, my argument is that understanding the requirements of due process in civil proceedings is a critical one. That is why, as said, the main expected contribution of this book is in the field of legal procedure design and it is targeted to those in charge of such responsibility.

To construct this theoretical framework, I use different empirically oriented methodologies. First, however, I describe due process as a complex jurisprudential concept and provide a preliminary version of the two models I will use. The idea is to acknowledge the challenging task ahead while testing the lens through which I will study how due process is applied in practice.

In the second part I justify the research ahead by describing and exemplifying the problem which will serve as a working hypothesis. I begin by providing an account of the sense of crisis in comparative civil procedure literature that is due to the concerns expressed by the access to justice movement. As I will argue, while this literature demanding a more accessible civil justice is not new at all, it is still quite applicable to many countries around the world where the current situation of civil justice is described as "in crisis". On this point, besides describing the literature that claims for a generalized dissemination of this perception of crisis, I focus later on Latin America to introduce the civil justice reform movement and its challenges. Finally, in this part, I use a comparative law methodology to show how due process as a constitutional requirement differs between Chile and California and how this produces different outcomes in terms of legal procedures as barriers of access to justice. My purpose is to introduce the problem and to explain why facing this crisis requires an understanding of due process requirements in civil procedure.

In the third part, I describe and compare the answers provided in the field of International Human Rights Law, which is critical for today's understanding of fair trial requirements, especially in this age of the convergence of legal systems.[4] With this purpose, I analyze the answers provided by two regional systems of human rights protection, using an empirical mixed method approach to study the case law of their two main tribunals, the Inter-American Court of Human Rights (IACHR) and the European Court of Human Rights (ECHR). I will analyze each system's response to the question of how due process applies to non-criminal matters in general, and to civil justice in particular. I will show that there are subtle but important differences in the answers they provide by identifying the application of the checklist and flexible models. Based on the case law of both regional systems I will describe and compare two different approaches: the expansive doctrine of the Inter-American system, and the concrete analysis of effectiveness of its European counterpart.

In the fourth part, I will analyze how the checklist and fairness ideal types of due process are at the origin of due process as a legal institution and how they have been followed until the present day in American jurisprudence. On this topic, I will explore how conceptions of justice and fairness were crystallized for the first time in the Magna Carta and later incorporated into the United States Constitution in its due process clause. This historical perspective and a comparison between criminal and non-criminal matters will exemplify the different conceptions of fair trial expressions of procedural due process. It also provides an opportunity to identify several factors that might explain how the two analytical models of due process have been in continuous interplay in different moments and contexts.

With these objectives in mind, I explore first the origins of the due process clause in the Magna Carta until its incorporation in the 14th Amendment. Particularly relevant in this point will be to explain why much of the development on procedural due process has been in the criminal justice arena. Second, I will develop the approaches followed by the Supreme Court of the United States (SCOTUS or simply the Supreme Court) in deciding on the procedure that is due. Particularly relevant in this regard is the conception of the adversarial mode of trial required by due process. For this purpose, I relied in a review of the specialized literature which was crucial to identify the relevant case law that I analyze in these chapters. I will describe the

[4]Merryman (1981), pp. 357–388.

different approaches, from early case law more focused on tradition and history to a more flexible approach based on the idea of a fundamental fairness test. I explore also from this point of view some modern debates on the application of the clause in non-criminal matters. Finally, I will explore on the relation of the due process clause and access to justice in the American legal system.

In the fourth part, based on the findings of the previous chapters, I will develop a theoretical framework on how fair trial should be understood and applied in civil matters. With this in mind, first I will argue that civil justice needs to escape the shadow of criminal justice. Procedural fairness, in this regard, not only requires procedural rights in order to ensure accurate determination of fact as a proxy for a quality outcome, but also to ensure a legal need has been satisfied, a dispute solved, a right protected. With the right to a court at the center of due process, the social cost of providing a legal procedure, far from being an exogenous element of a theory of procedural fairness it must be an inherent part of it.[5] Then I will describe the features of this understanding of procedural fairness using the categories of the flexible and the checklist models and explain how this theory fits with the common use of due process both in the international and national jurisdictions studied in the previous chapters. Finally, I will provide a basic exercise by using this analytical tool on the main legislative product of the Chilean civil justice reform, as an example of how the proposed theoretical framework can be applied in particular contexts.

References

Bone R (2003) Agreeing to fair process: the problem with contractarian theories of procedural fairness. Boston Univ Law Rev. 83:485–552

Galligan D (1996) Due process and fair procedures. A study of administrative procedures. Clarendon Press, Oxford

Merryman J (1981) On the convergence (and divergence) of the Civil Law and the common law. Stan J Int Law 17:357–388

Miller C (1977) The forest of due process of law. In: Pennock R, Chapman J (eds) Due process, Nomos, vol XVIII. New York University Press, New York, pp 3–68

Raz J (1995) Ethics in the public domain. Essays in the morality of law and politics, revised edn. Oxford University Press, Oxford

Sampford C (2005) Reconceiving the rule of law for a globalizing world. In: Zifcak S (ed) Globalisation and the rule of law. Routledge, Great Britain, pp 9–31

Scanlon T (1977) Due process. In: Pennock R, Chapman J (eds) Due process, Nomos, vol XVIII. New York University Press, New York, pp 94–106

Waldron J (2011) The rule of law and the importance of procedure. Nomos 50:3–31

[5]Bone (2003), p. 515.

Part I
An Introduction of Two Ideal Types. The Checklist and Flexible Models of Procedural Due Process

Chapter 2
Due Process as a Subject of Special Jurisprudence. The Checklist and Flexible Models of Procedural Due Process

The answer to the question of which procedure is provided by the right to due process may have a critical impact on the design of a civil procedure. In terms of access to justice, to provide a simple, flexible, fast, and low-cost mechanism to solve civil disputes—in a way that does not sacrifice other goals of a fair procedure—requires, first, a conception of what due process elements may and may not be sacrificed in order to fulfill such a goal. The main purpose of this book is to provide an understanding of the right to a fair trial for civil matters which allows these competing goals to be reconciled.

This is not an easy task. Fair trial, as an expression of procedural due process, is a complex concept from the point of view of jurisprudence. It draws on profound philosophical ideas of procedural and substantive justice that have changed over time. These ideas derive from different historical and political traditions concerning the relationship between individuals and the State, and specifically the protection of individuals against arbitrary actions by State authorities.[1]

Of course, whether an individual is being treated fairly or not may be analyzed from different perspectives, ranging from essentialism,[2] individual psychological perception or "party satisfaction,"[3] dignitary theories,[4] etc. From a normative point of view, particularly relevant is the distinction between process-based and outcome-based theories, depending on whether the analysis of fairness considers the outcomes of the legal procedure or is completely independent of them.[5]

Due process is a complex concept, also, because it addresses different types of public authorities that are mandated to follow its requirements in their relationships

---

[1] Miller (1977), p. 3. See also: Galligan (1996), p. 166.

[2] See: Fuller and Winston (1978).

[3] See: Tyler (1994).

[4] See: Mashaw (1981).

[5] Bone (2003), pp. 508–516.

R. Lillo Lobos, *Understanding Due Process in Non-Criminal Matters*, Ius Gentium: Comparative Perspectives on Law and Justice 97,
https://doi.org/10.1007/978-3-030-95534-2_2

with citizens. As such, due process is a mandate that applies to courts but also to legislatures. Regarding courts, due process presents specific issues that are important to analyze for at least two reasons. First, courts are supposed to be impartial and independent third parties that are empowered to determine whether another public authority's decision against a citizen was arbitrary from a procedural or a substantive perspective.[6] Evidently, it would be hardly considered fair if the same public authority that decides on people's rights were also in charge of resolving disputes about its own decisions. But the judiciary and judges themselves are equally bound by due process requirements in the way they treat individuals. Consequently, the legal process by which the judiciary decides or determines people's rights must be conducted in accordance with basic minimum conditions. This second dimension has its particularities and a complex structure consisting of different procedural guarantees, which in turn must be applied as standards depending on various factors. But, as courts decide cases following a legally established procedure, fair trial standards are mandates directed as much to judges as to legislators. During the design of legal proceedings, those in charge of enacting this regulation would be constitutionally mandated to establish and provide safeguards for the required fair trial standards.

According to an outcome-based conception of fairness, Dworkin characterizes the legislative dimension of procedural due process as a right to have the institution acting in such capacity (which might be a court or a parliament) to fix civil procedures that correctly assess the risk and importance of moral harm.[7] Moral harm, the "injustice factor" as he calls it—the risk that either might suffer from an erroneous assessment and application of law to a given factual situation—must be equally distributed between the parties.[8] From this point of view, procedural fairness relates to the reliability of the outcome. I will come back to this definition in the last part of this book. I see it as critical in answering my research question.

In the chapters that follow, I will pursue an approach that is somewhat different from the traditional one. My idea is to construct a theoretical framework to understand fair trial as an expression of procedural due process based on inductive reasoning. I will explore how this concept evolved into what it is known to be in central countries, such as in the modern American conception of the due process clause and in the field of international human rights law, which has been an important source for standards now shared among nations. By studying how procedural due process evolved in time and in particular how it has been understood in different jurisdictions I will propose a conception of procedural due process, especially concerning its application in civil justice.

---

[6] Regarding courts role against public authorities' arbitrariness, see: Scanlon (1977), pp. 94–106.

[7] Dworkin (1985), p. 93.

[8] According to Dworkin, to determine the procedural rights to which parties are entitled is relevant the moral harm beyond the bare harm, which are related to gains and losses which emerges from utilitarian calculations. That is why its determination would be a matter of principle not policy, because it is a question of an entitlement to a right to win a lawsuit if the law is on the party's side, even if the society overall loses thereby. See: Dworkin (1985), pp. 89, 92–96.

As I will show, beyond the philosophical roots of due process as a demand of procedural justice or as a dimension of morality, and specifically as a legal institution, there are two ways of applying procedural due process. One way is to understand due process as a strict minimum set of conditions that must be met for a legal procedure to be considered as the one that is due as a right. According to this model, due process requirements are applied without any reference to the underlying values or conceptions of justice that someone may have, even though it is perfectly possible that its requirements were designed to protect such values. The other way is to conceive due process as a general principle whose content will vary in each case, taking the necessary form required for its legal procedure to be considered "fair." Such a decision will be taken according to the values of the right to a fair trial inherent to each specific legal system, or even according to the discretion of the decision maker. I conceive these two models as two ideal types in the Weberian sense and as opposed versions that exist in tension with one another.[9] I have found that this conception is similar—and as such appealing for my purposes—to the work done by Cass Sunstein in "Two Conceptions of Procedural Fairness," where he distinguishes between a conception of fairness based on rule-bound decisions as compared to individualized treatment decisions.[10]

Later in this book, using the opposition between these two different understandings of due process and the requirements of fairness, I shall explain how I plan to tackle what Robert Bone calls the puzzle of a rights-based theory of procedural fairness. According to Bone, and following Ronald Dworkin, the puzzle is "how to make room for arguments of social cost without stripping the right of its force as a right."[11] My answer, which I will develop in the last chapter, is that an inherent element of procedural due process is the requirement of access to the legal procedure and the capacity to pursue it to its conclusion. In this sense, a procedure would also be unfair if, no matter how accurate it might be or how protective of procedural guarantees, it is too costly or ineffective to be useful. In this regard, the social cost of providing a legal procedure is not an exogenous element of a theory of procedural fairness but it must be an inherent part of it.[12]

For example, one way to frame this debate is to consider that fairness trumps or constrains aggregative metrics such as economic efficiency. A right to due process as an expression of the fairness of legal procedures, under this view, is concerned with how individuals are treated. As such, it provides reasons to trump or constrain the pursuit of aggregate social goals if they will be promoted at the expense of treating some individuals unfairly.[13] From the other side, the access to justice movement calls for simple civil procedures since in that way judicial resources would become available for more individuals. If the claim for a more accessible civil justice is taken

[9] See: Weber (1949), pp. 91–92.

[10] Sunstein (2006).

[11] Bone (2010), p. 1015.

[12] Bone (2003), p. 515.

[13] Bone (2003), p. 487.

as an efficiency argument, and as such based on purely utilitarian grounds, it is easy to see the problem.

In what follows I will describe this analytical framework I have constructed as the lens that I will use to analyze different conceptions on how procedural due process is conceived and applied in the following chapters. I shall call them the *checklist* and the *flexible* models. I conceive these as two ideal types in the Weberian sense and as opposed versions that exist in tension with one another. They will aid and guide me during the rest of the book and, finally, in proposing an answer to my main question: how to harmonize the requirements of due process with demands for access to civil justice.

2.1 The Checklist Model

In the checklist model, procedural due process is reduced to a set of procedural guarantees considered to be the minimum requirement for any legal proceedings that might affect an individual's legal rights to be regarded as a due procedure. Of course, the specific guarantees to be considered part of due process might vary between legal systems, and within them in terms of their application to different types of legal procedures. Nevertheless, under this conception, what seems to be more important is that its content is fixed by legislation. Whether statutory, constitutional, customary, or of any other source, what is considered "fair treatment" is decided ex ante by a rule-making authority.

The right to a fair trial, under such a conception, is equal to the sum of procedural guarantees that are recognized for all legal procedures, as well as specific ones. That is why I call this version of procedural due process the "checklist" model, since to assess whether a procedure is due the analysis would consist of "checking" that each protection on the list is guaranteed.

Under this conception, the content of due process is whatever law says, no more but no less. Since this content is decided ex ante, a great deal of work in "legal design" is required. The rule-maker in this regard will tend to rely more on rules that are abstract, general, and as clear as possible.[14] This will mean that procedural safeguards will take the form of legal directives construed more as legal rules, that is, as a mandate that is applicable in all-or-nothing fashion.[15]

In terms of its interpretation and subsequent application, the official in charge of its application must respond to the directive by assessing the presence of a list of easily distinguishable factual aspects of a situation and then intervene accordingly. This is what Ihering calls "formal realizability."[16] Clear-cut legal rules of this type, it

[14] Sunstein (2006), p. 620.

[15] Following Ronald Dworkin account for the differences between legal principles and rules. See: Dworkin (1967), pp. 22–29; Dworkin (1977), pp. 22–31.

[16] Kennedy (1976), p. 1687.

is said, provide better restraint over official arbitrariness[17] and allow less room for judicial discretion.[18]

This does not mean that every type of legal procedure will have the same procedural guarantees. In the checklist model, there is room for flexibility but only if the legislator has provided ex ante for broad categories of cases. The maxim in this regard is that similar situations demands similar treatment.[19] Therefore, it is perfectly possible under the checklist approach for a procedural regulation—let us say a code of civil procedure—to provide for different procedures, affording different procedural guarantees based on factors such as monetary value or the complexity of evidence. Moreover, it would be possible to find a specific legal procedure full of exceptions where one or more guarantees will not apply. Notwithstanding such regulation, the conception will still be characterized by clear, abstract, and general legal rules.

For this model to work, the interpretive choices[20] will tend to be based on textualism and originalism, that is, centered on the primacy of the text and or legislative intention.[21] Text will be as clear as possible so the decision-maker will have less room to deploy his own conceptions of the rule but, on the contrary, as far as possible rules will be applied strictly to a set of facts. The idea is for the decision-maker to apply such a rule even though the rationale behind it does not apply.[22] The decision-maker will resemble an officer inspector, checking that every procedural guarantee afforded in a specific legal procedure has been observed.

Thus, if the text is not as clear as desired, the role of the decision maker will be to ponder whatever notion of "fairness" the rule-maker entertained. In this regard, the checklist approach is neutral in terms of any underlying values or notions of justice. The legislator may have a purely utilitarian conception in establishing a simplified procedure or a consideration for human dignity when requiring that before depriving anyone of a social right there must be "some kind" of hearing.

A model like this might have advantages in deciding what procedural guarantees must be afforded by the right to a fair trial. The most obvious is the legal certainty it provides for private actors. If this model is followed, citizens are able to know in advance what to expect in a legal procedure and act and plan their activities accordingly.[23] This, in turn, might reduce decision costs for those potential litigants,[24] but also at the end it might impact on the duration, accuracy, and economic costs of the legal procedure and therefore be attractive for both private and public budgets.

[17] Kennedy (1976), p. 1688.

[18] Kennedy (1976), p. 1690.

[19] Sunstein (2006), p. 619.

[20] On interpretive choices, see: Vermeule (2000), p. 82.

[21] Between the relation among the two in its modern conceptions, see: Eskridge (2013).

[22] Sunstein (2006), p. 629.

[23] Kennedy (1976), p. 1688.

[24] Sunstein (2006), p. 629.

For private individuals, it might also protect against arbitrariness or bias of those officers in charge of deciding that procedural guarantees are afforded or of enforcing the law. According to Sunstein, an example in this regard are the Miranda rules, which through a clear prophylactic protocol avoid police arbitrariness.[25] At the same time, a clear checklist of what rights are to be afforded might simplify the accountability of such officers and enforceability by individuals, since such rules turn individuals into right-holders.[26]

2.2 The Flexible Model

In the flexible model the content of due process is not fixed but is flexible, less restrained by the ties of history and in its application more dependent on the circumstances. In this regard, to decide on what is the procedure that is due, there is a case-by-case approach in which details matter.

In this regard, procedural due process will be construed in a broad language, avoiding rigid rules. Using the conception developed by Ronald Dworkin,[27] due process and its content will be interpreted more as a legal principle or, as Robert Alexy would call it, as a mandate of optimization.[28] A legal principle in this regard is a type of norm which states a reason that argues in one direction but does not prescribe a particular decision.[29] As a matter of degree, Raz conceives of principles as norms that prescribe unspecific types of behavior, that is, types of acts that can be performed on different occasions by the performance of a great many heterogeneous generic acts on each occasion.[30]

Beyond the type of behavior prescribed, and especially according to authors such as Dworkin or Alexy, legal principles are distinguished from rules in the way of solving conflicts between norms. While legal principles are subject to a dimension of weight and the conflict between them may be solved by an exercise of "weighing" their merits, conflicts between rules are subject to a criterion of validity.[31] Also, like any norm but particularly as a legal principle, the use of due process in practical settings involves a critical interpretation of its meaning, instead of a mechanical binary answer as in the case of legal rules.

---

[25] Sunstein (2006), p. 631.

[26] Sunstein (2006), p. 632.

[27] Dworkin (1967), pp. 23–29.

[28] See: Alexy (2014), p. 68.

[29] Braithwaite (2002), p. 50.

[30] Raz (1972), p. 838. Notwithstanding, the main difference between rules and principles according to Raz is about the roles each type of norm serve in a legal system. See Raz (1972), pp. 839–843.

[31] Dworkin (1967), p. 27; Alexy (2014), pp. 70–79. Raz points out that this conflict solving criteria proposed by Dworkin as defining character of principles. See: Raz (1972), p. 833. Notwithstanding is not my purpose to solve this issue here, and I will use this character to try to define my analytical models, I believe it is important to acknowledge its limitations.

Interpretive choice weighs heavily on the decision-maker, who is required to decide what will be considered as due in a specific legal procedure. The labor would be not to "check" all of the elements on the laundry list but will be closer to what Dworkin calls *creative interpretation*, that is providing purpose in order to make it the best possible example of the form or genre to which is taken to belong. Interpretation, in his account, is a matter of interaction between purpose and object.[32] In this sense, the flexible model is a value-oriented approach.[33] Nevertheless, the flexible approach does not necessarily specify which values or notion of justice are those which the interpreter must use. From utilitarian conceptions of justice, natural law-based theories, even process-based and dignitary conceptions, all would be open to inclusion.[34]

This is not to say necessarily that the decision-maker will have full discretion in deciding which procedure is due. The admissible values might be those inherent to a specific legal system. In this regard, history, and especially legislative history, will have only a limited value since what will be considered "fair" might not be considered as such for times to come and especially for the case at hand. On the contrary, history might have a value in determining which values are inherent to the system, reflected in the settled practices.[35]

There are many reasons why a flexible approach would be desirable. Even though the decision-maker may or not have full discretion, what is certain is that he or she will be the one weighing up the specific circumstances and factors in order to specify which procedural guarantees are afforded. The idea, is that unlike legal rules, often criticized for being under or over-inclusive and therefore producing unfairness when applied to unanticipated circumstances, here particularities must be taken into account. Here the maxim is that those in different situations must be treated differently to be equal.[36]

While sometimes the use of legal rules to make decisions on what is a due procedure might reduce cost, sometimes it might increase it. For example, if it is established that for a legal procedure all parties must have legal representation, this might be more expensive than providing it under a specific circumstances approach only to those that really require it. In this regard, the flexible approach might imply greater decision cost but less transactional cost.

In many situations, a good design of clear-cut rules might be a challenge to achieve. For example, it might be quite complex to determine how long a legal procedure should take to be considered acceptable, especially taking into consideration that factors such as human resources or dockets change over time. In such cases, a flexible approach may even diminish decision cost.

---

[32] Dworkin (1986), p. 52.

[33] Regarding, value oriented theories of procedural due process, see: Saphire (1978).

[34] See: Mashaw (1981).

[35] Redish and Marshals (1986), pp. 474–475. See also: Dworkin (1985), p. 90.

[36] Sunstein (2006), p. 633.

According to Sunstein, rules also drive discretion underground. People in an authority or in an advantaged position would be more easily able to undercut legal rules without being caught and such deviation identified and sanctioned, than in comparison with regular or sporadic users.[37] This applies not just to officers but also to private individuals in position of power such as repeat players in a judicial procedure.

A flexible approach, by considering the particularities of the individuals, might also improve perception of the overall fairness of a given legal procedure, and in that regard promote responsiveness to the outcomes.[38]

Kadish, referring to conceptions of due process of law in the American Constitution and the case law of the Supreme Court, distinguishes between two main approaches, one that searches to fix the content of the clause, and the other a flexible one. The latter, which I will describe in Chap. 9, is described as required by changing social and economic conditions, the flux of science, technology, and communications, which creates new problems of government and leave others obsolescent. Therefore, a fixed or frozen meaning of due process destroys its chief virtue, its generality and elasticity.[39]

As pointed out, the above are ideal types in the Weberian sense. For example, a legal system closer to the flexible model might have established specific procedural guarantees as well as having a more general basic legal norm. Yet these specific protections are understood as a *specification* of the general principle and not as coterminous with it. Why a legal system would prefer to use the normative language of a standard instead of a legal rule is that application of a rule involves sacrificing precision in achieving the objectives of the procedural protections it establishes.[40] For example, authors argue that if the type of action to be regulated is simple, stable (not changing unpredictably over time) and does not involve large economic interests, rules regulate with greater certainty than principles. On the other hand, in complex actions in changing environments in which large economic interests are at stake, principles are more likely than rules to provide legal certainty.[41]

In the chapters that follow, I will describe my working hypothesis based on the literature about the crisis of civil justice and justify its relevance in providing a theoretical framework to understand due process. The idea is to study when and how both approaches are used in practice, and finally, in the last chapter, to develop a theory that, by encompassing both approaches, will allow me to answer the main question of how due process and access to justice can be reconciled.

[37] Sunstein (2006), p. 634.

[38] Sunstein (2006), p. 634.

[39] Kadish (1957), p. 341.

[40] Kennedy (1976), p. 1689.

[41] Braithwaite (2002), pp. 52–60.

References

Alexy R (2014) Teoría de los derechos fundamentales (trans: Carlos Bernal). Centro de Estudios Políticos y Constitucionales, Madrid

Bone R (2010) Procedure, participation, rights. Boston Univ Law Rev 90:1011–1028

Bone R (2003) Agreeing to fair process: the problem with contractarian theories of procedural fairness. Boston Univ Law Rev 83:485–552

Braithwaite J (2002) Rules and principles: a theory of legal certainty. AJLP 27:47–82

Dworkin R (1967) The model of rules. Univ Chicago Law Rev 35:14–46

Dworkin R (1977) Taking rights seriously. Harvard University Press, Cambridge

Dworkin R (1985) A matter of principle. Harvard University Press, Cambridge

Dworkin R (1986) The law's empire. The Belknap Press of Harvard University Press, Cambridge

Eskridge W (2013) The new textualism and normative canons. Columbia Law Rev 113:531–592

Fuller L, Winston K (1978) The forms and limits of adjudication. Harv Law Rev 92(2):353–409

Galligan D (1996) Due process and fair procedures. A study of administrative procedures. Clarendon Press, Oxford.

Kadish S (1957) Methodology and criteria in due process adjudication. A survey and criticism. Yale Law J 66(3):319–363

Kennedy D (1976) Form and substance in private law adjudication. Harv Law Rev 89(8): 1685–1778

Mashaw J (1981) Administrative due process: the quest for a dignitary theory. Boston Univ Law Rev 61:885–931

Miller C (1977) The forest of due process of law. In: Pennock R, Chapman J (eds) Due process, Nomos, vol XVIII. New York University Press, New York, pp 3–68

Raz J (1972) Legal principles and the limits of law. Yale Law J 8(5):823–854

Redish M, Marshall L (1986) Adjudicatory independence and the values of procedural due process. Yale Law J 95(3):455–503

Saphire R (1978) Specifying due process values: toward a more responsive approach to procedural protection. Univ Pa Law Rev 127(1):111–195

Scanlon T (1977) Due process. In: Pennock R, Chapman J (eds) Due process, Nomos, vol XVIII. New York University Press, New York, pp 94–106

Sunstein C (2006) Two conceptions of procedural fairness. Soc Res 73(2):619–646

Tyler T (1994) Psychological models of the justice motive: antecedents of distributive and procedural justice. J Pers Soc Psychol 67(5):850–863

Vermeule A (2000) Interpretive choice. New York Univ Law Rev 75(1):74–149

Weber M (1949) The methodology of the social sciences (trans: Shils E). The Free Press, Illinois.

Part II
Legal Procedure as a Barrier for Access to Justice: Why Understanding Due Process and Its Requirements Over Civil Procedure Matters

Chapter 3
The Crisis of Civil Justice. Criticism from the Access to Justice Movement and the Reform Movement in Latin America

3.1 The Crisis of Civil Justice, Access to Justice and Unmet Legal Needs. Comparative Perspectives

In this chapter, I begin by describing my working hypothesis based on the idea of the crisis of civil justice. Specifically, I will provide an account of this sense of crisis in comparative civil procedure literature and from the access to justice movement, claiming the need for a more accessible civil procedure in the context of resource constraints. In this regard, as I will explain, there is an internationally shared perception that civil justice is in crisis in Civil law as well as in Common law countries.[1] Recently, while criticizing the lack of good empirical studies on the matter, Genn has also emphasized how a common rhetoric and vocabulary has been adopted increasingly in many jurisdictions and legal cultures.[2]

This crisis perception is based mainly on the inability of the judicial system to provide accessible means to solve conflicts or satisfy unmet legal needs of low and middle-income individuals.[3] Every legal procedure tries to balance time, cost, and accuracy.[4] Of course, this a complex equation influenced by the legislative and value-oriented priorities adopted by each specific legal system. The solution to the puzzle affects how effectively a specific legal procedure is used to protect or enforce legal rights. For example, reducing factors such as time and cost to improve access

---

[1] Zuckerman (1999), pp. 12–14. See also: Buhai (2009), p. 1008; Wolf (2012), p. 763; Kiesiläinen (2008), p. 29; Pleasence and Balmer (2012), pp. 36–40.

[2] Genn (2010), pp. 27–29.

[3] There is literature also describing a crisis of relevance of the civil justice. In this regard, even those who might access the civil court are not using it to solve their legal conflicts (or they are using other dispute resolution devices), and in this sense civil justice is becoming increasingly less significant in some legal systems. See, e.g.: Galanter (2006); Genn (2010), pp. 29–38.

[4] Zuckerman (1999), p. 3.

R. Lillo Lobos, *Understanding Due Process in Non-Criminal Matters*, Ius Gentium: Comparative Perspectives on Law and Justice 97,
https://doi.org/10.1007/978-3-030-95534-2_3

might affect rightness or accuracy. Alternatively, on the other side, focus on pure accuracy, that is the ability to determine facts in order to apply the law, might create an expensive mechanism that ends by diminishing its availability for use by potential litigants.[5] This is especially true for less complex cases if the value of the expected outcome is surpassed by the cost of litigation.

The literature urging for more access to justice is not a recent phenomenon. In the United States, for example, the first half of the Twentieth century saw how Small Claims Courts were first proposed and then implemented through the country as an informal, inexpensive, and simplified legal procedures aimed to "...relieving the legal and monetary difficulties experienced by the poor litigant and the individual with a valid but minor monetary claim."[6] Such courts, in turn were proposed based on previous experiences from Canada and England and Wales during the Nineteen Century, and even older models such as the Conciliation Courts, established in Norway in 1797.[7] Well into the second half of the Twentieth century, the ground breaking comparative work by Mauro Cappelletti and Bryant Garth, epitomizes all the emergence of the access to justice movement and the different trends followed in many different countries.[8] Notwithstanding, as expressed by Sandefur, access to justice themes have remerged around the world as an object of academic interest and as "...a social movement and a value commitment that motivates study and action".[9]

It is not the purpose of this chapter, nor of this book, to answer empirically whether such resurgence is effective, or if so, how far reaches. Not is to understand whether if there is a reemergence or if it is a matter that has continuously surrounded the literature on civil justice but perhaps during past decades just diminished its relevance on the political agenda. Notwithstanding, and as I will describe, I believe there is enough cumulated evidence around the world at least to reaffirm that such perception exists, and it is enough I believe, to justify the purpose of this work.

In this regard, the basic idea derived from a comparative study by Adrian Zuckerman published at the end of the Twentieth century, is that both Civil law and Common law countries have been unable to provide accessible means to solve conflicts or satisfy unmet legal needs of low and middle-income individuals, especially regarding relatively simple but prevalent justiciable problems of the population.[10]

---

[5]Zuckerman (1999), pp. 10–12.

[6]Kosmin (1976), p. 936.

[7]Pagter et al. (1964), pp. 876–877; Vance (1917), pp. 108–109; Kosmin (1976), p. 936.

[8]See: Cappelletti and Garth (1978).

[9]Sandefur (2009), p. ix.

[10]Zuckerman (1999), p. 12.

In Common law countries most critiques point to the high cost of civil litigation.[11] In the United States, the usual suspect in this regard are discovery proceedings.[12] Among other procedural and evidentiary complexities, substantive law complexity also plays a part. Altogether, it seems that the American civil justice system has been designed to require a well-educated lawyer to operate effectively,[13] and lawyers are expensive.[14] Notwithstanding that these critiques might be mitigated by the contingency fees system, which allows attorneys to recover litigation fees upon results, this system is only available in tort cases and is attractive mainly when punitive damages are expected.[15] On the contrary, in other civil cases where the expected monetary return may not be as high as the cost of litigation and since the common rule is that each party pays her own attorney fees, that might turn accessibility as not as a rational option to pursue at least for low-and-middle income Americans. This crisis is especially serious for non-poor American with small contracts cases, tort cases, consumer, or other civil cases with strong potential claims on the merits but where the expected benefit of their cases is lower than the required investment but higher to the jurisdictional limit of other venues such as small claims courts.[16]

Accordingly, access to justice literature in countries such as the United States describes their civil justice system as one of people of means having access to lawyers and the courts –but also to other private means of dispute resolution-, while low-and-middle income groups of population experiencing legal needs either do not using the civil justice system or navigating it by their own.[17]

Beyond courts and procedure complexity, the American civil justice crisis results from an imbalance between demand—those experiencing legal needs and requires legal services- and those in charge of providing these services.[18] According to Wenstein, while the private bar—which is the primary provider and where most lawyers practice- is too expensive for low-and-middle income Americans, other sources such as publicly funded legal services providers, the pro bono work of the private bar, and other non-lawyer legal assistance, runs short.[19]

---

[11] In England, these problems influenced a deep judicial reform process. See: Michalik (1999), pp. 156–157. These reforms have been criticized of not being radical enough. See: Zander (1995), pp. 79–96.

[12] See, e.g.: Marcus (1999), pp. 92–95.

[13] Barton and Bibas (2017), p. 65.

[14] Estimating litigation cost is a complex task. An estimation of median costs in several civil cases are available at the National Center for States Courts. Available at: http://www.courtstatistics.org/other-pages/caseload_highlights.

[15] But punitive damages are increasingly being restricted because of the high variability specially in cases decided by civil juries. See: Zuckerman (1999), pp. 19–21. See also: Kagan (2003), pp. 108–109.

[16] Croley (2017), p. 127.

[17] Weinstein (2016), p. 4.

[18] Weinstein (2016), p. 4.

[19] Weinstein (2016), p. 13.

Pro se litigation in America today represents an important part of the civil docket.[20] In many simple cases it proves a workable alternative for many people. For example, in uncontested divorce cases, there are States where technology might ease the procedure using publicly available forms or through on-demand online forms providers. On the contrary, contested or slightly complicated divorces for low-and-middle income Americans are something else. While substantive and procedural reasons turn these cases to be lawyer dependent, for many there are simply no lawyer they can afford, pro bono work in family law is limited, and online forms are not much help since they are designed for simple divorces. In consequence, there are many Americans who decide to navigate the system by their own or simply to "lump it."[21]

Similarly, Attiyah and Summers, in a comparative study of England and the United States, found that the two most common barriers in both countries were the high cost of litigation and the excessive workload of the courts.[22] While in Canada, because of the high prices for legal services and the income ceiling on legal aid coverage, there is a lack of access to justice for middle-income citizens, those whose household income is too high to be eligible for legal aid while at the same time too low to be able to hire an attorney to go to the courts in civil matters.[23]

Alongside the high cost of litigation, many Common law countries such as England and Wales or Australia have been facing cuts in legal aid in several matters, including issues pertaining to civil and family law.[24] In England and Wales, for example, in 2013 the spending on civil legal aid was greatly reduced by a third in comparison with the period of 2009–2010 when the total civil legal aid scheme stood at £900 million. The restriction imposed great limitations on the scope of legal representation in several civil matters or changed the way by which the service was provided.[25]

High costs as an access to justice barrier are not a problem only in Common law countries. Across continental Europe, litigation cost becomes an access to justice barrier especially in the context of small claims. According to Nagy, in such cases—where the expected value at stake is low and costs tends to outweigh the expected value—for several reasons, in practice, individual claims cannot reach the courts. Legal cost which can't be shifted into the losing party, the existence of unrecoverable expenses, the cost borne by the lack of information on preliminary

---

[20] Barton and Bibas (2017), p. 52. In U.S. District courts, pro se litigation represented the 29% of filings in civil cases. Available at: https://www.uscourts.gov/statistics-reports/judicial-business-2017-tables. In States Courts an accurate estimation of civil cases handled by pro se litigants is difficult, but there are estimations that at least 75% of all civil cases includes at least one pro-se litigant and therefore they represent the majority user of the courts. Available at: https://www.srln.org/node/548/srln-brief-how-many-srls-srln-2015.

[21] Barton and Bibas (2017), pp. 46–43.

[22] Atiyah and Summers (1987), p. 188.

[23] Trebilcock et al. (2012), p. 4.

[24] See: Flynn and Hodgson (2017), pp. 1–22.

[25] Byrom (2017), pp. 221–224.

legal assessment, and the inherent risk of litigation (which in small claims impacts disproportionately on the decision to file a claim) creates a scenario where many potential plaintiffs are not seeking recovery at least at individual level.[26]

Notwithstanding, in Continental law countries such as France, Italy, Portugal, or Spain, main critiques are directed at the excessive delay of their civil proceedings, where formalism reigns over substance to such a degree that civil courts become useless for litigants.[27] In Italy, for example, the Council of Europe has urged for the adoption of legislative measures necessary to shorten civil trials and several studies have tried to identify factors for its delay.[28] According to Chiarloni, Italian civil justice is largely useless for those seeking to satisfy their legal needs. Besides the lack information resulting from the resistance of the legal profession to share technical knowledge, this strong accusation comes from the extremely long duration of the civil procedure.[29] For Silvestri, excessive delay has been a problem of the Italian justice since long ago and while it has prompted many legal reforms the issue has not been resolved.[30] In this regard, while studies made in the 1990's estimated an average for the first instance in 1200 days and the duration of the appeal up to ten years,[31] in 2011 the average length of adjudication was estimated in seven years.[32] According to data published by the European Commission for the Efficiency of Justice (CEPEJ), in 2018 civil litigation had a disposition time of 527 days in first instance and 863 days at the second instance, the highest of the member states with available information.[33] Even though the Italian system has incorporated a compensation scheme for excessive length of proceedings -known as the Pinto Act-,[34] the resort to the European Court of Human Rights is still frequently used as a mean of protection on this regard. As I will discuss in Chap. 7, Italy is one of the countries of the Council of Europe with most decisions of the court on the right to a fair trial, most of them cases involving length of proceedings. In fact, the proportion of violations on this regard is similar to the sum of the rest of the countries.[35]

In Latin America, Gargarella identifies high cost, lack of information about substantive rights and also on how to vindicate them,[36] formalism of proceedings,

---

[26]Nagy (2019), pp. 12–13.

[27]Zuckerman (1999), pp. 13–14.

[28]Nissi et al. (2019), pp. 396–397.

[29]Chiarloni (1999), pp. 264–268.

[30]Silvestri (2014), p. 237.

[31]Chiarloni (2014), p. 771.

[32]Silvestri (2014), p. 237.

[33]Available at: https://www.coe.int/en/web/cepej/cepej-stat.

[34]According to data collected by the CEPEJ, in 2018, 16247 condemnations were decided for excessive length of proceedings for a total of 98,602155 euros. Available at: https://www.coe.int/en/web/cepej/country-profiles/italy.

[35]ECHR, The ECHR in Facts & Figures 2018, 2019, pp. 6–8. Available at: https://echr.coe.int/Pages/home.aspx?p=reports/factsfigures&c=.

[36]Regarding this access to justice barrier in Latin-America, and analyzing several studies which has gathered information in different countries of the region, see: OCCA (2018), pp. 89–94.

the delay of the litigation, and even the geographic location of the courts as factors influencing the lack of access to justice in this region.[37] Especially in terms of formalism and delay, they have been described among Latin American countries,[38] or established as challenges for judicial reform.[39]

In Colombia, the largest and latest unmet legal needs research published in 2014 shown that two out of five Colombians experienced a legal need in the last four years. Two thirds of these were mostly thefts and scams, but also related to health and other public services and familiar and neighborhood related problems. Only 15% of experienced legal needs had a judicial outcome, since most of the potential claimants decided not to pursue or they filed a claim, but their cases are pending on the legal system. Most of these results did not come from a judge, who only receive a small fraction of such cases (only 2.8% among conflicts handed to a third party for resolution).[40] The main barriers faced by those experiencing these justiciable problems were the fact of pertaining to specific groups of population—such as the poor, women, LGBTI population or victims of armed conflicts—, the lack of legal empowerment (including low awareness on rights and their enforcement mechanisms) and the malfunctioning of the legal system. In this regard, it is mentioned the length of the proceedings as one of the causes on why many individuals are not seeking legal procedure as a mean to satisfy their legal needs.[41] In fact, one of the main critics on the civil justice in Colombia that led to the reform of 2012 and the enactment of a new procedural code[42]—the General Code of Procedure—was the lack of access to justice and efficiency. Notwithstanding, the new civil justice has been criticized for its inability to solve the crisis on this regard.[43]

Similarly, in Brazil, the constitutional reform of 2004 and mostly the civil procedure of 2014 were focused on improving justice efficiency,[44] meaning improving access to justice, judicial protection of fundamental rights and speedy proceedings, but also legal certainty. Both were seen as a solution for an overburdened judiciary[45] which resulted in excessive delay accounting for a "denial of justice" in practice.[46]

A Chilean study published in 2021, which followed closely the "Path of Justice" tradition led by Hazel Genn in the 1990s—as I will refer more in the next chapter—shown that most of adult population in Chile (76.6%) experienced a justiciable

[37] Gargarella (2002), pp. 2–12.
[38] OCCA (2018), pp. 40–49, 101–102.
[39] Iberian American Institute of Procedural Law (1988), pp. 17–24.
[40] La Rota et al. (2014), pp. 368–370.
[41] La Rota et al. (2014), pp. 373–393.
[42] Act N° 1564 of 2012.
[43] See, Rueda (2017), pp. 44–57.
[44] Silva and de Barros (2017), p. 24.
[45] Gidi and Zaneti (2021), pp. 56–57.
[46] Trejos (2004), p. 20.

problem on the last two years (prior to the study).[47] Most frequent justiciable problems experienced by respondents where consumer issues associated to goods and services (52.7%), money and finances (30.2%) or health (27.7%).[48]

Therefore, the level of involvement of people who experiences legal needs with formal dispute resolution mechanisms are low and of judicial mechanisms seems even lower in Latin America.[49] Later in this chapter, I return to Latin-America to explain how civil procedure may become a barrier of access to justice. Before embarking into such project, I believe it is important to explain why a well-functioning civil justice matter, which will be the focus on the next section.

According to the OECD, in 2013 access to civil justice was widest in the Nordic countries, as well as in the Netherlands and Germany. Italy, Mexico and Turkey were the OECD member countries with the lowest scores on civil justice.[50] This coincides with Zuckerman's research, which found that Netherlands and Germany have better outcomes in terms of access to civil justice. This success results mainly from a healthy balance between efficiency and the interests of the legal profession, for example by limiting the monopoly of the legal services, by regulations establishing fixed rates, or as a result of the availability of litigation insurance. Italy was found to have poor results in terms of both factors.[51] Moreover, the OECD found that among member countries performance in access to civil justice was the lowest on average of the four key contributors to the rule of law index (limited government powers, fundamental rights, regulatory enforcement and access to civil justice).[52]

After reviewing several surveys of unmet legal needs in various countries, Pleasence and Balmer found that, even with different methodologies and taking into consideration the limitations of these studies, they tend to show the same phenomenon. Although people with different income levels suffer similar legal problems, the attitude towards them and the vindication of their rights varies, depends not only on the type of legal problem but also on the income of the individuals affected. Pleasence and Balmer found that higher income people tend to have higher rates of involvement with legal services in order to solve their problems of a civil nature.[53] This is even more important bearing in mind that the majority of injustices faced by people today involve civil rather than criminal issues.[54]

---

[47] CAPJ (2021), p. 43. This study follows the concept of justiciable problem as defined by Sandefur (2015), p. 443 and based on the groundbreaking work of Genn (1999), p. 12.

[48] CAPJ (2021), pp. 43, 53.

[49] OCCA (2018), pp. 121–122.

[50] OECD (2013).

[51] Zuckerman (1999), pp. 23–25; 43–45.

[52] OECD (2013).

[53] Pleasence and Balmer (2012), pp. 36–40.

[54] OECD and Open Society Foundations (2016), p. 10.

For Cappelletti and Garth, paradoxically the courts have been critical of the expansion and recognition of legal rights during recent decades, for example in the international human rights law arena, which has created a complex scenario to uphold those rights. The problem, according to these authors, is that the courts' own features usually make them an ineffective alternative for the common population, especially in individual cases. More generally, Joseph Raz has pointed out how a bureaucratic conception of the rule of law tends, by itself, to create a gap between the legal system and citizens. The emphasis on meticulous and complex proceedings creates a need for legal services provided by trained and costly legal experts. Legal practice tends to give rise to highly technical language shared only by those engaged in the practice, and, in that regard, far removed from regular or even well-educated citizens.[55] According to Raz, this problem is to some extent unavoidable but every legal system should be aware of it and provide answers to mitigate it as much as possible.[56]

Even if at the end of the trial a right is recognized for one of the parties, the outcome will have less value for the person whose right has been vindicated if judicial proceedings are inefficient, costly, and excessively long. The inefficiencies of the judicial system may thus discourage future litigants from bringing their cases to the courts.[57] Of course, some cost and length of legal proceedings might be inevitable but also desirable, since they may be necessary to reach a correct decision. The problem arises when cost and delay reach proportions that threaten the justice system[58] because they make it inaccessible and useless for ordinary citizens. In the end, this will undermine the legitimacy of the justice system,[59] since the fact that judicial authority comes from a valid legal source is insufficient justification for it.[60]

According to Cappelletti and Garth, some of the main barriers to accessing civil justice are the high cost of the judicial process (whether monetary or caused by delays), and the imbalance of power among litigants. In this regard, it is particularly serious when ordinary citizens are pitted against what they call the "repeat players."[61]

These problems are especially troubling in non-complex civil cases, especially because the lower the cost and complexity associated with a case, the higher the proportional cost of litigation. In fact, in many of these cases, it is usual that the cost (in attorney's fees, for example) will be higher than the expected return if the case is

---

[55] Raz (1995), pp. 371–372.

[56] Raz (1995), p. 378.

[57] Atiyah and Summers (1987), p. 195.

[58] Zuckerman (1999), p. 12.

[59] Solum (2004), pp. 275–276.

[60] Yein (2007), pp. 20–22. For instance, according to Habermas, the legitimacy of a legal system requires a general right to equal liberties (reciprocity), correlative membership rights, and guaranteed legal remedies to enforce legal rights. See: Habermas (1996), pp. 122–125.

[61] Cappelletti and Garth (1978), pp. 181–292, 186–195.

won, as the excessive length of the proceedings in small claims may constitute another serious barrier for weaker parties.[62]

3.2 The Right of Access to Justice and the Functions of Civil Justice for the Rule of Law

A well-functioning civil justice is important. First, because the access to justice, as a basic right, means an effective right of an individual to advance in appropriate forum a legitimate legal claim or defenses against claims by others. Second, because the civil justice serves important functions to maintain the rule of law.[63] Most conceptions on this institution share this feature as a basic support.

From the point of view of access to justice, it is not an easy task to define the contours of this entitlement as a human right. Most international treaties on the subject does not provide an express provision on this regard.[64] On the contrary, its construction comes mainly from the institutions in charge of their interpretation, such as the Human Rights Committee for the International Covenant on Civil and Political Rights,[65] the Inter-American Court of Human Rights in the case of the Inter-American System,[66] or the European Court of Human Rights at the level of the Council of Europe.[67]

Cappelletti and Garth define access to justice as the means by which people may vindicate their rights and/or resolve their disputes under the general auspices of the State.[68] Currently, it means more than a formal right to litigate or defend a legal right, but it is also recognized as a pre-condition for exercising such rights effectively.[69]

Based on International Human Rights Law standards, states must "...guarantee not rights that are theoretical and illusory but rights that are practical and effective."[70] The idea is that people cannot effectively exercise their rights without having access to a State mechanism to protect them. In this regard, as an international

[62] Cappelletti and Garth (1978), pp. 181–292, pp. 187–189. For this authors, every fees system, looser pays everything, or each party pays its fees, may produce barriers to Access to civil justice.

[63] Trebilcock et al. (2012), p. 3.

[64] It was until the Treaty of Lisbon of the European Union which in 2007, which provides this right expressly in its articles 61.4: "The Union shall facilitate access to justice, in particular through the principle of mutual recognition of judicial and extrajudicial decisions in civil matters."

[65] See, Human Rights Committee, General Comment No. 32, CCPR/C/GC/32, 23 August 2007, pp. 3, 4.

[66] I/A Court H.R., Case of Cantos v. Argentina. Merits, Reparations and Costs. Judgment of November 28, 2002. Series C No. 97, par. 54.

[67] ECHR, Case of Golder v. United Kingdom, no. 4451/70, Judgment of 21 February 1975, par. 36.

[68] Cappelletti and Garth (1978), p. 185.

[69] Cappelletti and Garth (1978), pp. 183–186.

[70] Van Dijk and Van Hoof (1998), p. 74.

obligation, access to justice is a human right which entails positive and negative obligations from the State. Contraventions of this right might come from legal barriers but also from practical barriers that might turn into obstacles.[71]

Access to justice means providing access to a proper and effective mechanism to resolve complex and non-complex civil cases. These types of cases might have different names depending on the criteria used. For example, Small Claims if the factor is the amount of the allegation, or Neighborhood Justice if it is dedicated to the conflicts that tend to arise in the context of day-to-day problems in residential areas.[72] Particularly regarding International Human Rights Law, what is relevant is to satisfy the State obligations to ensure and guarantee the protection of substantive rights no matter their nature, as long as they are provided by the legal system.

As a human right, access to the courts to seek protection of rights that must be available to all persons regardless of their economic status, social origin, or other condition. Lack of access to justice, particularly for those in circumstances that make them vulnerable, therefore implies a violation of the international standards established in many instruments and especially of what has been called an effective judicial protection. Thus, as a right, access to justice implies an obligation to provide the conditions for the protections of rights. Beyond legal recognition, rights require to be enjoyed effectively.

The fact that common legal needs do not reach the civil courts is a concern not just for the individuals involved, but also because it affects society as a whole. As Genn has pointed out, besides solving disputes civil justice "...provides the architecture for the economy to operate effectively, for agreements to be honored and for the government to be scrutinized and limited."[73] In this regard, access to justice is also fundamental to maintaining and strengthening the rule of law. As Genn describes them, these functions served by civil justice are essential because they affirm that we live in a society where there are rights and protections which are enforceable and, in the end, effective.[74] Crucial to this argument is the idea that the civil justice system is comprised not just of substantive rights but also procedural provisions that allow citizens to bring civil claims, as they have a right of action and the machinery to enforce those rights and make them effective.[75]

In a recent article, Lucy argues that access to justice comprises three key elements: (i) the production and promulgation of legal knowledge; (ii) guidance on what the law requires; (iii) a legal forum that serves as dispute resolution mechanism provided by the State.[76] While this author sees a direct link between the first element

[71] ECHR, Case of Golder v. United Kingdom, no. 4451/70, Judgment of 21 February 1975, par. 26; I/A Court H.R., Case of Fernández Ortega et al. v. Mexico. Preliminary Objection, Merits, Reparations, and Costs. Judgment of August 30, 2010. Series C No. 215, par. 201.

[72] For an empirical study on Small Claims Courts, see: Lillo (2016).

[73] Genn (2010), p. 3.

[74] Genn (2010), p. 3.

[75] Genn (2010), p. 11.

[76] Lucy (2020), pp. 381–382.

on his account of access to justice and the classical Lon Fuller's list of eight key desiderata of the rule of law—specially with the generality and promulgation desiderata—the other two flows from the complexity that modern legal systems entail and the incentives for the addresses to want to know and to contests law's content, and the need for a fora in which to resolve contested claims, which follows from reciprocity—the eight desiderata general purpose.[77]

According to Rawls, the rule of law is firmly based on its regular and impartial administration, what he called "justice as regularity." In this regard, a legal order is administered more fairly if it follows the principles of the rule of law. Then, to make the rule of law effective, a judicial process is required that can reasonably be expected to establish the truth by means proportional to other goals of the legal system.[78] In this regard, the rule of law requires, not just the existence of a legal order, but also that its norms, besides being enacted, must be effectively enforced and applied in practice. The problem is, then, that the law on the books may differ from the law in action if, for whatever reason, there is lack of access to the judicial bodies in charge of that function.

Civil justice fulfils a key role on several of the elements of the rule of law, especially if the emphasis is, following Waldron, on the relevance of its formal or procedural dimension.[79] Zifcak, building on Hayek's classical determination of the rule of law's essential features, proposes five core values: legality, equality, legitimacy, accountability, and commitment to fundamental human rights.[80] In particular, for him, equal rights imply not just equal treatment but also equal access, because rights and entitlements are of little value if the opportunity for their vindication is lacking.[81] While critical on how the slogan of the rule of law has gone too far,[82] Raz's account of the principles that follow from its basic ideal also includes access to the courts, since the central role they play in ensuring the rule of law. As such, "[L] ong delays, excessive costs, etc., may effectively turn the most enlightened law to a dead letter and frustrate one's ability effectively to guide oneself by the law."[83] This importance, as noted by Lucy, arise from the particular circumstances of complexity at the social and legal levels.[84]

The relevance of civil justice it is not just in the adjudication of claims, but in the availability itself of the legal procedure. The preservation of a public forum to solve

[77] Which Lucy summarize as holding that rules must be (a) made with some degree of generality; (b) promulgated; (c) consistent; (d) non-retrospective; (e) must not require the impossible; (f) be radically unclear; (g) not contradictory; (h) congruent with official action. Lucy (2020), p. 386. See: Fuler (1969), p. 39.

[78] Rawls (1999), pp. 206–208.

[79] Waldron (2011), pp. 9–11.

[80] Zifcak (2005), p. 36.

[81] Zifcak (2005), p. 36.

[82] Raz (1979), pp. 210–211.

[83] Raz (1979), p. 217.

[84] Lucy (2020), p. 401.

disputes peacefully provides support for social stability and economic growth, since agreements and life in society in general are possible only if rights and obligations are covered by a clear framework and the effective possibility to enforce them.[85] Moreover, as stated by Resnik, beyond historical legal institutions associated with democracy such as juries, the courts themselves can be thought of as democratic forums where through the adjudication process individuals participate, redistribute, and curb power among disputants who disagree in public about the importance of legal rights. Litigants, however dissimilar outside the courtroom, must treat each other as equals. In this regard, the adjudication process allows popular participation in an egalitarian practice that serves to constrain public and private power.[86]

To confront the crisis we have referred to, the first step is to understand that the way in which we conceive the role of the courts and how they work has implications for the rights of the citizens to have their cases heard. Consequently, the issue today is how to make those rights effective.[87] With the growing importance of law in our societies, access becomes increasingly critical.[88] The central question to answer, then, is how to provide a simple, flexible, fast, and low-cost mechanism to provide access to justice, but in a way that does not sacrifice the other goals of a fair procedure and ascertaining the truth, while respecting fundamental guarantees.

In this regard, the correctness of a decision—i.e. how to apply the law to a given set of facts—will always be an essential objective of the legal procedure. However, as Zuckerman says, this does not mean that states have an absolute obligation to provide the most accurate system regardless of the cost: "It would be absurd to say that we are entitled to the best possible legal procedure, however expensive, when we cannot lay a credible claim to the best possible health service or to the best possible transport system."[89]

In addition, as stated by Scanlon, the legal process must provide not only correct decisions but also effective protection against arbitrary ones. "The procedures with which we are familiar in civil and criminal trials, disciplinary proceedings, and administrative hearings serve a variety of different functions in addition to the general one of providing protection against arbitrary power; and some of the features of the proceedings may be explained by these additional purposes. For example, many hearings are not merely fact-finding or rule-applying mechanisms; they also serve an important symbolic function as public expressions of the affected parties' right to demand that official acts be explained and justified."[90]

Besides these goals, it is important to keep proceedings simple and effective in order to enable people's access to justice. The specific design of civil procedure has a direct impact on whether people decide to use the justice system. No matter how

[85] Genn (2010), p. 3. See also: Zangl (2008), pp. 828–830.

[86] Resnik (2014), p. 10.

[87] Cappelletti and Garth (1978), pp. 239–241.

[88] Rhode (2004), p. 8.

[89] Zuckerman (1995), p. 160.

[90] Scanlon (1977), p. 99.

many due process safeguards—such as the right to professional representation or the right to challenge a judicial decision—are established, people will use other non-judicial mechanisms or no mechanisms at all to satisfy their legal needs if they believe the proceeding would consume too much time or money.

3.3 The Civil Procedure as a Barrier of Access to Justice in Latin America. The Reform Movement

During the second half of the twentieth century many Latin American countries began a profound reform process of the justice sector, inspired by an aspiration to update their justice systems to "modern" standards. Even though different waves of reforms began as early as the 1960s (and one could argue even before that), it was not until the 1980s, a time of the formation of new democracies, that this movement became a regional phenomenon and one with an unstoppable momentum. Indeed, these reforms have been described as part of a regional movement rather than just as isolated efforts.[91] In civil justice terms, these reforms had the goal, among others, of improving access to justice[92] in the region, not just by replacing civil procedure itself but also through the incorporation of alternative dispute resolution and other mechanisms such as neighborhood justice, "Houses of Justice", itinerant justice, consumer protection agencies, among others.[93]

In this section, I will describe, first, how the traditional civil procedure still in force in Latin American countries originated in the Middle Ages in continental Europe, and trace how the critics who originated the reform movement emerged. Second, I'll describe the main features and origins of the proposed Ibero-American Model Code of Civil Procedure system, which has been the normative basis for the reforms.

3.3.1 The Civil Procedure of the Ius Commune

The civil procedure that due for replacement in Latin America has its origins in the old procedure of the *Ius Commune*, one of the colonial legacies of Spain (or Portugal in the case of Brazil).[94] Even after the independence movement at the beginning of

[91] See e.g.: Hammergren (2005).

[92] Soleto and Fandiño (2017), pp. 19–21.

[93] Lillo et al. (2016), pp. 14, 20.

[94] Most procedural regulations come from the *Ley de las Siete Partidas*, the recompilation of regulations for the *Indias* in documents like the one called *Novísima Recopilación*. See: Iberian American Institute of Procedural Law (1988), p. 26, note 16; Couture (2014), pp. 18–20; Duce et al. (2008), p. 13.

the nineteenth century, in terms of procedural regulation countries kept faithful to the laws of *Castilla* in force in Spanish America during the colonial era.[95]

The civil procedure of the *Ius Commune*, developed in Europe during the Middle Ages has two main sources: (*i*) Roman law, especially the *Corpus Iuris Civile* of Justinian, and its interpretation during the medieval renaissance in European universities; (*ii*) the Roman Catholic Church and canon law, which influenced the law of procedure by adapting its dispute resolution mechanism to the judicial structures of the epoch.[96]

For the old *Ius Commune* model, the case file has an extraordinary importance. The judicial process in general, and the trial itself were held through several separated sessions where the contact between the judges and the parties was mediated by what Damaška calls a "documentary curtain."[97] Based on these written materials, judges assessed the evidence and solved the dispute in front of them. This fetishism for the written case file or dossier has been criticized for the incentives it creates to delegate pure judicial functions to clerks and, in that respect, increases the distance between the judge, the evidence, and the parties.[98] For this kind of procedure and decision-making process, a bureaucratic agency managed entirely by public officers, who handled their work using technical language and complex procedures was necessary which ended up excluding nonprofessionals almost entirely from the legal process.[99]

While one might think that Latin American basic procedural regulations could be identified with those in force in other Civil law countries (because of their Hispanic origins), the truth is that they differ profoundly. By the end of the nineteenth and the beginning of the twentieth century many countries in Western Europe—but not Spain which is probably why it was not introduced to this region—reformed their civil procedures.[100] They followed a trend termed by legal scholars the "orality" movement, which, even though it meant more than just the introduction of

[95]This was the case, for example of the *Código de Procederes* of Bolivia (1830), the *Ley de Procedimientos* of Ecuador (1835), the *Ley de Enjuiciamiento* of Venezuela (1836), the so called *Leyes Marianas* in Chile (1837), and the *Código de Procedimiento del Perú* (1852). This is the case too of the Spanish *Ley de Enjuiciamiento Civil* of 1855, which was based on old castellan regulations which were in force too on the colonies, and which explain its rapid dissemination in the new procedural regulations of the region, for example in the Chilean Code of Civil Procedure of 1902, still in force. In some other cases (like the *Código de Procedimientos Civiles* of Perú enacted in 1912 and in force until 1993) the inspiration was mainly the revised version of the Spanish text made in 1881. See: Lira (1984), pp.47–48; Nuñez (2005), p. 175; Couture (2014), pp.18–20; Oteiza (2011), p. 226.

[96]See: Damaška (1986), p. 207. See also: Merryman and Pérez-Perdomo (2007), p. 9–12; Glyn (1999), p. 370.

[97]Damaška (1986), pp. 50–53.

[98]Pereira (2015), p. 95.

[99]Damaška (1986), pp. 50–51.

[100]Vescovi (2006), pp. 21–34.

concentrated trial hearings, was designed in opposition to the old and extreme written procedure of the *Ius Commune*.[101]

In the last few decades, the civil justice reform movement in Latin America has tried to adopt the ideas of this nineteenth century continental European movement. In this regard, the Iberian American Model Code of Civil Procedure (hereinafter, the Model Code) published in 1988 by the Iberian American Institute of Procedural Law tried to update the old *Ius Commune* civil procedure by following this trend started in Europe.[102]

3.3.2 The Iberian American Model Code of Civil Procedure

This section describes the procedural system followed by this model code, its main ideas and inspirations. The Iberian American Model Code of Civil Procedure tried to update the old *Ius Commune* civil procedure following[103] a general trend started, as already described, by most European Countries at the end of the 19th and the beginning of the 20th centuries in what has been called the "orality" movement. As a reflection of the new post-World War II context, constitutionalism, and the propagation of international human rights law instruments, a key goal was to reinforce the due process and fail trial standards already guaranteed by many Latin American constitutions by ratifying the Universal Declaration of Human Rights, or at regional level, the American Convention on Human Rights.[104]

While Latin America has an established history of codification and influences mainly from France and Spain, and especially from the latter as far as procedural regulation is concerned, the ideas expressed in the Model Code have a different origin. Its main ideas were forged by a group of scholars from Uruguay and Argentina (known as the School of Río de la Plata) who incorporated ideas from the Italian school of procedural law (composed by Chiovenda, Carnelutti, Liebman, and Calamandrei), followed in turn by German scholars like Windsheid, Muther, Wach, Degenkolb, and others.

The key actor in this regard was Eduardo Couture, probably the main or at least one of the most famous scholars on civil procedure from Latin America.[105] His project for a code of civil procedure for Uruguay dating from 1945, and mainly his work with treatises like *Fundamentos del Derecho Procesal Civil* or his essay called *Las Garantías del Derecho Procesal Civil*, were as noted, a major source for the Model Code but they also continue to be part of the essential curricula of many law schools until the present day. A central idea of Couture's work for the reform,

[101] Cappelletti (1971), p. 853.

[102] Oteiza (2011), p. 229.

[103] Oteiza (2011), p. 229.

[104] Oteiza (2011), p. 233.

[105] Alcalá-Zamora y Castillo (1956), p. 101.

because of the context of democratization in the region, was the relation between the constitution, especially in terms of fundamental rights, and the civil procedure.[106] As he expressly recognized, unlike in criminal procedure scholars had paid no attention to this issue in the civil justice arena.[107] Thus, the challenge was how to harmonize the civil procedure with the requirements expressed in the documents, especially considering that many of them were influenced to different degrees by the Universal Declaration of Universal Rights and other International Human Rights treatises.[108] The old civil procedure conceptions in force in this part of the world were too outdated to satisfy this requirement. The problem, for Couture, was that the democratic states at that time had not yet designed specific procedural formulae that could be called a product of their constitutions. As an example, he mentions that the written characteristics of Latin American civil procedures infringe the principle of publicity which is essential for a democracy, and that the high cost of civil justice contravenes the basic principle that every person is equal under the law.[109] His answers are built on basic ideas not only from the European "orality" movement already described, but also on conceptions derived from the common law tradition, and especially those expressed by the Constitution of the United States and developed by its Supreme Court.

The Iberian American Institute of Procedural Law was created in 1957 during the first Latin American Conference on Procedural Law, held in Montevideo, Uruguay, in memory of Eduardo J. Couture.[110] This institution was created following the integration efforts begun by many countries of this region with the creation of the Organization of American States (OAS).

The Model Code was a product created exclusively by procedural law legal scholars. At the fourth Iberian American Conference on Procedural Law held in Venezuela in 1967 the Iberian American Institute of Procedural Law appointed the Uruguayan professors Enrique Vescovi and Adolfo Gelsi, to prepare a first draft of the Model Code (at the same time the professors Alfredo Vélez Mariconde and Jorge Clariá Olmedo were appointed to prepare its criminal counterpart).[111]

This first draft was approved with modifications during the fifth Iberian American Conference of Procedural Law held in Bogotá, 1970, and in its base the same authors, with the addition of Luis Torello, were put in charge of preparing a new draft which was presented at the eighth Conference in 1982. One important antecedent used in the drafting process was the so called "Act of Urgent Reforms" made in 1984 to try to introduce modifications to the traditional Spanish Civil Procedure Act of 1855.

---

[106] Alcalá-Zamora y Castillo (1956), p. 85.

[107] Couture (1946), p. 154.

[108] See: Levit (1999), pp. 292–301.

[109] Couture (1946), p. 154–155.

[110] Available at: Instituto Iberoamericano de Derecho Procesal (2019) Presentación institucional. http://www.iibdp.org/es/presentacion-institucional/. See also: Langer (2007), p. 642.

[111] Vescovi (2006), p. 10.

The first important feature of the Model Code was the incorporation of a procedure based on hearings in which the judge and the parties communicate directly. In this sense, the procedure was structured into two main hearings: preliminary and trial. Orality, as noted, was a necessary consequence of the reform's goal, to achieve immediacy between the parties and the judge, the concentration of proceedings to reduce delay, and transparency.[112] Nevertheless, this procedure has been described as a "mixed system" because most of the initial phase (complaint, pleadings, response, etc.) and some documentary evidence must be filed in written form.[113]

The second feature of the Model Code was to strengthen the role and power of the judge. If with the old model the civil procedure and its movement was in charge exclusively of the parties and the judge was absolutely passive in terms of an ability to speed things up, now the judge was seen as an active participant or as the "manager" of the case. In this regard, although Latin American authors had described this reform trend in terms that, despite the civil procedure, was still guided by the idea of the "dispositive principle," now the judge became an active participant, with an ability, for example, to seek evidence on his own initiative or to take all necessary measures to prevent the process from excessive delay.[114] This feature, as Cappelletti has stated, was a major innovation of the Austrian Code, a role that was meant both to expedite the proceedings and to promote the social aim of effective equality of the parties.[115] In Iberian American countries, reforms moving in this direction were previously incorporated in Spain by the Act of Urgent Reforms, as well as in México D.F. and in Venezuela.[116]

As we will see later, one of the trends of judicial reform in non-criminal matters is the creation of special courts or venues to attend to some special subjects traditionally considered to be "civil matters" like family law or labor law. Many countries had extracted such cases from the competence of civil justice and placed them under these new courts. Many of these new procedures had incorporated the same principles of the orality movement and converted procedures into hearings.[117] Instead, the Model Code had an explicit objective of counteracting that trend and it proposed a common procedural regulation for all such non-criminal matters by establishing only three types of proceedings: ordinary, extraordinary, and the order for payment procedure (procedimiento monitorio).[118]

The Model Code has been highly influential in the civil justice reform in the region. In this regard, the Uruguayan Civil Procedure Code of 1988, the Peruvian Civil Procedure Code of 1993, the Honduran Civil Procedure Code of 2007, the

[112] Iberian American Institute of Procedural Law (1988), p. 25.

[113] Vescovi (2006), pp. 14, 15.

[114] Pereira (2015), p. 96.

[115] Cappelletti (1971), p. 854.

[116] Iberian American Institute of Procedural Law (1988), p. 32.

[117] Vargas (2007), p. 29.

[118] Vargas (2007), p. 34.

Colombian Civil Procedure Code of 2012, the Brazilian Civil Procedure Code of 2015, and the Nicaraguan Code of 2015 have all followed the main ideas of the Model Code.

Critics have pointed out that one of the problems of the Model Code and associated reforms is that they are inspired by an "orality" movement consisting of reforms that were designed for another social and economic context, that prevailing in Europe in the nineteenth century. The European "orality" reforms of civil procedure of the nineteenth century were based on a liberal and individualistic paradigm, in which the law was supposed to be designed with precision to provide uniformity in its enforcement. There was no flexibility to take into account problems of social justice.[119]

Furthermore, studies in Latin America have criticized the "orality" model not only in theory, but also for how it has worked in practice. Critics have complained that, in many respects, the procedural practices under the new Latin American codes inspired by the Model Code have not succeeded in eliminating the prior heavy reliance on a written case file and on written documentation.[120] This literature calls not just for procedural reform but also for a robust implementation process of new reforms that truly transform the organizational and legal cultures associated with the *Ius Commune* civil procedure model.[121]

Whether in terms of a procedural model or their functioning in actual practice, the new civil procedure reforms inspired in the Model Code have been criticized for their inability to provide answers relevant to current social conditions. As previously said, in Latin America, just like in many other jurisdictions, there is a widely shared perception among Latin American scholars and institutions that civil justice is in crisis.[122] International actors have also called for urgent steps to improve civil justice to fulfill the legal needs of newly empowered citizens in Latin American democracies in which, for many, human rights are a universal aspiration.[123]

---

[119]Guilherme et al. (2010), pp. 4–9. As described by Álvarez, nineteenth century law's apparent egalitarianism in practice favored those in power, the owners and members of the mercantile class. Regarding the dominant ideas of law and legislation during the first half of the nineteenth century, see: Álvarez (1918).

[120]For an empirical research on the practices of non-criminal reforms in Chile, Uruguay, and Perú, see: Ríos (2013), pp. 95–166.

[121]Justice Studies Center of the Americas (2008), p. 9.

[122]In Latin-America, see, e.g.: Justice Studies Center of the Americas (2017), pp. 9–17.

[123]Rowat et al. (1995); Justice Studies Center of the Americas (2017), p. 5. On human rights as a universal aspiration, see, e.g., Kinley (2005), p. 99.

References

Alcalá-Zamora y Castillo N (1956) Calamandrei y Couture. UNAM/RFD 24:81–113

Álvarez A (1918) Dominant legal ideas in the first half of the century after the French Revolution. In: Various authors. The progress of continental law in the Nineteenth Century. The Continental Legal History Series, vol 11. Association of American Law Schools, Boston, part I, pp 3–18

Atiyah P, Summers R (1987) Form and substance in Anglo-American law. A comparative study of legal reasoning, legal theory, and legal institutions. Oxford University Press, Oxford

Barton B, Bibas S (2017) Rebooting justice. More technology, fewer lawyers, and the future of law. Encounter Books, New York

Buhai S (2009) Access to justice for underrepresented litigants: a comparative perspective. Loy Los Angeles Law Rev 42:979–1020

Byrom N (2017) Cuts to civil legal aid and the identity crisis in lawyering: lessons from the experience of England and Wales. In: Flynn A, Hodgson J (eds) Access to justice and legal aid. Comparative perspectives on unmet legal need. Hart Publishing, Oxford, pp 221–238

CAPJ (2021) Necesidades jurídicas y cursos de acción del ciudadano ante las barreras de acceso a la justicia. Informe final. Available at: http://decs.pjud.cl/direccion-de-estudios-realiza-coloquio-sobre-resultados-del-estudio-necesidades-juridicas-y-cursos-de-accion-del-ciudadano-ante-las-barreas-de-acceso-a-la-justicia/

Cappelletti M (1971) Social and political aspects of civil procedure: reforms and trends in western and eastern Europe. Mich Law Rev 69(5):847–886

Cappelletti M, Garth B (1978) Access to justice: the newest wave in the worldwide movement to make rights effective. Buff Law Rev 27:181–292

Chiarloni S (1999) Civil justice and its paradoxes: an Italian perspective. In: Zuckerman A (ed) Civil justice in crisis. Comparative perspectives of civil procedure. Oxford University Press, Oxford, pp 263–290

Chiarloni S (2014) A comparative perspective on the crisis of civil justice and on its possible remedies. REDP 13:769–796

Couture E (1946) Las garantías constitucionales del proceso civil. In: Estudios de derecho procesal en honor de Hugo Alsina. EDIAR, Buenos Aires, pp 153–213

Couture E (2014) Fundamentos del derecho procesal civil, 4th edn. Editorial IBdeF Buenos Aires

Croley S (2017) Civil justice reconsidered. Toward a less costly, more accessible litigation system. New York University Press, New York

Damaška M (1986) The faces of justice and state authority. Yale University Press, New Haven

Duce M, Marín F, Riego C (2008) Reforma a los procesos civiles orales: consideraciones desde el debido proceso y calidad de la información. In: Justicia civil: perspectivas para una reforma en américa latina. Justice Studies Center of the Americas, Santiago, pp 13–94

European Court of Human Rights (2019) The ECHR in facts & figures 2018. Available at: https://echr.coe.int/Pages/home.aspx?p=reports/factsfigures&c=

Flynn A, Hodgson J (2017) Access to justice and legal aid cuts: a mismatch of concepts in the contemporary Australian and British legal landscapes. In: Flynn A, Hodgson J (eds) Access to justice and legal aid. Comparative perspectives on unmet legal need. Hart Publishing, Oxford, pp 1–22

Fuler L (1969) The morality of law. Revised edn. Yale University Press

Galanter M (2006) A world without trials. J Disp Resol 2006(1):1–33

Gargarella R (2002) Too far removed from the people. Access to justice for the poor: the case of Latin America. Available at: http://citeseerx.ist.psu.edu/viewdoc/download?doi=10.1.1.407.7047&rep=rep1&type=pdf

Genn H (1999) Paths of justice: what people do and think about going to law. Hart Publishing, Oxford

Genn H (2010) Judging civil justice. Cambridge University Press, Cambridge

Gidi A, Zaneti H (2021) The cost of access to justice revisited—the "age of austerity" in Brazilian civil procedure five years later. Winds of change? Univ Miami Inter-Am Law Rev 52(2):49–103
Glyn T (1999) An historical introduction to modern civil law. Ashgate, Great Britain
Guilherme L, Pérez Á, Nuñez R (2010) Fundamentos del proceso civil. Hacia una teoría de la adjudicación. AbeledoPerrot, Santiago
Habermas J (1996) Between facts and norms. Contributions to a discourse theory of law and democracy (Trans: Regh W). The MIT Press, Cambridge
Hammergren L (2005) Expanding the rule of law: judicial reform in Latin America. Wash Univ Global Stud Law Rev 4:601–608
Iberian American Institute of Procedural Law (1988) El Código Procesal Civil Modelo Para Iberoamerica, Montevideo
Justice Studies Center of the Americas (2008) Justicia civil: perspectivas para una reforma en América Latina. Santiago
Justice Studies Center of the Americas (2017) Derecho de acceso a la justicia: aportes para la construcción de un acervo latinoamericano. Santiago
Kagan R (2003) Adversarial legalism. The American way of law. Harvard University Press, Cambridge
Kiesiläinen J (2008) Effiency and justice in procedural reforms: the rise and fall of the oral hearing. In: van Rhee C, Uzelac A (eds) Civil justice between efficiency and quality: from Ius Commune to the CEPEJ. Intersentia, Oxford, pp 29–46
Kinley D (2005) The universalizing of human rights and economic globalization. What roles for the rule of law? In: Zifcak S (ed) Globalisation and the rule of law. Routledge, Great Britain, pp 96–118
Kosmin L (1976) The small claims court dilemma. Hous Law Rev 13:934–982
La Rota M et al (2014) Ante la justicia. Necesidades jurídicas y acceso a la justicia en Colombia. DeJusticia, Bogotá
Langer M (2007) Revolution in Latin American criminal procedure: diffusion of legal ideas from the periphery. Am J Comp Law 55:617–676
Levit J (1999) The constitutionalization of human rights in Argentina: problem or promise? Columbia J Transnatl Law 37:281–355
Lillo R (2016) Access to justice and small claims courts: supporting Latin American civil reforms through empirical research in Los Angeles county, California. Rev Chil de Derecho 43(2): 955–986
Lillo R et al (2016) Mecanismos alternativos al proceso judicial para favorecer el acceso a la justicia en América Latina. In: Fandiño M (Coord.) Guía para la implementación de mecanismos alternativos al proceso judicial para favorecer el acceso a la justicia. Justice Studies Center of the Americas, Santiago, pp 11–125.
Lira B (1984) El derecho indiano después de la independencia en América española: legislación y doctrina jurídica. Historia 19:5–51
Lucy W (2020) Access to justice and the rule of law. Oxf J Leg Stud 40(2):377–402
Marcus R (1999) Malaise of the litigation superpower. In: Zuckerman A (ed) Civil justice in crisis. Comparative perspectives of civil procedure. Oxford University Press, Oxford, pp 71–116
Merryman J, Pérez-Perdomo R (2007) The civil law tradition. An introduction to the legal systems of Europe and Latin America, 3rd edn. Stanford University Press, California
Michalik P (1999) Justice in crisis: England and Wales. In: Zuckerman A (ed) Civil justice in crisis. Comparative perspectives of civil procedure. Oxford University Press, Oxford, pp 117–165
Nagy CI (2019) Collective actions in Europe. A comparative, economic and transsystemic analysis. SpringerOpen, Switzerland
Nissi E, Giacalone M, Cusatelli C (2019) Soc Indic Res 146:395–407. https://doi.org/10.1007/s11205-018-1892-5
Nuñez R (2005) Crónica sobre la reforma del sistema procesal civil chileno (fundamentos, historia y principios). Rev Est Jus 6:175–189. https://doi.org/10.5354/0718-4735.2011.15072

OCCA (2018) Conflictividad civil y barreras de acceso a la justicia en América Latina. Informe de vivienda y tierras. Justice Studies Center of the Americas, Santiago
OECD (2013) Government at a Glance 2013.
OECD, Open Society Foundations (2016) Leveraging the SDGs for inclusive growth: delivering access to justice for all. Available at: https://www.oecd.org/governance/delivering-access-to-justice-event.htm
Oteiza E (2011) Disfuncionalidad del modelo proceso civil en América Latina. In: López L (ed) Garantismo y crisis de la justicia. Universidad de Medellín, Medellín, pp 213–241
Pagter C, McCloskey R, Reinis M (1964) The California small claims court. Cal Law Rev 52(4): 876–898
Pereira S (2015) Justice systems in Latin America: the challenge of civil procedure reforms. Leg Inf Manag 15(2):95–99
Pleasence P, Balmer N (2012) Justiciable problems and the use of lawyers. In: Trebilcock M, Duggan A, Sossin L (eds) Middle income access to justice. University of Toronto Press, Canada, pp 27–54
Rawls J (1999) A theory of justice, Revised edition. The Belknap Press of Harvard University Press, Cambridge
Raz J (1979) The authority of law. Essays on law and morality. Oxford University Press, Oxford
Raz J (1995) Ethics in the public domain. Essays in the morality of law and politics, revised edition. Oxford University Press, Oxford
Resnik J (2014) Reinventing courts as democratic institutions. Daedalus 143(3):9–27
Rhode D (2004) Access to justice. Oxford University Press, New York
Ríos E (2013) La oralidad en los procesos civiles en América Latina. Reflexiones a partir de una observación práctica. In: Aportes para un diálogo sobre el acceso a la justicia y reforma civil en América Latina. Justice Studies Center of the Americas, Santiago, pp 95–166
Rowat M, Malik W, Dakolias M (1995) Judicial reform in Latin America and the Caribbean. Proceedings of a World Bank conference. The World Bank, Washington DC
Rueda M (2017) La raíz del Código General del Proceso: una movida concéntrica. In: Cruz H (coord.) El proceso civil a partir del Código General del Proceso, 2nd edition, Ediciones Uniandes, Bogotá, pp 33–78
Sandefur R (2009) Access to justice: classical approaches and new directions. In: Sandefur R (ed) Access to justice: sociology of crime, law, and deviance, vol 12, pp ix–xvii
Sandefur R (2015) What we know and need to know about the legal needs of the public. South Carolina Law Rev 67(2):443–460
Scanlon T (1977) Due process. In: Pennock R, Chapman J (eds) Due process, Nomos, vol XVIII. New York University Press, New York, pp 94–106
Silva A, de Barros G (2017) Acesso à justiça no brasil: panorama e perspectivas diante da jurisprudência interna e da corte internacional de direitos humanos. In: Derecho de acceso a la justicia: aportes para la construcción de un acervo latinoamericano. Justice Studies Center of the Americas, Santiago, pp 19–68
Silvestri E (2014) Italy: civil procedure in crisis. In: van Rhee C, Yulin F (eds) Civil litigation in China and Europe. Essays on the role of the judge and the parties. Springer, Switzerland, pp 235–255
Soleto H, Fandiño M (2017) Manual de mediación civil. Justice Studies Center of the Americas, Santiago
Solum L (2004) Procedural justice South Cal Law Rev 78: 181–322
Trebilcock M, Duggan A, Sossin L (eds) (2012) Middle income access to justice. University of Toronto Press, Toronto
Trejos D (2004) Civil justice reform in the Americas: lessons from Brazil. Fla J Int Law 16(1): 19–27
Van Dijk P, Van Hoof G (1998) Theory and practice of the European convention on human rights, 3rd edn. Kluwer Law International, The Hague
Vance W (1917) A proposed court of conciliation. Minn Law Rev 1:107–116

Vargas J (ed) (2007) Nueva justicia civil para Latinoamérica: aportes para la reforma. Centro de Estudios de Justicia de las Américas, Santiago

Vescovi E (2006) Teoría general del proceso, 2nd edn. Temis, Colombia

Waldron J (2011) The rule of law and the importance of procedure. Nomos 50:3–31

Weinstein I (2016) Access to civil justice in America: what do we know? In: Estreicher S, Radice J (eds) Beyond elite law. Access to civil justice in America. Cambridge University Press, New York, pp 3–20

Wolf M (2012) Collaborative technology improves access to justice. New York Univ J Legis Public Policy 15:759–789

Yein G (2007) Quality of judicial organization and checks and balances. Intersentia, Antwerp

Zander M (1995) Why Lord Woolf's proposed reforms of civil litigation should be rejected. In: Zuckerman A, Cranston R (eds) Reform of civil procedure. Essays on 'access to justice'. Clarendon Press, Oxford, pp 79–96

Zangl B (2008) Judicialization matters! A comparison of dispute settlement under GATT and the WTO. Int Stud Q 52(4):825–854

Zifcak S (2005) Globalizing the rule of law. Rethinking values and reforming institutions. In: Zifcak S (ed) Globalisation and the rule of law. Routledge, Great Britain, pp 32–64

Zuckerman A (1995) A reform of civil procedure: rationing procedure rather than access to justice. J Law Soc 22(2):155–188

Zuckerman A (1999) Justice in crisis: comparative dimensions of civil procedure. In: Zuckerman A (ed) Civil justice in crisis. Comparative perspectives of civil procedure. Oxford University Press, Oxford, pp 3–52

Chapter 4
Preliminary Exercise of a Comparative Perspective. Different Approaches on How the Right to a Fair Trial Has Been Applied to Common Legal Needs

4.1 The Path of Justice Tradition, the Concept of Unmet Legal Needs and a Hypothetical Case for the Comparative Exercise

Even though there are examples from as early as 1938,[1] studies on the identification of legal needs prevalent among the population grew and expanded increasingly in the 1960s, 1970s and 1980s in North America, Europe, and beyond.[2] During the 1990s a new movement gained force, beginning with the groundbreaking work done by Hazel Genn, known as the "Paths of Justice" tradition. This movement promoted this type of research even further,[3] mainly relying on public surveys through carefully crafted questionnaires focused on the prevalence of experiences or situations that they may have encountered within certain range of time.[4] Despite differences in methodology, these studies have points in common. One such is a broad approach that considers not only current legal problems under court litigation, but also events that the population experiences without taking legal action or even identifying them as legally relevant. Thus, as defined by Genn, a *justiciable event* means "...a matter experienced by a respondent which raised legal issues, whether

[1] According to Pleasence et al., in 1938 Clark and Corstvet's published the first study of this kind in the United States. See: Pleasence et al. (2013), p. 3.

[2] Genn (1999), p. 5. For example, in Australia by the work done by Cass and Sackville in 1973. See: Curran and Noone (2007), p. 65. Regarding this type of studies in Latin-America, see: OCCA (2018), pp. 40–49.

[3] According to Pleasence et al, between 1994 and 2012, 26 large-scale national surveys were conducted in at least 15 separate jurisdictions. Pleasence et al. (2013), p. 3. The most updated repository of such studies may be found at the World Justice Project Atlas of Legal Needs Surveys, which includes more than 90 studies conducted in 108 countries and jurisdictions available at: https://worldjusticeproject.org/legal-needs-atlas.

[4] Sandefur (2015), p. 444.

R. Lillo Lobos, *Understanding Due Process in Non-Criminal Matters*, Ius Gentium: Comparative Perspectives on Law and Justice 97,
https://doi.org/10.1007/978-3-030-95534-2_4

or not it was recognized by the respondent as being 'legal' and whether or not any action taken by the respondent to deal with the event involved the use of any part of the civil justice system."[5] As expressed by Sandefur, this concept refers to everyday situations faced by common individuals in a broad range aspects of their lives—such as work, finances, social benefits, etc.—sharing the same basic feature: they are all "justiciable" problems.[6]

Even though we should be cautious in generalizing results from a comparison of these studies, it is still possible to find some common trends relevant for my research purpose. For example, one basic idea found in many of these studies is that every kind of person may suffer or experience legal needs, they do not impact in the same way across different groups of population. We know, for example, they weight heavier on disadvantaged groups of populations, creating or exacerbating their disadvantages.[7] We don also know that their frequency and especially people's involvement could be greater within higher levels of integration into economic and social life. In this regard, routine every day activities correlate with the kind of problems most frequently reported.[8] Yet, as stated in the previous chapter, attitudes towards them can differ widely. According to Pleasence and Balmer, apart from the nature, value, and seriousness of a person's problem, whether they seek vindication of their rights varies according to the income of the individuals affected. Higher income people tend to have higher rates of involvement with legal services to solve their problems of a civil nature.[9]

These common trends, which it is possible to identify from these studies, are useful to describe the types of cases that the population experience and could eventually try to solve by resorting to the courts. In this regard, these studies tend to show, for example, that civil related justiciable problems are more common than criminal.[10] From the former, and among the usual subjects surveyed, the most frequent categories are related to consumer problems (such as disputes over defective goods and services) and those involving issues between neighbors such as pecuniary disputes.[11] Based on this idea, and just as a starting point, I provide a hypothetical case for use in later comparisons of how different legal procedures of a civil nature would approach such a case, with a focus on procedural guarantees.

[5] Genn (1999), p. 12.

[6] Sandefur (2015), p. 443.

[7] Sandefur (2015), p. 446; OECD and Open Society Foundations (2019), pp. 31–32.

[8] Pleasence et al. (2013), p. 28.

[9] Pleasence and Balmer (2012), pp. 36–40; Pleasence et al. (2013), p. 33.

[10] OECD and Open Society Foundations (2016), p. 2.

[11] Pleasence et al. (2013), p. 29; OECD and Open Society Foundations (2019), p. 31.

4.1.1 The Butchers

Erick Rivers is a 25-year-old amateur musician. He usually plays at local bars with his cover band called "The Butchers". Their set list is composed mainly of rock music from the 1970s and the 1990s. He recently bought his first semi-professional electric guitar from a new brand called "Fester Guitars" at a local store located in his hometown. The storeowner, Mr. Shredder, highly recommended the new brand for its quality and affordable price. Erick paid US$ 4.000 for the guitar.

Right after this purchase, for the band's next gig in the local pub called "The Corner Music Bar", Erick decided to use his new guitar. That is when Erick's problems began. The guitar's sound quality was extremely poor no matter how hard Erick fiddled with different cables and amps. The music produced by the band, caused by the horrible sound of Erick's guitar made public to leave the place screaming and booing. Finally, after the brief concert the owner of the bar, Ms. Morris, fired the band and decided not to pay what they had agreed to verbally: 10% of the revenue of the sale of the tickets (which could be valued at no more than US$ 1.000). Of course, Erick felt terrible because he spent a lot of money on a useless guitar, failed his band mates, and more importantly disappointed their local fans.

He decided to approach both Mr. Shredder and Ms. Morris to try to remedy his problem from a legal point of view. First, because he considered that the product had a defect no matter if it was the manufacturer or seller's fault, he went directly to the store to return the guitar and ask for his money back. As expected, Mr. Shredder said he would not return the money because it was a manufacturer's problem since the capsules of the guitar were made for domestic and not for professional use, and that kind of issue was not covered by the store's refund policy. Second, he decided to talk to the owner of the bar because despite the bad outcome of the concert, the bar sold tickets and the band played, so he felt the band was entitled to what was promised. Ms. Morris refused and what is more, she decided to forbid the band from playing again on the premises.

Two different civil actions and substantive laws are raised by this cameo, one related to consumer protection and the other to contractual remedies. If Erick decides to sue Mr. Shredder for civil liability by filing a claim in his local courts or in any other any other administrative agency, ¿what kind of procedure would be due under constitutional or legal procedural rights?

4.2 Comparing California and Chile

To show differences between conceptions of due process in non-criminal matters, it is useful to compare the United States, especially California, and Chile. The idea is to review the applicable legal procedures focusing on the procedural guarantees afforded or required by the conception of a right to a due process in each case.

There are some good reasons for this comparison. First, they are two systems of civil procedure I am familiar with, not just in terms of my graduate studies but also as research subjects.[12] Secondly, because both jurisdictions may be considered representative of two different legal traditions.

On the California side, the California Code of Civil Procedure, enacted in 1872 following the New York Code of Procedure of 1848 (the so called Field code) and later amended to incorporate main parts of the Federal Rules of Civil Procedure,[13] provides an adversarial setting commonly associated with the Anglo-American legal tradition despite its Mexican-Spanish heritage.[14] The same is true, notwithstanding its special features, of the specific legal procedure applicable to the case at hand, the Small Claims Court procedure regulated in Chapter 5.5 of the code, known as the Small Claims Court Act. This specific procedure, established in 1921 as an integral part of the general court system throughout the State,[15] as in many others, follows the adversarial model for litigation as the norm, but with an essential modification of the judge's role, which tends to me more active than the common passive umpire.[16]

On the Chilean side, the applicable legal procedure would be the one established by the Code of Civil Procedure enacted in 1902 which closely follows the Spanish Civil Procedure Act of 1855. Both are typical examples of the old procedure of the *Ius Commune* developed in Europe during the Middle Ages, in which the legal process in general, and the trial itself is held through several separate sessions in which the contact between the judges and the parties is mediated by what Damaška calls a "documentary curtain."[17]

It is a good comparison also because there is existing literature on comparative law between the Chilean and the American civil procedures. Richard Cappalli published in 1990 an informative article called "Comparative South American Civil Procedure: A Chilean Perspective.". He describes similarities and differences between both jurisdictions, and also comments on how many South American codes are very similar.[18] Because the Californian civil procedure—like that of many States—resembles the one established at the Federal level, and the Chilean resembles those of other Latin-American countries which have not yet reformed their civil procedure codes, both are good proxies for a broad comparison of the civil justice in the two traditions.

Finally, Cappalli in his work argues for the practicality of the comparison between United States and South-American civil procedure for legal practitioners

---

[12]Regarding California small claims courts system, see: Lillo (2016). Regarding Chilean civil courts, see: Lillo (2020).

[13]Clermont (2009), pp. 26, 27; Clark (1958), p. 435.

[14]The debates over the European conciliation court model in California are enlightening in this regard. See: Kessler (2017), pp. 233–236.

[15]Its current version date from 1990.

[16]Lillo (2016), p. 959.

[17]Damaška (1986), pp. 50–53.

[18]Cappalli (1990), p. 242.

in both hemispheres and their clients.[19] He focuses on the growing exchange in the 1980s, especially in export/import from the United States, now widely surpassed following the signing of the Free Trade Agreement between both countries in 2003.[20] However, connections between Chile and California go further back than the recent surge of trade.[21] According to Edward Dallam, connections between California and Chile began in 1786 when Jean- François de Galaup de La Pérouse brought potatos by ship from central Chile to the Franciscan mission at San Carlos Borromeo in Carmel, California. This event inaugurated a long trend of environmental and social displacements, exchanges and influences that have endured for more than two centuries between the country and the State, marked by their similar geography but opposed agricultural seasons.[22]

That said, first I will describe the substantive law applicable to both legal issues in the cases against Mr. Shredder and Ms. Morris, both due process clauses and provisions, and finally their legal procedures. I will also provide some statistical data that illustrate my point even further.

4.2.1 Applicable Substantive Law

The case against Mr. Shredder would be subject to specific regulations related to consumer protection, both in California and in Chile.

In the case of California, the applicable regulation would be, in general, the one related to the "Implied Warranty of Merchantability" by which it is presumed that consumer goods are fit for the ordinary purposes for which such goods are used.[23] The idea is that under the California Consumer Warranty Act, every sale of consumer goods that are marketed at retail in the state shall be accompanied by the manufacturers' and the retail sellers' implied warranty that the goods are merchantable.[24] Although the implied warranty does not provide for absolute satisfaction

---

[19]Cappalli (1990), p. 241.

[20]Cappalli describe how in 1986 the exports from the United States to Argentina, Bolivia, Brazil, Chile, Colombia, Ecuador, Paraguay, Peru, Uruguay, and Venezuela totaled US$11.8 billion while imports amounted to US$19.8 billion. See: Cappalli (1990), p. 214, footnote 2. According to the Office of the United States Trade Representative, U.S. goods exports solely to Chile in 2013 were US$17.6 billion while imports totaled US$10.4 billion. Available at: https://ustr.gov/map/countriesaz/cl.

[21]Exports from California to Chile in 2013 amounted US$2.2 billion, being the second State exporting to Chile. See: International Trade Administration, U.S.-Chile Bilateral Trade Analysis. Available at: https://build.export.gov/build/idcplg?IdcService=DOWNLOAD_PUBLIC_FILE&RevisionSelectionMethod=Latest&dDocName=eg_main_017585.

[22]Dalam (2015), pp. 1–11.

[23]West's Ann. Cal. Civ. Code § 1791.1, § 1792, § 1792.2. See also: Unif. Commercial Code § 2-314.

[24]West's Ann. Cal. Civ. Code § 1792.

from the buyer, it does provide for a minimum level of quality.[25] In *Music Acceptance Corp. v. Lofing*, the Court of Appeal stated that in the event of a breach of the implied warranty of merchantability, the buyer is entitled to cancel the contract and recover any amounts paid toward the purchase of the good.[26] According to the Civil Code, any buyer of consumer goods may bring an action for the recovery of damages and other relief in the face of a failure to comply with the obligations under the implied warranty, which may include the reimbursement of the payment among other costs and expenses.[27]

In our case, Erick must prove that he bought the guitar from Mr. Shredder; that at the time of the purchase the defendant was in the business of selling those guitars to retail buyers; and that this consumer good was not fit for the ordinary purposes for which these goods are used, that is, to be usable for playing guitar at a small venue. The critical test, in this regard, is *fitness for the ordinary purpose*, where the "crucial inquiry" is "whether the product conformed to the standard performance of like products used in the trade."[28]

Under Chilean legislation, Erick is protected by the Legal Warranty established by the Consumer Rights Protection Act. According to it, every consumer who has suffered because of a defect of a product has the non-renounceable right to choose between replacement, repair, or refund, plus recovery for damages.[29] This warranty applies to goods defective due to their manufacture or to their materials, or in cases where their quality makes them unfit for their common use.[30] Goods will be in this category if the features the buyer thought the product had are missing and they were important for his or her to give consent. Unfit products are those that are inadequate, simply do not work or work imperfectly when in common use.[31] This action may be pursued against the seller from the moment of the sale or subsequently for up to three months, providing evidence of the sale or the contract.[32] In our case, Erick would be entitled to go directly to the seller, Mr. Shredder, and require at least a refund, just as Erick did. Besides going to the National Consumer Service and filing a request for a mediation process between buyer and seller, he would be entitled to initiate a special civil action in a municipal Court where he could require the refund plus damages.[33]

---

[25] American Suzuki Motor Corp. V. Superior Court, 44 Cal.Rptr.2d 526, 529, 37 Cal.App.4th 1291, 1296 (Cal.app. 2 Dist., 1995).

[26] Music Acceptance Copr. V. Lofing, 39 Cal.Rptr. 2d 159, 165, 32 Cal.App.4th 610, 621 (Cal. App. 3 Dist., 1995).

[27] West's Ann. Cal. Civ. Code § 1794.

[28] Isip v. Mercedes-Benz USA, LLC, 65 Cal. Rptr.3d 695, 700, 155 Cal.App.4th 19, 27 (Cal. App. 2 Dist., 2007); Pisano v. American Leasing, 194 Cal. Rptr. 77, 80, 146 Cal. App.3d 194, 198 (Cal. App. 1 Dist. 1983).

[29] Consumer Rights Protection Act N 19496, Art. 20. See, also: Barahona (2014), p. 394.

[30] Consumer Rights Protection Act N 19496, Art. 20 (c) and (f).

[31] Barrientos (2010), p. 116.

[32] Consumer Rights Protection Act N 19496, Art. 21.

[33] Consumer Rights Protection Act N 19496, Art. 50 H, 58 (f).

In this regard, the extension of the compensation to be recovered covers not just material but also immaterial damages.[34]

On the California side, the case against Mr. Morris is a civil action over a breach of contract. In California, this civil action arises in the face of the unjustified or unexcused failure to complete a contract.[35] In California, any breach, total or partial, which causes a measurable injury gives the injured party a right to damages as compensation.[36] According to the Civil Code of California, the measure of this remedy "...is the amount which will compensate the party aggrieved for all the detriment proximately caused thereby or which, in the ordinary course of things, would be likely to result therefrom."[37] In this regard, Erick Rivers would be entitled at least to the amount due under the terms of the obligation (his US$1,000) plus interest.[38] The essential elements of his claim that he would be required to satisfy are: (1) the existence of a contract, (2) the plaintiff's performance or excuse for nonperformance, (3) the defendant's breach, and (4) the resulting damages to the plaintiff.[39]

In the case of Chile, civil liability over a breach of contract is quite similar. It is regulated by the Civil Code in the Title XXV of its Book IV, where in article 1556 it is provided that a breach of a contract might arise if an obligation of the contract is not fulfilled in its totality, or if it was satisfied but only imperfectly, or if its satisfaction was delayed. In every case, there is an obligation for the party to compensate for damages and lost profit,[40] from the moment the party is in default. That is, when the defendant has not performed in time according to the contract, or in any other case when the creditor has demanded satisfaction judicially.[41] As in the case of the California Civil Code, the plaintiff's performance or their excuse is an element that must be satisfied as a condition of compensation, since any party is considered in default if the other has not performed as agreed.[42] Chilean scholars have established that under a contract, a party would be liable if all the following elements are satisfied: (1) an event giving rise to an act or an omission by the debtor; (2) the existence of damages suffered by the creditor; (3) a causal link between that event and the damages; (4) the debtor must be in default of satisfying their

---

[34]Barahona (2014), p. 399.

[35]1 Witkin, Summary 11th Contracts § 872 (2018).

[36]Brawley v. J.C. Interiors, Inc., 74 Cal.Rptr.3d 832, 838, 161 Cal.App.4th 1126, 1134 (Cal.App 5 Dist., 2008).

[37]CA CIVIL § 3300.

[38]CA CIVIL § 3302.

[39]Coles v. Glaser, 205 Cal.Rptr.3d 922, 927, 2 Cal.App.5th 384, 391 (Cal. App. 1 Dist., 2016); General Sec- Services Corp. v. County of Fresno, 815 F.Supp.2d 1123, 1134 (E.D. Cal., 2011); Oasis West Realty, LLC v. Goldman, 250 P.3d 1115, 1121, 124 Cal.Rptr.3d 256, 263, 51 Cal.4th 811, 821 (Cal., 2011); Reichert v. General Ins. Co. of America, 442 P.2d 377, 381, 69 Cal. Rptr. 321, 325, 68 Cal.2d 822, 830 (Cal. 1968).

[40]Civil Code, Art. 1556.

[41]Civil Code, Art. 1551.

[42]Civil Code, Art. 1555.

obligations under the contract.[43] Regarding the event giving rise to the liability of the debtor, case law and scholars have established through article 1547 of the Civil Code, that this act or omission requires a subjective element of negligence or intent.[44]

4.2.2 *Due Process/Fair Trial Applicable Provisions*

In this section I will try to answer the question whether Erick has a right to pursue the enforceability or to be compensated over a violation of his substantive rights in each jurisdiction. If this is so, the next question arises as to the conditions under which Erick might initiate a legal proceeding by filing a claim in each case. In other words, what kind of legal procedure and under what minimum conditions he may do so in terms of the procedural guarantees afforded.

In the context of California, it is a complex answer, especially in terms of the relation between the federal and state constitutions. In terms of the right of access to the courts, it is a right guaranteed by the Constitution; if not expressly guarantee, as I will explain in Chap. 10, has been derived from other provisions such as the First Amendment right to petition the government for redress of grievances[45] and as an inherent part of the due process clause derived from both the Fifth and Fourteenth Amendments.[46] Both clauses are incorporated in the Constitution of the State of California. The former in article I section 3[47] and the latter in section 7.[48] In this regard, in *Payne v. Superior Court*, the Supreme Court of California found that "...an indigent prisoner seeking to defend a civil suit, has a due process right of access to the courts...The state has the burden of demonstrating a compelling state interest to justify the infringement...The denial of access also constitutes a prima facie equal protection violation"[49]

---

[43] Urrejola (2011), p. 29.

[44] Civil Code, Art. 1547.

[45] Jersey v. Jhon Muir Medical Center, 118 Cal. Rptr. 2d 807, 812, 97 Cal.App. 4th 814, 821 (Cal. App. 1 Dist., 2002); Church of Sientology v. Wollersheim, 49 Cal.Rptr. 2d 620, 631, 41 Cal. App. 4th 628, 647 (Cal. App. 2m Dist., 1996).

[46] Chang Doua Yang v. Kong Meng Lee, 2017 WL 4988174, at.*7 (Cal. App. 5 Dist., 2017).

[47] Article I, Section 3 (a): "The people have the right to instruct their representatives, petition government for redress of grievances, and assemble freely to consult for the common good."

[48] Article I, Section 7 (a): "A person may not be deprived of life, liberty, or property without due process of law or denied equal protection of the laws; provided, that nothing contained herein or elsewhere in this Constitution imposes upon the State of California or any public entity, board, or official any obligations or responsibilities which exceed those imposed by the Equal Protection Clause of the 14th Amendment to the United States Constitution with respect to the use of pupil school assignment or pupil transportation..."

[49] Payne v. Superior Court, 553 P.2d 565, 573, 132 Cal.Rptr. 405, 413, 17 Cal.3d 908, 919 (Cal. 1976). Regarding the right to access to the courts as part of the right of petition, see: Teachers Ass'n v. State of California, 975 P.2d 622, 632, 84 Cal.Rptr.2d 425, 435, 20 Cal.4th 327, 339 (Cal.1999).

Having established the right of access to the courts as a constitutional right in California, the next question is what type of legal procedure Erick would be entitled to, or what conditions should be satisfied in order to consider it the procedure that is "due." As I explain in Chap. 10, in the United States the common understanding of the due process clause, as a constitutional provision, is that it applies to any type of proceeding where a person could be affected in their life, liberty or property[50] by a governmental or public action.[51] Only when this condition is met does the second question of the minimum requirements of legal procedures arises.[52] As in the case of section 29 of the Constitution of the State of California, many current constitutional provisions related to fair trial expressly mention criminal procedure.[53] Yet, it is clear that the general clause of the Fifth and the Fourteenth Amendments, as section 7 of the Constitution of the State of California, applies to civil procedures as well.

In cases between private actors, or at least where there is no direct governmental intervention, the due process clause would not apply because of the state action doctrine, which is criticized on Chap. 10. Of course, that is not to say that a legal procedure between private individuals may not provide minimum conditions to be considered fair. As I will argue later, there might be good reasons to think that constitutional requirements apply even in such cases. For now, it is not necessary to enter this debate, since in California, in the context of membership applications to private associations or exclusions from them, similar protections have been afforded, if not by the Constitution, under the common law duty of fair procedure. In *Pinsker v. Pacific Coast Society of Orthodontists*, the Supreme Court of California held: "We thus recognized that a basic ingredient of the 'fair procedure' required under the common law is that an individual who will be adversely affected by a decision be afforded some meaningful opportunity to be heard in his defense. Every one of the numerous common law precedents in the area establishes that this element is indispensable for a fair procedure".[54] In this setting, beside the basic notion of notice and hearing providing the party a meaningful opportunity to present his or her case or defend himself or herself, other rights or procedural protections such as the right

---

[50] As I'll explain in subsequent chapters, early case law was centered in determining the importance of the interest while categorization between life, liberty, or property. It was fruit of the late twentieth century case law, which focused more on the nature of the interest at issue. Sullivan and Massaro (2013), p. 40.

[51] On the contrary, inaction or omission from public agencies (e.g., providing protection against private wrongdoings) is a much more debatable trigger of the clause. See: Strauss (1989), pp. 53–86.

[52] Galligan (1996), p. 190.

[53] Section 29 of the Constitution of the State of California, provides a speedy and public trial as other procedural guarantees such as the right to compel the attendance of witnesses, the assistance of a counsel, among others, but in such a language that refers only to in criminal cases.

[54] Pinsker v. Pacific Coast Society of Orthodontists, 526 P. 2d 253, 263, 116 Cal.Rptr. 245, 255, 12 Cal. 3d 541, 555 (Cal. 1974).

to counsel, to cross-examine, to an unbiased trier of facts, and others, will depend on the circumstances of the particular case.[55]

In Chile, as in California, the right of access to the courts is not expressly established in the Constitution but rather is a judicial and doctrinal interpretation derived from two Constitutional provisions, articles 19 N° 3 and 76.[56] The former guarantees equal protection in the exercise of rights. In paragraph 6, it establishes a due process clause in the following terms: "...Every decision of a body vested with jurisdiction must be based upon previous legally based proceedings. It will be the responsibility of the legislator to establish, at all times, the guarantees for a rational and fair investigation and procedure."[57] The second key provisions is article 76, which provides the judiciary with exclusive power to adjudicate cases and enforce compliance of judgments, but at the same time it mandates that "...Courts may not excuse themselves from exercising their authority if their intervention is requested in a legal manner and in connection with affairs of their jurisdiction, not even in the absence of a law to resolve the dispute or issue submitted to their decision."[58]

The other relevant source are the international human rights treatises signed by the State. The latter is an important source of rights according to article 5 of the Chilean Constitution of 1980, which provides that rights emanating from human nature constitute a limit to sovereignty and are mandatory for public bodies to guarantee no matter whether those rights are established in the Constitution or in international human rights treatises currently in force.[59] Particularly relevant are the American Conventions on Human Rights, the Universal Declaration on Human Rights, and the International Covenant on Civil and Political Rights. The former establishes in Article 8.1 its due process clause[60] and in article 25 provides an effective remedies provision called the right to effective judicial protection.[61] The

---

[55] Cruz (1986), pp. 74–75.

[56] García Contreras (2013), p. 247.

[57] Unofficial translation by the author on the basis of: Couso, Javier et al., Constitutional Law in Chile, Great Britain, Wolters Kluwer, 2011, p. 212.

[58] Unofficial translation by: Couso et al. (2011), p. 115.

[59] Couso et al. (2011), p. 171.

[60] Article 8.1. Every person has the right to a hearing, with due guarantees and within a reasonable time, by a competent, independent, and impartial tribunal, previously established by law, in the substantiation of any accusation of a criminal nature made against him or for the determination of his rights and obligations of a civil, labor, fiscal, or any other nature.

[61] Article 25. 1. Everyone has the right to simple and prompt recourse, or any other effective recourse, to a competent court or tribunal for protection against acts that violate his fundamental rights recognized by the constitution or laws of the state concerned or by this Convention, even though such violation may have been committed by persons acting in the course of their official duties.

2. The States Parties undertake:

a. to ensure that any person claiming such remedy shall have his rights determined by the competent authority provided for by the legal system of the state;

Inter-American Court of Human Rights has established a right of access to the courts as upheld by both articles of the Convention.[62]

Because of the lack of an explicit provision, it has been up to local legal scholars and the case law of the Constitutional Court to give content to this right. For example, in 1995 the Constitutional Court described access to justice as an inherent part of the rule of law, and as a consequence of the prohibition of individuals from taking justice into their own hands.[63] Much of the development refers to the relation between this right and others such as the right of action, judicial protection, or to the due process of law.[64] Regarding the relation between access to justice and due process, the Constitutional Court has said that access to justice would be a pre-requisite to provide effectiveness to other due process guarantees. For example, in 2009 it said that access to justice is "...one of the rights guaranteed by the N° 3 of the article 19 of the Constitution. Notwithstanding it is not provided expressly in its written text, it would be meaningless for the Fundamental Chart to provide for equal protection of the law in the exercise of the rights, the right to legal assistance, the right to be tried by a natural judge, or the right to a rational and fair procedure, without a prior right which is a basic presupposition for its legal existence. That is the right of every person to be tried, to an appearance in front of a judge without barriers or conditions inhibiting, delaying or impeding it in an arbitrary or in illegitimate way".[65]

In Chile, there is a constitutional right of access to the courts in order to be able to fully exercise a right to a procedure under conditions considered to be rational and fair. In this regard, the expression already described that "...guarantees for a rational and fair investigation and procedure" is the clause which embeds the idea of the right to a due process of law. In fact, that specific name was replaced by the current provision to provide the same protection but without using the Anglo-Saxon name for it. By doing that, it was said, courts and practitioners would not get confused with the incorporation of foreign case law pertaining to a different tradition.[66] However, it is clear how much influence the United States Constitution's due process clause and international sources such as the Universal Declaration of Human Rights had in

b. to develop the possibilities of judicial remedy; and
c. to ensure that the competent authorities shall enforce such remedies when granted.

[62] Medina (2016), pp. 355–358. See, e.g.: Inter-American Court of Human Rights, Case of Claude Reyes et al. v. Chile, Judgment of September 19, 2006, Series C No. 151, par. 127.

[63] Constitutional Court of Chile, Case N° 205-1195, January 31, 1995, c.9.

[64] Bordalí (2011), p. 312.

[65] Unofficial translation. Constitutional Court of Chile, Case N° 1470-2009, October 27, 2009, c. 9. See also: Constitutional Court of Chile, Case N° 1046-2008, June 22, 2008, c. 20; Constitutional Court of Chile, Case N° 1061-2008, August 28, 2011, c.15, and Constitutional Court of Chile, Case N° 2438-2013, April 10, 2014, c. 11.

[66] Official Acts of the Constitutional Committee, Session 101st, January 9th, 1975, p. 14.

giving shape to and influencing the enactment of the due process clause in the Chilean Constitution.[67]

The due process clause has been described as a complex right in terms of its composition. In this regard, the clause is composed of a set of procedural guarantees that would be required for an individual to be tried in a legal proceeding.[68] Today it is clear that the Constitution gives a broad conception to the due process clause in terms of its application to every legal procedure.[69] To provide content to the general clause, the Constitutional Court has had an originalism approach to the debates of the Constitutional Committee. On this basis, the Constitutional Court has found that the legislator is the body in charge of determining the minimum requirements that must be satisfied for a procedure to be considered rational and fair. Notwithstanding, there are some basic guarantees which must be present whatever the nature of the case: a right to notice and to have the opportunity to confront the allegations of the counterpart, to produce proofs, and to appeal to the decisions of an impartial judge of a court pre-established by law.[70]

Currently, besides the general due process clause of article 19 N° 3 protecting a rational and fair investigation and procedure, this article also provides for specific procedural guarantees. The independence and impartiality of the bodies which investigate and prosecute; quality in the interpretation and application of the law; guarantees of counsel and defense whenever it is required; certainty on the concept and delimitation of deadlines; the non-retroactivity of criminal laws and their configuration by the legislature, etc.[71] This list, according to legal scholars, must be complemented with the international human rights treatises,[72] for example by adding the procedural guarantees of article 8 of the American Convention of Human Rights. This provision establishes a general clause of the right to be heard under basic due process standards, like judicial independence or impartiality, in the substantiation of any accusation of a criminal nature or "...for the determination of ...rights and obligations of a civil, labor, fiscal, or any other nature."[73] In turn,

[67] See: Official Acts of the Constitutional Committee, Session 100th, January 6th, 1975, p. 4; Official Acts of the Constitutional Committee, Session 101st, January 9th, 1975, pp. 6–8.

[68] Duce et al. (2008), p. 17.

[69] Duce et al. (2008), p. 85.

[70] Constitutional Court of Chile, Case N° 481-06, July 4th, 2006, c. 7.

[71] Couso et al. (2011), p. 201.

[72] Bordalí (2011), pp. 266–268.

[73] Different from the solution given by the European Convention of Human Rights, which in its article 6.1 provides basic guarantees for the determination of "...civil rights and obligations" and in consequence generating a fruitful but no less complex case law from the European Court of Human Rights but also from the highest courts of the member States interpreting the meaning of this expression. See, in this regard: Cross (2010), p. 366; European Court of Human Rights, Case of Ringeisen v. Austria, 16 July 1971, par. 94; European Court of Human Rights, Case of König v. Germany, 28 June 1978, par. 89; European Court of Human Rights, Case of Le Compte, Van Leuven and De Meyere v. Belgium, 23 June 1983, par. 46–47; European Court of Human Rights, Case Elles and Others v. Switzerland, 16 March 2011, par. 20; European Court of Human Rights,

article 8.2 provides more specific minimum guarantees expressly reserved for the *accused of a criminal offense* such as the presumption of innocence; to be assisted without charge by a translator; adequate time and means for the preparation of his or her defense; the right of the accused to defend himself or herself personally or to be assisted by legal counsel; an inalienable right to be assisted by counsel provided by the state if the accused does not defend himself personally or engage his own counsel; the right of the defense to examine witnesses present in the court and to obtain the appearance, as witnesses, of experts or other persons who may throw light on the facts; the right not to be compelled to be a witness against himself or to plead guilty; and the right to appeal the judgment to a higher court.[74] Moreover, others have described how, as mentioned previously, article 25 provides a right to an effective judicial protection and incorporates the right to a simple and effective appeal within the guarantees of a fair and rational procedure.[75]

As explained in Chap. 6, this broad conception of due process allowed by an expansive doctrine and the Inter-American Court of Human Rights, shared by Chilean scholars and reflected in case law, applies the same protections of due process in criminal matters to non-criminal proceedings.

In Chile, the addition of this expansive doctrine and the Constitutional protections to those recognized in International Treatises of Human Rights, may be exemplified by two particular procedural guarantees. First, notwithstanding its origins in the special focus on criminal matters,[76] that of a right to professional legal assistance as mandatory or at least as a general rule in every type of legal proceeding.[77] The case of the appeal as a resort to a two-tier system, common in Continental Law countries,[78] goes even further in Chile. There are authors who consider that the Article 19 N° 3 Due Process Clause, and also Article 8° of the American Convention of Human Rights,[79] provide for an appeal against the final decision as an inherent procedural guarantee in civil cases.[80] Likewise the Constitutional Court, which has considered an appeal against final decisions an inherent part of the due process clause in the Constitution.[81]

Case of Shapovalov v. Ukraine, 31 July 2012, par. 43–45; European Court of Human Rights, Case of Fazia Ali v. the United Kingdom, 20 January 2016, par. 53–54.

[74] American Convention on Human Rights, Art. 8.2.

[75] Couso et al. (2011), p. 201.

[76] Cea (2012), p. 158.

[77] The Article 1 of the Act N° 18.120, provides for a general rule of a mandatory system of legal representation: The first presentation of each party or claimant in disputed or voluntary matters at any Court of the Republic, being a common jurisdiction court, arbitral or special, shall be sponsored by an attorney admitted to the bar (Unofficial translation).

[78] Merryman and Pérez (2007), pp. 120,121.

[79] Both, mandatory legal assistance and a right to appeal are part of the list of procedural guarantees exclusively provided for the accused in the article 8.2. of the American Convention of Human Rights.

[80] Astorga (2017), pp. 241–242. See, also: Palomo (2010), pp. 496–501.

[81] Constitutional Court of Chile, Case N° 205-1995, January 31, 1995, c.8.

4.2.3 The Applicable Legal Procedure in California. Empirical Data on the Small Claims Court of Los Angeles, California

In California the applicable legal procedure in both civil actions will fall under the general jurisdiction of the Superior Court of the specific county where both contracts (sale and performance) were made or where the obligations or liability arose, or the breaches occurred. Moreover, both defendants, Mr. Shredder and Mr Morris, could be sued in the county where the principal places of business were located (assuming that it was in the same locality where Erick lives).[82]

In terms of legal procedure, there are two available tracks for Erick. First, the Limited Civil Cases procedure regulated by the Code of Civil Procedure, which applies to cases not exceeding $25,000. No matter that it has some features that make it less expensive than the general civil procedure for unlimited civil cases, it has other requirements in terms of pleadings, motions, and discovery, that are allowed and in the end make it unfit for this specific case.

Since the amount in Erick's case is much lower it would not make much sense to litigate under that regulation. Nevertheless, it is important to take into consideration that the regular procedure has been highly criticized from the point of view of access to justice. A review of several unmet legal needs' studies carried out in the United States, according to Barton and Bibas, shows that many low and middle-income Americans are living with legal problems that could be solved by a court. However, because of the high cost of legal services and the complexities of pro se litigation, unless is a simple matter—such as an uncontested divorce- most American prefer to "lump it," that is, just endure the problem without doing anything about it. For these authors, part of the problem causing the lack of legal services is procedural complexity, which boosts the prices of a market highly monopolized by the legal profession.[83] For example, according to Kagan, it is the adversarial feature of pretrial discovery, which puts powerful fact-finding tools in the hands of entrepreneurial lawyers, that makes American litigation especially costly, unpredictable, and alienating.[84]

Taking into consideration the above criticisms, because of the small amount at stake in both civil actions the applicable civil procedure in California would be the Small Claims Courts, regulated under the provisions of the Code of Civil Procedure.[85] This mechanism was designed in order to resolve minor civil disputes

---

[82] West's Ann. Cal. C.C.P. § 395.5.

[83] Barton and Bibas (2017), pp. 46–57; 65–68. Similarly, see: Croley (2017), pp. 117–134.

[84] Kagan (2003), p. 100.

[85] It may also applies the Limited Civil Cases procedure regulated by the Code of Civil Procedure, which applies to cases not exceeding 25,000. Notwithstanding, because of the amount in Erick's case is much lower, it would not make much sense to litigate under that regulation. No matter it has son some features which makes it less expensive or costly that the general civil procedure for unlimited civil cases, it still have other requirements in terms of the pleadings, motions, discovery,

expeditiously, inexpensively, and fairly, as a forum accessible to all the parties directly involved in these types of disputes.[86] The Small Claims Court was introduced in the United States at the beginning of the twentieth century. In 1920, Massachusetts was the first state to pass a statewide implementation of this type of court.[87] Since these early developments, the model experienced an important expansion throughout the country. By 1959 there were 34 states with Small Claims Courts (plus the District of Columbia)[88] and currently all 50 states have Small Claims Courts.[89]

As Yngvesson and Henessey point out, the Small Claims Court model was designed "…to be a simplified and streamlined version of due process, with a view to self-representation by the litigants. There was to be a minimum of formality, delay and expense…"[90] The main goal of this type of tribunal was to provide access to justice to "poor" litigants through the establishment of informal and simplified proceedings where expenses and delay should be greatly reduced.[91] Notwithstanding when referring to poor people, advocates meant "plain, honest men," such as "small tradespeople, lodging housekeepers and wage-earners".[92] Then, it was understood as "…not the indigent, but the great majority of all people, those who find it hard to get through each year without debt, and so cannot endure the extravagance of litigation."[93]

In California a general establishment of Small Claims Court for the entire state passed, following Massachusetts, in 1921.[94] Following important modifications during the century, a current small claims court law was enacted in 1990 and, as said, occupies sections 116.110 to 116.950 of the California Code of Civil Procedure.[95]

As with many other States, in California the Small Claims Courts are part of the ordinary court system. In fact, the Small Claims filings occupied in 2018 the 19% of the civil docket of the Judiciary of California.[96] For this purpose, each superior court has a small claims division (called Small Claims Courts even when they are not considered a separate tribunal). Since 2005, the current limit of the claim amount is

---

that are allowed and at the end makes it unfit for this specific case. See: West's Ann. Cal. C.C.P. Pt. 1, T. 1, Ch. 5.1, Art. 2.

[86]West's Ann. Cal. C.C.P. § 116.120.

[87]Pagter et al. (1964), p. 877.

[88]Best and Zalesne (1993), pp. 347–348.

[89]Lillo (2016), p. 957.

[90]Yngvesson and Henessey (1975), p. 222.

[91]Kosmin (1975), p. 936.

[92]Yngvesson and Henessey (1975), p. 221.

[93]Yngvesson and Henessey (1975), p. 222.

[94]1921 Cal. Stat. ch. 125.

[95]Lillo (2016), p. 962.

[96]Judicial Council of California (2018), p. 94.

$10,000 if the action is brought by a natural person (individual or sole proprietor).[97] This is the general rule for individual plaintiffs but there are other special exceptions as well. For example, in cases related to damages for bodily injures resulting from a car accident, the limit is $7500 if the defendant has an insurance policy covering a duty to defend.[98] For corporate plaintiffs the court has jurisdiction only in cases up to $5000. Finally, some other restrictions or limitations apply when the defendant is a guarantor.[99]

To initiate a small claims action, and in accordance with the general model of Small Claims Courts, no formal pleading (other than the claim itself) is necessary and pretrial discovery procedures are not permitted.[100] To simplify the claim a standard form is provided (physically or electronically), which provides basic information regarding the defendant, amount and basis of the claim, that the plaintiff understands that the judgment on his or her claim will be conclusive and without a right of appeal,[101] and that the plaintiff may not be represented by an attorney, etc.[102]

After the claim is filed and received, the court clerk will issue an order to appear and will schedule the trial hearing no earlier than 20 days but not more than 70 days from the date of the order.[103] This order to appear together with the claim will be served to the defendant, who may elect to file a counterclaim within the same limitations.[104] The proceeding is designed to be resolved through a single informal hearing. Witnesses are allowed in this hearing, but in an innovation from normal court proceedings, the court may consult witnesses informally and otherwise investigate the controversy with or without notice to the parties.[105] The general rule is pro se litigation, which means that no attorney may take part in the conduct or defense of a small claims action (with some exceptions e.g. if one of the parties is an attorney but is not representing a third party).[106] If a party does not understand English sufficiently, an interpreter will be provided.[107]

The case may be disposed of by dismissal, settlement, or judgment. Awards, although made in accordance with substantive law, are often based on the application of common sense; a spirit of compromise and conciliation informs the proceedings.[108] In this regard, when judgment is entered, the court can order compensation for damages, equitable relief, or both within the jurisdictional limits.

[97] Cal. Code Civ. Proc. § 116.221 (2006).

[98] Cal. Code Civ. Proc. § 116.224 (2006).

[99] Cal. Code Civ. Proc. § 116.220 (2006).

[100] Cal. Code Civ. Proc. § 116.310 (2006).

[101] Cal. Code Civ. Proc. § 116.320 (2006).

[102] Cal. Code Civ. Proc. § 116.320 (2006).

[103] Cal. Code Civ. Proc. § 116.330 (2006).

[104] Cal. Code Civ. Proc. § 116.360 (2006).

[105] Cal. Code Civ. Proc. § 116.520 (2006).

[106] Cal. Code Civ. Proc. § 116.530 (2006).

[107] Cal. Code Civ. Proc. § 116.550 (2006).

[108] Sanderson v. Niemann, 17 Cal. 2d 563, 110 P.2d 1025 (1941).

Table 4.1 Type of Party in Small Claims Court, Stanley Mosk Courthouse (Lillo 2016, p. 967)

Type of party	Corporations	Government agencies	Individuals
Plaintiffs	38%	5%	57%
Defendants	33%	2.5%	64.5%

Table 4.2 Cases by type in Small Claims Court, Stanley Mosk Courthouse (Lillo 2016, p. 974)

Case type	N° of cases (%)
Auto repair	4 (3)
Breach of contract	13 (9.7)
Car accident	20 (14.9)
Debt collection	56 (41.8)
Defamation, slander or other related	2 (1.5)
Defective products	3 (2.2)
Government services	4 (3)
Insufficient fund	6 (4.5)
Landlord/Tenant	17 (12.7)
Other	7 (5.2)
Other torts	2 (1.5)

Judges can make any orders as to the time of payment or otherwise as the court deems just and equitable for the resolution of the dispute.[109] The plaintiff has no right to appeal the judgment, but a plaintiff who did not appear at the hearing may file a motion to vacate the judgment. In contrast, the defendant may appeal the judgment to the superior court.[110] At this stage, the parties can be represented by lawyers.

According to my previous research done in Stanley Mosk Courthouse in Los Angeles, this setting allows that in this type of legal procedure individuals constitute the principal type of actor bringing claims to this jurisdiction.[111] In my database, plaintiffs were individuals 57% of the time, while corporations were plaintiffs in 38% of the cases. On the opposing side, individuals were the defendant in 64.5% (because both corporations and individuals filed claims against them more often), while corporations were the defendants in 33.5% of cases (see Table 4.1).[112]

In terms of the types of case, the docket analyzed shows that the uses made of the Small Claims Court are diverse. They depend greatly on the type of defendant. Although debt collections occupy a majority of the cases (41.8%), this is because corporations overwhelmingly sue within this category. The next most common cases were those coded as car accidents (14.9%), landlord and tenant conflicts (12.7%) and those related to breach of contract (9.7%) (see Table 4.2).

[109] Cal. Code Civ. Proc. § 116.610 (2006).

[110] Cal. Code Civ. Proc. § 116.710 (2006).

[111] The database used consisted of 200 cases randomly selected from the Stanley Mosk Courthouse for the period 2010-2013 (25 cases each year). Lillo (2016), p. 966.

[112] Lillo (2016), pp. 967, 968.

Table 4.3 Repeat players by type of plaintiff in Small Claims Court, Stanley Mosk Courthouse (Lillo 2016, p. 967)

	Repeat player		
Type of plaintiff	No	Yes	Total
Corporations (%)	20 (21.5)	32 (80)	52 (39.1)
Government agencies (%)	1 (1.1)	6 (15)	7 (5.3)
Individuals (%)	72 (77.4)	2 (5)	74 (55.7)
Total (%)	93 (70)	40 (30)	133 (100)

In this study, I called "repeat players" those who filed more than 12 small claims in the last 12 months in California. From the totality of cases where this information was available (133), 30% were repeat players. Examining only the repeat players, 80% were corporations, 15% government agencies and only 5% were individuals. This finding is important because although corporations are not a majority of the plaintiffs in the entire dataset, they are the parties that most frequently use the Small Claim Courts (Table 4.3).[113]

An important number of the corporations that sue for debt collections are repeat players. Individuals, on the other hand, who represent the majority of the plaintiffs, tend to use it for bringing different types of claims.[114] Therefore, if the majority of cases filed at the Small Claims Court are debts collections, it is mainly because corporate plaintiffs file these claims 80.8% of the time. These cases were mostly related to balances owed on installment contract agreements by the defendants who were mainly individuals. In comparison, individuals filed this type of claim only 12% of the time. The nature of the debts also varied greatly with individual plaintiffs, ranging from cases in which the claimant was pursuing the payment for a services or products provided to but not paid for by the defendants, family cases where one of the parents fail to pay agreed commitments, parties that failed to repay money borrowed, etc. All such cases were against other individuals. In contrast to corporations, cases involving individual plaintiffs tend to be diverse. Individuals sued for car accident-derived conflicts 26.7% of the time, for issues derived from landlord-tenant relationships 21.3% of the time, and for breach of contract 13.3% of the time.[115]

The average duration of the cases in this dataset was 55 days, which means that the range of time permitted by law (no less than 20 and no more than 70 days) is regularly respected. Regarding cases terminated by judgment, which may or may not be entered at the same first hearing, the average amount of days between filing and disposition was 80.4 days. The median is 61.5 which means that the average is probably being raised by the cases closest to the maximum amount of days registered (356). For all cases of the dataset with any type of disposition the numbers are similar. The median is 62.5 days, which means that most of the cases were disposed of in less than 70 days. The mean is 86.8 days, which is likely influenced by hearings scheduled closer to the maximum number of days (399). The minimum was 15 days,

[113]Lillo (2016), p. 969.
[114]Lillo (2016), p. 976.
[115]Lillo (2016), p. 975.

Table 4.4 Days between filing, first hearing, and disposition in Small Claims Court, Stanley Mosk Courthouse (Lillo 2016, p. 979)

	Median	Mean	Minimum	Maximum
Days between Filing and First Hearing	55	56.3	30	118
Days between filing and disposition (by judgment)	61.5	80.4	30	356
Days between filing and disposition (by any type of disposition)	62.5	86.8	15	399

which can be explained by cases that were resolved before the first hearing (Table 4.4).[116]

The main conclusion of this research was that with proper safeguards to avoid systematic abuse—such as limitations on corporations and on the amount of claims allowed to be filed by year—Small Claims Courts may help improve access to civil justice by providing informal and flexible responses for common citizens. Notwithstanding, this is not necessarily the case of all the Small Claims Court in the United States, which are present in the fifty States with different configurations. Moreover, it has not always been the case in California. In this regard, there is a series of empirical studies, mostly carried out in the 1960s and 1970s, which were mostly critical of this special court.[117] For example, a study conducted in 1969 denounced how the individual litigant appeared most frequently as a defendant and how the real beneficiaries of this mechanism were business interests and government agencies, many of whom filed multiple claims as a regular part of their collection activities.[118] Moreover, another study in Los Angeles County found plaintiffs were businesses in about 60% of the cases, and that almost all of them were suing private individuals, not other companies.[119] These criticisms led to a series of reforms to the Small Claims Courts, such as limitations on the participation of corporate plaintiffs in terms of the amount of claims that could be brought, the imposition of fees, and improvements to the support provided for defendants in the preparation of their cases (but not necessarily allowing lawyers to represent them).[120] These reforms, according to my findings at least, seems to have worked in the sense I describe here.

[116] Lillo (2016), pp. 975–976.

[117] Lillo (2016), p. 961.

[118] Moulton (1969), p. 1659.

[119] Graham and Snortum (1976), p. 264.

[120] Lillo (2016), p. 962.

4.2.4 *The Applicable Legal Procedure in Chile. Empirical Data on the Civil Courts of Santiago*

To describe the Chilean legal procedure that is applicable to each legal issue is rather more complex, especially because each civil action must be filed in a different type of court.

The claim against Mr. Shredder under the Consumer Protection Act, as described, must be filed in the Municipal Court corresponding to the location where the consumer has his home address or where the seller is located.[121] These courts are not part of the judiciary,[122] but belong to the local governments, known as Municipalities, into which each province in Chile is divided.[123] The main jurisdiction of these courts are contraventions and misdemeanors[124] in subjects related to transit, alcohol, and local regulations. These proceedings are structured to decide over the imposition of sanctions, while civil remedies are only optional. In fact, according to the National Institute of Statistics, in 2016 only 0.12% of the cases were cases concerning Consumer Protection Act contraventions,[125] which are not necessarily associated with a civil claim. On the contrary, most of the cases filed in these courts come from local authorities, mostly police or the municipal officer in charge of traffic and local regulations.

In terms of the procedure to be followed in the case of filing the civil action in the Municipal Courts, the claim is made in writing. Special motions are admissible, but they will be processed together and will be solved at the final judgment. Parties are admitted to incorporate proof, including witnesses, for which purposes a written list of names may be filed until the beginning of a hearing in front of a judicial officer (who, depending on the court, will be the judge); the parties may examine the witnesses. At this stage, the judge decides to distribute the burden of proof depending on the availability and simplicity of gathering evidence; another hearing will be scheduled to introduce such evidence. Verdict and judgment will be issued by the judge no later than 30 days after the last hearing, unless there is other evidence pending incorporation.[126] Other procedural regulation will be the same as the one established in Act No. 18.287 which regulates the general procedure to be used in this Municipal Courts and the Code of Civil Procedure.[127]

Although the Consumer Protection Act—in an exception from the general rule in civil proceedings in Chile—allows pro se litigation, which might be interpreted as a

---

[121] Consumer Rights Protection Act N 19496, Art. 50 H.

[122] Notwithstanding the Judiciary have the supervision of these courts, an attribution that is seldom used. Besides that, the Courts of Appeal have jurisdiction to hear appeals from these courts in many cases. See: Act No 18.287, art. 32,33.

[123] See: Couso et al. (2011), p. 61.

[124] Act No 18.287, art. 1.

[125] Available at: http://www.ine.cl/estadisticas/sociales/justicia.

[126] Consumer Rights Protection Act N 19496, Art. 50 H.

[127] Consumer Rights Protection Act N 19496, Art. 50 B.

way to improve access to justice, in these cases it produces the opposite effect.[128] Most of these cases, which as previously said are quite low on the docket of these courts, begin with a complaint without a civil claim, because of lack of information on the part of consumers. In those cases, most Municipal Courts follow the proceedings established in Act No 18.287, which are designed for cases of misdemeanors, or contraventions initiated by the authorities and local officials (such as Municipal inspectors, police officers, and the like. This means that as part of the proceedings, the seller will be interrogated through investigative activities directed by the court (as in inquisitive types of proceedings) more similar to criminal proceedings than civil in nature.[129] Moreover, in cases like Erick's involving over 25 UTM (approximately USD$1,800), appeal is allowed and the two-tier system, common in civil procedure regulation in Chile, will be applied in response.[130]

Because these Municipal Courts do not belong to the judiciary but to each Municipality, they differ greatly on budgets, human resources, and how they deal with their case flow. But primarily, this makes it difficult to gather data to compare and study their functioning. In practice. However, because many features of the Municipal Courts' procedure follow the Code of Civil Procedure—which also provides the common civil procedure applicable to the case against Ms. Morris—I think it is more useful to focus my analysis of the Chilean case on its main features in terms of the procedural guarantees afforded.

In this second case, the claim of Erick falls under the jurisdiction of the Civil Courts, which are first-tier courts of common jurisdiction meant to deal with most civil actions according to Chilean legislation. The applicable legal procedure in these courts is provided in the Code of Civil Procedure enacted in 1902, which follows closely the Spanish Civil Procedure Act of 1855. This resembles the old *Ius Comune* model of civil procedure, described previously. In Chile, scholars have criticized the legislator of that epoch for lack of innovation by sticking to an inefficient and outdated procedural model compared to other available alternatives that already existed like those of the "orality" movement already described.[131]

First, and especially for American lawyers, it must be remembered that this legal procedure is almost in its entirety in writing and is held through several stages or phases. These phases are three: discussion, a term to introduce evidence, and decision. Each stage is characterized by an exchange of documents, motions, pleadings, orders of the court, etc., which are advanced by the parties until the case, or the file is ready for judgment. This is not provided in a trial hearing as in the case of an American trial where the trier of fact will hear the arguments and evidence of the parties and decide. Arguments and evidence, as previously said, are introduced in writing at different moments of the two main phases, and at the end the judge in isolation will write a final decision declaring the winner.

---

[128] Guerrero (2005), p. 180.

[129] Guerrero (2005), p. 178.

[130] Consumer Rights Protection Act N 19496, Art. 50 H.

[131] Nuñez (2005), p. 175.

The Code of Civil Procedure provides a "common procedure", applicable to most of cases of declarative nature. For cases between 10 and 500 UTM (approximately USD$700 to USD$ 35,000), the applicable procedure is the "common procedure" but with some special features aimed at speeding up the process somewhat. For example, the main discussion of the parties is restricted to the lawsuit and reply (limiting a reply of the plaintiff and a rejoinder by the defendant) and many phases like the one to reply, or the one to introduce evidence, are shortened.[132]

As Cappalli describes the Chilean civil procedure, the case is initiated by the plaintiff's lawsuit, which must comply with a series of formal requisites such as providing information about parties and representatives, containing a clear statement of the supporting facts and legal grounds, and specifying the relief sought in precise and clear terms. Along with the lawsuit, the plaintiff may also incorporate documentary proof at the beginning.[133] The reply of the defendant must be served in fifteen days after the service of the claim, with additional time in cases where the defendant's domicile is far from the court.[134] In the case of the ordinary procedure for the amount in our case, this term is shortened to eight days with the same option of adding time but it cannot surpass twenty days in total.[135] Of course, alongside the reply the defendant may also file a counterclaim.

Both the lawsuit and the reply (or the counterclaim) as part of the initial pleading (in general) of the judicial process must be signed by a lawyer and include their full name and address. As previously said, this is the general rule in Chile, where professional representation in civil cases is mandatory. Any initial pleading without this requirement is considered null and void.[136] This system of mandatory legal representation is considered by scholars in Chile to be a matter of due process and within the procedural guarantee of the right to a defense established in article 19 No 3 of the Chilean Constitution.[137] Of course, there are exceptions, such as the one established in the Municipal Courts act, but this is almost nonexistent because of how the legal procedure functions in practice.[138]

As described by Cappalli, in the main a Chilean trial is a paper process in which the judge's decision is based on facts found by studying documents.[139] Most of this proof is incorporated by the parties during the term especially allocated by the Code of Civil Procedure, which in Erick's case would be fifteen days with the possibility

[132] Code of Civil Procedure, art. 698.

[133] Code of Civil Procedure, art. 254. Regarding its similarities with the Federal Rules of Civil Procedure, see: Cappalli (1990), pp. 259–260.

[134] Cappalli (1990), p. 260.

[135] Code of Civil Procedure, art. 698.

[136] Act No 18.120, art. 1.

[137] See, e.g.: Romero (2017), p. 73.

[138] Based on the database gathered for a research I conducted in the civil courts of Santiago, I was able to identify that only 13.3% of the plaintiffs who were able to pro se litigate in landlord and tenant proceedings, decided to pursue their claim in this way.

[139] Cappalli (1990), p. 267.

of adding more days for the party whose domicile is far away from the Court.[140] Following the discussion phase, if there is no settlement in front of the Court, the judge will decide if there are disputed points of facts between the parties, and if she or he considers such facts to be substantial and relevant, will order the parties to present their evidence during that term.[141] As might be perceived, one major difference between the Chilean Civil Procedure is the lack of discovery. As explained by Cappalli, Chile follows the Civil law tradition of eschewing discovery mechanisms such as pre-trial depositions, interrogationss, document inspections, and medical examinations.[142]

The evidence the parties may produce are strictly regulated by the Code. For example, regarding witnesses to be summoned, the party must present a list with the names and addresses along with the points of fact for which they will provide testimony (with a maximum of six witness for each point of fact[143]) The list must be presented up to five days after the last service of the decision of the judge which begins the proof-taking stage.[144] As for the witnesses, the Code outlines which people may not to be summoned as witnesses because of their relation with the parties, and who may be excluded by the parties.[145] Regarding the examination of witnesses, the parties submit the questions and the judge will pose these questions to witnesses.[146] As explained by Cappalli, the U.S. trial mechanism of direct examination and cross-examination by the lawyers does not exist. In fact, there is not a single hearing in which witnesses will be deposed and questioned by the lawyers in front of the judge or court officer. Instead, the Chilean practice resembles juror *voir dire* in U.S. federal court, where the common practice is for the judges to qualify jurors using their own questions and those submitted by the lawyers.[147] A court functionary, called "the receptor", who is a private officer paid for by the parties, summarizes the answers given by the witness to each question, which is quite unlike the U.S. practice of verbatim stenography.[148] According to article 370, testimonies are written down trying to maintain the verbal expressions of the witness but reduced as much as possible. These summaries of testimony are read aloud by the receptor and signed by the witness, the judge, and the parties present.[149]

After all evidence is gathered—during the term for proof-taking and in some cases subsequently if all the evidence was not produced in time, but has at least been requested—or if the judge decides to order more evidence on their own if the

[140] Code of Civil Procedure, art. 698.
[141] Code of Civil Procedure, art. 318.
[142] Cappalli (1990), p. 268.
[143] Code of Civil Procedure, art. 372.
[144] Code of Civil Procedure, art. 320.
[145] Code of Civil Procedure, art. 366.
[146] Code of Civil Procedure, art. 365.
[147] Cappalli (1990), p. 365.
[148] Cappalli (1990), p. 365.
[149] Code of Civil Procedure, art. 370; Cappalli (1990), p. 365.

evidence produced by the parties was not enough,[150] the parties will have a term of ten days (or six in the cases of the amount of Erick's claim) to present a written plea called "observations that an examination of the proof suggests to them."[151] These written documents have the purpose of summarizing and analyzing the evidence introduced regarding the points of facts to be proven. According to Cappalli, this activity resembles closing arguments in U.S. civil trials.[152]

Finally, the judge will schedule parties to hear judgment and from that moment will have a term of sixty days or fifteen days in Erick's type of proceeding to render judgment.[153] Of course, in practice civil courts tend to take much more time than that established in the Civil Procedure Code to render judgment; to be considered final, it must take into account the appeal process. In fact, one of the most common critiques of civil courts is the delays civil trial are subject to.[154] According to a study of the Justice Studies Center of the Americas published in 2012, the average length of a civil trial under the common procedure was 217 days. Taking only those cases with final judgment, which includes cases with appeal proceedings into account, the average length was 821 days.[155]

When compared to the data gathered on the Small Claims Court in Los Angeles, data from the Civil Courts of Santiago show a quite different reality. In the courts where Erick would have filed his claim, 92% of cases are debt collection enforcement proceedings (which in Chile is a judicial proceeding). Only 6.4% were cases under the common procedure, the one described above and applicable to Erick's case, and of those, 68% were debt collections. Summary procedures, applicable in cases where urgency is required and in other specific cases according to Chilean legislation, occupy no more than 1.5%.[156,157]

From a random sample of files,[158] I have found that the 93.2% of the plaintiffs in enforcement proceedings and 88.1% in the common procedure were corporations. Only in summary proceedings (which occupy no more than 1.5% of the case docket) was this not the case (Table 4.5).

To try to characterize better the type of corporations who are the regular plaintiffs in Chilean civil courts, I used as a proxy of the size of such corporations the public record pertaining to the Internal Tax Service (SII), in which tax payers can file a

[150] Code of Civil Procedure, art. 159.

[151] Cappalli (1990), p. 277; Code of Civil Procedure, art. 430, 680.

[152] Cappalli (1990), p. 277.

[153] Code of Civil Procedure, art. 162, 680.

[154] See, in this regard: Riego and Lillo (2015), pp. 30–48.

[155] Justice Studies Center of the Americas (2012), p. 46.

[156] Chilean Code of Civil Procedure, Art. 680.

[157] Lillo (2020), p. 126.

[158] In this section, I rely on the finding of an empirical study I conducted in the Civil Court of Santiago. The research was made on a base of a random sample of cases taken from the total list of filings between 2014 and 2016 in the Civil Courts of the jurisdiction of the Court of Appeal of Santiago, Chile. The cases were classified in four types of procedures to overrepresent, since as said, more than 92% were enforcement proceedings. In total, 1000 were selected. See: Lillo (2020).

Table 4.5 Corporations as plaintiffs by type of procedure (Lillo 2020, p. 130)

Plaintiff corporation	Enforcement proceedings (%)	Common procedure (%)	Summary proceedings (%)
No	6,8	11,9	65,7
Yes	93.2*	88.1*	34.3*
Total	100	100	100
* = Confidence Interval at 95% Z-Test	90.14131–96.22233 $P = 0.000$	84.13792–92.01593 $P = 0.000$	28.29085–40.3284 $P = 0.000$

Table 4.6 Corporation registered as Small and Medium Enterprises (PYME) (Lillo 2020, p. 132)

PYME	Enforcement proceedings	Common procedure	Summary proceedings
No	92.68	93.89	59.76
Yes	7.32	6.11	40.24
Total	100	100	100
* = Confidence Interval at 95% Z-Test	4.06284–10.57131 $P = 0.000$	3.01056–9.21651 $P = 0.000$	29.62982–50.85798 $P = 0.0772$

register voluntarily identifying themselves as Small and Medium Enterprises (PYME). According to this indicator, I was able to determine that approximately 7% in the enforcement proceedings and 6% in common procedure, such plaintiffs were PYMEs. Only in the summary proceedings, where plaintiffs were corporations (which, as I have said, were a minority under this type of procedure), the proportion of PYMEs is higher and may even reach the half of the plaintiffs (Table 4.6).[159]

Using the same database of the SII, I was able to gather data on the main economic activity of the plaintiffs. Most of the corporations who claim in the civil courts belong to the sector of banks and other financial institutions (76% under the enforcement proceedings and 48% in the common procedure).[160]

Finally, I classified corporation who filed more than 10 claims in the period between 2014 and 2016 as "repeat players," and then coded whether the specific claim was filed by a repeat player or not. According to this, 66.3% in the enforcement proceedings, and 71.6% in the common procedure were cases initiated by repeat players. Only in the summary proceedings were most of the claims filed by claimants who were not repeat players (72%).[161]

In looking at who are the defendants, it is possible to affirm that in the civil courts of Santiago not only are plaintiffs mostly big corporations suing in debt collection related proceedings, but also that they do so against individual defendants. The exception is the summary procedure, where most plaintiffs and defendants are individuals suing each other. Notwithstanding, as shown above, this procedure is

[159] Lillo (2020), pp. 133–134.

[160] Lillo (2020), pp. 133–134.

[161] Lillo (2020), p. 136.

Table 4.7 Individual as defendants by type of procedure (Lillo 2020, p. 138)

Individual as defendants	Enforcement proceedings	Common procedure	Summary proceeding
No	3.8	15.8	19.3
Yes	96.2*	84.2*	80.8*
Test Chi^2	100	100	100
*= Confidence Interval at 95% Z-Test	93.90931–98.51494 $P = 0.000$	79.80079–88.66075 $P = 0.000$	75.75499–85.75128 $P = 0.000$

Table 4.8 Defendant type of response by type of proceeding (Lillo 2020, p. 142)

Defendant response	Enforcement proceedings	Common procedure	Summary proceedings
Answer or file another pleading	3.8	7.7	33.1
Do not answer in time but it was served	6.4	5.4	22.4
Do not answer because it was not served	89.4	86.9	44.7
Do not answer, but it was served and it's on time	0.4	0	2.5
Total Test Chi^2 $P = 0.000$ Fisher" exact $P = 0.0026$	100	100	100

used only in specific cases and occupies only a small proportion of the case docket (Table 4.7).

In the civil courts of Santiago, while most defendants are individuals, in general they do not act in courts. Especially in enforcement proceedings and in the common procedure, they do not answer or file another type of pleadings, not necessarily because they prefer not to but, on the contrary, because they are not even served (89% and 87%, respectively). Only in the summary proceedings is the proportion of defendants who do not answer despite being able to do so larger (22.4%) and many of them in fact respond in court (33%).[162] Of course, this may be explained by the fact that, as we saw, the type of case and the type of parties acting in this procedure is quite different from the other two. Nevertheless, as can be seen they occupy a minor proportion of the docket (Table 4.8).

It is not easy to explain the current state of civil justice in Chile. Some possible explanations have been advanced by Chilean scholars as to why the main users of the system are corporations in legal procedures related to debt collection. For example, it has been said that there are tax regulations and especial statutes of limitation on this type of collection.[163] Moreover, it is possible that civil justice in Chile could be part

[162] Lillo (2020), p. 142.

[163] Pontificia Universidad Católica de Valparaíso (2012), pp. 13–14.

of a broad collection strategy, of which the filing of a claim is just one part (for example, to threaten debtors and force payment agreements). In Chile, no fees are payable to the courts and big corporations may take advantage of economy of scale by hiring massive legal services at low hourly rates. In addition to the lack of knowledge regarding regulations, and how to make rights effective, all these features make the system very attractive to this type of plaintiff. This might also explain why such a high number of defendants are not even served.

On the other hand, why these types of corporations are not using the system to solve other type of dispute in the courts is less clear. One alternative in this regard, is the growing availability of private arbitration. Sadly, there is a lack of data or even basic descriptive statistics on private adjudication, so this is an area for urgent empirical research.[164]

Why ordinary people do not use the civil courts is another story. The literature in Chile and abroad, as I explained before, has pointed to several barriers that hinder access to justice such as the lack of information, the location of courts, formalism and lack of flexibility of the legal procedures, delays, and the mandatory requirement of legal representation. These barriers create a situation whereby under a cost-benefit analysis the sporadic individual decides not to solve their legal need through civil justice. This explanation can be applied as well to small and medium corporations, themselves probably sporadic litigants who cannot afford the luxury of litigation as a regular conflict-solving mechanism. On this too, empirical research is lacking.

In summary, the data summarized here suggests that the current access to justice situation in Chile is critical, and supports the many criticisms made since the 1990s that the Chilean civil justice is inaccessible to many groups of the population and especially for simple civil cases like those I exemplified at the beginning of this chapter.[165]

References

Astorga P (2017) Algunas consideraciones sobre la casación civil, fórmulas para su racionalización y su relación con el ius litigatoris. In: Palomo D (dir.) Recursos procesales. Problemas actuales. Ediciones DER, Santiago, pp 239–264

Barahona J (2014) La regulación contenida en la ley 19.496 sobre protección de los derechos de los consumidores y las reglas del código civil y Comercial sobre contratos: un marco comparativo. RChD 41(2):381–408

Barrientos F (2010) La responsabilidad civil del fabricante bajo el artículo 23 de la ley de protección de los derechos de los consumidores y su relación con la responsabilidad del vendedor. RChDP 14:109–158

Barton B, Bibas S (2017) Rebooting justice. More technology, fewer lawyers, and the future of law. Encounter Books, New York

[164] Notwithstanding, there are some Chilean authors who provide a description on this expansive phenomenon. See, e.g.: Leturia (2006), p. 266.

[165] Riego and Lillo (2015), pp. 12–17.

Best A, Zalesne D (1993) Peace, wealth, happiness, and small claims courts: a case study. Fordham Urban Law J 21:343–379
Bordalí A (2011) Análisis crítico de la jurisprudencia del Tribunal Constitucional sobre el derecho a la tutela judicial. RChD 38(2):311–337
Cappalli R (1990) Comparative south American civil procedure: the Chilean perspective. Univ Miami Inter-Am Law Rev 1990:239–310
Cea J (2012) Derecho constitucional chileno, vol II. Ediciones UC, Santiago
Clark C (1958) The feral rules of civil procedure: 1938-1958. Two decades of the Federal Civil Rules. Columbia Law Rev 58(4):435–451
Clermont K (2009) Principles of civil procedure, 2nd edn. Thomson/Reuters, St. Paul
Couso J, Coddou A, Lovera D, Guiloff M (2011) Constitutional law in Chile. Wolters Kluwer, Great Britain
Croley S (2017) Civil justice reconsidered. Toward a less costly, more accessible litigation system. New York University Press, New York
Cross T (2010) Is there a "Civil Right" under Article 6? Ten principles for public lawyers. Judicial Rev 15(4):366–376
Cruz M (1986) The duty of fair procedure and the hospital medical staff: possible extension in order to protect private sector employees. Capital Univ Law Rev 16:59–86
Curran L, Noone M (2007) The challenge of defining unmet legal need. J Law Soc Policy 21:63–89
Dalam E (2015) Strangers on familiar soil. Rediscovering the Chile-California connection. Yale University Press, New Haven
Damaška M (1986) The faces of Justice and State authority. Yale University Press, New Haven
Duce M, Marín F, Riego C (2008) Reforma a los procesos civiles orales: consideraciones desde el debido proceso y calidad de la información. In: Justice Studies Center of the Americas, Justicia civil: perspectivas para una reforma en América Latina. Santiago, pp 13–94.
Galligan D (1996) Due process and fair procedures. A study of administrative procedures. Clarendon Press, Oxford.
García G, Contreras P (2013) El derecho a la tutela judicial y al debido proceso en la jurisprudencia del Tribunal Constitucional chileno. Estudios Constitucionales. 11(2):229–282
Genn H (1999) Paths of justice: what people do and think about going to Law. Hart Publishing, Oxford
Graham B, Snortum J (1976) Small claims court, where the little man has his day. Judicature 60: 260–267
Guerrero J (2005) Acciones de interés individual en protección al consumidor en la ley 19496 y la incorporación de mecanismos alternativos de resolución de conflictos. RDPUCV 26(2): 165–185
Judicial Council of California (2018) Court statistics report. Statewide caseload trends 2008-09 through 2017-18. Available at: https://www.courts.ca.gov/12941.htm#id7495
Justice Studies Center of the Americas (2012) Estudio de análisis de trayectoria de las causas civiles en los tribunales civiles de Santiago. Informe final. Ministerio de Justicia, Santiago
Kagan R (2003) Adversarial legalism. The American way of law. Harvard University Press, Cambridge
Kessler A (2017) Inventing American exceptionalism. The origins of American adversarial legal culture, 1800–1877. Yale University Press, New Haven
Kosmin L (1975) The small claims court dilemma. Houston Law Rev 13:934–982, p. 936
Leturia F (2006) Ampliación del ámbito del arbitraje: una solución estructural para algunos de los problemas de la justicia civil. In: Silva J et al (ed) Justicia civil y comercial: una reforma pendiente. Bases para el diseño de la reforma procesal civil. Libertad y Desarrollo, Pontificia Universidad Católica de Chile, Santiago, pp 263–312
Lillo R (2016) Access to justice and small claims courts: supporting Latin American civil reforms through empirical research in Los Angeles County, California. RChD 43(3):955–986
Lillo R (2020) La justicia civil en crisis. Estudio empírico en la ciudad de Santiago para aportar a una reforma judicial orientada hacia el acceso a la justicia (formal). RChD 47(1):119–157

Medina C (2016) The American Convention on Human Rights, crucial rights and their theory and practice, 2nd edn. Intersentia, Cambridge
Merryman J, Pérez R (2007) The civil law tradition, 3rd edn. Stanford University Press, California
Moulton B (1969) The persecution and intimidation of the low-income litigant as performed by the small claims court in California. Stanford Law Rev 21(6):1657–1684
Nuñez R (2005) Crónica sobre la reforma del sistema procesal civil chileno (fundamentos, historia y principios). REJ 6:175–189
OCCA (2018) Conflictividad civil y barreras de acceso a la justicia en America Latina. Informe de vivienda y tierras. Justice Studies Center of the Americas, Santiago
OECD, Open Society Foundations (2016) Understanding effective access to justice. Available at: https://www.oecd.org/gov/understanding-effective-access-to-justice-workshop.htm
OECD, Open Society Foundations (2019) Legal Needs Surveys and Access to Justice. Available at: https://www.oecd.org/gov/legal-needs-surveys-and-access-to-justice-g2g9a36c-en.htm
Pagter C, McCloskey R, Reinis M (1964) The California small claims court. California Law Rev 52(4):876–898
Palomo D (2010) Apelación, doble instancia, y proceso civil oral. A propósito de la reforma en trámite. Estudios Constitucionales 8(2):465–524
Pleasence P, Balmer N (2012) Justiciable problems and the use of lawyers. In: Trebilcock M, Duggan A, Sossin L (eds) Middle income access to justice. University of Toronto Press, Toronto, pp 27–54
Pleasence P, Balmer N, Sandefur R (2013) Paths to justice. A past, present and future road map. UCL Centre for Empirical Legal Studies, London
Pontificia Universidad Católica de Valparaíso (2012) Informe final. Diseño de un modelo de oficial de ejecución. Ministerio de Justicia, Valparaíso
Riego C, Lillo R (2015) ¿Qué se ha dicho sobre el funcionamiento de la justicia civil en Chile? Aportes para la reforma. RChDP 25:9–54
Romero A (2017) Curso de derecho procesal civil. Los presupuestos procesales relativos a las partes, vol III, 3rd edn. Editorial Jurídica de Chile, Santiago
Sandefur R (2015) What we know and need to know about the legal needs of the public. South Carolina Law Rev 67:443–459
Strauss D (1989) Due process, government inaction, and private wrongs. Supreme Court Rev 1989: 53–86
Sullivan T, Massaro T (2013) The arc of Due process in American constitutional law. Oxford University Press, New York
Urrejola S (2011) El hecho generador del incumplimiento contractual y el artículo 1547 del código civil. RChDP 17:27–69
Yngvesson B, Henessey P (1975) Small claims, complex disputes: a review of the small claims literature. Law Society Rev 9(2):219–274

Part III
The Requirements of Fairness in Civil Procedure. Procedural Due Process in International Human Rights Law. Answers from Two Regional Systems

Chapter 5
A Methodology to Study Two Regional Human Rights Protection Systems

Analyzing the fair trial requirements as developed by international human rights tribunals is important. Today the right to a court is a universally recognized human right, which entails international State obligations to ensure and guarantee the effective enjoyment of the legal rights provided. Crucial to this argument is the idea that the legal system is comprised not just of substantive rights but also procedural rights that allow individuals to put in motion the machinery of the State to enforce those rights and make them effective.[1] International Human Rights Law has been an important source for the development of fair trial standards now shared among nations. The relationship between international treatises and its supervisory bodies has accounted for a challenge where domestic law and its interpretation by local courts are not just local anymore but more and more a reflection of a common understanding.[2]

For this project, it was relevant to understand not just current trends of case law in each regional court but on the contrary to have a picture of the whole and then to focus on specific topics. Since this approach required a comprehensive selection and a method to analyze a bulk of cases, I created a database from scratch for each of the courts and applied a set of variables.

As the definition of what might be considered civil matters might vary from one jurisdiction to another, for research purposes I use an operational definition to distinguish them from cases which are purely criminal or punitive in nature. This excludes from my analysis legal procedures to decide if a criminal offence has been committed or to impose an administrative sanction. It does, however, include claims for damages even when determined by a criminal court,[3] the determination of

[1] Genn (2010), p. 11.

[2] See: Slaughter (1994), pp. 106–111; De S.-O.-L' E. (2010), p. 159.

[3] I acknowledge there might be an issue with punitive damages, but since there are no cases on any of the regional Court I analyze in this Chapter, I believe this is not the place or time to engage in that debate.

R. Lillo Lobos, *Understanding Due Process in Non-Criminal Matters*, Ius Gentium: Comparative Perspectives on Law and Justice 97,
https://doi.org/10.1007/978-3-030-95534-2_5

parental rights and obligations, adoption proceedings, employment relations, expropriation proceedings, and others.

Using this criterion, I made a database comprising the 19 cases I was able to find from the IACHR and 303 decisions from the ECHR. I studied this database following a mixed method approach by construing several variables that I applied to the text of the decisions. In this chapter, I provide some methodological insights which will be used in the next chapters when exploring each of the regional tribunals. In the last chapter of this third part I will compare the results and provide some conclusions and possible explanations for my findings.

5.1 An Operational Definition of Civil Justice

As a starting point, I acknowledge the challenging task of defining what civil justice is. It is challenging primarily because determining what types of legal issue will be brought to it will depend on the substantive law definition of "civil matters," and in that regard might vary from one jurisdiction to another.

One solution to this puzzle is to understand civil justice just as a mechanism for resolving disputes between individuals and, in that regard, it consists of substantive matters related to private law only. However, there are many countries in which civil justice covers areas where disputes are deeply intertwined with public law matters, such as family law or those employment relations not covered by special labor courts.[4] Moreover, there are jurisdictions in which many civil matters are not even "disputes" between parties, such as non-contentious matters. From an economic perspective, civil justice has been defined as an instrument which contributes to "...the production of legal norms which help to tackle the problems caused by market failures".[5] I found particularly relevant the definition of civil justice provided by Genn, for whom it comprises partly substantive rights but more importantly "...the provision that society makes for citizens and business to bring civil suits – the *right of action* and the *machinery to make good* that right".[6] Michael Zander provides a negative definition expressing that "[C]ivil justice concerns the handling of disputes between citizens arising out of civil, as opposed to criminal, law".[7] To compare the answer provided by the regional courts, I follow Zander's approach by constructing an operational negative definition of civil matters as those opposed to proceedings that are punitive in nature. However, I have not limited my study to cases dealing with disputes between private citizens because civil justice also comprises claims for the effectiveness of substantive rights against public bodies,

---

[4]Refering to the goals of civil justice more than a definition of civil matters, see: Uzelac (2014), p. 17.

[5]Visscher (2012), p. 71.

[6]Genn (2010), p. 11.

[7]Zander (2000), p. 27.

which are quite important in the International Human Rights Law arena. Basically, then, I have included cases in which the legal issues were related to private law, such as civil claims to protect private property, or to public law—like employment relations with public employers or adoption proceedings. I have excluded criminal or administrative proceedings related to the determination of acts or omissions to be considered as forbidden by legal order and which entail a negative consequence to be applied by the legitimate authority in the form of a sanction or of a "punitive nature".[8]

Although my original purpose was to analyze the regional human rights standards on the requirements of fair trial in civil matters at both regional levels, I have focused my attention mainly on the case law of their courts as an expression of the former idea. Unlike traditional case law studies, I was interested in understanding not just current trends of case law but on the contrary to have a picture of the whole and then to focus on specific topics. That approach required a comprehensive selection and a method to analyze a bulk of cases and, with that purpose, I created a database from scratch for each of the courts and applied the set of variables I describe in the next section.

5.2 Variables to Apply to Databases of Each Court

In each of the setlists created for the case law of both regional tribunals, I applied two sets of variables. First, variables of basic data to better describe the case, such as the date of the decision, country, legal tradition, and outcome. To gather information on the type of the case decided, I coded the main legal issue in dispute in the local proceeding that originated the petition. I have classified these legal issues in cases in which the dispute arose between private parties and those where a public body was a party. Now, the right to a fair trial is a complex human right, in the sense that is a right by itself but is also comprised of several "sub-rights," which in turn might be operationalized or analyzed in terms of specific procedural elements. Therefore, to describe better whether one or the other were analyzed by the court in a specific decision, I created two type variables distinguished by their level of abstraction. First, in what I shall call here a "dimension", I included broad "sub-rights" which traditionally include the right to a fair trial such as judicial independence, impartiality, the right to a defense, access to justice, and the like. Second, to describe a more specific or narrow procedural feature under analysis, I created a variable for "procedural elements." For example, a public hearing, the composition of the court, the use of court fees, a right to an appeal, are included in this type of coding. A list of these descriptive variables are shown in Table 5.1.

[8]Useful in this regard is the classic work of H.L.A. Hart and his model of orders backed by threats. See: Hart (1994), p. 27

Table 5.1 Variables to describe cases

Variable	Content
Date of decision	DD-MM-YYYY
Country	Name
Legal tradition	Common law
	Civil law
Outcome (Finding violation)	Yes or No
Type of case (depends on the dispute and parties)	Administrative
	Civil
Main legal issue	Access to information proceedings
	Arbitration proceedings
	Audit proceedings
	Capacity to exercise private rights
	Change of the use of land
	Contracts
	Damages
	Discrimination
	Dissolution of associations
	Electoral proceedings
	Employment relations/Labor associations
	Free market protection/Economic cases
	Freedom of expression ban proceedings
	Insolvency
	Intellectual property and other registration proceedings
	Inter-state application, military occupation
	Judicial review of administrative fines
	Land registry proceedings
	Land/Environment protection
	Libel/Defamation
	Limitation on right of property
	Nationality annulment
	Parental rights/adoption proceedings
	Partition proceedings
	Payment proceedings
	Personal liberty
	Public contract termination proceedings
	Public employment application
	Residence/asylum application
	Right of private property
	Right to education
	Right to practice professional/economic activity
	Separation/divorce
	Social security

(continued)

Table 5.1 (continued)

Variable	Content
	Subsidy application
	Tenancy/Rent
Dimensions of the right to a fair trial according to the court	Effective remedy
	Equality of arms
	General fairness
	Independence and/or impartiality
	Opportunity to be heard
	Reasonable time
	Right to an adversarial proceeding
	Right to a court/Access to justice
	Right to defense
Procedural elements analyzed by the court	Access to evidence materials
	Active judge
	Admissibility of appeal
	Admission of evidence
	Application over non-contentious proceedings
	Claim filing
	Competent court/natural judge
	Court composition
	Court fees
	Curator ad litem or other types of special representation
	Decision based on documentary evidence
	Duty to state reasons
	Equality of arms
	Expert witness neutrality
	Public hearing
	Independent fact-finding
	Information for pro se litigants
	Judicial decision enforcement
	Final judicial decision and res iudicata
	Judicial control of administrative decision.
	Legal personality prior to initiate proceedings
	Litigation costs other than court fees
	Opportunity to present evidence
	Prior communication/notification
	Proceedings complexity
	Proper evaluation and interpretation of law
	Public judgment
	Retrial
	Right to a lawyer/legal assistance
	Right to defense and access to case file
	Time limits/Statute of limitations

Table 5.2 Variables to identify checklist or flexible models

Checklist model	Flexible model
The Court applies a procedural guarantee from the criminal prong of the clause over non-criminal cases	The Court considers the complexity of the case or its particular circumstances as a factor to determine whether a procedural guarantee was required
The Court considers that the legal procedure as provided by regulation is the one that is due	The Court is more concerned with practical effectiveness than formal recognition
The Court considers a specific procedural element or dimension as strict minimum required by the right to a fair trial	The Court expresses the view that there is greater latitude in civil than in criminal cases
The Court interpret the procedural element or dimension as a clear-cut rule	The Court considers that a less formalistic approach is required
The Court considers the entire content of the clause to be applied to every type of proceeding	The Court analyzes if a procedural guarantee is required attending to the nature of the particular proceeding
The Court analyze a restriction in an all-or-nothing fashion	The Court considers that the due process clause does not have a strict catalog of guarantees
	The Court analyze a restriction of a procedural guarantee using proportionality

Besides coding variables to describe the cases, I was interested in identifying the conceptions of the requirements of fair trial in these matters used by both regional courts. So, in the second place, I created several variables to operationalize the ideal types presented in the first part of this book, the checklist or the flexible approaches. As explained there, I believe there are contexts in which the protection of fairness demands clear cut rules to be applied as a strict minimum—like within the checklist model. Other situations might demand a flexible approach where the content of due process or its procedural protections must be understood as legal principles, less restrained by the ties of history and in its application and interpretation more dependent on the type of case or legal procedure and in balance with other goals of the legal system. While presenting both models in extreme positions, they are not necessarily in opposition for there may be situations in which they are superimposed on one another. With this purpose, and following the description I provided for each model, I created a preliminary set of variables to serve as proxies for both ideal types, which I further modified and improved as I progressed with the coding phase (Table 5.2).

I used these variables, which I coded in each decision, and latter analyzed focused on the relations across the set list. I present the results of this process for each court in the chapters that follow.

References

De S.-O.-L' E M (2010) Is the separation of powers the basis for the legitimacy of an internationalised judiciary? In: Muller S, Richards S (eds) Highest courts and globalization. Hague Academic Press, The Hague, pp 149–162

Genn H (2010) Judging civil justice. Cambridge University Press, Cambridge

Hart H (1994) The concept of law, 2nd edn. Clarendon Press, Oxford

Slaughter A (1994) A typology of transjudicial communication. Univ Richmond Law Rev 29(1): 99–138

Uzelac A (ed) (2014) Goals of civil justice and civil procedure in contemporary judicial systems. Springer, Switzerland

Visscher L (2012) A law and economics view on harmonisation of procedural law. In: Kramer X, van Rhee C (eds) Civil litigation in a globalising world. The Hague, T.M.C. Asser Press, pp 65–91

Zander M (2000) The state of justice. Sweet & Maxwell, London

Chapter 6
The Inter-American Court of Human Rights Case Law on Due Process Over Civil Matters

The Inter-American system of human rights protection consists of two main bodies, the Inter-American Commission of Human Rights (the Commission from now on), founded in 1959, and the Inter-American Court of Human Rights (IACHR or the Court)., created in 1969 by the American Convention on Human Rights (ICHR) which entered into force in 1978 when enough states had ratified it. The IACHR began its operation a year after.[1]

Traditionally in this regional system, two distinct provisions of the basic document of the system, the ICHR, provide what we might call a modern conception of a right to have a trial with the due guarantees. First, article 8 guarantees expressly a right to a fair trial by a general clause in its first paragraph: "Every person has the right to a hearing, with due guarantees and within a reasonable time, by a competent, independent, and impartial tribunal, previously established by law, in the substantiation of any accusation of a criminal nature made against him *or for the determination of his rights and obligations of a civil, labor, fiscal, or any other nature*." Paragraphs 2, 3, 4, and 5 provide a list of specific guarantees to enhance or emphasize the protection of anyone accused of a crime such as the right to be presumed innocent, the right to defense in its several dimensions, a right to appeal, a right to public criminal proceeding, etc.[2] Second, article 25 of the Convention provides a right to judicial protection: "Everyone has the right to simple and prompt recourse, or any other *effective* recourse, to a competent court or tribunal for protection against acts that violate his fundamental rights recognized by the constitution or laws of the state concerned or by this Convention, even though such violation may have been committed by persons acting in the course of their official duties." In this regard, the States must ensure "a)...that any person claiming such remedy shall have his rights determined by the competent authority provided for by

[1] Alston and Goodman (2013), p. 980.

[2] Medina (2016), p. 242.

R. Lillo Lobos, *Understanding Due Process in Non-Criminal Matters*, Ius Gentium: Comparative Perspectives on Law and Justice 97,
https://doi.org/10.1007/978-3-030-95534-2_6

the legal system of the state; b) to develop the possibilities of judicial remedy; and c) to ensure that the competent authorities shall enforce such remedies when granted." Most of the cases on the matter tend to analyze both and find violations in conjunction.[3]

The formula of providing two separated but inherently intertwined provisions is at the origin of the system. During the Ninth International Conference of American States held in Bogotá in 1948, when the Organization of American States (OAS) was formally established, the American Declaration of the Rights and Duties of Men was also approved. This instrument, notwithstanding its non-binding nature, was a clear expression of the goals of the organization to promote and protect human right across the region.[4] The Charter in its Article XVIII "a right to fair trial",[5] is quite similar to article 25 of the Convention, and in its Article XXVI "a right to a due process of law",[6] is equivalent to current article 8 but clearly directed at criminal proceedings only. In the *travaux préparatoires* of the Convention, it is clear how these provisions were discussed and modified into what they are today.[7]

Both articles are of great importance in the case law of the Inter-American Court of Human rights. In her recent book, Cecilia Medina, former President of the regional tribunal, analyzes decisions on the merits between 2004 and 2014, and concludes that the vast majority find a violation of article 8 and/or 25.[8] Using the search engine of the Center for Justice and International Law,[9] with the descriptors "Fair Trial" and "Judicial Protection" 152 and 173 results come up, respectively, from a total of 241 decisions on the merits.[10] Many of the Advisory Opinions of the ICHR, a quite relevant source of interpretation of the Convention,[11] are devoted to one or both provisions.[12]

[3] Medina (2016), p. 75.

[4] See: Charter of the Organization of American States. Available at: http://www.oas.org/en/sla/dil/inter_american_treaties_A-41_charter_OAS.asp#Chapter_I.

[5] Article XXVI. Every person may resort to the courts to ensure respect for his legal rights. There should likewise be available to him a simple, brief procedure whereby the courts will protect him from acts of authority that, to his prejudice, violate any fundamental constitutional rights.

[6] Article XXVI. Every accused person is presumed to be innocent until proved guilty.

Every person accused of an offense has the right to be given an impartial and public hearing, and to be tried by courts previously established in accordance with pre-existing laws, and not to receive cruel, infamous or unusual punishment.

[7] See: OEA/Ser.K/XVI/1.2. Available only in Spanish at: http://www.oas.org/es/cidh/mandato/Basicos/Actas-Conferencia-Interamericana-Derechos-Humanos-1969.pdf.

[8] Medina (2016), p. 240.

[9] Availble at: https://sidh.cejil.org/.

[10] In its Spanish version the results are even higher. From the same 241 decisions on the merits, 231 hits for both terms "Garantías Judiciales" and "Protección Judicial".

[11] Buergenthal (1985), p. 2.

[12] See e.g.: I/A Court H.R., habeas corpus in emergency situations (Arts. 27(2), 25(1) and 7-(6) American Convention on Human Rights). Advisory Opinion OC-8/87, Series A No. 8 (1987); I/A Court H.R., exceptions to the exhaustion of domestic remedies (Arts. 46(1), 46(2)(a) and 46(2)(b) American Convention on Human Rights). Advisory Opinion OC-11/90, Series A No.11 (1990);

Despite the relevance of due process in the IACHR, most of its case law concerns legal proceedings that are criminal or punitive in nature.[13] Using the digest of the IACHR,[14] I have found only 12 decisions on the merits where the main legal issue was a civil matter according to my operational definition. Due to the lack of a comprehensive and reliable search engine, I supplemented these with another seven cases pointed out by experts in the Inter-American system. I analyze these 19 cases in the next section.

Following this procedure, I ended up with 19 cases dealing with legal issues fitting my operational definition of civil matters, from 299 decisions on the merits as of August 2019.[15] For this task, I have used the search engines provided by the court website and the one provided by the Center for Justice and International Law.[16] I acknowledge the relevance of the Inter-American Commission on Human Rights reports on the petition system, which filters most cases before filing a claim to the Court and where there is a priority criterion according to the nature and seriousness of the violation.[17] I decided to analyze in depth only court decisions, there being no reliable search engine for the case reports of the Commission. That might explain the amount of cases I was able to find in comparison with the European system, especially taking into consideration that less than 1% of the petitions received are sent to the IACHR each year.[18] However, I tried to compensate for this regional system by using also the Advisory Opinions of the court and the thematic reports of the Commission to support the study of the court's case law.

In the following sections, I explore the developments in this regional system. First, I acknowledge the relevance of the work done by the Commission and its thematic reports, before embarking on an analysis of the case law of the court and applying the set of variables I described in the methodological chapter.

I/A Court H.R., judicial guarantees in states of emergency (Arts. 27(2), 25 and (8) American Convention on Human Rights). Advisory Opinion OC-9/87, Series A No. 9 (1987); I/A Court H.R., the right to information on consular assistance in the framework of the guarantees of the due process of law. Advisory Opinion OC-16/99, Series A No.16(1999); I/A Court H.R., juridical condition and human rights of the child. Advisory Opinion OC-17/02, Series A No.17 (2002); I/A Court H.R., juridical condition and rights of the undocumented migrants. Advisory Opinion OC-18/03, Series A No.18 (2003).

[13] See, e.g.: ICHR, second progress report of the special rapporteurship on migrants workers and their families in the hemisphere, OEA/Ser.L/V/II.111, Doc. 20 rev. (2001), par. 91. Available at: https://www.cidh.oas.org/annualrep/2000eng/chap.6a.htm.

[14] The Digest is a project carried on between the IACHR and the cooperation agency of the German government, GIZ. Its serves as a repository of every decisi6n of the IACHT regarding the articles 1, 2, 4, 8, and 25 of the American Convention on Human Rights. Available only in Spanish at: http://www.corteidh.or.cr/cf/themis/digesto/.

[15] See: http://www.corteidh.or.cr/cf/Jurisprudencia2/busqueda_casos_contenciosos.cfm?lang=es.

[16] Available at: https://sidh.cejil.org/.

[17] Rules of Procedure of the Inter-American Commission on Human Rights, art. 45. Available at: http://www.oas.org/en/iachr/mandate/Basics/rulesiachr.asp.

[18] See: https://www.oas.org/en/iachr/multimedia/statistics/statistics.html.

6.1 The Role of the Inter-American Commission on Human Rights and Its Thematic Reports

Apart from its competence in the mechanisms of petitions, and complaints over violations of the Conventions that it might eventually submit to the Court, the Commission plays a role promoting respect for and the defense of human rights.[19] Especially important in this regard are its functions on thematic and national reports,[20] many of them focusing on the judicial protection of vulnerable groups.[21] Because of this, to understand the right of a fair trial in this regional system, not only is the case law of the IACHR important, but also the progress on the issue made by this OAS body due to its role in the petition and reporting system. Here I focus especially on its thematic reports.

In its thematic report on Access to Justice as a Guarantee of Economic, Social, and Cultural Rights, the Commission had the opportunity to develop the content of article 8 and 25 beyond the scope of the criminal justice system. For example, this report reviews the standards on the right to a free counsel as an essential minimum judicial guarantee of constitutional proceedings because of their inherent complexity.[22] In other types of cases, the Commission had established several guidelines to determine its applicability as a requirement of the right to a fair trial: (a) the resources available to the person concerned; (b) the complexity of the issues involved; and (c) the significance of the rights involved.[23]

In terms of the range of applicability of both articles 8 and 25, according to the Commission there is no question about the regional standards: they apply to every type of legal proceeding involving or affecting the determination of rights.[24] More arguable are the specific guarantees which may constitute the minimum content of the right. According to the Commission, the minimum guarantees to be applied or

[19] See. American Convention on Human Rights, Arts. 44 et seq.

[20] See, American Convention on Human Rights, Art. 41.

[21] See, e.g.: ICHR, access to justice for women victims of violence in the Americas, OEA/Ser.L/V/II., Doc. 68 (2007). Available at: https://www.oas.org/en/iachr/reports/thematic.asp; ICHR, access to justice as a guarantee of economic, social and cultural rights: a review of the standards adopted by the Inter-American System of Human Rights, OEA/Ser.L/V/II.129, Doc. 4 (2007). Available at: https://www.oas.org/en/iachr/reports/thematic.asp; ICHR, indigenous peoples, afro-descendent communities, and natural resources: human rights protection in the context of extraction, exploitation, and development activities, OEA/Ser.L/V/II. Doc. 47/15 (2015). Available at: https://www.oas.org/en/iachr/reports/thematic.asp.

[22] ICHR, access to justice as a guarantee of economic, social and cultural rights: a review of the standards adopted by the Inter-American System of Human Rights, OEA/Ser.L/V/II.129, Doc. 4 (2007), p. 13. Available at: https://www.oas.org/en/iachr/reports/thematic.asp.

[23] ICHR, access to justice as a guarantee of economic, social and cultural rights: a review of the standards adopted by the Inter-American System of Human Rights, OEA/Ser.L/V/II.129, Doc. 4 (2007), p. 19. Available at: https://www.oas.org/en/iachr/reports/thematic.asp.

[24] ICHR, access to justice as a guarantee of economic, social and cultural rights: a review of the standards adopted by the Inter-American System of Human Rights, OEA/Ser.L/V/II.129, Doc. 4 (2007), p. 45. Available at: https://www.oas.org/en/iachr/reports/thematic.asp.

what it calls the right's "core components"[25] are the right to a hearing, to a decision within a reasonable time, the right to have a judicial control of administrative decisions, the right to an attorney, the right to a reasoned decision, and publicity of proceedings. For example, regarding administrative proceedings for the determination of social rights, the Commission summarizes the content of this right as applicable in full to administrative proceedings just like they must be observed in all proceedings for the determination of obligations and rights.[26]

By identifying a "core component", the Commission does not distinguish between administrative proceedings of criminal or punitive natures and those that are not. For example, by determining that one of these components is a right to a hearing, which in turn comprises several procedural guarantees, such as legal advice, the Commission cites cases related to the imposition of administrative sanctions.[27] It seems, because the first question of applicability is resolved "in full" that would mean at the same time that these proceedings must ensure the minimum core component "in full" as well.

In this report, the Commission summarizes the regional fair trial standards on judicial proceedings concerning social rights. As a mechanism to enhance its enforceability, it is required to afford proceedings conducted within a reasonable time, with an effective equality of arms, and a proper judicial control of administrative decisions.[28] The key concept in this regard is *effectiveness*. The Inter-American standards established an important connection between the real possibility of access to justice and respect, protection, and assurance of the right to a fair trial in social rights proceedings.[29] The minimum contents of the fair trial must be analyzed from this point of view. In this regard, for example, the justification for enhancing equality of arms comes from disadvantage inherent in the unequal economic or social status of litigants against the State.[30]

---

[25] ICHR, access to justice as a guarantee of economic, social and cultural rights: a review of the standards adopted by the Inter-American System of Human Rights, OEA/Ser.L/V/II.129, Doc. 4 (2007), p. 34. Available at: https://www.oas.org/en/iachr/reports/thematic.asp.

[26] ICHR, access to justice as a guarantee of economic, social and cultural rights: a review of the standards adopted by the Inter-American System of Human Rights, OEA/Ser.L/V/II.129, Doc. 4 (2007), p. 20. Available at: https://www.oas.org/en/iachr/reports/thematic.asp.

[27] ICHR, access to justice as a guarantee of economic, social and cultural rights: a review of the standards adopted by the Inter-American System of Human Rights, OEA/Ser.L/V/II.129, Doc. 4 (2007), pp. 35-37. Available at: https://www.oas.org/en/iachr/reports/thematic.asp.

[28] ICHR, access to justice as a guarantee of economic, social and cultural rights: a review of the standards adopted by the Inter-American System of Human Rights, OEA/Ser.L/V/II.129, Doc. 4 (2007), p. 46. Available at: https://www.oas.org/en/iachr/reports/thematic.asp.

[29] ICHR, access to justice as a guarantee of economic, social and cultural rights: a review of the standards adopted by the Inter-American System of Human Rights, OEA/Ser.L/V/II.129, Doc. 4 (2007), p. 64. Available at: https://www.oas.org/en/iachr/reports/thematic.asp.

[30] ICHR, access to justice as a guarantee of economic, social and cultural rights: a review of the standards adopted by the Inter-American System of Human Rights, OEA/Ser.L/V/II.129, Doc. 4 (2007), pp. 48-52. Available at: https://www.oas.org/en/iachr/reports/thematic.asp.

In other reports, a separation between criminal and non-criminal legal proceedings has been advanced. In the Second Progress Report of the Special Rapporteur on Migrant Workers and their Families in the Hemisphere, it is recognized that in non-criminal proceedings against a migrant worker, a "certain quantum" of due process must be respected. This "quantum" depends on the expected outcomes in terms of liberty restrictions: "As the importance of the values at stake diminishes, the content of due process may also decline to a degree compatible with the general principle and the celerity and efficacy of decisions."[31] In this regard, a degree of flexibility is recognized in order to harmonize the different goals to be pursued by legal proceedings. Moreover, in the Report on Terrorism and Human Rights it is recognized that the "...full complement of due process protections applicable in a criminal proceeding may not necessarily apply in all other processes, but rather will depend upon the potential outcome and effects of the proceedings. The principle of due process, with this degree of flexibility, applies not only to court decisions, but also to decisions made by administrative bodies."[32]

6.2 The Case Law of the Inter-American Court of Human Rights

As described before, most of the case law on the right to a fair trial at the IACHR concern criminal cases or at least of punitive nature. Even in the administrative law arena, most of the cases found are related to the imposition of sanctions over individuals by public bodies. Some cases refer to deportations,[33] disciplinary proceedings against public officials,[34] and even impeachment proceedings against constitutional court judges of the State members.[35]

In these cases, which might be catalogued as administrative but punitive or criminal in nature, the IACHR has established that the minimum guarantees of the second paragraph of article 8, established for criminal procedures, are applied as well in proceedings whether judicial or not. In this regard, the court had held that "...the

[31] ICHR, second progress report of the special rapporteurship on migrants workers and their families in the hemisphere, OEA/Ser.L/V/II.111, Doc. 20 rev. (2001), par. 95. Available at: https://www.cidh.oas.org/annualrep/2000eng/chap.6a.htm.

[32] ICHR, report on terrorism and human rights, OEA/Ser.L/V/II.116 Doc. 5 rev. 1 corr. (2002), par. 401. Available at: http://www.cidh.org/terrorism/eng/toc.htm.

[33] E.g.: I/A Court H.R., Case of Vélez Loor v. Panama. Preliminary Objections, Merits, Reparations, and Costs. Series C No. 218, Judgment of November 23, 2010.

[34] E.g.: I/A Court H.R., Case of López Lone et al. v. Honduras. Preliminary Objection, Merits, Reparations and Costs. Series C No. 302, Judgment of October 5, 2015.

[35] I/A Court H.R., Case of the Constitutional Court v. Peru. Merits, Reparations and Costs. Series C No. 71, Judgment of January 31, 2001; I/A Court H.R., Case of the Constitutional Tribunal (Camba Campos et al.) v. Ecuador. Preliminary Objections, Merits, Reparations and Costs. Series C No. 268, Judgment of August 28, 2013.

full range of minimum guarantees stipulated in the second paragraph of this article are also applicable in those areas and, therefore, in this type of matter, the individual also has the overall right to the due process applicable in criminal matters."[36]

However, there are cases where the punitive nature is not as clear as it might be. The most cited and relevant case from this group is *Ricardo Baena et. al.* v. Panama. In this case, the alleged victims were 270 public employees, dismissed after being accused of complicity in a military coup after they had participated in a demonstration for labor rights, which coincided temporally with the military uprising.[37] Many of these workers were dismissed by written notice issued in most cases by the Director General or the Executive Director of the public entity, by order of the President of the Republic.[38] Under the existing law, the dismissed workers could initiate an administrative complaint or judicial proceedings in the labor jurisdiction. The latter comprised a claim to the Conciliation and Decision Board, an appeal to the Superior Labor Court and eventually to a constitutional remedy claim at the Supreme Court.[39] On the contrary, other workers were dismissed after the enactment of new legislation, the "Law 25," which, applied retroactively, authorized that their appointments be terminated upon identification of their participation in the demonstration. For these workers, the only available recourse was a motion for reconsideration to the same authority that ordered the dismissal, followed by an appeal to the superior authority. Only after that appeal, could they file contentious administrative proceedings before the Third Chamber of the Supreme Court.[40]

As said, the nature of the termination of these workers is not purely and clearly punitive. In fact, according to the Court, "Law 25" does not refer to criminal matters since it does not characterize an offence and the consequent sanction through the imposition of a punishment. It deals, rather, with an administrative or labor relation matter.[41]

From the judgement, it can be read that this fact is not material for the Court. Article 8's application is not limited to judicial remedies in a strict sense. It applies to any procedural stage where a State action could *affect* the rights of a person, whether

[36] I/A Court H.R., Case of the Constitutional Court v. Peru. Merits, Reparations and Costs. Series C No. 71. Judgment of January 31, 2001, par. 70.

[37] ICHR, access to justice as a guarantee of economic, social and cultural rights: a review of the standards adopted by the Inter-American System of Human Rights, OEA/Ser.L/V/II.129, Doc. 4 (2007), p. 21. Available at: https://www.oas.org/en/iachr/reports/thematic.asp.

[38] I/A Court H.R., Case of Baena Ricardo et al. v. Panama. Merits, Reparations and Costs. Series C No. 72, Judgment of February 2, 2001, p. 60.

[39] I/A Court H.R., Case of Baena Ricardo et al. v. Panama. Merits, Reparations and Costs. Series C No. 72, Judgment of February 2, 2001, p. 61.

[40] ICHR, access to justice as a guarantee of economic, social and cultural rights: a review of the standards adopted by the Inter-American System of Human Rights, OEA/Ser.L/V/II.129, Doc. 4 (2007), p. 21. Available at: https://www.oas.org/en/iachr/reports/thematic.asp.

[41] I/A Court H.R., Case of Baena Ricardo et al. v. Panama. Merits, Reparations and Costs. Series C No. 72, Judgment of February 2, 2001, par. 123.

of a punitive administrative, or of a judicial nature.[42] What is more, article 8 is not only applicable, but must be applied in "full." This means that the minimum guarantees established in section 2 of the provision applies to the realms identified in the first paragraph, that is, "...in the determination of his rights and obligations of a civil, labor, fiscal, or any other nature."[43] Therefore, the test to be applied is the possibility of a procedure ending in a decision that may *affect* the rights of persons.[44] To be fair, it must be taken into consideration that *Ricardo Baena et. al.* v. Panama was the first non-criminal case decided by the Court, and that might explain these caveats.

I have identified more than twenty cases where the Court applied the Article 8–25 formula to proceedings which can be considered to be non-criminal and thus fit into my operational conception of civil matters. Although there were some other candidates, I ended up by excluding some of them.[45] The best known of these was the case of Ricardo Baena because even though its punitive nature might be debatable, it is clear from the judgement that the Court treated it as if it was. In any case, for my purposes I was interested in cases where the discussion of the legal issue was not related to the possible imposition of a sanction by public authorities, judicial, administrative, or even congressional. From this point of view, 16 of the 19 cases were administrative but not punitive. Only three case were purely civil. Two of them concerned proceedings on vertical family relations and one of them was a defamation case with a civil and criminal side (which I excluded from the analysis). The summary of these cases is listed in Table 6.1.

From the administrative non-punitive arena, in eight cases the legal issues debated concerned different forms of limitation on the right to property. One of these cases was *Barbani Duarte et. al. v. Uruguay,* which arose from the banking crisis of that country during the first half of 2002. This crisis was a result of capital controls imposed by the Argentine government and deposit freezes on the bank accounts of their nationals, which resulted in many Argentines withdrawing their deposits from Uruguayan banks. Because of the crisis, three banks had liquidity problems and were finally suspended and dissolved, among them the Banco de

[42] I/A Court H.R., Case of Baena Ricardo et al. v. Panama. Merits, Reparations and Costs. Series C No. 72, Judgment of February 2, 2001, 124.

[43] I/A Court H.R., Case of Baena Ricardo et al. v. Panama. Merits, Reparations and Costs. Series C No. 72, Judgment of February 2, 2001, par. 124.

[44] I/A Court H.R., Case of Baena Ricardo et al. v. Panama. Merits, Reparations and Costs. Series C No. 72, Judgment of February 2, 2001, par. 127.

[45] I excluded some article 25 cases because the only analysis was the lack of remedies but not of a specific legal procedure or judicial guarantees. See, e.g.: I/A Court H.R., Case of the Saramaka People. v. Suriname, Preliminary Objections, Merits, Reparations, and Costs. Series C No. 172, Judgment of November 28, 2007; I/A Court H.R., Case of Castañeda Gutman v. Mexico, Preliminary Objections, Merits, Reparations, and Costs. Series C No. 184, Judgment of August 6, 2008. I also excluded a criminal proceeding where a civil action was an issue, but only because of the undue delay of the criminal proceedings under analysis of the Court. I/A Court H.R., Case of Ximenes Lopes v. Brazil, Merits, Reparations and Costs. Series C No. 149, Judgment of July 4, 2006.

Table 6.1 Summary of cases of the IACHR

Case	Type of the case	Main legal institution	Decision
Ivcher Bronstein v. Peru	Administrative	Nationality annulment	Violation art. 8–25
The Mayagna (Sumo) Awas Tingni Community v. Nicaragua	Administrative	Limitation on right of property	Violation art. 25
Cantos v. Argentina	Administrative	Payment proceedings against State	Violation art. 8–25
The "Five Pensioners" v. Peru	Administrative	Social security	Violation art. 25
The Yakye Axa Indigenous Community v. Paraguay	Administrative	Limitation on right of property	Violation art. 8–25
Yatama v. Nicaragua	Administrative	Electoral proceedings	Violation art. 8–25
Sawhoyamaxa Indigenous Community v. Paraguay	Administrative	Limitation on right of property	Violation art. 8–25
Claude Reyes et al. v. Chile.	Administrative	Access to information	Violation art. 8–25
Salvador Chiriboga v. Ecuador	Administrative	Limitation on right of property	Violation art. 8–25
Xákmok Kásek Indigenous Community v. Paraguay	Administrative	Limitation on right of property	Violation art. 8–25
Barbani Duarte et al. v. Uruguay	Administrative	Limitation on right of property	Violation art. 8–25
Atala Riffo and Daughters v. Chile	Civil	Parental rights/adoption proceedings	Violation art. 8
Fornerón and Daughter v. Argentina	Civil	Parental rights/adoption proceedings	Violation art. 8–25
The Kichwa Indigenous People of Sarayaku v. Ecuador	Administrative	Limitation on right of property	Violation art. 8–25
Furlán and Family v. Argentina	Administrative	Damages	Violation art. 8–25
Mémoli v. Argentina	Civil	Libel/Defamation	Violation art. 8
The Pacheco Tineo family v. Bolivia.	Administrative	Asylum proceedings	Violation art. 8–25
The Xucuru Indigenous People and its members v. Brazil	Administrative	Limitation on right of property	Violation art. 8–25
Colindres Schonenberg v. El Salvador	Administrative	Public employment termination	Violation art. 8

Montevideo.[46] The Government enacted Act N° 17.613 with a provision, article 31, that created a special administrative procedure before the Central Bank to

[46] I/A Court H.R., Case of Barbani Duarte et al. v. Uruguay. Merits, Reparations and Costs. Series C No. 234, Judgment of October 13, 2011, par. 63, 64.

determine the rights of "depositors" of the dissolved banks whose savings "had been transferred to other institutions" "without their consent." This administrative proceeding would grant them the possibility of claiming their inclusion as creditors of the bank with the same rights as those granted to depositors with checking, savings or fixed term accounts.[47] Upon decision an appeal for annulment was available before the Contentious-Administrative Tribunal.[48]

In this case, the IACHR analyzed the right to be heard from two dimensions. First, from a formal aspect which ensures access to the competent body to determine the legal right, and, second, from a material aspect of protection, meaning that the State must guarantee that the decision produced by the proceedings meets the purpose for which it was conceived.[49] This second element calls for an analysis of *effectiveness*. In this particular case, the proceeding lacked it since the administrative body decided not to analyze one of the elements of article 31, the required consent, which had a direct impact on the decision on whether to accept the petitions of the alleged victims or not.[50]

Based on a difference in treatment between the case of two petitioners and other cases, it was determined that an "adequate reasoning" was not guaranteed, in the sense that the proceeding allowed verification that the criteria to determine that the requirement of absence of consent were met, were applied objectively.[51]

Regarding the appeal for annulment before the Contentious-Administrative Tribunal, the Court had the opportunity to refer to article 25. According to this article, there is a violation of the right to an effective remedy if the tribunal in charge of the judicial control of an administrative body decision, is prevented from determining the main object of the dispute. For example, if it is restricted by factual or legal determinations made by the administrative body that would have been decisive in the case.[52] In this regard, the IACHR held that the administrative body, the tribunal responsible for deciding the judicial remedy, made an incomplete examination of the

[47] I/A Court H.R., Case of Barbani Duarte et al. v. Uruguay. Merits, Reparations and Costs. Series C No. 234, Judgment of October 13, 2011, par. 124, 133.

[48] I/A Court H.R., Case of Barbani Duarte et al. v. Uruguay. Merits, Reparations and Costs. Series C No. 234, Judgment of October 13, 2011, par. 101.

[49] I/A Court H.R., Case of Barbani Duarte et al. v. Uruguay. Merits, Reparations and Costs. Series C No. 234, Judgment of October 13, 2011, par. 122.

[50] The requirements of article 31 of Law 17,613 were: (1) to be a "depositor" of the Banco de Montevideo or the Banco La Caja Obrera; (2) whose savings had been transferred to other institutions, and (3) without his consent. I/A Court H.R., Case of Barbani Duarte et al. v. Uruguay. Merits, Reparations and Costs. Series C No. 234, Judgment of October 13, 2011, par. 141, 142, 153.

[51] I/A Court H.R., Case of Barbani Duarte et al. v. Uruguay. Merits, Reparations and Costs. Series C No. 234, Judgment of October 13, 2011, par. 183, 184.

[52] I/A Court H.R., Case of Barbani Duarte et al. v. Uruguay. Merits, Reparations and Costs. Series C No. 234, Judgment of October 13, 2011, par. 204.

claims submitted by the petitioner and therefore the judicial control of the administrative decision was not effective.[53]

Another six cases of administrative proceedings concern limitations imposed on the right of property, and are representatives of one of the topics on which the Inter-American system of human rights protection has been particularly innovative. The cases of the *Mayagna (Sumo) Awas Tingni Community v. Nicaragua*, the *Yakye Axa Indigenous Community*, the *Sawhoyamaxa Indigenous Community*, and *Xákmok Kásek Indigenous Community*, the three of them against Paraguay, the *Kichwa Indigenous People of Sarayaku v. Ecuador*, and the *Xucuru Indigenous People and its members v. Brazil*, are paradigmatic cases on collective rights.[54] In these cases, indigenous communities initiated proceedings to protect their ancient right to property over recognized indigenous territories against public or private decisions that could affect them.

The first of these cases, against Nicaragua, is the only one from those identified as non-criminal where there was a declaration of a violation of article 25 without taking article 8 into consideration. The analysis, here, was exclusively one of effectiveness of the existing titling proceedings and of the constitutional claim proceedings initiated by the community (*amparo*). The issue was not the inexistence of a normative recognition of indigenous communal property but a lack of a specific proceeding to protect it since the one existing does not establish a specific procedure for demarcation and titling of lands held by indigenous communities, taking into account their specific characteristics.[55] Regarding the constitutional proceedings, the violation arose from the unjustified delay in reaching a decision. In this regard, the Court says "...amparo remedies will be illusory and ineffective if there is unjustified delay in reaching a decision on them."[56] Consequently, it did not include the analysis of the particular procedural guarantees as a content of a right to a fair trial.

The cases of the Yakye Axa, the Sawhoyamaxa, and the Xákmok Kásek indigenous communities are related to a series of administrative proceedings to protect their rights over ancestral lands. In the first two, the proceedings included the request for the recognition of their leaders and the legal identity of the community, as claims for the recovery of territorial rights.[57] In all of them, violations of article 8 and

[53] I/A Court H.R., Case of Barbani Duarte et al. v. Uruguay. Merits, Reparations and Costs. Series C No. 234, Judgment of October 13, 2011, par. 220.

[54] The topics related to the rights of indigenous peoples, such as those related to the collective right to land, have been one of the main contributions of this regional system. See: Alston and Goodman (2013), p. 1009.

[55] I/A Court H.R., Case of the Mayagna (Sumo) Awas Tingni Community v. Nicaragua. Merits, Reparations and Costs. Series C No. 79, Judgment of August 31, 2001, par. 122, 123.

[56] I/A Court H.R., Case of the Mayagna (Sumo) Awas Tingni Community v. Nicaragua. Merits, Reparations and Costs. Series C No. 79, Judgment of August 31, 2001, par. 134.

[57] I/A Court H.R., Case of the Yakye Axa Indigenous Community v. Paraguay. Merits, Reparations and Costs. Series C No. 125, Judgment of June 17, 2005, par. 66; I/A Court H.R., Case of the Sawhoyamaxa Indigenous Community v. Paraguay. Merits, Reparations and Costs. Series C No. 146, Judgment of March 29, 2006, par. 81.

25 were found. First, from the undue delay of the proceedings taken as a whole, all of which lasted more than a decade. The reasonableness of the duration of the proceedings, in the case of the Yakye Axa community, was assessed taking into account three aspects: (a) the complexity of the matter, (b) the procedural initiative of the interested party and (c) the conduct of the judicial authorities. By contrast, in the case of the Sawhoyamaxa, because the case lasted two years more than that of the Yakye Axa, the duration was unreasonable by itself.[58] In the case of the Xákmok Kásek, despite the fact that it lasted longer than the two previous cases, a fact noted by the Court, it applied the same three factors as in the case of the Yakye Axa community, but included a fourth one, the effects on the legal situation of the person concerned.[59] Secondly, the violation came from the clear lack of efficacy of the existing proceedings to address the claims by the members of these communities to the land they consider their traditional and ancestral habitat.[60] The standard to be applicable for indigenous peoples is that effective protection must take into account their specificities, their economic and social characteristics, as well as their situation of special vulnerability, their customary law, values, and customs.[61]

The case of *Ivcher Bronstein v. Peru* is also worth a mention. The petitioner, Mr. Baruch Ivcher originally from Israel, was a naturalized Peruvian citizen and the main shareholder, director and president of a Peruvian television network. During transmission his TV channel denounced violations of human rights perpetrated by members of the Army Intelligence Service, and acts of corruption reputedly committed by its officers.[62] Soon after, the Military authorities denounced Mr. Ivcher for conducting a defamatory campaign of libel against the Armed Forces,[63] and the Peruvian Executive issued an administrative regulation establishing the possibility

[58] I/A Court H.R., Case of the Yakye Axa Indigenous Community v. Paraguay. Merits, Reparations and Costs. Series C No. 125, Judgment of June 17, 2005, par. 65; I/A Court H.R., Case of the Sawhoyamaxa Indigenous Community v. Paraguay. Merits, Reparations and Costs. Series C No. 146, Judgment of March 29, 2006, par. 95.

[59] I/A Court H.R., Case of the Xákmok Kásek Indigenous Community. v. Paraguay. Merits, Reparations and Costs. Series C No. 214, Judgment of August 24, 2010, par. 133, 134.

[60] I/A Court H.R., Case of the Yakye Axa Indigenous Community v. Paraguay. Merits, Reparations and Costs. Series C No. 125, Judgment of June 17, 2005, par. 96, 97; I/A Court H.R., Case of the Sawhoyamaxa Indigenous Community v. Paraguay. Merits, Reparations and Costs. Series C No. 146, Judgment of March 29, 2006, par. 108; I/A Court H.R., Case of the Xákmok Kásek Indigenous Community. v. Paraguay. Merits, Reparations and Costs. Series C No. 214, Judgment of August 24, 2010, par. 144, 145.

[61] I/A Court H.R., Case of the Yakye Axa Indigenous Community v. Paraguay. Merits, Reparations and Costs. Series C No. 125, Judgment of June 17, 2005, par. 62; I/A Court H.R., Case of the Sawhoyamaxa Indigenous Community v. Paraguay. Merits, Reparations and Costs. Series C No. 146, Judgment of March 29, 2006, par. 83.

[62] ICHR, access to justice as a guarantee of economic, social and cultural rights: a review of the standards adopted by the Inter-American System of Human Rights, OEA/Ser.L/V/II.129, Doc. 4 (2007), p. 24. Available at: https://www.oas.org/en/iachr/reports/thematic.asp.

[63] I/A Court H.R., Case of Ivcher Bronstein v. Peru. Merits, Reparations and Costs. Series C No. 74, Judgment of February 6, 2001, par. 76.k).

of canceling the citizenship of naturalized Peruvians. On the next day, a "Directorial Resolution" signed by the Director General of Migration and Naturalization was issued, annulling Mr. Ivcher's citizenship without any prior contact or communication with the petitioner.[64] As a direct result of his nationality annulment, he would lose control over the company because under Peruvian legislation it was necessary to be a Peruvian national to own a licensed television company.[65] The IACHR found violations of articles 8 and 25 not just in the administrative procedure that terminated in the nationality annulment, if there was one, but also in the judicial proceedings initiated by the petitioner to remedy his situation.

Regarding the administrative proceedings, the Court said not only that article 8 was applicable but also that it must be applicable in full, "so that a person may defend himself adequately against any act of the State that could affect his rights."[66] In this regard, the Court followed its case law by establishing that "...although this article does not stipulate minimum guarantees in matters which concern the determination of the rights and obligations of a civil, labor, fiscal or any other nature, the minimum guarantees established in paragraph 2 of the article should also apply to those categories and, therefore, in that respect, a person has the right to due process in the terms recognized for criminal matters, to the extent that it is applicable to the respective procedure."[67] This means, that against an act of the State, no matter whether punitive or not—because that was not the case, or at least it was not specified as such by the Court— the individual must be afforded all the procedural guarantees established in article 8. In this specific case, it was found that Mr. Ivcher's rights were affected without him being afforded any chance to intervene in the process, and to be fully informed in all the stages, despite being the person whose rights were being determined.[68]

On the judicial proceedings pursued by Mr. Ivcher, the Court found that the tribunal did not satisfy the minimum requirements of independence and impartiality of Article 8.1, necessary to obtain a decision in accordance with the law. Moreover, because the recourses were not effective either, the Court not only found a violation of article 8, but also of article 25 as well.[69]

---

[64] ICHR, access to justice as a guarantee of economic, social and cultural rights: a review of the standards adopted by the Inter-American System of Human Rights, OEA/Ser.L/V/II.129, Doc. 4 (2007), p. 24. Available at: https://www.oas.org/en/iachr/reports/thematic.asp.

[65] I/A Court H.R., Case of Ivcher Bronstein v. Peru. Merits, Reparations and Costs. Series C No. 74, Judgment of February 6, 2001, par. 76.e).

[66] I/A Court H.R., Case of Ivcher Bronstein v. Peru. Merits, Reparations and Costs. Series C No. 74, Judgment of February 6, 2001, par. 102.

[67] I/A Court H.R., Case of Ivcher Bronstein v. Peru. Merits, Reparations and Costs. Series C No. 74, Judgment of February 6, 2001, par. 103.

[68] I/A Court H.R., Case of Ivcher Bronstein v. Peru. Merits, Reparations and Costs. Series C No. 74, Judgment of February 6, 2001, par. 107.

[69] I/A Court H.R., Case of Ivcher Bronstein v. Peru. Merits, Reparations and Costs. Series C No. 74, Judgment of February 6, 2001, par. 137, 139.

The case of *Colindres Schonenberg v. El Salvador*, relates to a series of disciplinary administrative proceedings pursued by the Salvadorian Congress against a Mr. Colindres, a judge from the electoral court. Notwithstanding the clear criminal nature of the main proceeding, this case was considered because in 1999 Mr. Colindres filed a civil claim against the first act of destitution against the State. Despite a first instance civil court decision in favor of the claimant, the appeal stage lasted until 2009 and only in 2014 was a payment of USD $114.285,71 for damages made for Mr. Colindres. The petitioner alleged a violation of his right to a hearing within a reasonable time, and the Court found that it was not necessary to analyze the traditional factors in this case, since it was apparent that fifteen years for a decision and its enforcement was a violation in itself.[70]

From the point of view of access to justice as an element of due process, the case of *Cantos v. Argentina* is particularly important. On July 4, 1986, Mr. Cantos filed a claim with the Supreme Court for "payment of amounts owed" against the government of the Province of Santiago del Estero and the Argentine State, derived from an agreement signed in 1982.[71] The case was ended only 1996 with a ruling from the Supreme Court dismissing the claim on formal grounds, the non-payment of the court fees which amounted to USD$ 83,400,459 approximately (the fee is a flat rate consisting of 3% of the amount claimed), and a corresponding fine which amounted to 50% of the filing fee for not paying within five days after filing the claim. The IACHR found this amount unreasonable, even though in mathematical terms it represents 3% of the amount being claimed. The idea was that while the right of access to a court is not absolute and therefore may be subject to certain discretional limitations set by the State, the means used must nevertheless be proportional to the aim sought. Consequently, with the amount charged, there was no relationship of proportionality between the means employed and the aim being sought by Argentine law.[72]

According to this judgement, any domestic law or measure that imposes costs, or in any other way obstructs individuals' access to the courts beyond what is reasonably needed for the administration of justice, implies a violation of Article 8(1) of the Convention. Moreover, it also infringes article 25, since it is not enough that an appeal mechanism formally exists, for it must be effective.[73] The Court says: "[T]he fact that a proceeding concludes with a definitive court ruling is not sufficient to satisfy the right of access to the courts. Those participating in the proceeding must be able to do so without fear of being forced to pay disproportionate or excessive sums because they turned to the courts. The problem of excessive or disproportionate

---

[70] I/A Court H.R., Case of Colindres Schonenberg v. El Salvador. Merits, Reparations and Costs. Series C No. 373, . Judgment of February 4, 2019, par. 53-55, 114–119.

[71] I/A Court H.R., Case of Cantos v. Argentina. Merits, Reparations and Costs. Series C No. 97, Judgment of November 28, 2002, par. 44.

[72] I/A Court H.R., Case of Cantos v. Argentina. Merits, Reparations and Costs. Series C No. 97, Judgment of November 28, 2002, par. 53, 54.

[73] I/A Court H.R., Case of Cantos v. Argentina. Merits, Reparations and Costs. Series C No. 97, Judgment of November 28, 2002, par. 50, 52.

filing fees is compounded when, in order to force payment, the authorities attach the debtor's property or deny him the opportunity to do business."[74]

The case of *Furlán and Family v. Argentina* is another claim for damages against the State of Argentina. It was initiated in 1990 by Mr. Danilo Furlan to claim compensation for the damages stemming from the disability of his son, Sebastián Furlan, due to an accident at an abandoned military camp where he used to play as a child.[75] The Court noted that the civil proceeding lasted almost ten years, and the enforcement phase lasted another 1 year and 9 months until effective payment of the compensation. Accordingly, the Court analyzed the right to a reasonable duration of the proceeding, following the traditional criteria described before—the adverse effect on the judicial situation of the interested party and impact on his personal integrity—and concluded that there had been a violation.[76] At the administrative enforcement stage, the payment of the compensation was issued under a legal scheme which made the petitioner unable to receive immediately the 130,000 Argentine pesos decided by the local courts in his favor. Instead, once court costs and legal fees had been discounted, and the bonds by which he was paid cashed out, Sebastián Furlan finally received a sum equivalent to approximately $38.000 Argentine pesos. For the Court, this meant that the judicial decision had not been fully implemented. Taking into account Sebastián Furlán's disability and the financial situation of his family which called for a special degree of diligence, this resulted in a lack of effective judicial protection of the victim, and a violation of article 25.[77]

The petitioner also alleged a violation of Sebastián Furlan's right to be heard. According to the Court, even though Sebastián Furlán personally appeared a couple of times, he was not heard by the court in the damages claim. Consequently, the judge was not able to consider his opinions on the matter and, more especially, confirm his specific situation as a person with a disability.[78] Secondly, it was alleged that despite being a requirement in local regulations, the representative of the Juvenile Defender's Office was not notified of the proceedings. According to the Court, given the victim's reduced participation and personal and family situation, this officer would have provided a mechanism to address Sebastián Furlan's vulnerability and effectively protects his rights. This amounted to a violation of his right to a fair trial.[79]

---

[74] I/A Court H.R., Case of Cantos v. Argentina. Merits, Reparations and Costs. Series C No. 97, Judgment of November 28, 2002, par. 55.

[75] I/A Court H.R., Case of Furlan and family v. Argentina. Preliminary Objections, Merits, Reparations and Costs. Series C No. 246, Judgment of August 31, 2012, par. 78, 99.

[76] I I/A Court H.R., Case of Furlan and family v. Argentina. Preliminary Objections, Merits, Reparations and Costs. Series C No. 246, Judgment of August 31, 2012, par. 147–204.

[77] I/A Court H.R., Case of Furlan and family v. Argentina. Preliminary Objections, Merits, Reparations and Costs. Series C No. 246, Judgment of August 31, 2012, par. 213–223.

[78] I/A Court H.R., Case of Furlan and family v. Argentina. Preliminary Objections, Merits, Reparations and Costs. Series C No. 246, Judgment of August 31, 2012, par. 232.

[79] I/A Court H.R., Case of Furlan and family v. Argentina. Preliminary Objections, Merits, Reparations and Costs. Series C No. 246, Judgment of August 31, 2012, par. 242, 243.

Finally, it is interesting that the IACHR considered that, taken together, all these violations amounted to a lack of effective access to justice in this case. Taking the special situation of inequality of Sebastian Furlán and his family, compensatory measures were required to reduce or eliminate the obstacles and deficiencies that impaired or diminished an effective defense of their own interests. Their situation amounted to de facto discrimination and the Court declared that the State failed to comply with its obligation to guarantee, without discrimination, their right of access to justice.[80]

Only three cases involved a dispute between private parties. In the case of *Mémoli v. Argentina*, Pablo Mémoli and Carlos Mémoli were defendants in a civil and criminal complaint for libel and defamation, over a series of statements made around 1990 in newspaper articles and radio shows against the complainants and plaintiffs Antonio Guarracino, Humberto Romanello and Juan Bernardo Piriz.[81] The allegations refer to alleged fraud and other illegal activities in the context of irregular sales of burial niches in the local cemetery. Allegedly, these offences were committed while the complainants were acting as officers of a mutual association in the town of San Andrés de Giles.[82] The local criminal court delivered the judgment in first instance in 1994, finding both Carlos and Pablo Mémoli guilty of the charge of defamation, and sentencing the former "...to a suspended sentence of one month's imprisonment, with costs," and the latter to "...to a suspended sentence of five months' imprisonment, with costs."[83] In 1995, the Appeal Chamber confirmed the decision of the first instance court in full,[84] and further attempts to revoke those decisions were rejected.[85,86] Regarding the civil proceedings, in 1997 the complainants filed a claim for damages against both petitioners, based on the final criminal convictions handed down against them.[87] This civil claim was still pending by

[80] I/A Court H.R., Case of Furlan and family v. Argentina. Preliminary Objections, Merits, Reparations and Costs. Series C No. 246, Judgment of August 31, 2012, par. 268, 269.

[81] I/A Court H.R., Case of Mémoli v Argentina, Preliminary Objections, Merits, Reparations and Costs. Series C No. 265, Judgment of August 22, 2013, par. 74.

[82] I/A Court H.R., Case of Mémoli v Argentina, Preliminary Objections, Merits, Reparations and Costs. Series C No. 265, Judgment of August 22, 2013, par. 1.

[83] I/A Court H.R., Case of Mémoli v Argentina, Preliminary Objections, Merits, Reparations and Costs. Series C No. 265, Judgment of August 22, 2013, par. 84.

[84] I/A Court H.R., Case of Mémoli v Argentina, Preliminary Objections, Merits, Reparations and Costs. Series C No. 265, Judgment of August 22, 2013, par. 87.

[85] These attempts were rejected even though the IACHR had order Argentina to update its legislation to the Convention in this matter. See: I/A Court H.R., Case of Kimel v. Argentina. Merits, Reparations and Costs. Series C No. 177, Judgment of May 2, 2008.

[86] I/A Court H.R., Case of Mémoli v Argentina, Preliminary Objections, Merits, Reparations and Costs. Series C No. 265, Judgment of August 22, 2013, par. 89, 90.

[87] I/A Court H.R., Case of Mémoli v Argentina, Preliminary Objections, Merits, Reparations and Costs. Series C No. 265, Judgment of August 22, 2013, par. 95.

August 2012 when the IACHR decided the case and during that time, it issued precautionary measures to protect the petitioner's properties.[88]

The petitioners alleged violation of article 8.1 of the Convention in conjunction with article 13 (freedom of expression). Before analyzing the claimants' allegations, the Court acknowledged that this case, unlike most others, concerned a dispute between two private persons in which the State was not a party. Notwithstanding, it reiterated its case law on the range of application of article 8 by expressing "...that all the organs that exercise functions of a jurisdictional nature, whether criminal or not, have the obligation to take decisions based on full respect for the guarantees of due process established in Article 8 of the American Convention."[89] In terms of the specific violations, the petitioners alleged first that the duration of the civil proceeding were unreasonable, taking into consideration that they had lasted more than 15 years and, as described before, were still pending while precautionary measures were in force.[90] To decide on the duration of the civil proceedings, the Court recalled that this analyzes is based on the particular circumstances of the case, specifically on the following factors: "(a) the complexity of the matter; (b) the procedural activity of the interested party; (c) the conduct of the judicial authorities, and (d) the impact on the legal situation of the individual involved in the proceeding."[91] Secondly, the petitioners alleged several procedural irregularities during the proceedings. Among them, they argued that a payment they allegedly had to make following the inadmissibility of the remedy of complaint against the proceedings violated their right of access to justice.[92] The Court dismissed this argument because "...charging a sum of money for the rejection of the remedy of complaint before the Supreme Court of Justice of the Nation does not constitute per se an obstruction of access to justice. On the contrary, the representatives would have to show that this charge was unreasonable or represented a serious prejudice to their financial capacity, which they have not done in this case."[93] The test to be applied is one of proportionality, as "...the right of access to justice is not absolute and, consequently, may be subject to some discretional limitations by the State, which should ensure correspondence between the means used and the objective pursued."[94]

[88] I/A Court H.R., Case of Mémoli v Argentina, Preliminary Objections, Merits, Reparations and Costs. Series C No. 265, Judgment of August 22, 2013, par. 108–112.

[89] I/A Court H.R., Case of Mémoli v Argentina, Preliminary Objections, Merits, Reparations and Costs. Series C No. 265, Judgment of August 22, 2013, par. 171.

[90] I/A Court H.R., Case of Mémoli v Argentina, Preliminary Objections, Merits, Reparations and Costs. Series C No. 265, Judgment of August 22, 2013, par. 167–168.

[91] I/A Court H.R., Case of Mémoli v Argentina, Preliminary Objections, Merits, Reparations and Costs. Series C No. 265, Judgment of August 22, 2013, par. 174–180.

[92] I/A Court H.R., Case of Mémoli v Argentina, Preliminary Objections, Merits, Reparations and Costs. Series C No. 265, Judgment of August 22, 2013, par. 193.

[93] I/A Court H.R., Case of Mémoli v Argentina, Preliminary Objections, Merits, Reparations and Costs. Series C No. 265, Judgment of August 22, 2013, par. 193.

[94] I/A Court H.R., Case of Mémoli v Argentina, Preliminary Objections, Merits, Reparations and Costs. Series C No. 265, Judgment of August 22, 2013, par. 193.

The cases of *Fornerón and Daughter v. Argentina*, and *Atala Riffo and Daugthers v. Chile*, are both concerned with family law issues. The first case arose from a series of legal proceedings initiated by the petitioner trying to gain access and guardianship over his daughter. Her former partner decided to give her daughter in custody for future adoption and initially denied the petitioner paternity. Therefore, besides initiating a filiation claim, he later had to request access and custody and finally he had to oppose the adoption proceedings initiated by the custodians.[95] The first legal issue analyzed by the IACHT was whether the proceedings on legal guardianship and the visiting regime complied with the requirement of reasonable time, which lasted three and ten years respectively. While deciding on the basis of the traditional factors used to access such claims, including the special circumstances of the petitioner, the court linked this due process requirement with the right of access to justice in the sense that it must ensure that the rights of the individual are determined within a reasonable time.[96] The second case, *Atala Riffo and Daugthers v. Chile*, related to the sexual discrimination that the petitioner suffered in the legal dispute over the custody of the daughters that she and her partner had in common, but also in the subsequent disciplinary proceeding conducted against Ms. Atala in her capacity as a judge.[97] For the purpose of this project, I will focus on the debate surrounding the custody trial since the disciplinary proceeding concerned a legal issue which may be considered as criminal in nature according to the operational definition provided previously. In this case, among other due process claims, the petitioners alleged a violation of the right to be heard regarding both girls in the custody proceeding. The court analyzed this due process dimension in conjunction with article 12 of the Convention on the Rights of the Child, which contains appropriate stipulations for facilitating the child's intervention according to age and maturity, while ensuring that it does not harm its genuine interest.[98] The Court found, however, that the first instance court in the custody proceeding complied with its obligations arising from the child's right to be heard in a judicial proceeding that affects them, since it is clearly stated that the views of the three girls were taken into account, bearing in mind their maturity and capacity at that time. It found no evidence that the girls were heard again by the Supreme Court of Justice of Chile in the context of the decision on the remedy of complaint, nor is there any mention in the ruling issued by the Supreme Court regarding the decision to set aside the wishes expressed by the girls during the proceedings. While a new hearing was not necessary since the nature of the proceeding, at least the Supreme Court of Justice

[95] I/A Court H.R., Case of Fornerón and daughter v. Argentina. Merits, Reparations and Costs. Series C No. 242, Judgment of April 27, 2012, par. 31–43.

[96] I/A Court H.R., Case of Fornerón and daughter v. Argentina. Merits, Reparations and Costs. Series C No. 242, Judgment of April 27, 2012, par. 65, 66.

[97] I/A Court H.R., Case of Atala Riffo and daughters v. Chile. Merits, Reparations and Costs. Series C No. 239, Judgment of February 24, 2012, par. 3, 29.

[98] I/A Court H.R., Case of Atala Riffo and daughters v. Chile. Merits, Reparations and Costs. Series C No. 239, Judgment of February 24, 2012, par. 196.

had to explain in its judgment how it assessed or took into consideration the statements and preferences expressed by the girls and included in the case file.[99]

6.3 Requirements Over Civil Matters in the Inter-American Court of Human Rights. The Expansive Approach

Of these 19 cases containing a limb that is non-criminal in nature, the first common element is that in most of them the Court decided on the effectiveness of the proceedings based on an analysis that takes article 25 in conjunction with article 8. The only exception is the case of *"Five Pensioners" v. Peru*, which found a violation of article 25 only, and the cases of *Atala Riffo and Daugthers v. Chile, Mémoli v. Argentina*, and *Colindres Schonenberg v. El Salvador*, in which the Court found a violation of article 8 only (at least for the non-criminal side of these cases). All the others followed the general approach of the Court to analyze both articles in conjunction. This approach might be problematic because it is not easy to determine whether the IACHR in these cases analyzes the effectiveness of a procedural guarantee in the context of a specific legal procedure or, on the contrary, it determines if the legal procedure by itself proved to be an effective remedy against the alleged violation.

The second common element of the right to a fair trial in these cases was the right to a reasonable duration of the proceedings. It was present in ten of the cases, that dealt with limitation of the property rights of indigenous communities (*Yakye Axa Indigenous Community v. Paraguay*, *Sawhoyamaxa Indigenous Community v. Paraguay*, *Xucuru Indigenous People and its members v. Brazil*), expropriation proceedings (*Salvador Chiriboga v. Ecuador*), civil claims for damages against the State (*Furlan and family v. Argentina*), parental rights or adoption proceedings (*Fornerón and daughter v. Argentina*), defamation (*Mémoli v Argentina*), payment proceedings against the State (*Cantos v. Argentina*), or the termination of public employment relations (*Colindres Schonenberg v. El Salvador*).

The third common element of due process was the right to a court or access to justice, analyzed in six of the 19 cases. Most of these concerned disputes between private individuals and a State body, and because of that, I coded them as administrative. The legal proceedings that originated the petitions were related to asylum proceedings (*Pacheco Tineo family v. Bolivia*), limitations over the right of property in the context of bank accounts (*Barbani Duarte et al. v. Uruguay*), administrative nationality annulments (*Ivcher Bronstein v. Peru*), payment proceedings against the State (*Cantos v. Argentina*), or the termination of public employment relations (*Colindres Schonenberg v. El Salvador*). The only case between private individuals where access to justice was a legal issue was *Fornerón and Daughter v. Argentina*, a

[99] I/A Court H.R., Case of Atala Riffo and daughters v. Chile. Merits, Reparations and Costs. Series C No. 239, Judgment of February 24, 2012, par. 203, 204, 208.

case concerning paternity rights and opposition to an adoption. However, here the court mentioned access to justice not to analyze it in its own terms but solely in connection with the right to a decision in a reasonable time.[100]

Four cases concerned the right to an opportunity to be heard. In the case of *Ivcher Bronstein v. Perú*, described above, the court found (by applying article 8 in full) that the decision of his nationality annulment was conducted without any opportunity for the petitioner to intervene, and be fully informed in all the stages, despite being the person whose rights were being determined.[101] Similarly, in *Yatama v. Nicaragua*, a case concerning the exclusion from participation in municipal elections of the indigenous regional political party "YATAMA" as a result of a decision issued by the Supreme Electoral Council, the court found that when deciding that the organization did not comply with the registration requirements, the electoral body gave this organization no opportunity to correct the existing defect.[102] In the case of *Atala Riffo and Daughters v. Chile*, as described before, the violation of the right to be heard was not of Ms. Atala but of her daughters in the custody proceedings. Finally, in *Furlán and Family v. Argentina,* it was found that although the victim personally appeared in the civil court he was not heard in the suit for damages, especially important considering his situation as a disabled person.[103]

In summary, the most frequent elements of the right to a fair trial were the effectiveness of the legal proceeding as a remedy (15 out to 19), followed by the right to have legal proceedings completed within a reasonable time (10 out of 19), the right to a court or access to justice (6 out of 19), and to an opportunity to be heard (4 out of 19). Finally, there were two cases where independence and impartiality were briefly discussed (*Ivcher Bronstein v. Perú* and *Atala Riffo and Daugthers v. Chile*) and one case where there was an issue concerning the right of equality of arms (*Barbani Duarte et al. v. Uruguay*) (Table 6.2).

In terms of the variables to operationalize both models, the flexible and the checklist approach, of the 19 cases, in 14 I used a variable that I have identified as pertaining to the flexible approach. The most recurrent was the variable I coded as effectiveness (found in 12 cases), which I constructed for those cases where the Court was more concerned with the practical effectiveness than formal recognition. From these cases, it was mostly applied in decisions where one of the elements analyzed was whether the legal procedure as a whole was an effective remedy under article 25,[104] but also used to analyze procedural guarantees such as the judicial

[100] I/A Court H.R., Case of Fornerón and daughter v. Argentina. Merits, Reparations and Costs. Series C No. 242, Judgment of April 27, 2012, par. 66.

[101] I/A Court H.R., Case of Ivcher Bronstein v. Peru. Merits, Reparations and Costs. Series C No. 74, Judgment of February 6, 2001, par. 107.

[102] I/A Court H.R., Case of Yatama v. Nicaragua. Preliminary Objections, Merits, Reparations and Costs. Series C No. 127, Judgment of June 23, 2005, par. 2, 162.

[103] I/A Court H.R., Case of Furlan and family v. Argentina. Preliminary Objections, Merits, Reparations and Costs. Series C No. 246, Judgment of August 31, 2012, par. 232.

[104] See: I/A Court H.R., Case of the Mayagna (Sumo) Awas Tingni Community v. Nicaragua. Merits, Reparations and Costs. Series C No. 79, Judgment of August 31, 2001, par. 127; I/A Court

Table 6.2 Dimensions of the right to a fair trial and procedural elements analyzed by the Court

Case	Dimension of the right to a fair trial	Procedural elements
Ivcher Bronstein v. Peru	Right to a court/ Access to justice Independence/impartiality Opportunity to be heard	Present evidence/argument Prior notification Competent court/natural judge
The Mayagna (Sumo) Awas Tingni Community v. Nicaragua	Effective remedy	
Cantos v. Argentina	Effective remedy Reasonable time Right to a court/ Access to justice	Court fees
The "Five Pensioners" v. Peru	Effective remedy	Judicial decision enforcement
The Yakye Axa Indigenous Community v. Paraguay	Effective remedy Reasonable time	Legal personality prior to initiate proceedings
Yatama v. Nicaragua	Effective remedy Opportunity to be heard	Reasoned decision Judicial control of administrative decision Prior notification
Sawhoyamaxa Indigenous Community v. Paraguay	Effective remedy Reasonable time	Legal personality prior to initiate proceedings
Claude Reyes et al. v. Chile.	Effective remedy	Reasoned decision
Salvador Chiriboga v. Ecuador	Effective remedy Reasonable time Right to a court/ Access to justice	
Xákmok Kásek Indigenous Community v. Paraguay	Reasonable time Effective remedy	
Barbani Duarte et al. v. Uruguay	Effective remedy Equality of arms Right to a court/ Access to justice	Reasoned decision Judicial control of administrative decision Present evidence/argument Proper evaluation/ interpretation
Atala Riffo and Daughters v. Chile	Independence/impartiality Opportunity to be heard	
Fornerón and Daughter v. Argentina	Reasonable time Effective remedy Right to a court/ Access to justice	
The Kichwa Indigenous People of Sarayaku v. Ecuador	Effective remedy	Judicial decision enforcement

(continued)

Table 6.2 (continued)

Case	Dimension of the right to a fair trial	Procedural elements
Furlán and Family v. Argentina	Reasonable time Effective remedy Opportunity to be heard	Judicial decision enforcement
Mémoli v. Argentina	Reasonable time	Proper evaluation/ interpretation
The Pacheco Tineo family v. Bolivia.	Effective remedy Right to a court/ Access to justice	Reasoned decision Judicial control of administrative decision Proper evaluation/interpretation Legal assistance Translation Access to materials to prepare defense Public hearing
The Xucuru Indigenous People and its members v. Brazil	Reasonable time Effective remedy	
Colindres Schonenberg v. El Salvador	Reasonable time	

control of administrative decisions[105] or the enforcement of judicial decisions.[106] For example, in *Barbani Duarte et al. v. Uruguay*, the Court decided whether the legal proceedings at the Contentious-Administrative Tribunal against the administrative decisions were effective, since it was an appeal for annulment and not a full-blown appeal. The court dismissed this allegation stating that this type of judicial review could have been considered effective had the annulment of the administrative decision protected the alleged victims from the decision that violated their rights,

H.R., Case of Yatama v. Nicaragua. Preliminary Objections, Merits, Reparations and Costs. Series C No. 127, Judgment of June 23, 2005, par. 168, 169; I/A Court H.R., Case of the Sawhoyamaxa Indigenous Community v. Paraguay. Merits, Reparations and Costs. Series C No. 146, Judgment of March 29, 2006, par. 108; I/A Court H.R., Case of the Xákmok Kásek Indigenous Community. v. Paraguay. Merits, Reparations and Costs. Series C No. 214, Judgment of August 24, 2010, par. 124; I/A Court H.R., Case of Fornerón and daughter v. Argentina. Merits, Reparations and Costs. Series C No. 242, Judgment of April 27, 2012, par. 111; I/A Court H.R., Case of the Xucuru Indigenous People and its members v. Brazil. Preliminary Objections, Merits, Reparations and Costs. Series C No. 346, Judgment of February 5, 2017, par. 130.

[105] I/A Court H.R., Case of Yatama v. Nicaragua. Preliminary Objections, Merits, Reparations and Costs. Series C No. 127, Judgment of June 23, 2005, par. 174; I/A Court H.R., Case of Barbani Duarte et al. v. Uruguay. Merits, Reparations and Costs. Series C No. 234, Judgment of October 13, 2011; I/A Court H.R., Case of Mémoli v Argentina, Preliminary Objections, Merits, Reparations and Costs. Series C No. 265, Judgment of August 22, 2013.

[106] See: I/A Court H.R., Case of Furlan and family v. Argentina. Preliminary Objections, Merits, Reparations and Costs. Series C No. 246, Judgment of August 31, 2012, par. 219.

even when the judicial body was not empowered to analyze all aspects of an administrative decision.[107]

In deciding on the duration of legal proceedings, the IACHR applied in most cases a flexible approach, by analyzing the traditional factors already mentioned that refer to the particular circumstances of the case. For example, in *Sawhoyamaxa Indigenous Community v. Paraguay*, the Court found a violation of article 8.1 because the petition for recognition of the "legal personality" of the Sawhoyamaxa Community took four years, ten months and fourteen days. To decide that this was a violation, the Court took into consideration that said proceedings were not complex and that the State had not justified such a delay.[108] Similarly, in *Fornerón and Daugthers v. Argentina*, the IACHR decided that the legal proceedings, which lasted more than 10 years, were unreasonably long by applying the specific facts of the case to each of the elements: (a) the complexity of the matter; (b) the procedural activities of the interested party; (c) the conduct of the judicial authorities, and (d) the effects on the legal situation of the individual involved in the proceedings.[109]

It also used the mentioned approach to decide a violation of the right to a court and access to justice. In the case of *Mémoli v. Argentina*, regarding one of the allegation of the petitioners concerning a payment that the presumed victims had to make following the inadmissibility of the complaint, the Court expressly said: "...the right of access to justice is not absolute and, consequently, may be subject to some discretional limitations by the State, which should ensure correspondence between the means used and the objective pursued and, in short, cannot suppose the negation of this right. In this regard, the Court considers that charging a sum of money for the rejection of the remedy of complaint before the Supreme Court of Justice of the Nation does not constitute per se an obstruction of access to justice. To the contrary, the representatives would have to show that this charge was unreasonable or represented a serious prejudice to their financial capacity, which they have not done in this case."[110] Similarly, in the case of *Cantos v. Argentina*, the Court argued that a filing fee is not per se a violation, but "...while the right of access to a court is not an absolute and therefore may be subject to certain discretional limitations set by the State, the fact remains that the means used must be proportional to the aim sought."[111]

Although most cases dealt with a right to an effective remedy claim in connection with the requirements of due process, which calls for a flexible approach, in 12 of the

---

[107] I/A Court H.R., Case of Barbani Duarte et al. v. Uruguay. Merits, Reparations and Costs. Series C No. 234, Judgment of October 13, 2011, par. 210–213.

[108] I/A Court H.R., Case of the Sawhoyamaxa Indigenous Community v. Paraguay. Merits, Reparations and Costs. Series C No. 146, Judgment of March 29, 2006, par. 88–89.

[109] /A Court H.R., Case of Fornerón and daughter v. Argentina. Merits, Reparations and Costs. Series C No. 242, Judgment of April 27, 2012, par. 66–77.

[110] I/A Court H.R., Case of Mémoli v Argentina, Preliminary Objections, Merits, Reparations and Costs. Series C No. 265, Judgment of August 22, 2013, par. 193.

[111] I/A Court H.R., Case of Cantos v. Argentina. Merits, Reparations and Costs. Series C No. 97, Judgment of November 28, 2002, par. 54.

19 cases the Court used at least one of the variables I identified as pertaining to the checklist model. In one case, a specific guarantee of article 8.2's list of procedural guarantees for the accused was expressly applied to a non-criminal proceeding. This case was *Ivcher Bronstein v. Peru*, in which the Court found that the victim was not properly informed, nor had access to the relevant materials of the administrative proceeding whose outcome was the annulment of Mr. Ivcher's nationality.[112] In other cases, although the IACHR did not expressly apply guarantees of article 8.2, it considered that the entire clause of article 8 was applicable to every type of legal proceeding.[113] Moreover, it interpreted a specific procedural element or due process dimension as a strict minimum in eight cases[114] and, in other three cases, it interpreted a procedural requirement as a legal rule calling for a binary application.[115] For example, in *Colindres Schonenberg v. El Salvador*, the IACHR considered that it was not necessary to analyze the particularities of the case because it was manifest that fifteen years to decide and enforce a claim for damages constitutes a violation of the right to a judicial hearing within a reasonable time.[116]

---

[112] I/A Court H.R., Case of Ivcher Bronstein v. Peru. Merits, Reparations and Costs. Series C No. 74, Judgment of February 6, 2001, par. 103–107.

[113] I/A Court H.R., Case of Ivcher Bronstein v. Peru. Merits, Reparations and Costs. Series C No. 74, Judgment of February 6, 2001, par. 102; I/A Court H.R., Case of Yatama v. Nicaragua. Preliminary Objections, Merits, Reparations and Costs. Series C No. 127. Judgment of June 23, 2005, par. 149; I/A Court H.R., Case of Claude Reyes et al. v. Chile. Merits, Reparations and Costs. Series C No. 151, Judgment of September 19, 2006, par. 116; I/A Court H.R., Case of Barbani Duarte et al. v. Uruguay. Merits, Reparations and Costs. Series C No. 234, Judgment of October 13, 2011, par. 116; I/A Court H.R., Case of Mémoli v Argentina, Preliminary Objections, Merits, Reparations and Costs. Series C No. 265, Judgment of August 22, 2013, par. 171.

[114] I/A Court H.R., Case of Ivcher Bronstein v. Peru. Merits, Reparations and Costs. Series C No. 74, Judgment of February 6, 2001, par. 104; I/A Court H.R., Case of the "Five Pensioners" v. Peru. Merits, Reparations and Costs. Series C No. 98. Judgment of February 28, 2003, par. 138; I/A Court H.R., Case of Yatama v. Nicaragua. Preliminary Objections, Merits, Reparations and Costs. Series C No. 127. Judgment of June 23, 2005, par. 164; I/A Court H.R., Case of Claude Reyes et al. v. Chile. Merits, Reparations and Costs. Series C No. 151, Judgment of September 19, 2006, par. 122; I/A Court H.R., Case of Kichwa Indigenous People of Sarayaku v. Ecuador. Merits and Reparations. Series C No. 245, Judgment of June 27, 2012, par. 263; I/A Court H.R., Case of Furlan and family v. Argentina. Preliminary Objections, Merits, Reparations and Costs. Series C No. 246, Judgment of August 31, 2012, par. 232; I/A Court H.R., Case of the Pacheco Tineo family v. Bolivia. Preliminary Objections, Merits, Reparations and Costs. Series C No. 272, Judgment of November 25, 2013, p. 159; I/A Court H.R., Case of Colindres Schonenberg v. El Salvador. Merits, Reparations and Costs. Series C No. 373, Judgment of February 4, 2019, par. 87.

[115] I/A Court H.R., Case of the Sawhoyamaxa Indigenous Community v. Paraguay. Merits, Reparations and Costs. Series C No. 146, Judgment of March 29, 2006, par. 95; I/A Court H.R., Case of Claude Reyes et al. v. Chile. Merits, Reparations and Costs. Series C No. 151, Judgment of September 19, 2006, par. 122; I/A Court H.R., Case of Colindres Schonenberg v. El Salvador. Merits, Reparations and Costs. Series C No. 373, Judgment of February 4, 2019, par. 118.

[116] I/A Court H.R., Case of Colindres Schonenberg v. El Salvador. Merits, Reparations and Costs. Series C No. 373, Judgment of February 4, 2019, par. 118.

Finally, regarding specific procedural protections, the case with more procedural elements analyzed by the Court was the case of the *Pacheco Tineo family v. Bolivia*, a case concerning asylum proceedings involving an administrative decision and the corresponding judicial control of that decision. In this regard, the IACHR provided a strict minimum list of procedural guarantees that should be afforded to asylum seekers,[117] but also took into account the nature of the procedure which calls for an enhanced protection. On the contrary, seven cases did not analyze specific procedural features at all, which might be a consequence of the approach of the Court of deciding most cases over the effectiveness of the proceedings as remedies for a violation of the right to a fair trial as a whole.

In cases where specific procedural guarantees were analyzed as a legal issue, the most common was the duty to state reasons. Most of these cases also involved the judicial control of administrative decisions. In Yatama, the decision on this requirement followed the flexible approach with reference to the circumstances and the nature of the proceedings. In this regard, the IACHR held that the Supreme Electoral Council should have indicated the specific requirements that the political party had failed to comply with, indicating the corresponding norm, and the reasons for that conclusion. This requirement was especially important since the new electoral regulation had entered into force approximately nine months before the date set for holding the elections and it was the first electoral process organized under this law, which involved significant changes to the previous one.[118] On the contrary, in *Claude Reyes et al. v. Chile*, this requirement was applied using a checklist approach interpreting this requirement of article 8.1. as a strict legal rule applicable in full to "...domestic bodies that could affect human rights".[119]

In three cases the IACHR decided on issues related to the enforcement of judicial decisions. These cases followed a flexible approach by considering the effectiveness of a remedy by its enforcement and compliance by the State, but at the same time considering it as a strict minimum for effectiveness. For example, in the case of *The Kichwa Indigenous People of Sarayaku v. Ecuador*, the IACHR held that to comply with article 25 the States must guarantee effective mechanisms to execute the decisions or judgments issued by judicial authorities, "...since the effectiveness of the judgments and the judicial orders depends on their execution. Anything to the contrary would entail the denial of the right concerned."[120]

---

[117] I/A Court H.R., Case of the Pacheco Tineo family v. Bolivia. Preliminary Objections, Merits, Reparations and Costs. Series C No. 272, Judgment of November 25, 2013, par. 159.

[118] I/A Court H.R., Case of Yatama v. Nicaragua. Preliminary Objections, Merits, Reparations and Costs. Series C No. 127, Judgment of June 23, 2005, par. 159–160.

[119] I/A Court H.R., Case of Claude Reyes et al. v. Chile. Merits, Reparations and Costs. Series C No. 151, Judgment of September 19, 2006, par. 116–122.

[120] I/A Court H.R., Case of Kichwa Indigenous People of Sarayaku v. Ecuador. Merits and Reparations. Series C No. 245, Judgment of June 27, 2012, par. 263. Similar strict approach might be seen in: I/A Court H.R., Case of the "Five Pensioners" v. Peru. Merits, Reparations and Costs. Series C No. 98, Judgment of February 28, 2003, par. 138; I/A Court H.R., Case of Furlan

This analysis shows that the case law of the IACHR in non-criminal matters and the fair trial requirements in these legal procedures, moves between the two ideal types already described. In some cases, a more flexible approach is applied and in others a strict checklist model can be found. If we imagine these two models in their ideal or extreme versions, I would probably locate the Inter-American case law somewhere between the two, but with an important retention of the checklist model.

Expert doctrine on the matter had advanced some possible explanations. As described by Elizabeth Salmón, due process in the Inter-American Court of Human Rights case law has experienced an expansive effect. First, a horizontal expansion, that is, by applying the content of the right to a fair trial to proceedings that are not judicial in nature if a right is affected. Second, a vertical expansion, recognizing guarantees not expressly mentioned in the provision of article 8.1, for example, by applying those guarantees to someone accused of a crime.[121]

Regarding the first horizontal expansive effect, it has been justified in the wording of the article 8.1 of the Convention, which establishes the right fair trial "...*for the determination of* ...*rights and obligations of a civil, labor, fiscal, or any other nature*.[122] Thus, the IACHR has given this "expansive effect" with the purpose of providing judicial protection to other situations where rights or obligations are concerned but not necessarily determined.[123] The rationale behind this expansion is that its guarantees apply to every kind of proceeding that may *affect* human rights and not, as expressly mandated by the Convention, only to those that entail the *determination of rights and obligations*.[124] Regarding the vertical expansion, it is clear since the early days of the Court that article 8.2 applies to proceedings concerning the determination of rights and obligations of civil, labor, fiscal, or of any of other character.[125]

The described mode of interpretation, as expressed by Medina, "...requires States to establish *all* minimum guarantees for accused persons in *all* types of proceedings. This would at times appear to be excessive."[126] On the contrary, according to this author, the specific provision of Article 8.2 should be reserved for cases of a criminal nature and where the final decision leads to a penal sanction. Other types of proceedings should fall under the generic clause of Article 8.1 that entails a more concrete and case by case approach.[127]

---

and family v. Argentina. Preliminary Objections, Merits, Reparations and Costs. Series C No. 246, Judgment of August 31, 2012, par. 209.

[121] Salmón and Blanco (2012), p. 84.

[122] Different from the solution given by the European Convention of Human Rights, as I will explain in the next chapter.

[123] García (2012), pp. 23–24.

[124] Medina (2016), pp. 251–261.

[125] García (2012), pp. 23–24.

[126] Medina (2016), p. 260.

[127] Medina (2016), pp. 260–261.

While Medina is right in her interpretation of the IACHR case law—and how could it be otherwise if she is a former judge and president of the court and a recognized expert on the matter—I believe this approach must be nuanced a little. This idea might be true in administrative proceedings, especially in those of a punitive nature, but at least in non-criminal matters, as I showed, the IACHR tends to have a more flexible approach. Even so, this expansive doctrine is characteristic of the case law of the IACHR in comparison with its European counterpart, as I will show later.

References

Alston P, Goodman R (2013) International human rights. The successor to international human rights in context: law, politics and morals. Oxford University Press, Oxford

Buergenthal T (1985) The advisory practice of the Inter-American Human Rights Court. Am J Int Law 79(1):1–27

García S (2012) El debido proceso. Criterios de la jurisprudencia interamericana, Porrúa, Mexico

Medina C (2016) The American Convention on Human Rights. Crucial rights and their theory and practice, 2nd edn. Intersentia, Cambridge

Salmón E, Blanco C (2012) El derecho al debido proceso en la jurisprudencia de la Corte Interamericana de Derechos Humanos. IDEHPUCP, GIZ, Perú

Chapter 7
The European Court of Human Rights Case Law on Due Process Over Civil Matters

The human rights protection system of the Council of Europe emerged from a shared understanding that a strong protection system was crucial to avoid new gross human right violations after the Second World War. It was the first regional response and affirmation of a belief that governments respecting human rights are less likely to wage war on their neighbors.[1] There was also a common assumption that the best way to ensure that Germany would be for peace was through regional integration unlike the harsh measures that followed World War One. Finally, there was a common desire to bring the non-communist countries of Europe together with a common ideological framework to counteract the "communist threat."[2] At its origins a true political will existed to implement a functional system. This understanding led to the founding members' decision to admit new members only upon acceptance of the rule of law and respect for human rights, and to enact a document not just a mere declaration but a binding human right treaty as soon as this could be achieved.[3] That is how the European Convention on Human Rights, technically called the Convention for the Protection of Human Rights and Fundamental Freedoms, the primary source of fundamental rights in Europe,[4] was adopted in 1950 and entered into force in 1953. Of course, this context contrasted with the Inter-American counterpart, which was created with a strong sense of distrust, especially from Latin and South American countries, of the United States, which is reflected in the non-intervention principle commonly used at the regional level.[5] This lack of political will is reflected in the scarce political and financial support for the OAS,[6] and in the fact that two

[1] Alston and Goodman (2013), p. 891.

[2] Alston and Goodman (2013), p. 892.

[3] Alston and Goodman (2013), pp. 894–895.

[4] Hazelhorst (2017), p. 126.

[5] Goldman (2009), pp. 857–858.

[6] Alston and Goodman (2013), p. 985.

R. Lillo Lobos, *Understanding Due Process in Non-Criminal Matters*, Ius Gentium: Comparative Perspectives on Law and Justice 97,
https://doi.org/10.1007/978-3-030-95534-2_7

decades were necessary to begin its full operation, in comparison with the 6 years it took for the European Court of Human Rights (ECHR or the Court), which began its work in 1959.

The original procedure at the ECHR could be initiated only by a complaint filed by the European Commission on Human Rights, the victims' State, or the denounced State member. For that purpose, and just like the Inter-American system in its current legal procedure, an individual could file a petition to the Commission which, would consider whether a complaint was admissible, try to settle the case between the parties, and, eventually, prepare a report on the findings. This report went to the committee of Ministers, a political body in charge of endorsing or rejecting it. Only thereafter could the Commission or a State could bring a case to the Court. The complaints procedure was accepted for all the State members in 1990, and subsequently, as new states became members of the system, it was evident that deep reforms were needed to deal with the increasing workload.[7]

In 1998 the system was reformed by Protocol N° 11 with the purpose of streamlining the complaints procedure. The most important change was that the individual petition system became compulsory and the Commission ceased to exist.[8] With the current mechanism, a member State, individuals, or NGOs may file a claim directly to the Court, which will hear cases in a single-judge formation, in committees of three judges, in chambers of seven judges and in a Grand Chamber of seventeen judges.[9] Its judgements are binding for the member States and currently the only function of the Committee of Ministers is to supervise the enforcement of Court decisions.[10] The modifications introduced by Protocol 11 resulted in a great increase in the number of applications filed, and consequently in an increasing backlog of pending cases at the Court.[11] Accordingly, in 2010 a new Protocol 14 came into force, with new measures to deal more effectively with repetitive cases, such as introducing new admissibility criteria and strengthening the capacity to filter clearly inadmissible cases.[12] Finally, to streamline the case processing, a Filtering Section was established in 2011. This section was to carry out a thorough analysis of the applications to ensure they were placed on the appropriate procedural track, might submit the case to a single judge for prompt decision or send it to await

[7] Alston and Goodman (2013), p. 898.

[8] Alston and Goodman (2013), p. 898.

[9] European Convention on Human Rights, art. 26–31.

[10] Alston and Goodman (2013), p. 898.

[11] See: Scheinin (2007), p. 136.

[12] Council of Europe (2004) Explanatory report to protocol no. 14 to the Convention for the Protection of Human Rights and Fundamental Freedoms, amending the control system of the Convention, pp. 2–3. Available at: https://www.coe.int/en/web/conventions/full-list/-/conventions/treaty/194.

examination by a committee of three judges, or Chamber, in accordance with the Court's prioritization policy.[13]

Since its inception in 1959 until 2018, the Court has decided by judgment 21,651 cases, most of them concerning Turkey (3532), the Russian Federation (2501) and Italy (2396). According to the last Annual Report of the Court, in 2018 43,075 applications were filed, of which 2738 were decided by judgment. The rest of those petitions were declared inadmissible or struck off the list.[14]

Because the enormous number of judgments produced by the ECHR on article 6 (more than 10,000, including the Chamber and the Great Chamber decisions), I decided to collect and analyze a sample of cases. Using the excellent HUDOC search engine of the ECHR, I selected a list of cases based on the filters provided by the system. I used keywords related to the civil limb of article 6 and only kept cases of high importance. With this purpose, I kept those cases which the system calls "Key cases" (judgments since 1998 selected for publication in the Court official selection), and of level 1 importance (cases published in the reports before 1998 or those unpublished after 1998 but which made a significant contribution to the development, clarification or modification of case law).[15] That search gave me 326 results. After expunging from the list cases in which the Court did not analyze article 6.1 (for example, because it considered it unnecessary or was not competent to do so), I ended up with a list of 303 cases. This includes decisions in which the court analyzed article 6.1 in its civil limb no matter if a violation was found or not.

7.1 The Right to a Fair Civil Trial. Scope of Application and General Description of Its Case Law

Like its American equivalent, article 6 of the European Convention on Human Rights provides a general right to a fair trial in its first paragraph and further procedural guarantees applicable specifically over criminal proceedings in its Sects. 6.2 and 6.3. Despite these similarities, it is important to note a slight but important difference between the provisions. The article 6.1 wording might seem more restricted than the American functional equivalent. It says: "[I]n the determination of his *civil rights and obligations* or of any criminal charge any criminal charge against him, everyone is entitled to a fair and public hearing within a reasonable time by an independent and impartial tribunal established by law..." In comparison, as we saw previously, article 8.1's wording expressly applies to

[13]European Court of Human Rights (2013a) Filtering Section speeds up processing of cases from highest case-count countries. Available at: https://www.echr.coe.int/Documents/Filtering_Section_ENG.pdf.

[14]European Court of Human Rights (2019) The ECHR in facts & figures 2018, pp. 6–8. Available at: https://echr.coe.int/Pages/home.aspx?p=reports/factsfigures&c=.

[15]See: http://www.corteidh.or.cr/cf/Jurisprudencia2/busqueda_casos_contenciosos.cfm?lang=es.

proceedings for the determination of rights and obligations of a "civil, labor, fiscal or any other nature".

The basic requirement, which triggers the applicability of article 6 in its civil limb, is the existence of a *dispute* over rights and obligations, at least arguably, recognized under domestic law.[16] This requirement comes from the French version of the covenant which uses the word "contestation" instead of "determination".[17] This excludes from the range of application non-contentious proceedings. In addition, the dispute must be serious in terms of what is a stake for the petitioner.[18] In *Károly Nagy v. Hungary*, the Court said that what matters most is that there must be a real and serious dispute over the legality of an act that interferes with the exercise of a right of civil character, which might be related to its existence or range of application.[19] Lastly, the results of the denounced proceedings must be directly decisive for the right in question,[20] in terms that a remote or weak connection between the proceeding and the determination of a right is not enough to engage the protections of the article 6.1.[21] In this regard, has been decided that if a proceeding does not imply a disposition of a right it might be not be decisive for the purpose of article 6.1.[22]

Only exceptionally, article 6.1 may apply in interim measures, which are not determinative of civil rights. In *Micallef v. Malta*, the ECHR held to be applicable to these measures, first, the right at stake in both the main and the injunction proceedings should be "civil" according to its case law, and secondly, the nature of the interim measure, its object and purpose as well as its effects on the right in question should be scrutinized. However, in cases where the effectiveness of the measure

[16] European Court of Human Rights (2013b) Guide on Article 6 of the European Convention on Human Rights. Right to a fair trial (Civil limb), p. 6. Available at: https://www.echr.coe.int/documents/guide_art_6_eng.pdf.

[17] Hazelhorst (2017), p. 127.

[18] Hazelhorst (2017), p. 127.

[19] ECHR, Case of Károly Nagy v. Hungary, no. 56665/09, Judgment of 2 May 2016, par. 65.

[20] European Court of Human Rights (2013b) Guide on Article 6 of the European Convention on Human Rights. Right to a fair trial (Civil limb), p. 7. Available at: https://www.echr.coe.int/documents/guide_art_6_eng.pdf. See also: ECHR, Case of Masson and Van Zon v. the Netherlands, no. 15346/89;15,379/89, Judgment of 28 September 1995, par.17; ECHR, Case of Balmer-Schafroth and Others v. Switzerland, no. 67\1996\686\876, Judgment of 26 August 1997, par. 32; ECHR, Case of Le Calvez v. France, no. 73/1997/857/1066, Judgment of 29 July 1998, par. 56; ECHR, Case of Emine Araç v. Turkey, no. 9907/02, Judgment of 23 September 2008, par. 16; ECHR, Case of Micallef v. Malta, no. 17056/06, Judgment of 15 October 2009, par. 74; ECHR, Case of Boulois v. Luxembourg, no. 37575/04, Judgment of 3 April 2012, par. 90; ECHR, Case of Fazia Ali v. the United Kingdom, no. 40378/10, Judgment of 20 January 2016, par. 53.

[21] ECHR, Case of Le Compte, Van Leuven and De Meyere v. Belgium, no. 6878/75; 7238/75, Judgment of 23 June 1983, par. 46–47.

[22] ECHR, Case of Fayed v. United Kingdom, no. 17101/90, Judgment of 21 September 1990, par. 61.

depends upon a rapid decision-making process it may be possible not to comply immediately with all the requirements of Article 6.[23]

Even though the dispute must concern a civil right recognized by domestic law, under the European approach, what may or may not be regarded as "civil" must be determined by reference to the substantive content and effect of the right. In this sense, it is an autonomous concept that prevails over domestic law and which must be interpreted in the light of present-day conditions.[24] The classification made by domestic legislation is important but not determinative. What matter most is the substantive content of the legislation and the effects it might produce in the context of the domestic order.[25] As a consequence, the ECHR case law has engaged in great detail in the question of determining what cases may or not be considered as "civil," so as to be included under the clause. This has led to a fruitful but no less complex case law from the ECHR itself but also from the governments and highest courts of the member States, interpreting the meaning of this expression.[26]

In my setlist for the ECHR, 68 out of the 303 decisions engaged in an analysis of whether the specific legal issue can be considered as a proceeding which triggers the application of article 6 under its civil limb, most of them classified as administrative but non-punitive in nature (50 out of 68).

Article 6's civil limb applies to all rights and obligations arising from private relations over disputes whose intended outcome is the determination of those civil rights and obligations. In this regard, there is no discussion that it covers ordinary civil litigation between private individuals, such as those arising out of tort, contract, and family law.[27] Not as simple as those but probably not as controversial as others, are claims on damages against the State. Given the pecuniary nature of these claims, in these cases the State acts as a defendant in a setting closer to the typical dispute between private parties. 47 out of 190 cases I classified as "administrative" in my setlist concerned claims of negligence or were derived from an injury caused by a breach of a legal duty of a public body.

---

[23] ECHR, Case of Micallef v. Malta, no. 17056/06, Judgment of 15 October 2009, par. 83–86.

[24] European Court of Human Rights (2013b) Guide on Article 6 of the European Convention on Human Rights. Right to a fair trial (Civil limb), p. 6. Available at: https://www.echr.coe.int/documents/guide_art_6_eng.pdf.

[25] ECHR, Case of König v. Germany, no. 6232/73, Judgment of 28 June 1978, par. 89. More recently: ECHR, Case of Fazia Ali v. the United Kingdom, no. 40378/10, Judgment of 20 January 2016, par. 53–54.

[26] See, in this regard: Cross (2010), p. 366; ECHR, Case of Ringeisen v. Austria, no 2614/65, 16 July 1971, par. 94; ECHR, Case of König v. Germany, no. 6232/73, Judgment of 28 June 1978, par. 89; ECHR, Case of Le Compte, Van Leuven and De Meyere v. Belgium, no. 6878/75; 7238/75, Judgment of 23 June 1983, par. 46–47; ECHR, Case Elles and Others v. Switzerland, no. 12573/06, 16 March 2011, par. 20; ECHR, Case of Shapovalov v. Ukraine, no. 45835/05, Judgment of 31 July 2012, par. 43–45; ECHR, Case of Fazia Ali v. the United Kingdom, Judgment of 20 January 2016, par. 53–54.

[27] Hazelhorst (2017), p. 127; European Court of Human Rights (2013b) Guide on Article 6 of the European Convention on Human Rights. Right to a fair trial (Civil limb), p. 9. Available at: https://www.echr.coe.int/documents/guide_art_6_eng.pdf.

Article 6 in its civil limb is not restricted to private law matters. It is settled from the early case law that neither the public or private nature of the domestic legislation governing the matter, nor the type of the invested authority taking the decision, are determinative.[28] In this regard, the Court has established as falling within its scope, proceedings which, in domestic law, fall under "public law" but whose results are decisive for private rights and obligations.[29] For example, it covers proceedings before professional bodies where the right to practice a profession is at stake, such as in *König v. Germany,*[30] *Le Compte, Van Leuven and De Meyere v. Belgium,*[31] or *Albert and Le Compte v. Belgium,*[32] *H v. Belgium,*[33] *Chevrol v. France,*[34] and *Kök v. Turkey.*[35] It also covers proceedings concerning administrative permissions in connection with occupations or economic activities, such as licenses for serving alcoholic beverages in *Tre Traktörer Aktiebolag v. Sweden,*[36] selling Liquid Petroleum Gas (LPG) in *Benthem v. The Netherlands,*[37] providing interurban transport services in *Pudas v. Sweden,*[38] and fishing permissions in *Posti and Rahko v. Finland.*[39] Two cases in my sample, *Jurisic and Collegium Mehrerau v. Austria*[40] and *Coorplan-Jenni GmbH and Hascic v. Austria,*[41] were related to employment permits requested by enterprises for a foreign workforce. Still, the Court has decided that article 6.1. applies even to civil-party complaints in criminal proceedings except where such civil actions were brought purely to obtain private vengeance or for punitive purposes.[42] Moreover, it has expressly considered bankruptcy and insolvency proceedings, even regarding financial institutions, to fall

[28]ECHR, Case of Ringeisen v. Austria, no 2614/65, Judgment of 16 July 1971, par. 94.

[29]European Court of Human Rights (2013b) Guide on Article 6 of the European Convention on Human Rights. Right to a fair trial (Civil limb), p. 9. Available at: https://www.echr.coe.int/documents/guide_art_6_eng.pdf.

[30]ECHR, Case of König v. Germany, no. 6232/73, Judgment of 28 June 1978.

[31]ECHR, Case of Le Compte, Van Leuven, and De Meyere v. Belgium, no. 6878/75; 7238/75, 23 June 1981.

[32]ECHR, Case of Albert and Le Compte v. Belgium, no. 7299/75; 7496/76, Judgment of 10 February 1983.

[33]ECHR, Case of H v. Belgium, no. 8950/80, Judgment of 30 November 1987.

[34]ECHR, Case of Chevrol v. France, no. 49636/99, Judgment of 13 February 2003.

[35]ECHR, Case of Kök v. Turkey, no 1855/02, Judgment of 19 October 2006.

[36]ECHR, Case of Tre Traktörer Aktiebolag v. Sweden, no. 10873/84, Judgment of 7 June 1989.

[37]ECHR, Case of Benthem v. The Netherlands, no. 8848/80, Judgment of 23 October 1985.

[38]ECHR, Case of Pudas v. Sweden, no. 10426/83, Judgment of 27 October 1987.

[39]ECHR, Case of Posti and Rahko v. Finland, no. 27824/95, Judgment of 24 September 2002.

[40]ECHR, Case of Jurisic and Collegium Mehrerau v. Austria, no. 62539/00, Judgment of 27 July 2006.

[41]ECHR, Case of Coorplan-Jenni GmbH and Hascic v. Austria, no. 10523/02, Judgment of 27 July 2006.

[42]European Court of Human Rights (2013b) Guide on Article 6 of the European Convention on Human Rights. Right to a fair trial (Civil limb), p. 9. Available at: https://www.echr.coe.int/documents/guide_art_6_eng.pdf.

under article 6, notwithstanding the relevant public interest associated with this matter. In this regard, in *Capital Bank AD v. Bulgaria*, the Court said: "[T]he fact that banks are legal entities and that the industry is tightly regulated in view of the important interests at stake, such as those of depositors and of the public at large, is not a sufficient reason for concluding that proceedings in respect of a bank fall outside the scope of Article 6 § 1. To hold otherwise would create an important lacuna in the system of human rights protection in that area."[43]

The ECHR have considered that article 6 applies even over proceedings where an administrative fine is under review and there is a close connection between such proceedings and the economic activity and, consequently, the pecuniary rights of the petitioner. Even though these proceedings may be considered as criminal in nature, since a fine could be considered an administrative sanction, in *Procola v. Luxembourg* the ECHR found article 6.1 applicable. It held it was applicable since there was a close connection between the proceedings brought by the petitioner and the consequences that the outcome of the proceeding might have had for one of its pecuniary rights and for its economic activities in general.[44]

More potentially controversial are those cases concerning public servants and their relationship with their employer, a State body, an issue commonly regulated under public law. The case law in this regard has evolved over time. A good summary of this progression is offered by the ECHR in the case of *Vilho Eskelinen and Others v. Finland*. This case concerned a group of police officers who lodged an application requesting compensation for their loss because of the abolition of a remote-area allowance and a subsequent reduction of salary after their duty station changed.[45] The original approach relating to the recruitment, careers and termination of service of civil servants is that they were, generally, outside the scope of Article 6.1.[46] On the contrary, that meant that the Court found it applicable in cases related to a "purely or essentially economic" right, such as payment of salary, and did not mainly call in question "the authorities discretionary powers".[47] However, the line dividing the applicability contained a degree of uncertainty for the member States that the Court tried to clarify in *Pellegrin v. France*.[48] In this case, it established an autonomous interpretation of the term "civil service," understanding this concept

---

[43]ECHR, Case of Capital Bank AD v. Bulgaria, no. 49429/99, Judgment of 24 November 2005, par. 88.

[44]ECHR, Case of Procola v. Luxembourg, no. 14570/89, Judgment of 28 September 1995, par. 39.

[45]ECHR, Case of Vilho Eskelinen and Others v. Finland, no. 63235/00, Judgment of 19 April 2007, par. 10–15.

[46]ECHR, Case of Vilho Eskelinen and Others v. Finland, no. 63235/00, Judgment of 19 April 2007, par. 43. As mentioned in this decision, there were cases where public employment relation triggered article 6.1 but only as they consisted in claims for purely pecuniary rights arising in law after termination of service. See: ECHR, Case of Francesco Lombardo v. Italy, no. 11519/85, Judgment of 26 November 1992, par. 17.

[47]ECHR, Case of Vilho Eskelinen and Others v. Finland, no. 63235/00, Judgment of 19 April 2007, par. 45.

[48]ECHR, Case of Pellegrin v. France, no. 28541/95, Judgement of 8 December 1999, par. 60.

irrespective of the domestic system of employment and, in particular, whatever the nature of the legal relation between the official and the administrative authority.[49] With this purpose, the ECHR developed a functional criterion based on the nature of the employee's services. As long as the employee's duties involved responsibilities in the general interest or participation in the exercise of powers conferred by public law, which entails a special bond of trust and loyalty, any dispute arising from these functions are excluded. On the contrary, in respect of other posts without this "public administration" aspect, there was no such interest and therefore article 6.1 would be applicable. A manifest example of such excluded activities were the armed forces and the police. In such cases, this functional criterion allowed one single exception: disputes concerning pensions because, on retirement, the employees found themselves in a situation exactly comparable to that of employees under private law as long as the special relationship of trust and loyalty binding them to the State had ceased to exist.[50]

The functional criterion of *Pellegrin*, for several reasons, soon proved to be ineffective in providing a better degree of certainty for member States, so the Court decided to further develop it in *Vilho Eskelinen and Others v. Finland*.[51] Under the new approach, there is a presumption that article 6 in its civil limb applies to ordinary labor disputes, such as those relating to salaries, allowances or similar entitlements, between public servants and the State in question. On the contrary, if the respondent State uses the public servant status to deprive the individual of the protection embedded in article 6, two conditions must be fulfilled. Firstly, the State in its national law must have expressly excluded access to a court for the post or category of staff in question. Secondly, the exclusion must be justified on objective grounds in the State's interest. As a consequence, it is not enough for the State to establish that the civil servant in question participates in the exercise of public power. It is also for the State to show that the subject matter of the dispute in issue is related to the exercise of State power or that it has called into question the special bond. The burden to demonstrate that both conditions are met would be on the State.[52] For example, in the subsequent case of *Cudak v. Lithuania*, the second condition was not met since the kind of duties that the petitioner had were not the kind of duties that could give rise to "objective grounds for the exclusion in the State's interest".[53]

The ECHR has found article 6.1 also applicable to other not strictly pecuniary matters like proceedings related to the protection of the environment or in access to

---

[49] ECHR, Case of Vilho Eskelinen and Others v. Finland, no. 63235/00, Judgment of 19 April 2007, par. 46.

[50] ECHR, Case of Vilho Eskelinen and Others v. Finland, no. 63235/00, Judgment of 19 April 2007, par. 48.

[51] ECHR, Case of Vilho Eskelinen and Others v. Finland, no. 63235/00, Judgment of 19 April 2007, par. 55, 56.

[52] ECHR, Case of Vilho Eskelinen and Others v. Finland, no. 63235/00, Judgment of 19 April 2007, par. 62.

[53] ECHR, Case of Cudak v. Lithuania, no. 15869/02, Judgment of 23 March 2010, par. 44.

public information proceedings. For example, in *Taşkin and Others v. Turkey*, the Court found it applicable in a petition for judicial review by a group of villagers of a Ministry of the Environment's decision to issue a permit for a gold mine operation. They argued on the dangers inherent in the company's use of cyanide to extract the gold, and especially the risks of contamination of the groundwater and destruction of the local flora and fauna.[54]

Particularly important as well are cases related to social matters of public or private nature—such as social security benefits, pensions, or insurances.[55] From my list of cases, I have identified 25 of these cases. I have only classified as civil the case of *Lukenda v. Slovenia*, a case concerning an employee injured at work in a lignite mine who was a recipient of disability benefits provided by the employer through an insurance company. The applicant instituted civil proceedings claiming an increase in his disability benefits on the basis of an expert medical opinion and alleged an infraction of article 6.1 due to the length of the proceedings.[56] By contrast, all the others were considered administrative because a public agency was a party in the proceeding. In these cases, the ECHR recognized that the private law aspects predominated over the public law side and that is why it found article 6.1 applicable.[57] For example, in *Feldbrugge v. The Netherlands*, a petitioner who had fallen ill and did not consider herself sufficiently recovered to work lost her sickness allowances. The Governing Board of the Occupational Association of the Banking and Insurance, Wholesale Trade and Self-Employment Sector in Amsterdam decided she was no longer entitled to the sickness allowances since the association's consulting doctor had judged her fit to resume work. She appealed this decision but the Appeal Board ruled against her and further efforts were declared inadmissible.[58] The Court recognized the public and private law nature of the matter according to domestic legislation, but found the latter to be predominant.[59] In *Salesi v. Italy*, the applicant instituted proceedings against the Minister of the Interior before a magistrate's court seeking payment of a monthly disability allowance that the Lazio social-security department had refused her.[60] The Government defense was that the case presented features of public law only, basically because the right claimed derived from an ordinary statute and not from a contract of employment and, secondly, because the

---

[54] ECHR, Case of Taşkin and Others v. Turkey, no. 46117/99, Judgment of 10 November 2004, par. 23, 130–132.

[55] European Court of Human Rights (2013b) Guide on Article 6 of the European Convention on Human Rights. Right to a fair trial (Civil limb), p. 10. Available at: https://www.echr.coe.int/documents/guide_art_6_eng.pdf.

[56] ECHR, Case of Lukenda v. Slovenia, no. 23032/02, Judgment of 6 October 2005, par. 6,7, 29.

[57] European Court of Human Rights (2013b) Guide on Article 6 of the European Convention on Human Rights. Right to a fair trial (Civil limb), p. 10. Available at: https://www.echr.coe.int/documents/guide_art_6_eng.pdf.

[58] ECHR, Case of Feldbrugge v. The Netherlands, no. 8562/79, Judgment of 29 May 1986, par. 11–14.

[59] ECHR, Case of Feldbrugge v. The Netherlands, no. 8562/79, Judgment of 29 May 1986, par. 40.

[60] ECHR, Case of Salesi v. Italy, no. 13023/87, Judgment of 26 February 1993, par. 8.

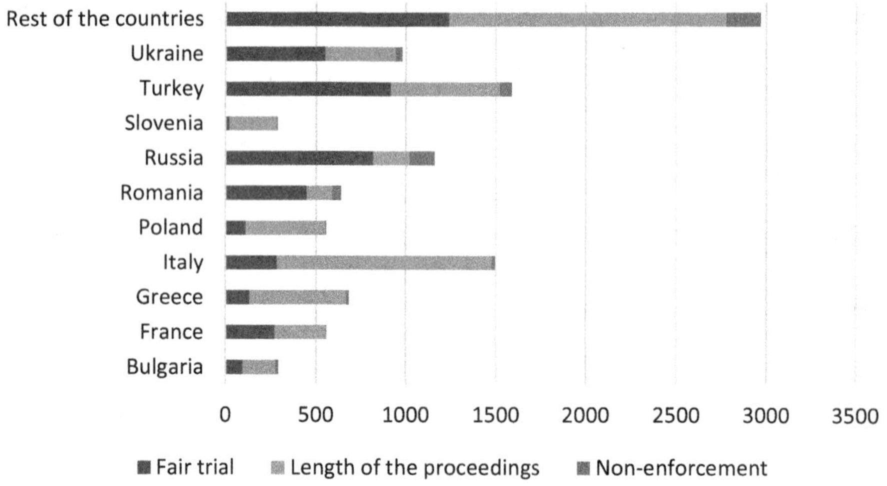

Fig. 7.1 Violations article 6 by country, 1959–2018 (European Court of Human Rights, The ECHR in facts & Figs. 2018, 2019, pp. 6–8)

subject matter was exclusively a governmental one since the State met the entire cost of financing the scheme.[61] The ECHR expressed the general rule that Article 6.1 does apply in the field of social insurance. Now, despite the fact that the present case concerned welfare assistance and not social insurance, as in Feldbrugge, the Court did not provide a different answer. Despite the public law features pointed out by the Government, the petitioner was not affected in her relations with the administrative authorities as such, acting in the exercise of discretionary powers, but she suffered an interference with her means of subsistence and was claiming an individual, economic right flowing from domestic legislation. That is why the protection scheme at judicial stage came within the jurisdiction of the ordinary courts.[62]

Article 6 cases (in both criminal and civil limbs) occupy an important position in ECHR case law. In fact, they hold first place in the number of violations found in its decisions, with approximately 37% of the total. Most violations of this right involved excessive length of the proceedings (20%).[63] The countries against the ECHR with most findings of article 6 violations were Turkey (14,2%), Italy (13.3%), Russia (10.4%), and Ukraine (8.7%). On cases involving the length of proceedings, Italy is particularly important. In fact, the proportion of cases against this country is similar to the rest of the countries of the Council of Europe not individually listed in Fig. 7.1.

Of the 303 cases I have identified under the scope of article 6.1, in approximately 80% the Court found at least one violation in any of the dimensions of the right to a

[61] ECHR, Case of Salesi v. Italy, no. 13023/87, Judgment of 26 February 1993, par. 18.

[62] ECHR, Case of Salesi v. Italy, no. 13023/87, Judgment of 26 February 1993, par. 19.

[63] ECHR, The ECHR in Facts & Figures 2018, 2019, pp. 6, 7. Available at: https://echr.coe.int/Pages/home.aspx?p=reports/factsfigures&c=.

Fig. 7.2 Cases by country, Article 6 civil limb

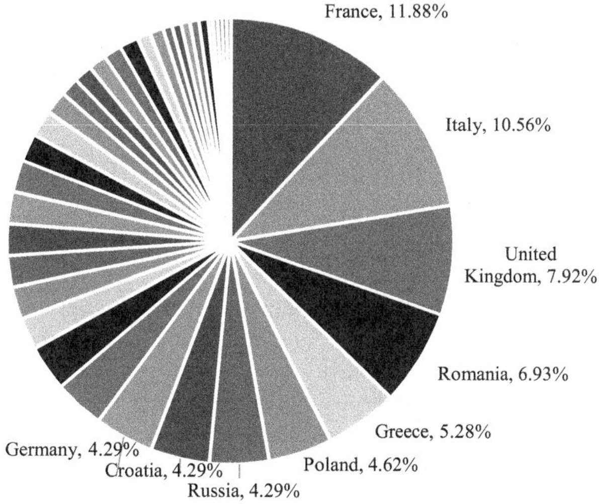

fair trial. Most cases concerned France (11.9%), Italy (10.6%), United Kingdom (7.92%), Romania (6.9%), Greece (5.3%), Poland (4.6%), Russia (4.3%), Croatia (4.3%), and Germany (4.3%) (Fig. 7.2).

The range of matters covered by this case law is quite broad. Those cases I have coded as administrative but non-punitive in nature, comprise approximately 63% of the set list. As described in section 1, these are cases involving decisions by a government agency, or a judicial procedure for a review of such decision, or any proceeding in which the State was a party. In any of these situations, the procedure in question was closely connected to the determination of a right that the court considered as "civil" for the purpose of article 6. In such cases, the most frequent type of legal matters were damage claims against public agencies or the State (24.7%), and proceedings related to decisions limiting the right of property of the petitioner (23.7%), such as expropriations against private individuals or companies. In a second tier, there are decisions concerning social benefits such as pensions, disability benefits, health care, etc. (12.6%), or related to the right to practice professional or economic activities (11.6%). In the same category, cases concerning labor relations with public servants are quite frequent as well (8.4%) (Table 7.1).

What I have coded as "typical civil proceedings"—which basically are every other type of legal issue that the ECHR considered a "civil matter" between private individuals or corporations—occupy 37.3% of my set list. The most frequent cases were those concerning vertical family relation matters such as parental rights and obligations and adoption proceedings (22.1%). Other cases involved damage claims (17.7%), the civil side of proceedings for libel or defamation (9.7%), debt and payment (8.9%), tenant and landlord related cases (7.1%), the protection of private property (6.2%), and employment relations including those with labor associations (6.2%) (Table 7.2).

Table 7.1 Types of proceedings in administrative cases

Main legal issue	Frequency	%
Access to information proceedings	3	1.58%
Audit proceedings	1	0.53%
Change of use of land	1	0.53%
Damages	47	24.74%
Discrimination	1	0.53%
Dissolution of associations	1	0.53%
Employment relations/labor associations	16	8.42%
Freedom of expression ban proceedings	3	1.58%
Insolvency	2	1.05%
Intellectual property and other registration proceedings	3	1.58%
Inter-state application, military occupation	1	0.53%
Judicial review of administrative fines	1	0.53%
Land/Environment protection	4	2.11%
Limitation on right of property	45	23.68%
Parental rights/adoption proceedings	1	0.53%
Payment proceedings	5	2.63%
Personal liberty	5	2.63%
Public contract termination proceedings	1	0.53%
Public employment competition	1	0.53%
Residence application proceedings	1	0.53%
Right to education	1	0.53%
Right to practice professional/economic activity	22	11.58%
Social security	24	12.63%
Subsidy application	1	0.53%
Total general	**190**	**100%**

Of the 303 cases of my set list, I have identified 294 instances in which the court decided on a dimension of the right to a fair trial. Of course, there are cases where more than one dimension was covered by the decision. Nevertheless, not every case involved an argument regarding one of these dimensions because there are some cases where a legal procedure is analyzed only through the general wording of article 6 and then focuses on specific procedural elements instead.

The most frequent element of the right to a fair trial in its civil limb analyzed by the Court is without a doubt the right to a court or to access to justice (45.2%). It was followed by the right to a reasonable length of proceedings (34.4%), cases concerning the dimensions of independence and impartiality (17.7%), and the opportunity to be heard (12.24%). Less frequently, the issue was equality of arms (7.1%) and the right to an effective remedy (6.5%) (Fig. 7.3). Regarding the latter, as I will explain later, the Court differs from the approach followed by the IACHR described in the previous sections.

Because of the importance of the right to a court or access to justice for the purpose of this project, I will provide a detailed account of this dimension in the next

Table 7.2 Types of proceedings in civil cases

Main legal issue	Frequency	%
Arbitration proceedings	1	0.88%
Capacity to exercise private rights	4	3.54%
Contracts	5	4.42%
Damages	20	17.70%
Discrimination	2	1.77%
Employment relations/Labor associations	7	6.19%
Free market protection/Economic cases	1	0.88%
Insolvency	2	1.77%
Insurance	1	0.88%
Inter-state application, military occupation	1	0.88%
Land registry proceedings	1	0.88%
Libel/Defamation	11	9.73%
Limitation on right of property	1	0.88%
Parental rights or obligations and adoption proceedings	25	22.12%
Partition proceedings	2	1.77%
Payment proceedings	10	8.85%
Right of private property	7	6.19%
Separation/divorce	4	3.54%
Tenancy/Rent	8	7.08%
Not determined	2	1.77%
Total general	**113**	**100%**

section. However, before analyzing this specific dimension of the right to a fair trial, it is useful to describe the procedural elements as well, as described in Fig. 7.4, which have been included in the petitions and decided by the ECHR. Of the decisions in my set list 56.4% included an analysis of a specific procedural element. They cover an extraordinarily broad range of features. Most frequently, the petition involved the right to a public hearing or the enforcement of a judicial decision as a requirement of the right of a fair trial. Other procedural elements included the opportunity to present evidence at trial, the admissibility of appeals, the right to a natural judge (or a tribunal established by law), the right to a lawyer (including legal aid), a right to a final decision (including *res iudicata* and legal certainty cases), the duty to state reasons, the judicial control of administrative decisions, the proper conditions for an effective defense (including access to the case file), among others.

7.2 The Right to a Court in the ECHR Case Law

In this section, I use the terms "right to a court" and "access to justice" as equivalents. I acknowledge that both concepts are not exactly synonymous. In fact, according to the ECHR, the right of access to justice is only one aspect that implies

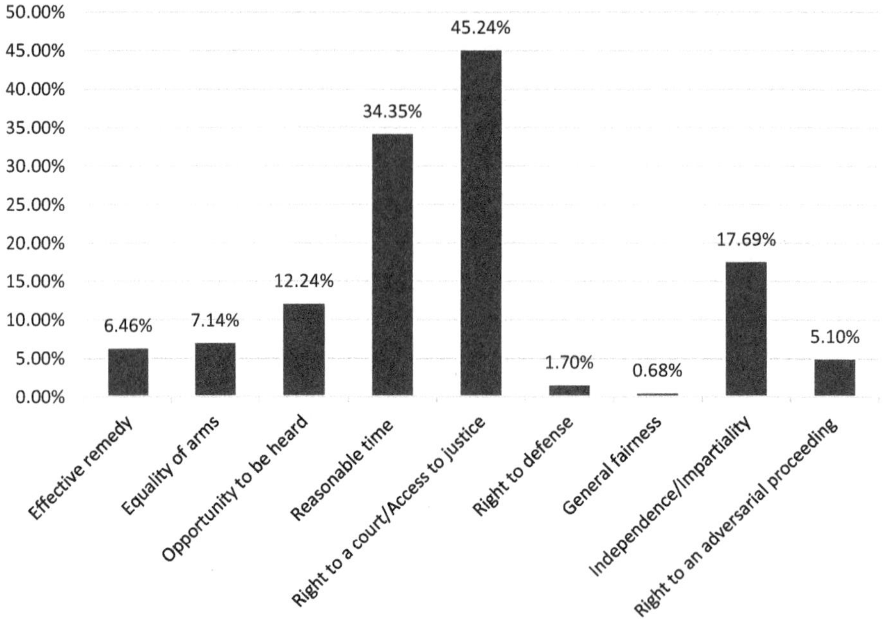

Fig. 7.3 Elements of the right to a fair trial according to the court

the possibility of initiating legal proceedings.[64] In this respect, the right to a court is a broader concept. However, I use both concepts as equivalent because what is more important here is the notion that the right to a court or of access to that court implies not just the possibility of filing a claim but also to pursue a case effectively until its conclusion. The contrary seems illogical. It would not make sense to have a right to a file a claim but not to continue the proceedings until a legal need has been effectively satisfied. There are cases in which the ECHR uses both terms interchangeably as well. In paragraph 36 of the decision in *Golder v. United Kingdom* the ECHR expressly says that article 6.1 "...secures to everyone the right to have any claim relating to his civil rights and obligations brought before a court or tribunal. In this way, the Article embodies the "right to a court", of which the right of access, that is the right to institute proceedings before courts in civil matters, constitutes one aspect only... To this are added the guarantees laid down by Article 6 para. 1 (art. 6-1) as regards both the organisation and composition of the court, and the conduct of the proceedings. In sum, the whole makes up the right to a fair hearing".[65] In subsequent cases, the ECHR has not necessarily used the term "access to justice" but it is clear that it is referring to it. For example, in the case of *Rasmusen v. Denmark*, concerning a proceeding to contest the paternity of a child, the court refers to the right to court or

[64] See: ECHR, Case of Golder v. United Kingdom, no. 4451/70, Judgment of 21 February 1975, par. 36.

[65] ECHR, Case of Golder v. United Kingdom, no. 4451/70, Judgment of 21 February 1975, par. 36.

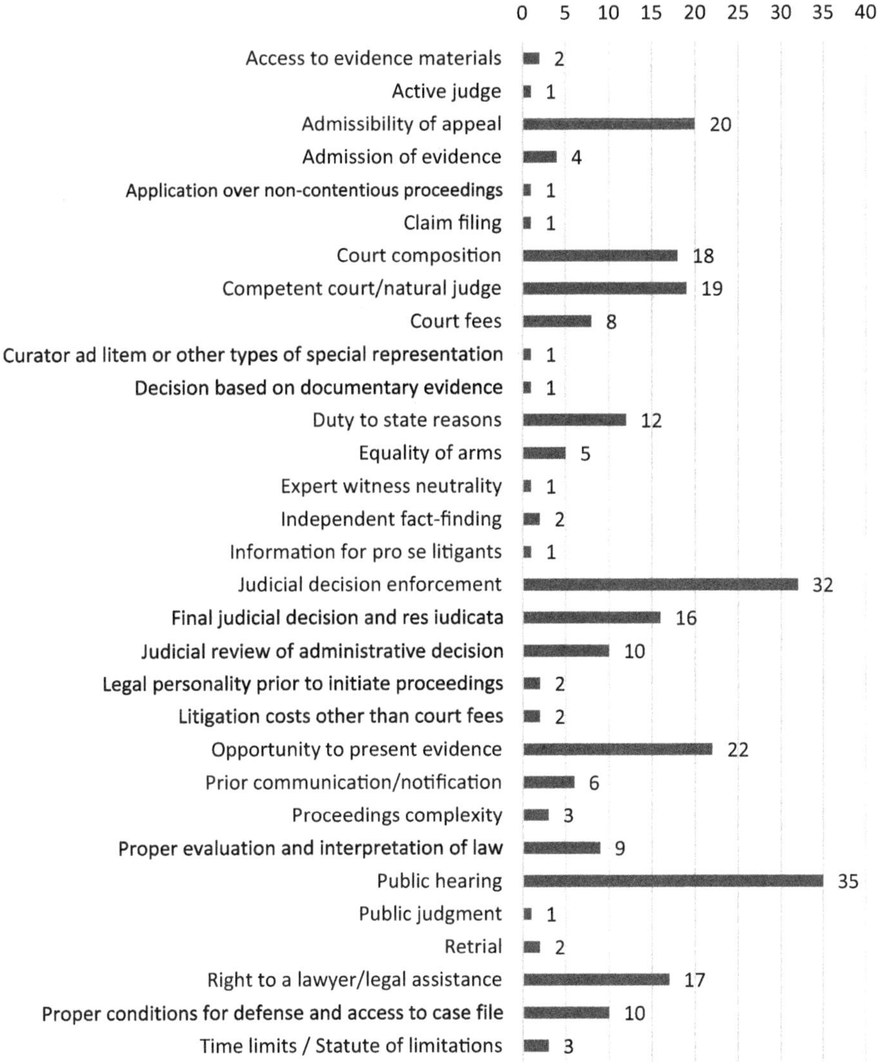

Fig. 7.4 Procedural elements analyzed as requirement of the right to a fair trial according to the court (number of cases)

tribunal and,[66] even though it does not refer to the right of access expressly, it does cite the same paragraph of *Golder v. United Kingdom* just quoted. I will come back to this point later while studying the scope or range of application and procedural guarantees covered by this right.

[66]ECHR, Case of Rasmusen v. Denmark, no. 8777/79, Judgment of 28 November 1984, par. 32.

In the 76.7% of the cases concerning the right to a court, the ECHR found a violation. I have catalogued most right to a court cases as administrative (62.4%) and involving the United Kingdom (15%) and Romania (11.3%). The most typical type of legal issue concerned claims of damages (22.6%), the limitation of property rights (19.6%) and parental rights or child adoptions (9%).

The case of *Golder v. United Kingdom*, relating to an inmate who sought to consult a solicitor to initiate civil proceedings for libel against a prison officer, has an extraordinary importance for the ECHR case law.[67] The European Convention does not expressly mention the right of access. This right did not get explicit recognition until this 1975 decision in which the Court said this right was implicit in the wording of article 6.1, as a necessary condition to exercise other procedural guarantees expressly provided there.[68] In this regard, it says "It would be inconceivable, in the opinion of the Court, that Article 6 para. 1 (art. 6-1) should describe in detail the procedural guarantees afforded to parties in a pending lawsuit and should not first protect that which alone makes it in fact possible to benefit from such guarantees, that is, access to a court. The fair, public and expeditious characteristics of judicial proceedings are of no value at all if there are no judicial proceedings."[69]

Further case law has refined the contours of this element of the right to a fair trial under article 6. For example, the ECHR has established that this right is not absolute. First, the interested person may waive this right.[70] In this regard, the limitation on this right may result from private action such as a voluntary surrender from the victim or an agreement between both parties to resort to arbitration. In these situations, the legal question to analyze would be whether such waiver satisfies the standards of due process.[71] In the recent case of *Mutu and Pechstein v. Switzerland*, the court recognized this right is not necessarily to be understood as access to a court of law of the classic kind, integrated within the standard judicial machinery of the country, but is compatible as well with mechanisms of dispute resolution such as arbitration proceedings. In this regard, by signing an arbitration clause the parties voluntarily waive certain rights secured by the Convention. Such a waiver is compatible with article 6 as long it is established in a free, lawful and unequivocal manner.[72]

---

[67] ECHR, Case of Golder v. United Kingdom, no. 4451/70, Judgment of 21 February 1975, par. 26.

[68] In fact, its incorporation into a human rights treaty is recent, being expressly mentioned for the first time in the European Union Treaty of Lisboa of 2007, at least in its English version.

[69] ECHR, Case of Golder v. United Kingdom, no. 4451/70, Judgment of 21 February 1975, par. 36.

[70] European Court of Human Rights (2013b) Guide on Article 6 of the European Convention on Human Rights. Right to a fair trial (Civil limb), p. 17. Available at: https://www.echr.coe.int/documents/guide_art_6_eng.pdf.

[71] Francioni (2017), p. 40.

[72] ECHR, Case of Mutu and Pechstein v. Switzerland, nos. 40575/10 and 67474/10, Judgment of 2 October 2018, par.94–96.

This right may not just be waived but also, under several conditions, restricted by the State.[73] For example, an exclusion by statue of suits under certain circumstances or in relation to a certain class of individuals. In *Lithgow and Other v. United Kingdom,* a case where it was necessary to process a large mass of claims related to a compensation for the nationalization of an entire sector of the economy,[74] the ECHR recognized that the right of access "by its very nature calls for regulation by the State, regulation which may vary in time and in place according to the needs and resources of the community and of individuals". Although limitations are allowed, "...[i]t must be satisfied that the limitations applied do not restrict or reduce the access left to the individual in such a way or to such an extent that the very essence of the right is impaired."[75] The limitation must pursue a legitimate aim. For example, the ECHR has held that some immunities or restrictions of filing civil cases against diplomatic officers or Parliament members are permissible. In *A v. The United Kingdom,* a case concerning defamation proceedings against a member of the parliament protected by immunity, this restriction was considered legitimate since it aimed to protect free speech in Parliament and maintain the separation of powers between the legislature and the judiciary.[76] In other cases, limitations in order to protect serviceman or works in sensitive sectors has been allowed as a legitimate goal. For example, in *Ashingdane* v. *The United Kingdom,* a statute protecting those responsible for the care of mental patients of being unfairly harassed by litigation was found to be a permissible restriction by itself—at least in relation to hospital staff as individuals-, and in this particular case against other public health authorities since in practice the alleged victim was not totally barred of courts protection.[77]

In this regard, to decide over the restriction imposed a test of proportionality must be applied between the measure imposed and the goals pursued.[78] Such principles,

---

[73] European Court of Human Rights (2013b) Guide on Article 6 of the European Convention on Human Rights. Right to a fair trial (Civil limb), p. 15. Available at: https://www.echr.coe.int/documents/guide_art_6_eng.pdf.

[74] Francioni (2017), p. 39.

[75] ECHR, Case of Lithgow and Other v. United Kingdom, no. 9006/80; 9262/81; 9263/81; 9265/81; 9266/81; 9313/81; 9405/81, Judgment of 8 June 1986, par. 194. See also: ECHR, Case of Fayed v. United Kingdom, no. 17101/90, Judgment of 21 September 1990, par. 65; ECHR, Case of Canea Catholic Church v. Greece, 143/1996/762/963, Judgment of 16 December 1997, par. 38; ECHR, Case of Kreuz v. Poland, no. 28249/95, 19 June 2001, par. 53; ECHR, Case of Forrer-Niedenthal v. Germany, no. 47316/99, Judgment of 20 February, 2003, par. 59; ECHR, Case of Weissman and Others v. Romania, no. 63945/00, Judgment of 24 May 2006, par. 34; ECHR, Case of Stankov v. Bulgaria, no. 68490/01, Judgment of 12 July 2007, par. 50. ECHR, Case of Stanev v. Bulgaria, no. 36760/06, Judgment of 17 January 2012, par. 230.

[76] ECHR, Case of A v. The United Kingdom, no. 35373/97, Judgment of 17 December 2002, par. 77. Same reasoning in: ECHR, Case of Fayed v. The United Kingdom, no. 17101/90, Judgment of 21 September 1990, par. 70.

[77] ECHR, Case of Ashingdane v. the United Kingdom, no. 8225/78, Judgment of 28 May 1985, par. 56–59; Francioni (2017), p. 40.

[78] See, in this regard: ECHR, Case of Fayed v. United Kingdom, no. 17101/90, Judgment of 21 September 1990, par. 65; ECHR, Case of Tinnelly & Sons Ltd. and Others and McElduff and

as recognized in *Fayed v. United Kingdom*, are "... inherent in the Court's task under the Convention, of striking a fair balance between the demands of the general interest of the community and the requirements of the protection of the individual's fundamental rights."[79]

What seems to be the key is that right needs to be practical and *effective*.[80] This might require from the State not merely the absence of an interference but various forms of positive action on its part.[81] Beginning with *Golder*, the early case law on this right was quite clear that a hindrance, whether in fact or by legal impediment, could rise to being an infringement of article 6.1.[82] Soon after *Golder*, in the case of *Airey v. Ireland* the court recalls: "...the Convention is intended to guarantee not rights that are theoretical or illusory but rights that are practical and effective...This is particularly so of the right of access to the courts in view of the prominent place held in a democratic society by the right to a fair trial".[83]

The effectiveness requirement should not be confused with the element of the right to an effective remedy under article 13 of the Convention.[84] Notwithstanding there are cases in which the right to an effective remedy has been analyzed under the right to a fair trial (6.5% of my set list), in two cases the ECHR has clearly distinguished the specific right to an effective remedy and the effectiveness

---

Others v. the United Kingdom, 62/1997/846/1052–1053, Judgment of 10 July 1998, par. 72.; ECHR, Case of García Manibardo, no. 38695/97, Judgment of 15 February 2000, par. 36; ECHR, Case of T.P. and K.M. v. The United Kingdom, no. 28945/95, Judgment of 10 May 2001, par. 98; ECHR, Case of Kreuz v. Poland, no. 28249/95, 19 June 2001, par. 55; ECHR, Case of Běleš and Others v. The Czech Republic, no. 47273/99, Judgment of 12 November 2002, par. 61; ECHR, Case of Ernst and Others v. Belgium, no 33400/96, Judgment of 15 July 2003; ECHR, Case of Musumeci v. Italy, no 33695/96, Judgment of 11 January 2005, par. 49; ECHR, Case of Weissman and Others v. Romania, no. 63945/00, Judgment of 24 May 2006, par. 36; ECHR, Case of Woś v. Poland, no. 22860/02, Judgment of 08 June 2006, par. 98; ECHR, Case of Hirschhorn v. Romania, no. 29294/02, Judgment of 26 July 2007, par. 50. ECHR, Case of Faimblat v. Romaine, no. 23066/02, Judgment of 13 January 2009, par. 28; ECHR, Case of Sâmbata Bihor Greek Catholic Parish v. Romania, no 48107/99, Judgment of 12 January 2010, par. 63; ECHR, Georgel and Georgeta v. Stoicescu v. Romania, no. 9718/03, Judgment of 26 July 2011, par. 68; ECHR, Case of Lupeni Greek Catholic Parish and Others v. Romania, no. 76943/11, Judgment of 29 November 2016, par. 89.

[79] ECHR, Case of Fayed v. United Kingdom, no. 17101/90, Judgment of 21 September 1990, par. 65. See also: ECHR, Case of Lupeni Greek Catholic Parish and Others v. Romania, no. 76943/11, Judgment of 29 November 2016, par. 89.

[80] European Court of Human Rights (2013b) Guide on Article 6 of the European Convention on Human Rights. Right to a fair trial (Civil limb), p. 10. Available at: https://www.echr.coe.int/documents/guide_art_6_eng.pdf.

[81] ECHR, Case of Kreuz v. Poland, no. 28249/95, 19 June 2001, par. 55; ECHR, Case of Apostol v. Georgia, no. 40765/02, Judgment of 28 November 2006, par. 59.

[82] ECHR, Case of Golder v. United Kingdom, no. 4451/70, Judgment of 21 February 1975, par. 26.

[83] ECHR, Case of Airey v. Ireland, no. 6289/73, Judgment of 9 October 1979, par. 24.

[84] Article 13. Right to an effective remedy Everyone whose rights and freedoms as set forth in this Convention are violated shall have an effective remedy before a national authority notwithstanding that the violation has been committed by persons acting in an official capacity.

requirement of the right to a court. In the case of *Assunção Chaves v. Portugal*, the ECHR said that when the right claimed is a civil right, the right to a fair trial under article 6.1 is *lex specialis* in relation to Article 13. In this regard, "…its requirements, which involve the full panoply of safeguards specific to judicial proceedings, are more than those of Article 13, which are absorbed by them.".[85] In *Turczanik v. Poland*, the petitioner claimed that the proceeding to determine the location where he was entitled to practice law had been excessively lengthy even though there was a previous decision ruling in his favor. In this regard, he alleged that, besides there being a violation in the length of the proceedings, there was a lack of an effective local remedy against undue delay and non-execution of the rulings in his favor. Here the ECHR clearly divided both issues. It considered the question of the lack of remedies to secure compliance with the court orders to fall under Article 6, but the complaint concerning the lack of a remedy for the excessive length of administrative proceedings to fall under Article 13.[86] As noted before, this marks an important difference with the IACHR's approach on this subject.

In most case law regarding the right to a court, the ECHR has decided on this right in conjunction with several procedural guarantees. First, in terms of the scope of the right to a court, the ECHR held that it goes further than solely to the possibility of instituting a legal procedure. That is, it consists of more than the right to knock on the door of a court, but also of a right to obtain a determination of the dispute by a court, and even the execution of judgments.[87]

In terms of a right to obtain a determination of the dispute by a court, I have found that 11 out of the 16 cases in this category were analyzed specifically from the perspective of a right to a court. The first case I found is *Kutic v. Croatia*, a claim for damages against the State resulting from an explosion considered a terrorist act, which destroyed the applicants' property. This action was barred after the enactment of a legislative amendment providing all such proceedings were to be stayed pending new legislation on the subject. That new legislation never came.[88] The ECHR said that the article 6.1. right of access to a court for the determination of civil disputes includes not only the right to institute proceedings but also the right to obtain a *final determination* of the dispute. Following the same reasoning that I have expressed above, the Court found it would be illusory if a domestic legal system allowed an individual to bring a civil action before a court without ensuring that the case would be determined by a final decision in the judicial proceedings.[89] This is another

[85]ECHR, Case of Assunção Chaves v. Portugal, no 61226/08, Judgment of 31 January 2012, par. 62. Unofficial translation, original is in French. See also: ECHR, Case of Tinnelly & Sons Ltd. and Others and McElduff and Others v. the United Kingdom, 62/1997/846/1052–1053, Judgment of 10 July 1998, par. 77.

[86]ECHR, Turczanik v. Poland, no. 38064/97, Judgment of 5 July 2005, par. 47, 48.

[87]European Court of Human Rights (2013b) Guide on Article 6 of the European Convention on Human Rights. Right to a fair trial (Civil limb), p. 15. Available at: https://www.echr.coe.int/documents/guide_art_6_eng.pdf.

[88]ECHR, Case of Kutić v. Croatia, no. 48778/99, Judgment of 1 March 2002, par. 8–11.

[89]ECHR, Case of Kutić v. Croatia, no. 48778/99, Judgment of 1 March 2002, par. 25.

example of those cases in which the court uses both terms, the right to a court or the right of access, indistinguishably.

The right to obtain a decision relates to the principle of legal certainty and *res iudicata*. The ECHR have highlighted the importance of this principle for the interpretation of procedural hurdles and regarding the immutability of a final judgment on the merits. In the case of *Běleš and Others v. The Czech Republic*, concerning a legal proceeding filed by members of a homeopathic association suing a medical society for damages, the ECHR found that a particularly strict interpretation of a procedural rule was an issue of legal certainty, which could amount to an infraction of the right to a court.[90] Regarding the legal institution of *res iudicata*, in *Nelyubin v. Russia*, the ECHR held that the right to a court "...would be illusory if a Contracting State's domestic legal system allowed a final and binding judicial decision to be quashed by a higher court on an application made by a State official whose power to lodge such an application is not subject to any time-limit, with the result that the judgments were liable to challenge indefinitely... The Court stresses that a binding and enforceable judgment should only be quashed in exceptional circumstances rather than for the sole purpose of obtaining a different decision in the case."[91] One of the most cited *res iudicata* decisions is *Brumărescu v. Romania*, concerning an action for recovery of possession filed by a private individual after a nationalization process. The Court of First Instance decided for the petitioner in a judgment, which became final since no appeal was lodged. Notwithstanding, after the legal procedure was finished, the Procurator General applied to the Supreme Court of Justice on the grounds that the Court of First Instance had exceeded its jurisdiction in examining the lawfulness of the application of the decree of nationalization. The Supreme Court of Justice allowed this request, quashing the judgment of the Court of First instance and dismissing the applicant's claim, arguing that it lacked jurisdiction on the matter.[92] The ECHR found a violation of the legal certainty, and said that the decision of the Supreme Court denying its jurisdiction to decide civil disputes such as the action for recovery of possession implied a self-exclusion contrary to the right of access to a tribunal.[93]

Moreover, the ECHR had held that where this kind of review of final decisions exists, this power should be used only to avoid a miscarriage of justice, but not to carry out a fresh examination. In other words, it cannot be exercised as an appeal in disguise.[94] For example, in *Protsenko v. Russia*, the Court found that the quashing of

[90]ECHR, Case of Běleš and Others v. The Czech Republic, no. 47273/99, Judgment of 12 November 2002, par. 50, 51.

[91]ECHR, Case of Nelyubin v. Russia, no. 14502/04, Judgment of 2 November 2006, par. 24, 28.

[92]ECHR, Case of Brumărescu v. Romania, no. 28342/95, Judgment of 28 October 1999, par.14–24.

[93]ECHR, Case of Brumărescu v. Romania, no. 28342/95, Judgment of 28 October 1999, par. 65. See also: ECHR, Case of Budescu and Petrescu v. Romania, no. 33912/96, Judgment of 2 July 2002, par. 37–39; ECHR, Case of Curutiu v. Romania, no. 29769/96, Judgment of 22 October 2002, par. 39–41.

[94]ECHR, Case of Oferta Plus S.R.L. v. Moldova, no. 14385/04, Judgment of 19 December 2006, par. 98.

a final judgment in the applicant's favor by way of supervisory review was justified since there was an interested third party who did not knew of the proceedings and therefore could not participate in a decision that adversely affected him. Under such circumstances, the quashing of the final judgment was not inconsistent with the principle of legal certainty.[95]

As pointed out, the right to a court does not include only the stage of a final decision, but also its enforcement though execution proceedings. Of the 133 cases concerning the right to a court, in 21 the ECHR decided on this procedural requirement. The leading case in this regard is *Hornsby v. Greece*, where the Court clearly specified that the right to execution of a decision given by any court is an integral part of the "trial" for the purposes of article 6. The ECHR adds: "...to construe article 6 (art. 6) as being concerned exclusively with access to a court and the conduct of proceedings would be likely to lead to situations incompatible with the principle of the rule of law which the Contracting States undertook to respect when they ratified the Convention."[96] This confirms what I concluded in the previous section, that the ECHR conceives the right of access to justice as going further than filing a claim. On the contrary, as decided in *Apostol v. Georgia*, it includes a right to have enforcement proceedings initiated.[97] In the case of *Burdov v. Russia*, the ECHR adds to this idea that a contrary position would deprive article 6 of all useful effect.[98]

From the 133 cases related to the right to a court, 19 concerned the admissibility of an appeal. In *Liakopoulou v. Greece*, the ECHR said that the general rule is that it is not mandatory for the States to establish courts of appeal or cassation under article 6. However, if such jurisdictions do exist, the guarantees of Article 6 must be respected, in particular by providing litigants with an effective right of access.[99] The limitations to this right, and especially as to the conditions of admissibility of an appeal, are permissible under article 6 since by its very nature, it calls for regulation by the State. In this regard, the compatibility of such limitations with the Convention depends on the particularities of the procedure in question and must be taken into account as a whole.[100]

The cases concerning the right to a lawyer and legal aid are quite important for the right to a court. In 16 out of 17 cases where this right was in dispute, the Court decided this particular procedural guarantee from the perspective of the right to a

[95] ECHR, Case of Protsenko v. Russia, no. 13151/04, Judgment of 31 July 2008, par. 29–33.

[96] ECHR, Case of Hornsby v. Greece, no. 18357/91, Judgment of 19 March 1997, par. 40.; ECHR, Scordino v. Italy (No 1), no. 36813/97, Judgment of 29 March 2006, par. 196. See also: ECHR, Case of Okyay and Others v. Turkey, no. 36220/97, Judgment of 12 July 2005, par. 72; ECHR, Case of Sukhobokov v. Russia, no. 75470/01, Judgment of 13 April 2006, par. 22; ECHR, Case of Beshiri and Others v. Albania, no. 7352/03, Judgment of 22 August 2006, par. 60; ECHR, Case of Jeličić v. Bosnia And Herzegovina, no. 41183/02, Judgment of 31 October 2006, par. 38; ECHR, Case of Hirschhorn v. Romania, no. 29294/02, Judgment of 26 July 2007 par. 49.

[97] ECHR, Case of Apostol v. Georgia, no. 40765/02, Judgment of 28 November 2006, par. 56.

[98] ECHR, Case of Burdov v. Russia, no. 59498/00, Judgment of 7 May 2002, par. 34,37.

[99] ECHR, Case of Liakopoulou v. Greece, no 20627/04, Judgment of 24 May 2006, par. 18,19.

[100] ECHR, Case of Liakopoulou v. Greece, no 20627/04, Judgment of 24 May 2006, par. 17.

court. The case law of the ECHR shows clearly that the right to a lawyer and provision of legal aid is not a strict minimum applicable to every case concerning "civil rights and obligations." Beginning with *Airey*, the ECHR has declared "...that there is no obligation under the Convention to make legal aid available for all disputes (contestations) in civil proceedings, as there is a clear distinction between the wording of Article 6 § 3 (c), which guarantees the right to free legal assistance...in criminal proceedings, and of Article 6 § 1, which makes no reference to legal assistance."[101] Moreover, to guarantee an effective right of access to the courts "...leaves to the State a free choice of the means to be used towards this end. The institution of a legal aid scheme...constitutes one of those means but there are others such as, for example, a simplification of procedure."[102]

The connection between the right to a lawyer and to access to a court arise in cases where the impossibility of obtain legal aid impairs the real chance of effectively pursuing and sustaining a legal procedure. For example, in *Golder*, the petitioner tried to contact a solicitor from prison to study the initiation of civil proceedings for libel against a prison warden. The authorities did not allow such contact based on prison regulations. According to the ECHR, without formally denying his right to institute proceedings before a court, the authorities did in fact prevent the petitioner from commencing an action.[103] In *Airey*, the petitioner alleged since legal aid was not at the time available in Ireland for seeking a judicial separation, nor indeed for any civil matters, and she could not afford the cost of litigation, her right to a court was denied.[104] The government, in this case, contended that her right to a court was not impaired since she was free to go before the courts without the assistance of a lawyer.[105] The Court rejected that argument because the right to a court is meant to be effective and not merely illusory. With that purpose, the question was whether Mrs. Airey's appearance without the assistance of a lawyer would be effective, in the sense of whether she would be able to present her case properly and satisfactorily.[106] The Court concluded that this was not realistic given

[101] ECHR, Case of Airey v. Ireland, no. 6289/73, Judgment of 9 October 1979, par. 26; ECHR, Case of Del Sol v. France, no. 46800/99, Judgment of 26 February 2002, par. 20; ECHR, Case of McVicar v. United Kingdom, no. 46311/99, Judgment of 7 May 2002, par. 47; ECHR, Case of Bertuzzi v. France, no. 36378/97, Judgment of 13 February 2003, par. 23; ECHR, Case of Siałkowska v. Poland, no. 8932/05, Judgment of 22 March 2007, par. 105; ECHR, Case of Staroszczyk v. Poland, no. 59519/00, Judgment of 22 March 2007, par. 127.

[102] ECHR, Case of Airey v. Ireland, no. 6289/73, Judgment of 9 October 1979, par. 26. See also: ECHR, Case of Steel and Morris v. The United Kingdom, no. 68416/01, Judgment of 15 February 2005, par. 60; ECHR, Case of Assunção Chaves v. Portugal, no 61226/08, Judgment of 31 January 2012, par. 70.

[103] ECHR, Case of Golder v. The United Kingdom, no. 4451/70, Judgment of 21 February 1975, par. 26.

[104] ECHR, Case of Airey v. Ireland, no. 6289/73, Judgment of 9 October 1979, par. 11, 20.

[105] ECHR, Case of Airey v. Ireland, no. 6289/73, Judgment of 9 October 1979, par. 24.

[106] ECHR, Case of Airey v. Ireland, no. 6289/73, Judgment of 9 October 1979, par. 24.

the nature of the issue, a judicial separation, which entails emotional involvement and complicated points of law and evidence.[107]

In *McVicar v. The United Kingdom* the ECHR applied the same reasoning of Airey in a libel proceeding where there was no procedural requirement of legal representation. The reasoning in this regard was that taking into consideration the circumstances of the litigation, the complexity of the case, the profession and education of the petitioner, he was not prevented from presenting his defense effectively to the High Court, nor was he denied a fair trial due to his ineligibility for legal aid.[108] On the contrary, in *Steel and Morris v. The United Kingdom*, another case of defamation, the Court found that notwithstanding the substantive matter in dispute was not inherently complex, the circumstances of the case made it so. Here, the petitioners were defendants against a big corporation (McDonalds) facing serious financial consequences if found liable in a trial which lasted more than 300 days involving extensive documentary evidence, 130 oral witnesses, expert witnesses, among others. Although well-articulated and having received some help from ad hoc advisers and latitude from judicial officers, all these circumstances made this case exceptionally demanding for the petitioners to present their case effectively without legal aid.[109]

If legal representation is mandatory by legislation, article 6 does require access to some kind of legal aid scheme. For example, in *Aerts v. Belgium*, since Belgian law required representation by counsel before the Court of Cassation, the ECHR found a violation of the right to a court by the Legal Aid Board's refusal to grant him legal aid for an appeal on points of law, on the ground that the appeal was ill-founded.[110] On the contrary, in *Gnahoré v. France*, where the petitioner alleged a similar violation, the court found there was no violation of article 6.1. In this case, the rules of civil procedure exempted cases such as that initiated by the petitioner, concerning education assistance measures, from the requirement that he be represented before the Court of Cassation. Moreover, there was a special proceeding without compulsory representation governed by special rules markedly simpler than the original procedure.[111] In this case, the ECHR concluded: "[T]he refusal of legal aid thus only denied the applicant free assistance from a lawyer, it did not ipso facto prevent him from pursuing his appeal."[112] In *Del Sol v. France*, a case concerning the appeal of a divorce decision which also provided for the liquidation and partition of the matrimonial property,[113] the ECHR found no violation of article 6 even

---

[107] ECHR, Case of Airey v. Ireland, no. 6289/73, Judgment of 9 October 1979, par. 24.

[108] ECHR, Case of McVicar v. The United Kingdom, no. 46311/99, Judgment of 7 May 2002, par. 51–62.

[109] ECHR, Case of Steel and Morris v. The United Kingdom, no. 68416/01, Judgment of 15 February 2005, par. 63–72.

[110] ECHR, Case of Aerts v. Belgium, 61/1997/845/1051, Judgment of 30 July 1998, par. 57, 60.

[111] ECHR, Case of Gnahoré v. France, no. 40031/98, Judgment of 19 September 2000, par. 38–40.

[112] ECHR, Case of Gnahoré v. France, no. 40031/98, Judgment of 19 September 2000, par. 39.

[113] ECHR, Case of Del Sol v. France, no. 46800/99, Judgment of 26 February 2002, par. 8.

though the refusal of the authorities to provide legal representation prevented the petitioner from filing his appeal. The main reason was that the Legal Aid scheme offered enough guarantees from arbitrariness taking such decisions.[114]

In *Bertuzzi v. France*, the petitioner wished to bring an action in damages against a lawyer.[115] He applied to legal aid, which was granted to him immediately, even though legal representation was not compulsory for the proceedings he wished to bring. However, as explained by the Court, that decision remained a dead letter because the three lawyers successively assigned to his case sought permission to withdraw because of personal links with the lawyer the applicant wished to sue. Not being able to secure for himself a lawyer he was forced into *pro se* litigation, and in these circumstances was prevented from sustaining the legal procedure.[116]

In summary, according to the ECHR case law, the applicable test is whether such assistance was indispensable for an *effective* access to court, that is, whether under the particular circumstances of the case, the individual was able to participate and to put forward the matters in support of his or her claims. Some of the factors to take into consideration in this regard are: (i) if representation is rendered compulsory by national legislation; (ii) the complexity of the procedure; (iii) the necessity to address complicated points of law or to establish facts including expert evidence and the examination of witnesses; (iv) the seriousness of what is at stake for the applicant, including his or her emotional involvement; (v) if the circumstances do not place him or her at a substantial disadvantage, such as in cases where the adversary is a lawyer.[117] Even though legal aid might be required, still, the right to a court is not absolute and may be subject to limitations. For example, by restricting legal aid to cases with prospects of success with the purpose of ensuring proper administration of resources.[118] In this regard, the structure and regulation of the legal aid scheme are also elements to take into consideration.[119]

---

[114]ECHR, Case of Del Sol v. France, no. 46800/99, Judgment of 26 February 2002, par. 20. See also: ECHR, Ilbeyi Kemaloğlu and Meriye Kemaloğlu v. Turkey, no. 19986/06, Judgment of 10 April 2012, par. 52, 53.

[115]ECHR, Case of Bertuzzi v. France, no. 36378/97, Judgment of 13 February 2003, par. 22.

[116]ECHR, Case of Bertuzzi v. France, no. 36378/97, Judgment of 13 February 2003, par. 24–31.

[117]ECHR, Case of Airey v. Ireland, no. 6289/73, Judgment of 9 October 1979, par. 24; ECHR, Case of Gnahoré v. France, no. 40031/98, Judgment of 19 September 2000, par. 38–40, ECHR, Case of McVicar v. The United Kingdom, no. 46311/99, Judgment of 7 May 2002, par. 46; ECHR, Case of P. C. And S. v. The United Kingdom, no. 56547/00, Judgment of 16 July 2002, par. 89–91; ECHR, Case of A. v. The United Kingdom, no. 35373/97, Judgment of 17 December 2002, par. 96, 97; ECHR, Case of Steel and Morris v. The United Kingdom, no. 68416/01, Judgment of 15 February 2005, par. 62, 69; ECHR, Case of Assunção Chaves v. Portugal, no 61226/08, Judgment of 31 January 2012, par. 70.

[118]ECHR, Case of P. C. And S. v. The United Kingdom, no. 56547/00, Judgment of 16 July 2002, par. 90; ECHR, Case of Del Sol v. France, no. 46800/99, Judgment of 26 February 2002, par. 25–27; ECHR, Case of Steel and Morris v. The United Kingdom, no. 68416/01, Judgment of 15 February 2005, par. 62.

[119]ECHR, Case of Siałkowska v. Poland, no. 8932/05, Judgment of 22 March 2007, par. 107; ECHR, Case of Staroszczyk v. Poland, no. 59519/00, Judgment of 22 March 2007, par. 129.

As described before, in *Mutu and Pechstein v. Switzerland*, the Court recognized that this right is not necessarily to be understood as access to a court of law of the classic kind, as part of the standard judicial machinery of the country, but is also compatible with mechanisms of dispute resolution such as arbitration proceedings.[120] However, the right to a court does includes the notion that in regard to a decision that might be determinative for civil rights, there is a right at least to have that decision reviewed by a court. For example, in *Pudas v. Sweden*, a dispute arose between the petitioner and the County Administrative Board that revoked his interurban transport license and the government decided it in final instance. Since lawfulness of this decision was not open to review by either the ordinary courts or the administrative courts, or by any other body that could be considered a "tribunal," the ECHR decided there was a violation of the article 6.1 right to a court.[121]

Eight cases concerned the payment of court fees as a requirement prior to initiate an action, to file some kind of appeal, or even prior to initiate enforcement proceedings. In *Kreuz v. Poland*, concerning a claim for damages against the State, the ECHR noted that its case law has never ruled out the possibility of imposing court fees as a financial restriction of access in the interests of the fair administration of justice. In this regard, article 6.1 does not include an unqualified right to obtain free legal aid from the State in a civil dispute, nor a right to free proceedings in civil matters.[122] As a consequence, the requirement to pay fees to civil courts cannot be regarded as a restriction that is incompatible *per se* with article 6.1. On the contrary, the legal issue to be answered is if, in the circumstances of the case, the fee actually charged constitutes a restriction that impairs the very essence of the right to a court. Factors such as the applicant's ability to pay the fee, and the phase of the proceedings at which that restriction is imposed, are material in this regard.[123] Moreover, in *Stankiewicz v. Poland*, the ECHR had the opportunity to say that not only can court fees amount to a violation of article 6.1 but also that there may also be situations in which the issues linked to the determination of litigation costs can be of relevance in that regard.[124]

---

[120] ECHR, Case of Mutu and Pechstein v. Switzerland, nos. 40575/10 and 67474/10, Judgment of 2 October 2018, par.94–96.

[121] ECHR, Case of Pudas v. Sweden, no. 10426/83, Judgment of 27 Octlober 1987, par. 12–15, 39–40. . See, also: ECHR, Case of Tre Traktörer Aktiebolag v. Sweden, no. 10873/84, Judgment of 7 July 1989, par. 47, 48; ECHR, Case of Woś v. Poland, no. 22860/02, Judgment of 08 June 2006, par. 92; ECHR, Case of Sâmbata Bihor Greek Catholic Parish v. Romania, no 48107/99, Judgment of 12 January 2010, par. 70.

[122] ECHR, Case of Kreuz v. Poland, no. 28249/95, 19 June 2001, par. 59.

[123] ECHR, Case of Kreuz v. Poland, no. 28249/95, 19 June 2001, par. 60, 61. See also: ECHR, Case of Weissman and Others v. Romania, no. 63945/00, Judgment of 24 May 2006, par. 34–37; ECHR, Case of Apostol v. Georgia, no. 40765/02, Judgment of 28 November 2006, par. 59; ECHR, Case of Bakan v. Turkey, no. 50939/99, Judgment of 12 June 2007, par. 67, 68; ECHR, Case of Stankov v. Bulgaria, no. 68490/01, Judgment of 12 July 2007, par. 51, 52; ECHR, Case of Anakomba Yula v. Belgium, no. 45413/07, Judgment of 10 March 2009, par. 32; ECHR, Georgel and Georgeta v. Stoicescu v. Romania, no. 9718/03, Judgment of 26 July 2011, par. 69.

[124] ECHR, Case of Stankiewicz v. Poland, no. 46917/99, Judgment of 26 July 2011, par. 60.

Although less frequent, there are some cases providing good examples of the type of procedural requirements that are related to the right of access to justice. In *Lawyer Partners a.s. v. Slovakia*, the applicant was obliged to sue persons who had refused to pay debts for which this company had acquired the right to recover. Because of the high number of payment orders to be issued against debtors, the actions were generated by means of computer software and recorded on DVDs. The DVDs were sent to the district courts concerned, accompanied by an explanatory letter. The courts refused to register such claims, indicating that they lacked the equipment to receive and process submissions made and signed electronically. At the end, they became statute barred.[125] By the approach just described, the Court found a violation of the right to a court because the refusal imposed a disproportionate limitation on the applicant company's right to present its cases to a court in an effective manner.[126]

Finally, in the case of *Canea Catholic Church v. Greece*, the ECHR referred to the requirement of legal personality to initiate legal proceedings, as an indirect restriction of the right to a court. Here, the petitioner alleged that the local court restricted its right to take legal proceedings to protect its property, on the sole ground that the church served the Catholic faith. The legal personality was called into question, and the petitioner alleged that formalities, with which it did not comply, were therefore an excuse.[127] According to the ECHR, by holding that the applicant church had no capacity to take legal proceedings, the Court of Cassation not only penalized the failure to comply with a simple formality for the protection of public order, but imposed a real restriction on the applicant from having any dispute relating to its property rights determined by the courts.[128]

7.3 The ECHR Concrete Analysis of Effectiveness

In 284 cases, I was able to identify at least one of the variables I use as a proxy to characterize both ideal types described previously, the checklist and the flexible approaches. Much more frequently applied in my set list is the flexible (86.6%) than the checklist model (32.8%). At this point, it is also important to take into consideration that there are cases in which the Court decided over more than one element of the right to a fair trial, which means both models might be present in the same case.

[125] ECHR, Case of Lawyer Partners a.s. v. Slovakia, nos. 54252/07, 3274/08, 3377/08, 3505/08, 3526/08, 3741/08, 3786/08, 3807/08, 3824/08, 15055/08, 29548/08, 29551/08, 29552/08, 29555/08 and 29557/08, Judgment of 16 June 2009, par. 8–11.

[126] ECHR, Case of Lawyer Partners a.s. v. Slovakia, nos. 54252/07, 3274/08, 3377/08, 3505/08, 3526/08, 3741/08, 3786/08, 3807/08, 3824/08, 15055/08, 29548/08, 29551/08, 29552/08, 29555/08 and 29557/08, Judgment of 16 June 2009, par. 52–55.

[127] ECHR, Case of Canea Catholic Church v. Greece, 143/1996/762/963, Judgment of 16 December 1997, par. 35, 36, 40.

[128] ECHR, Case of Canea Catholic Church v. Greece, 143/1996/762/963, Judgment of 16 December 1997, par. 41.

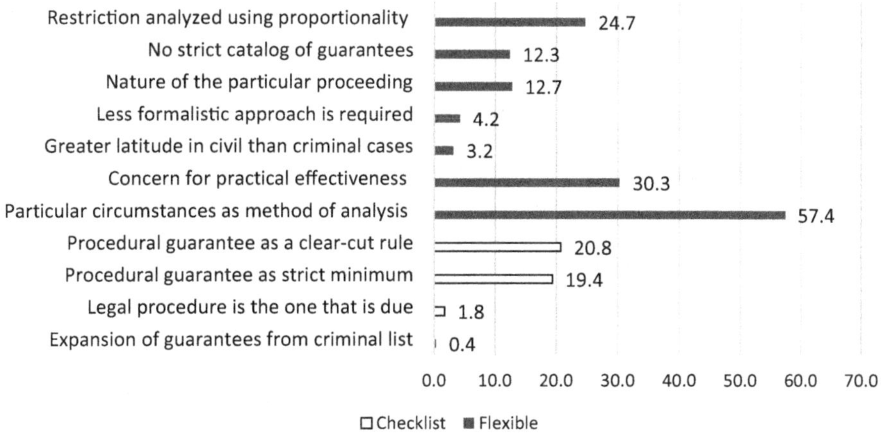

Fig. 7.5 Variables applied for the Checklist and Flexible models

From the total number of cases in which I was able to identify the use of at least one of the models, in 57.4% of them the variable identified was use of the particular circumstances of the case as a factor to determine whether a procedural guarantee was required. In 30.3% of the cases, the ECHR decided over a right to a fair trial dimension or regarding a particular procedural guarantee with greater concern for practical effectiveness than formal recognition. Quite relevant as well for this model is the use of proportionality criteria to analyze the restrictions imposed by local authorities. I applied this code in the 24.7% of the cases. These three variables explain why the most frequent model I was able to identify in the ECHR case law on article 6.1 in its civil limb was the flexible model. Yet, as shown in Fig. 7.5, there is significant proportion of cases in which a variable used as proxy for the checklist model was applied. In this regard, in 20.8% of the cases, the ECHR interpreted a procedural requirement as a clear-cut rule, and in the 19.4%, it understood it was a strict requirement by the right to a fair trial.

In the next section, I explore the different variables I have coded as identifiers for each model in the Court's decisions. I begin by describing the flexible model variables and then the checklist model variables. The idea is to pinpoint how several dimensions and/or procedural guarantees tend to be analyzed more frequently from one or another point of view.

7.3.1 The Flexible Model Approach Under the Civil Limb of Article 6.1

Under the flexible approach, a concrete analysis of the *particular circumstances* is the basic method to decide over the requirements of the right to a fair trial under article 6's civil limb. From the 246 cases in which I identified at least one of the variables I have coded as pertaining to the flexible model (recall Table 7.2), in 164 decisions the Court has considered the particular circumstances as the applicable approach. In fact, frequently, the other variables I coded as identifiers of the flexible model were used in conjunction with it. This is probably because many other variables, such as the nature of the particular proceeding, the effectiveness analysis, or the proportionality test, require a concrete analysis that means taking into consideration the particularities of the case.

The right to a reasonable duration is a good example, especially taking into consideration its importance for the case law on the right to a fair trial. These cases represent 33.3% of the cases, showing the highest rate of violations of all right to a fair trial dimensions (in 89.1% of the cases concerning the right to a reasonable duration, a violation was found).[129]

The profuse case law on this right has established, first, that the period to take into consideration covers the entirety of litigation, the whole proceedings. This means, for example, that administrative proceedings prior to the initiation of a judicial process are often included.[130]

To decide on the reasonableness of the duration, the ECHR uses an *ex post facto* concrete analysis of the circumstances of such proceedings. Beginning with *König v. Germany*, the ECHR established that these circumstances must be assessed in the light of several factors. One of them is the complexity of the case, which is also one of the variables I used to identify the flexible model and because of that, they are applied together. Other factors include the conduct of the parties and the relevant authorities, but also what was at stake for the applicant in the dispute.[131] These criteria do not necessarily have the same weight. For example, in *H v. The United Kingdom*, concerning parental rights and adoption proceedings, the ECHR gave special emphasis to the importance of what was at stake for the applicant since the proceedings were not only decisive for her future relations with her own child, but

[129] In fact, a simple logistic regression shows that this element of due process, in fact, increases the probability of finding a violation 1.27 times (at a p-value of.004) when compared with the other dimensions.

[130] ECHR, Case of Deumeland v. Germany, no. 9384/81, Judgment of 29 May 1986, par. 77. More recently: ECHR, Case of X v. France, no. 18020/91, Judgment of 31 March 1992, par. 31; ECHR, Case of Siegel v. France, no. 36350/97, Judgment of 28 November 2000, par. 42; ECHR, Case of Kress v. France, no. 39594/98, Judgement of 7 June 2001, par. 90.

[131] ECHR, Case of König v. Germany, no. 6232/73, Judgment of 28 June 1978, par. 99, 111; ECHR, Case of Buchholz v. Germany, no. 7759/77, Judgment of 6 May 1981, par. 49; ECHR, Case of Zimmermann and Steiner v. Switzerland, no. 8737/79, Judgment of 13 July 1983, par. 24; ECHR, Case of Deumeland v. Germany, no. 9384/81, Judgment of 29 May 1986, par. 78. More recently: ECHR, Case of Frydlender v. France, no. 30979/96, Judgment of 27 June 2000, par. 43; ECHR, Case of Boca v. Belgium, no. 50615/99, Judgment of 15 November 2002, par. 24; ECHR, Case of O'Sullivan McCarthy Mussel Development Ltd. v. Ireland, no. 44460/16, Judgment of 7 June 2018, par. 144.

were irreversible. Under such circumstances, the authorities are under a duty to exercise exceptional diligence.[132]

In cases where the State has justified the length of proceedings on the measures taken to prioritize cases other than the petitioners', such as *Zimmermann and Steiner v. Switzerland*, the ECHR has considered that only delays attributable to the State may justify a failure to comply with this requirement. This element of the right to a fair trial places a duty on the States to organize their legal systems to allow the courts to comply with it. A temporary backlog of business does not involve liability if the State take measures to remedy such a situation,[133] which includes prioritizing cases according to their degree of urgency and importance. Notwithstanding, if a state of affairs of this kind is prolonged and becomes a matter of structural organization, such methods no longer suffice.[134] In fact, even in legal procedures characterized by the principle that the procedural initiative lies with the parties, the parties' attitude does not excuse the courts from ensuring the expeditious trial that article 6 requires.[135] For example, in *Tierce v. San Marino*, the Court found the State was responsible for the length of the proceedings since it was mainly due to the complexity of San Marino's procedure, and to the fact that in civil matters the judge is not empowered to take the initiative in the event of inaction by the parties.[136]

Notwithstanding that most of cases on reasonable duration are analyzed according to this approach, as I shall explain later there are cases in which I have identified a checklist approach by the ECHR. I will return to this in the next section when studying the checklist model under the right to a fair trial in its civil limb.

Nevertheless, the use of the particular circumstances of the case to decide whether the right to a fair trial requires a procedural guarantee is also quite relevant for the decisions on other dimensions, such as the right to a court[137] and the right to an

[132] ECHR, Case of H v. The United Kingdom, 9580/81, Judgement of 8 July 1987, par. 85. See also: ECHR, Case of X. France, no. 18020/91, Judgment of 31 March 1992, par. 47; ECHR, Case of Süßmann v. Germamy, no. 20024/92, Judgment of 16 September 1996, par. 58, 61; ECHR, Case of Laino v. Italy, no. 33158/96, Judgment of 18 February 1999, par. 18; ECHR, Case of Nuutinen v. Finland, no. 32842/96, Judgment of 27 June 2000, par. 119; ECHR, Case of Frydlender v. France, no. 30979/96, Judgment of 27 June 2000, par. 45; ECHR, Case of Mikulić v. Croatia, no. 53176/99, Judgment 7 February 2002, par. 44; ECHR, Case of Szarapo v. Poland, no. 40835/98, Judgment of 23 May 2002, par. 40.

[133] ECHR, Case of Buchholz v. Germany, no. 7759/77, Judgment of 6 May 1981, par. 49.

[134] ECHR, Case of Zimmermann and Steiner v. Switzerland, no. 8737/79, Judgment of 13 July 1983, par. 27–29. See also: ECHR, Case of Francesco Lombardo v. Italy, no. 11519/85, Judgment of 26 November 1992, par. 20; ECHR, Case of Zwierzyński v. Poland, no. 34049/96, Judgment of 19 June 2001, par. 55.

[135] ECHR, Case of Sürmeli v. Germany, no. 75529/01, Judgment of 8 June 2006, par. 129.

[136] ECHR, Case of Tierce v. San Marino, no. 69700/01, Judgment of 17 June 2003, par. 31

[137] See, e.g.: ECHR, Case of Cordova v. Italy (no. 2), no. 45649/99, Judgment of 30 January 2003, par. 58 (regarding an analysis of a limitation imposed over access to justice by parlamentary immunity); ECHR, Case of Oferta Plus S.R.L. v. Moldova, no. 14385/04, Judgment of 19 December 2006, par. 108–111 (regarding judicial enforcement of a judicial decision as an inherent element of the right of a court).

independent and impartial judicial body.[138] Moreover, it has been important in deciding on specific procedural guarantees. Some of the most relevant concern the admissibility of appeal to a higher courts,[139] enforcement of the judicial decision,[140] access to legal aid,[141] the court composition as required by the right to an impartial and independent tribunal,[142] the duty to state reasons,[143] the opportunity to present evidence and argue the case,[144] and the right to a public hearing.[145]

The second relevant variable is the analysis of the procedural elements or the dimensions of the right to a fair trial under the criteria of effectiveness. In these cases, the Court was more concerned with practical effectiveness than formal recognition. In 86 decisions the ECHR used this criterion, of which, in 43% of the cases in which I applied the effectiveness variable I also applied the particular circumstances code. This is why I consider that the European Court of Human Rights' basic conception of the article 6.1 civil limb consists of the concrete analysis of effectiveness.

This effectiveness criterion has been used to analyze several procedural guarantees, most of them related to the right to a court, which as described above occupies an important part of the article 6.1 case law (58% of the total of these cases). As I explained earlier, the key to understanding the right to a court is the idea that this dimension need not to be theoretical or illusory, but practical and effective.[146] The

---

[138] See, e.g.: ECHR Case of Hirschhorn v. Romania, no. 29294/02, Judgment of 26 July 2007, par. 82–83 (analyzing whether petitioners' doubts as to the Independence and impartiality of the Court of Appeal could be said to be objectively justified under the particular circumstances of the case). Similarly, see: ECHR, Case of Wettstein v. Switzerland, no. 33958/96, Judgment of 21 December 2000, par. 45–49; ECHR, Case of Pétur Thór Sigurðsson v. Iceland, no. 39731/98, Judgment of 10 April 2003, par. 37–45; ECHR, Case of Pescador Valero v. Spain, no. 62435/00, Judgment of 17 June 2003, par. 27–28; ECHR, Case of San Leonard Band Club v. Malta, no. 77562/01, Judgment of 29 June 2004, par. 62; ECHR, Case of Puolitaival and Pirttiaho v. Finland, no. 54857/00, Judgment of 23 November 2004, par. 51–54.

[139] See, e.g.: ECHR, Case of Levages Prestations Services v. France, no. 21920/93, Judgment of 23 October 1996, par. 43–44.; ECHR, Case of Miragall Escolano and Others v. Spain, nos. 38366/97, 38688/97, 40777/98, 40843/98, 41015/98, 41400/98, 41446/98, 41484/98, 41487/98 and 41509/98, Judgment of 25 January 2000, par. 37.

[140] See, e.g.: ECHR, Case of Sukhobokov v. Russia, no. 75470/01, Judgment of 13 April 2006, par. 24; ECHR, Case of Oferta Plus S.R.L. v. Moldova, no. 14385/04, Judgment of 19 December 2006, par. 108–111.

[141] See, e.g.: ECHR, Case of Staroszczyk v. Poland, no. 59519/00, Judgment of 22 March 2007, par. 137–138; ECHR, Case of Steel and Morris v. The United Kingdom, no. 68416/01, Judgment of 15 February 2005, par. 61.

[142] See, e.g.: ECHR, Case of Denisov v. Ukraine, no. 76639/11, 25 September 2018, par. 61–63.

[143] See, e.g.: ECHR, Case of Tatishvili v. Russia, no. 1509/02, 22 February 2007, par. 62–63; ECHR, Case of Blücher v. Czech Republic, no 58580/00, Judgment of 11 January 2005, par. 55–57.

[144] See, e.g.: ECHR, Case of Blücher v. Czech Republic, no 58580/00, Judgment of 11 January 2005, par. 60–61; ECHR, Case of Yvon v. France, no. 44962/98, Judgment of 24 April 2003, par. 39–40; ECHR, Case of Stepinska v. France, no 1814/02, Judgment of 15 June 2004, par. 18.

[145] ECHR, Case of Helmers v. Sweden, no. 11826/85, Judgment of 29 October 1991, par. 36.

[146] ECHR, Case of Golder v. United Kingdom, no. 4451/70, Judgment of 21 February 1975, par. 26; ECHR, Case of Airey v. Ireland, no. 6289/73, Judgment of 9 October 1979, par. 24

cases concerning the right to a lawyer or the provision of legal aid in civil cases are good examples. In these, the Court usually decides on the real chances of effectively pursuing and sustaining a legal procedure without having such a recourse. But the effectiveness analysis goes beyond these legal aid cases. For example, the ECHR have held that a particularly strict interpretation of a procedural rule as a way as to prevent the applicants' action from being examined on the merits, such as in a constitutional appeal, might impair the right to the effective protection of the courts.[147]

As expected, the ECHR uses this approach in most cases of the effective remedy under article 6 analysis (18 cases). A good example are the so-called "Pinto Act" proceedings cases against Italy. This legislation provided a mechanism to claim for remedies in cases where the domestic courts finds that the length of a proceeding exceed what is reasonable. Many petitions filed at the ECHR argue that such proceedings were not effective to remedy the damages caused by the delay. For example, in *Simaldone v. Italy*, the petitioner filed a claim to the Rome Court of Appeal based on this statute over a civil procedure that lasted more than 10 years. He claimed a compensation of EUR 10.846 in respect of non-pecuniary damage. The Court of Appeal awarded the applicant EUR 700 in compensation for non-pecuniary damage and EUR 1000 to his lawyer for costs and expenses, but the execution of this decision took more than a year.[148] At the ECHR, the applicant complained both for the length of the civil proceedings and for the amount awarded by the Court of Appeal under the Pinto Act, which the petitioner found insufficient to remedy the injury caused by the violation of Article 6.1 of the Convention.[149] The ECHR decided that by taking more than 12 months before implementing the required measures to comply with the "Pinto" decision, the Italian authorities excluded article 6.1 any *effet utile*.[150] Besides these cases, a similar reasoning may be found in *Qufaj Co. Sh.p.k. v. Albania*. Here, the claimant had a decision in his favor in a compensation claim against a municipality, but the Ministry of Finance stayed it at execution for lack of funds. Against this administrative decision, the petitioner brought proceedings in the Constitutional Court, claiming that local governmental institutions were obliged to guarantee the enforcement of final judicial decisions. The Constitutional Court rejected this argument and excluded this matter from its jurisdiction.[151] The ECHR argued that, although a delay in the execution of a judgment may be justified in particular circumstances, it cannot impair the essence of the right to a

[147] ECHR, Case of Běleš and Others v. The Czech Republic, no. 47273/99, 12 November 2002, par. 68, 69.

[148] ECHR, Case of Simaldone v. Italy, no 22644/03, Judgment of 31 March 2009, par. 5–10.

[149] ECHR, Case of Simaldone v. Italy, no 22644/03, Judgment of 31 March 2009, par. 16.

[150] ECHR, Case of Simaldone v. Italy, no 22644/03, Judgment of 31 March 2009, par. 55.

[151] ECHR, Case of Qufaj Co. Sh.p.k. v. Albania, no. 54268/00, Judgment of 18 November 2004, par. 7–20.

court of which the enforcement stage is part.[152] Moreover, the Court noted that the Albanian legal system did afford a remedy—in the form of a complaint to the Constitutional Court for breach of the right to a fair trial—but it was not effective since this court did not consider the enforcement to be a part of it. In consequence, the ECHR found that the fair trial rules in Albania should have been interpreted in a way that guaranteed an effective remedy for an alleged breach of the requirement under Article 6.1 of the Convention.[153]

The proportionality test was used in 70 cases (28.5% of the cases where I identified the flexible approach), as a mechanism to decide if a restriction over this right is permissible under article 6 in its civil limb. Almost all these cases concerned the right to a court and, as could be expected, this variable was applied in conjunction with the effectiveness criteria. The case of *Lawyer Partners a.s. v. Slovakia* described previously, is a good example. While refusing to register claims because they lacked the equipment to receive and process submissions made and signed electronically, the local courts imposed a disproportionate limitation on the applicant company's right to present its cases to a court in an effective manner.[154]

In other cases concerning access to evidentiary materials, the ECHR had held that article 6 extends to situations where a person has, in principle, a civil claim but a legal provision prevents him or her from seeking redress before a court without appropriate justification.[155] In *K.H. and Others v. Slovakia*, the petitioners were eight women of Roma ethnic origin who feared that their infertility was a product of unauthorized sterilization procedures performed on them during their caesarean delivery by medical personnel. They requested access to medical records through their legal representatives for preparation of a claim against the medical institution, but were denied it. Through an access to information proceeding, the applicants were able to consult their records but not to obtain photocopies of such documents. These restrictions were considered necessary by local authorities in order to prevent abuse of personal data contained therein.[156] Before the ECHR, the petitioners argued that having copies of the files was important for later civil litigation, especially for compliance with the burden of proof, and for an assessment of the prospect of success. This was important since they were living on social benefits and would be ordered to reimburse the other party's costs if the courts dismissed their action.[157]

[152] ECHR, Case of Qufaj Co. Sh.p.k. v. Albania, no. 54268/00, Judgment of 18 November 2004, par. 38.

[153] ECHR, Case of Qufaj Co. Sh.p.k. v. Albania, no. 54268/00, Judgment of 18 November 2004, par. 40–42.

[154] ECHR, Case of Lawyer Partners a.s. v. Slovakia, nos. 54252/07, 3274/08, 3377/08, 3505/08, 3526/08, 3741/08, 3786/08, 3807/08, 3824/08, 15055/08, 29548/08, 29551/08, 29552/08, 29555/08 and 29557/08, Judgment of 16 June 2009, par. 52-55.

[155] ECHR, Case of K.H. and Others v. Slovakia, no. 32881/04, Judgment of 28 April 2009, par. 66.

[156] ECHR, Case of K.H. and Others v. Slovakia, no. 32881/04, Judgment of 28 April 2009, par. 6, 11–19.

[157] ECHR, Case of K.H. and Others v. Slovakia, no. 32881/04, Judgment of 28 April 2009, par. 59–61.

Following their usual case law on this regard, the ECHR examined whether this normative restriction impaired the essence of the right and, in particular, whether it pursued a legitimate aim, and if there was a reasonable relationship of proportionality between the means employed and the aim sought to be achieved.[158] In this analysis, the ECHR found that notwithstanding the statutory bar on making available copies of the records, this did not entirely bar the applicants from bringing a civil action, nor did it impose a disproportionate limitation on their ability to present their cases to a court in an effective manner.[159]

Both the particular circumstances methodology and the effectiveness analysis are good proxies to understand that the Court is more concerned with practical effectiveness than it is with formal recognition. Indeed, there are cases in which the ECHR expressly said that to decide whether a procedural requirement is required under the right to a fair trial, it is necessary to follow a less formalistic approach (another of the variables I coded as a proxy for the flexible approach). In the case of *Liakopoulou v. Greece*, a compensation claim for an expropriation procedure, the Court of Cassation dismissed an appeal on formal grounds relying on a procedural rule which established than an appellant had to specify the circumstances of the case the Court of Appeal relied on for rejecting the appeal.[160] The ECHR held that notwithstanding that the rules on the formalities for lodging an appeal are not by themselves contrary to article 6.1, in this case there was a violation since the Court of Cassation had an overly formalistic interpretation that prevented the applicant from even having the merits of her allegations examined.[161]

There are cases in which the ECHR has expressly recognized that in civil matters there is greater latitude than in criminal cases in deciding whether a procedural element was a requirement of the right to a fair trial. In six cases concerning the right to a lawyer, I have found that the ECHR had established that since article 6.1. had not expressly mentioned this right in civil cases, in this area the member States are not required to provide it as long as there are other ways to secure an effective participation. In some of them, which I have already mentioned, such as *Airey v. Ireland*, *Del Sol v. France* and *Bertuzzi v. France*, the ECHR says there is a clear distinction between article 6.3(c), which provides for a right to free legal assistance in criminal proceedings and of article 6.1. which makes no express reference to such right. Therefore, there is no obligation under the Convention to

[158]ECHR, Case of K.H. and Others v. Slovakia, no. 32881/04, Judgment of 28 April 2009, par. 64.

[159]ECHR, Case of K.H. and Others v. Slovakia, no. 32881/04, Judgment of 28 April 2009, par. 67.

[160]ECHR, Case of Liakopoulou v. Greece, no 20627/04, Judgment of 24 May 2006, par. 11.

[161]ECHR, Case of Liakopoulou v. Greece, no 20627/04, Judgment of 24 May 2006, par. 23, 24. Similarly, see: ECHR, Case of Sotiris and Nikos Koutras ATTEE v. Greece, no. 39442/98, Judgment of 16 November 2000, par. 22; ECHR, Case of Platakou, no. 38460/97, Judgment of 11 January 2001, par. 43; ECHR, Case of Dodov. Bulgaria, no. 59548/00, Judgment of 17 January 2008, par. 113; ECHR, Case of L'Erablière A.S.B.L. v. Belgium, no 49230/07, Judgment of 24 February 2009, par. 37, 38; ECHR, Case of RTBF v. Belgium, no 50084/06, Judgment of 29 March 2011, par. 71; ECHR, Case of Zubac v. Crotia, no. 40160/12, Judgment of 5 April 2018, par. 85.

make legal aid available for all disputes in civil proceedings,[162] unless it proves indispensable for effective access to a court, either because legal representation is rendered compulsory, or by reason of the complexity of the procedure or of the case.[163]

I have found the same reasoning in decisions concerning rules of evidence as a right to a fair trial requirement in these matters. In *Jokela v. Finland*, the petitioners claimed that they were denied the right to a fair trial in an expropriation proceeding since the Land Court had not taken into consideration that they had sought to examine two witnesses, having failed to register their request.[164] According to the ECHR, article 6.1. requires that a domestic court must conduct a "proper examination of the submissions, arguments, and evidence" adduced by the parties, but "[T]he requirements. . .are not necessarily the same in cases concerning the determination of civil rights and obligations as they are in cases concerning the determination of a criminal charge. This is borne out by the absence of detailed provisions such as paragraphs 2 and 3 of Article 6 applying to cases of the former category. Thus, although these provisions have a certain relevance outside the strict confines of criminal law, the Contracting States have greater latitude when dealing with civil cases concerning civil rights and obligations than they have when dealing with criminal cases."[165]

I identified 36 decisions in which the ECHR decided on a procedural guarantee based on the nature of the proceeding. That would mean that the specific procedural element is not considered as a strict minimum to be applied to every type of proceeding, and so is a proxy for the flexible approach. This variable has been frequently applied from a concrete analysis of the particular circumstances of the case.

Most of the cases where the ECHR followed this approach involved the right to a public hearing. A case worth mentioning is *Eisenstecken v. Austria*, concerning an administrative proceeding for an authorization to celebrate a contract for property to vest in a third person on the owner's death. The petitioner alleged that the Regional Real Property Transactions Commission had adopted its decision denying such authorization, without offering him the opportunity to present his arguments during an oral hearing before this body. At the ECHR, the government argued that the

---

[162] ECHR, Case of Airey v. Ireland, no. 6289/73, Judgment of 9 October 1979, par. 26; ECHR, Case of Del Sol v. France, no. 46800/99, Judgment of 26 February 2002, par. 20; ECHR, Case of Bertuzzi v. France, no. 36378/97, Judgment of 13 February 2003, par. 23; ECHR, Case of Siałkowska v. Poland, no. 8932/05, Judgment of 22 March 2007, par. 105; par. ECHR, Case of Staroszczyk v. Poland, no. 59519/00, Judgment of 22 March 2007, par. 127.

[163] ECHR, Case of A v. The United Kingdom, no. 35373/97, Judgment of 17 December 2002, par. 96; ECHR, Case of McVicar v. The United Kingdom, no. 46311/99, Judgment of 7 May 2002, par. 47.

[164] ECHR, Case of Jokela v. Finland, no. 28856/95, Judgment of 21 May 2002, par. 66.

[165] ECHR, Case of Jokela v. Finland, no. 28856/95, Judgment of 21 May 2002, par. 68. See also: ECHR, Case of Levages Prestations Services v. France, no. 21920/93, Judgment of 23 October 1996, par. 46.

applicant never requested a hearing and since there was no important question of fact or law to resolve, a public hearing was not required. The ECHR reasoning was twofold. First, it established that as a general rule there is an entitlement to a hearing under article 6.1 as long as a case does not fall into one of the permitted exceptions,[166] an approach closer to the checklist model (and in fact it was coded as such). Second, on the argument of the government that no public hearing was required, the ECHR found that *the matter at issue* was not a highly technical one better dealt with in written proceedings.[167] In this regard, there are cases where the ECHR had established that it takes into account the nature of the issues to be decided since procedures devoted exclusively to points of law or highly technical considerations can fulfill the conditions of Article 6 even in the absence of public debates.[168] It adds in *Miller v. Sweden*, that as along as a public hearing has been held at first instance, a less strict standard applies to the appellate level in general and in particular, if an oral hearing has been waived at first instance and requested only on appeal. The ECHR recognizes that in the interests of the proper administration of justice, it is normally more expedient that a hearing be held at first instance rather than only before the appellate court.[169] In a case concerning a proceeding to access to restricted information based on national security against an intelligence agency, *Kennedy v. The United Kingdom*,[170] the ECHR uses a more flexible language over this requirement. It says "...that the obligation to hold a hearing is not absolute. There may be proceedings in which an oral hearing is not required and where the courts may fairly and reasonably decide the case on the basis of the parties' submissions and other written materials. The character of the circumstances that may justify dispensing with an oral hearing essentially comes down to the nature of the issues to be decided by the competent national court."[171] In the recent case of *Mutu and Pechstein v. Switzerland*, the ECHR adds that there may be proceedings in which an oral hearing is not required under Article 6, for example where there are no issues of credibility or contested facts that necessitate a hearing. Moreover, it held that article 6 does not always "...requires a right to a public hearing irrespective of the nature of

[166] Article 6.1. establish the following: "...Judgment shall be pronounced publicly but the press and public may be excluded from all or part of the trial in the interests of morals, public order or national security in a democratic society, where the interests of juveniles or the protection of the private life of the parties so require, or to the extent strictly necessary in the opinion of the court in special circumstances where publicity would prejudice the interests of justice."

[167] ECHR, Case of Eisenstecken v. Austria, no. 29477/95, Judgment of 3 October 2000, par. 31–36. See also: ECHR, Case of Miller v. Sweden, no. 55853/00, Judgment of 8 February 2005, par. 29; ECHR, Martinie v. France, no. 58675/00, Judgment of 12 April 2006, par. 40–42.

[168] ECHR, Case of Ernst and Other v. Belgium, no 33400/96, Judgment of 15 July 2003, par. 66. More recently: ECHR, Case of Nikolova and Vandova v. Bulgaria, no. 20688/04, Judgment of 17 December 2013, par.70.

[169] ECHR, Case of Miller v. Sweden, no. 55853/00, Judgment of 8 February 2005, par. 30.

[170] ECHR, Kennedy v. The United Kingdom, no. 26839/05, Judgment of 18 May 2010, par. 8.

[171] ECHR, Kennedy v. The United Kingdom, no. 26839/05, Judgment of 18 May 2010, par. 188. See, also: ECHR, Case of Tommaso v. Italy, no. 43395/09, Judgment of 23 February 2017, par. 163.

the issues to be decided. There are other considerations, including the right to trial within a reasonable time and the related need for expeditious handling of the courts' caseload, which must be taken into account in determining the need for a public hearing."[172]

A similar approach has been used in cases concerning the admissibility of appeals by the applicants in civil proceedings but denied by local courts. In this regard, the ECHR had held that the admissibility of an appeal, as part of the right to access to a court, by its very nature calls for regulation by the State, enjoying a margin of appreciation in this regard. Of course, these limitations may not impair the very essence of the right, must pursue a legitimate aim and must have a reasonable relationship of proportionality between the means employed and the aim sought to be achieved.[173] In the case of *Annoni di Gussola and Others v. France*, the ECHR held that a provision allowing an appeal to be struck from the list of the high court may be legitimate if it is aimed to ensure protection for judgment creditors, avoiding dilatory appeals, reinforcing the authority of lower courts and relieving congestion in the Court of Cassation's list. Nevertheless, in this particular case, it found that by deciding without taking into consideration the precariousness of the financial circumstances of the applicant, as required, amounted to a disproportionate limitation of his right to a court.[174] The case of *Zubac v. Croatia* adds two additional rationales in analyzing a restriction on an appeal on a point of law under article 6. First, the extent to which the case was examined before the lower courts, the existence or not of issues related to the fairness of the proceedings before the lower courts, and the nature of the role of the court at issue. Second, limitations based on the amount of the claim have been considered legitimate and reasonable since the very essence of the Supreme Court's role is to deal only with matters of significance. In this analysis, the court will look into: "(i) the foreseeability of the restriction, (ii) whether it is the applicant or the respondent State who should bear the adverse consequences of the errors made during the proceedings that led to the applicant's being denied access to the Supreme Court and (iii) whether the restrictions in question could be said to involve 'excessive formalism'".[175]

A couple of cases on the duty to state reasons have also been decided using the nature of the proceedings in question. The ECHR had held that judicial decisions should adequately state the reasons on which they are based, but article 6.1 does not require a detailed answer to every argument. The extent of the requirement may vary

[172] ECHR, Case of Mutu and Pechstein v. Switzerland, nos. 40575/10 and 67474/10, Judgment of 2 October 2018, par. 177.

[173] ECHR, Case of Levages Prestations Services v. France, no. 21920/93, Judgment of 23 October 1996, par. 40; ECHR Case of García Manibardo v. Spain, no. 38695/97, Judgment of 15 February 2000, par. 36; ECHR, Case of Berger v. France, no. 48221/99, Judgment of 03 December 2002, par. 30; ECHR, Case of Ernst and Other v. Belgium, no 33400/96, Judgment of 15 July 2003, par. 74; ECHR, Case of Liakopoulou v. Greece, no 20627/04, Judgment of 24 May 2006, par. 17.

[174] ECHR, Case of Annoni di Gussola and Others v. France, nos. 31819/96 and 33293/96, Judgment of 14 November 2000, par. 50–57.

[175] ECHR, Case of Zubac v. Croatia, no. 40160/12, Judgment of 5 April 2018, par. 85–86.

according to the nature of the decision and must be determined in the light of the circumstances of the case. For example, a court, by dismissing an appeal, may in principle simply endorse the reasons for the lower court's decision without further justification. In such cases, the lower court or authority must have provided such reasons as to enable the parties to make effective use of their right of appeal.[176] Similar approach has been used when analyzed whether a departure from settled case law might amount to a violation of the right to a fair trial. According to Galič, for example, the existence of a well-established case law impose a duty on Supreme Courts –because of its specific function on a legal system- to provide a reasoned justification to such divergence, since different treatment on similar factual situations does not give rise a violation of article 6 per se. Factors that depends on specific circumstances of a given case, such as retroactive application or pending cases that might get affected, has to be considered.[177]

In 35 cases, the ECHR expressly said that the due process clause does not have a strict catalog of guarantees. In terms of right to a fair trial dimension, the best example is the right to a court since in its inception it was considered as inherent to article 6 no matter that it is not expressly mentioned.[178] Not as expressly as in Golder, there are other cases in which the ECHR held that the elements of the right to a fair trial under the clause of article 6.1. cannot be interpreted as demanding a strict set of requirements. For example, in *Forrer-Niedenthal v. Germany*' the ECHR held that notwithstanding that article 6 precludes interference by the legislature in the administration of justice to influence the judicial outcome of a case, the specific clause of its first paragraph cannot be interpreted as preventing any interference by the public authorities in pending judicial proceedings to which they are parties.[179] In *Blücher v. Czech Republic*, the petitioner alleged the unfairness of the proceedings he initiated for the restitution of nationalized properties he inherited, which were denied, according to him because of the excessive burden of proof imposed on him and from the manifestly arbitrary findings of the competent courts.[180] Here, the ECHR held that it is not its function to substitute the domestic courts' assessment of the facts and evidence, but only to ensure that the evidence has been presented in such a way as to guarantee a fair trial. While the right to a fair trial guaranteed by article 6.1 includes the right of the parties to the proceedings to submit the

---

[176]ECHR, Case of García Ruiz v. Spain, no. 30544/96, Judgment of 21 January 1999, par. 26, 29; ECHR, Case of Jokela v. Finland, no. 28856/95, Judgment of 21 May 2002, par. 72, 73; ECHR, Case of Buzescu v. Romania, no. 61302/00, Judgment of 24 May 2005, par. 63; ECHR, Case of Tatishvili v. Russia, no. 1509/02, Judgment of 22 February 2007, par. 58; ECHR, Case of Wagner and J.M.W.L. v. Luxembourg, no. 76240/01, Judgment of 28 June 2007, par. 90; ECHR, Case of Gorou v. Greece (No 2), no. 12686/03, Judgment of 20 March 2009, par. 37.

[177]Galič (2017), pp. 30–31.

[178]ECHR, Case of Golder v. United Kingdom, no. 4451/70, Judgment of 21 February 1975, par. 36.

[179]ECHR, Case of Forrer-Niedenthal v. Germany, no 47316/99, Judgment of 20 February 2003, par. 60.

[180]ECHR, Case of Blücher v. Czech Republic, no 58580/00, Judgment of 11 January 2005, par. 10, 11, 40.

observations they consider relevant to their case, it does not regulate admissibility, probative force and burden of proof, which are essentially matters of domestic law.[181] On the contrary, what is for the Court to assess, is to examine applications alleging that the domestic courts have failed to observe specific procedural safeguards laid down in article 6.1 or that the conduct of the proceedings as a whole did not guarantee the applicant a fair hearing.[182] Moreover, in cases concerning the right to a lawyer or legal aid such as *Steel and Morris v. The United Kingdom*, the ECHR had held that although article 6.1. provides guarantees intended to ensure that a litigant has the opportunity to present his or her case effectively and that he or she is able to enjoy equality of arms with the opposing side, it leaves the State a free choice of the means to be used in guaranteeing litigants the above rights. The institution of a legal aid scheme constitutes one of those means, but there may be others.[183]

7.3.2 The Checklist Model Approach in the Article 6.1. Civil Limb

Less frequent in the ECHR case law are the variables I used as a proxy to characterize the checklist model. As said, from the 284 cases in which I was able to identify one of the models, I applied at least one of its variables in 32.8% of them. The codes pertaining to this model I applied most were two. First, whenever the Court interpreted a procedural guarantee as being a clear-cut rule (20.8%) and, second, whenever it considered a specific procedural guarantee to be a strict minimum required by the right to a fair trial (19.4%). In many cases, I applied both codes at the same time, since when the ECHR decides that a procedural guarantee is a strict minimum requirement under article 6's civil limb, at the same time it interprets such a guarantee as a clear-cut type of rule.

In 59 cases, the ECHR analyzed a procedural guarantee as being a clear-cut rule. As described in Chap. 1, by this conception, the procedural guarantee to be interpreted as a legal directive, which contains a mandate that is applicable in an all-or-nothing fashion.[184]

---

[181] ECHR, Case of Blücher v. Czech Republic, no 58580/00, Judgment of 11 January 2005, par. 52, 53. See also: ECHR, Case of ECHR, Case of Tommaso v. Italy, no. 43395/09, Judgment of 23 February 2017, par. 170.

[182] CHR, Case of ECHR, Case of Tommaso v. Italy, no. 43395/09, Judgment of 23 February 2017, par. 171.

[183] ECHR, Case of Steel and Morris v. The United Kingdom, no. 68416/01, Judgment of 15 February 2005, par. 59, 60. See, also: ECHR, Case of Airey v. Ireland, no. 6289/73, Judgment of 9 October 1979, par. 26; ECHR, Case of Gnahoré v. France, no. 40031/98, Judgment of 19 September 2000, par. 38; ECHR, Case of McVicar v. The United Kingdom, no. 46311/99, Judgment of 7 May 2002, par. 48–50.

[184] Following Ronald Dworkin account for the differences between legal principles and rules. See: Dworkin (1967), pp. 22–29; Dworkin (1977), pp. 22–31.

As explained before, many of these cases concern the length of the proceedings in the context of systemic problems of delay in the respondent States. As explained, in such situations the ECHR does not necessarily analyze all the factors as described in the previous section but relies on previous cases and applies them as strict legal rules. In other words, in these cases the ECHR decides on a violation in an all-or-nothing fashion in the sense that it is only required to acknowledge the systemic problem to make a State responsible without further consideration of the criteria mentioned above. That is why I have coded these cases as pertaining to the checklist model. I have identified 19 cases where this has happened. Most of these are petitions against Italy. In this regard, in *Di Mauro v. Italy*, concerning a tenancy and eviction proceeding which lasted more than 13 years, the ECHR decided the matter based on the fact that between 1987 and 1997 it had already delivered 65 judgments finding an excessive duration of the proceedings in the civil courts of the various regions of Italy. This, and other facts, led the ECHR to conclude that the delay in the Italian legal system was a continuing situation, which by itself constituted a practice that was incompatible with the Convention,[185] and in consequence in this case it found a violation without necessarily arguing on the concrete circumstances of the case. Many other cases, some decided on the same date, as well as others decided later and even after the so called "Pinto Proceedings" (enacted in Italy as an attempt to provide remedy in these cases), followed the same reasoning.[186] Beyond these cases concerning systematical problems of efficiency, I have found a similar kind of reasoning in cases where the ECHR did not require a detailed account of the particular circumstances because it relied on similar previous cases or by findings of the national courts or the respondent government. For example, in *Kaic and Other v. Croatia*, the court did not analyze in depth the circumstances of the case (notwithstanding that the basic case law was mentioned) since the national Constitutional Court had already found the proceedings to be unreasonably long, the government did not contend this finding, and the ECHR had itself found the same in similar cases.[187]

---

[185] ECHR, Di Mauro v. Italy, no. 34256/96, Judgment of 28 July 1999, par. 23.

[186] ECHR, Case of Bottazzi v. Italy, no. 34884/97, 28 July 1999, par. 22; ECHR, Case of Mennitto v. Italy, no. 33804/96, Judgment of 5 October 2000, par. 30; ECHR, Case of Apicella v. Italy, no. 64890/01, Judgment of 29 March 2006, par. 116–118; ECHR, Case of Cocchiarella v. Italy, no. 64886/01 Judgment of 29 March 2006, par. 119–121; ECHR, Case of Giuseppe Mostacciuolo v. Italy (no. 1), no. 64705/01, Judgment of 29 March 2006, par. 115–119; ECHR, Case of Giuseppina and Orestina Procaccini v. Italy, no. 65075/01, Judgment of 29 March 2006, par. 115–119; ECHR, Case of Giuseppe Mostacciuolo v. Italy (no. 2), no. 65102/01, Judgment of 29 March 2006, par. 114–118; ECHR, Case of Musci v. Italy, no. 64699/01, Judgment of 9 March 2006, par. 117–121; ECHR, Case of Riccardi Pizzatti v. Italy, no. 62361/00, Judgment of 9 March 2006, par. 114–118; ECHR, Case of Scordino v. Italy (no. 1), no. 36813/97, Judgment of Judgment of 9 March 2006, par. 222–226; ECHR, Case of Simaldone v. Italy, no 22644/03, Judgment of 31 March 2009, par. 35–37.

[187] ECHR, Case of Kaic and Other v. Croatia, no. 22014/04, Judgment of 17 July 2008, par. 24–27. Similarly, see: ECHR, Case of Frerot v. France, no 70204/01, Judgment of 12 June 2007, par. 67–70; ECHR, Case of Gorou v. Greece (No. 2), no 70204/01, Judgment of 20 March 2009, par.

Besides these exceptional cases on the reasonable duration, another frequent element of the right to a fair trial where I applied this variable was the right to an independent and impartial tribunal. In terms of the independence requirement, to establish whether a tribunal may be considered "independent" for the purposes of Article 6.1, factors that must be taken into account include the manner of appointment of its members and their term of office, the existence of safeguards against outside pressures and the question whether it presents an appearance of independence *inter alia.*[188] Moreover, this requirement covers not just its autonomy of other powers of the State, the Executive or the Parliament,[189] but also of the parties. In this regard, in *Sramek v. Austria*, the ECHR held that in cases where a tribunal's members include a person who is in a subordinate position, vis-à-vis one of the parties, litigants may entertain a legitimate doubt about that person's independence and in that regard trigger a violation of this right.[190] This is the type of application in an all-or-nothing fashion I tried to identify with this variable.

In turn, impartiality denotes the absence of prejudice or bias on the part of the judge.[191] Impartiality is required from two points of view. First, the tribunal must be subjectively free of personal prejudice or bias. Secondly, a tribunal must offer sufficient guarantees to exclude any legitimate doubt of bias. This is what the ECHR calls the objective test. Under this perspective, it must be determined whether there are ascertainable facts, which may raise doubts as to the court's impartiality. In this respect, even appearances may be of a certain importance.[192] What is key under this approach is whether parties' fears regarding the judge's impartiality can be held to be objectively justified or not.[193] Notwithstanding, as pointed out before, that there are cases where this analysis is made clearly from the perspective of the particular circumstances (and in that regard from the flexible model approach), there are other cases where it is made from a stricter normative language, and because of that I coded those as fitting the checklist model. For example, in the case of *Micallef v. Malta*, the petitioner in a civil injunction case alleged that the Court of Appeal's three-judge panel that decided her case lacked impartiality since it was presided by the Chief Justice, who was the defendant attorney's uncle. In this

46 (referring to the arguments of the First section); ECHR, Case of Kenedi v. Hungary, no. 31475/05, Judgment of 26 May 2009, par. 37–39; ECHR, Martins Castro et Alves Correia de Castro v. Portugal, no 33729/06, Judgment 10 June 2008, par. 40; ECHR, Case of Turek v. Slovakia, no. 57986/00, Judgment of 14 February 2006, par. 98–99.

[188] ECHR, Case of Kleyn and Others v. The Netherlands, nos. 39343/98, 39651/98, 43147/98 and 46664/99, Judgment of 6 May 2003, par. 190.

[189] See, e.g.: ECHR, Case of Sovtransavto Holding v. Ukraine, no. 48553/99, Judgment of 25 July 2002, par. 80.

[190] ECHR, Case of Sramek v. Austria, no. 8790/79, Judgment of 22 October 1984.

[191] Hazelhorst (2017), p. 155.

[192] ECHR, Case of Kleyn and Others v. The Netherlands, nos. 39343/98, 39651/98, 43147/98 and 46,664/99, Judgment of 6 May 2003, par. 191.

[193] ECHR, Case of Micallef v. Malta, no. 17056/06, Judgment of 15 October 2009, par. 97; ECHR, Case of Driza v. Albania, no. 33771/02, Judgment of 13 November 2007, par. 80.

case, the Court found that, although there was no sufficient evidence on personal bias, it failed the objective test since the domestic legislation did not provided a safeguard mechanism for such circumstances and the close family ties between the opposing party's advocate and the Chief Justice sufficed to objectively justify fears that the presiding judge lacked impartiality.[194] In turn, in *Buscemi v. Italy*, the ECHR found a violation of the right to an impartial tribunal in a case where the court that heard the case was presided over by a person with whom the petitioner had an argument in the press. In this regard, it held "...that the judicial authorities are required to exercise maximum discretion with regard to the cases with which they deal in order to preserve their image as impartial judges. That discretion should dissuade them from making use of the press, even when provoked. It is the higher demands of justice and the elevated nature of judicial office which impose that duty....the fact that the President of the court publicly used expressions which implied that he had already formed an unfavourable view of the applicant's case ...objectively justify the applicant's fears as to his impartiality."[195] Moreover, this appearance doctrine has been applied in several cases against Belgium, France and Luxembourg in which petitioners allege a violation of the impartiality requirement by the participation of a government representative in the deliberations of the *Conseil d'Etat.*[196]

Although the elements of independence and impartiality differ from each other, they are closely linked, and in consequence, usually the ECHR decides both issues together.[197] I have applied the strict rule variable as well in such circumstances. In *Brudnicka and Others v. Poland*, the ECHR decided whether the Maritime Chambers, an administrative body in charge of incidents and accidents at the sea, provided enough guarantees to be considered an independent and impartial body since there was no further appeal or review of its decisions. The ECHR held that "[G]iven that the members of the maritime chambers are appointed and removed from office by the Minister of Justice in agreement with the Minister of Transport and Maritime Affairs, they cannot be regarded as irremovable, and they are in a subordinate position vis-à-vis the Ministers. Accordingly, the maritime chambers, as they exist in Polish law, cannot be regarded as impartial tribunals capable of ensuring compliance with the requirement of "fairness" laid down by Article 6 of the Convention. In the Court's view, the applicants were entitled to entertain objective doubts as to their independence and impartiality."[198]

---

194 ECHR, Case of Micallef v. Malta, no. 17056/06, Judgment of 15 October 2009, par. 101–103.

195 ECHR, Case of Buscemi v. Italy, no. 29569/95, Judgment of 16 September 1999, par. 64, 67–68.

196 ECHR, Case of Procola v. Luxembourg, no. 14570/89, Judgment of 28 September 1995, par. 44, 45; ECHR, Case of Kress v. France, no. 39594/98, Judgment of 7 June 2001, par. 81–85; ECHR, Case of Martinie v. France, no. 58675/00, Judgment of 12 April 2006, par. 53–55; ECHR, Case of Tedesco v. France, no 11950/02, Judgment of 10 May 2007, par. 63–65.

197 ECHR, Case of Kleyn and Others v. The Netherlands, nos. 39343/98, 39651/98, 43147/98 and 46664/99, Judgment of 6 May 2003, par. 192.

198 ECHR, Case of Brudnicka and Others v. Poland, no. 54723/00, Judgment of 03 March 2005, par. 41. See, also: ECHR, Case of Langborger v. Sweden, no. 11179/84, Judgment of 22 June 1989, par.

Less frequent but no less important are cases concerning *res iudicata* and the judicial determination of a case, and the enforcement of such decisions. In *Driza v. Albania*, the ECHR reaffirms its case law on the matter establishing that the principle of legal certainty requires that where the courts have finally determined an issue, their ruling should not be called into question. In this regard, powers of review by higher courts should be exercised to correct judicial errors and miscarriages of justice, but not to carry out a fresh examination. In this case, by granting request for leave to seek a review of a final judgment and by allowing the introduction of parallel sets of proceedings, the Supreme Court set at naught an entire judicial process, which had ended in a final and enforceable judicial decision, which was thus *res judicata*.[199] Regarding the enforcement of judicial decisions, in *Immobiliarie Saffi v. Italy*, the ECHR held that even although States may, in exceptional circumstances, intervene in enforcement proceedings, the consequence of such intervention should not be that execution is prevented, invalidated or unduly delayed, or still less that the substance of the decision is undermined.[200]

In 54 cases I have identified that the court used the strict minimum variable. Most of these cases concern the right to a public hearing. As described before, even though in many of these cases the ECHR analyze the circumstances and the nature of the proceeding to decide, there are many cases where it uses a stricter interpretation. In this regard, from the early case law on article 6.1 the ECHR had established that this right is a basic requirement that must be afforded in civil proceedings where the article 6.1 applies. The lack of a hearing can only be cured if a subsequent procedure of full review provides such opportunity.[201] The only permitted exceptions to this general rule are those provided by the second sentence of the clause,[202] or by a waiver of the right.[203] In the already mentioned case of *Eisenstecken v. Austria,*

32–35; ECHR, Case of McGonell v. The United Kingdom, no. 28488/95, Judgment of 8 February 2000, par. 52–57.

[199]ECHR, Case of Driza v. Albania, no. 33771/02, Judgment of 13 November 2007, par. 63–70. See, also: ECHR, Case of Brumărescu v. Romania, no. 28342/95, Judgment of 28 October 1999, par. 62.

[200]ECHR, Case of Immobiliare Saffi v. Italy, no. 22774/93, Judgment of 28 July 1999, par. 74. Similar reasoning may be found in: ECHR, Case of Okyay and Others v. Turkey, no. 36220/97, Judgment of 12 July 2005, par. 72–74.

[201]ECHR, Case of Malhous v. the Czech Republic, no. 33071/96, Judgment of 12 July 2001, par. 62.

[202]Article 6.1.: Judgment shall be pronounced publicly but the press and public may be excluded from all or part of the trial in the interests of morals, public order or national security in a democratic society, where the interests of juveniles or the protection of the private life of the parties so require, or to the extent strictly necessary in the opinion of the court in special circumstances where publicity would prejudice the interests of justice.

[203]ECHR, Case of Le Compte, Van Leuven and De Meyere v. Belgium, no. 6878/75; 7238/75, Judgment of 23 June 1981, par. 59, 60; ECHR, Case of Albert and Le Compte v. Belgium, no. 7299/75; 7496/76, Judgment of 10 February 1983, par. 34, 35; ECHR, Case of H. v. Belgium, no. 8950/80, Judgment of 30 November 1987, par. 54; ECHR, Case De Moor v. Belgium, no. 16997/90, Judgment of 23 June 1994, par. 55, 56.

although part of the reasoning of the ECHR is based on the particular circumstances of the case, it added two points that are important to mention. First, it held that in terms of a valid waiver it is irrelevant whether the petitioner has requested one when the applicable domestic law excludes the holding of such hearings. Second, it reiterates that an applicant is entitled, in principle, to a hearing under article 6.1 unless an admissible exception applies.[204] Based on the last sentence of article 6.1. which states for "special circumstances where publicity would prejudice the interests of justice", the ECHR case law has understood as an exception proceedings concerning exclusively legal or highly technical questions, which may be better decided in private or over purely written material.[205] For example, in *Schuler-Zgraggen v. Switzerland*, the ECHR held that a legal proceeding concerning social security, might be better dealt with by a private and written procedure. The court considered the legal issue to be a highly technical matter, and given its medical nature, a public proceeding may deter future applicants. Moreover, the ECHR recognized that in this sphere the national authorities should have regard to the demands of efficiency and economy.[206]

The strict minimum variable is quite important for the right to a tribunal established by law. From the 14 cases I found of such cases where one of the two models were identified, in eight the Court decided the case using this approach. Two questions arise in this regard. First, what can be considered a "tribunal," and second, what does it mean that a tribunal must be "established by law."

Considering the first of these questions, the ECHR had held that even if a tribunal is not considered as such under domestic law, it may be considered one, in the substantive sense, as long its function is to determine matters within its competence on the basis of rules of law, following proceedings conducted in a prescribed manner.[207] In cases of professional associations deciding over the right to practice, such as *H. v. Belgium*, the ECHR had held that even though such organs usually have many functions –administrative, regulatory, adjudicative, advisory and disciplinary –, that cannot in itself preclude an institution from being a "tribunal."[208] Then, by identifying an organ as a tribunal with full jurisdiction to decide over all matters of facts and law, it must satisfy the requirements of article 6.1. such as independence of the executive and of the parties to the case, duration of its members' term of office, guarantees afforded by its procedure, and others appearing in the text of Article

[204] ECHR, Case of Eisenstecken v. Austria, no. 29477/95, Judgment of 3 October 2000, par. 34. Similar approach may be found in: ECHR, Case of Göç v. Turkey, no. 36590/97, Judgment of 11 July 2002, par. 47–51.

[205] ECHR, Case of Jurisic and Collegium Mehrerau v. Austria, no. 62539/00, Judgment of 27 July 2006, par. 65–67; ECHR, Case of Koottummel v. Austria, no. 49616/06, Judgment of 10 December 2009, par. 19, 20; ECHR, Case of Nikolova and Vandova v. Bulgaria, no. 20688/04, Judgment of 17 December 2013, par. 69, 70.

[206] ECHR, Case of Schuler-Zgraggen v. Switzerland, no. 14518/89, Judgment of 24 June 1993, par. 58, 59.

[207] ECHR, Case of Sramek v. Austria, no. 8790/79, Judgment of 22 October 1984, par. 36.

[208] ECHR, Case of H. v. Belgium, no. 8950/80, Judgment of 30 November 1987, par. 50.

6.1.[209] In *Chevrol v. France*, a medical a doctor qualified in Algeria applied for registration to practice medicine in France. She was refused several times by the local and national medical association, and by the Minister for Health, because although she was French, she did not have a French medical qualification. She applied to the *Conseil d'Etat* for judicial review against the decision of the national medical association. The petitioner relied on a treaty called the "Evian Accords", which provided for reciprocal validation of academic diplomas and qualifications. However, the *Conseil d'Etat* considered it could not decide on this treaty provisions since, as expressed by the Legal Affairs Department of the Ministry of Foreign Affairs which submitted its observations by request, the reciprocity requirement had not been satisfied.[210] This opinion given by the government representative was not open to challenge by the applicant, because she was not given the opportunity to do so and her documentary evidence was not even considered by the *Conseil d'Etat.* The ECHR held that this organ considered itself to be bound by the opinion of the government representative, thereby voluntarily depriving itself of the power to examine and take into account factual evidence that could have been crucial for the practical resolution of the dispute before it. In consequence, the applicant could not be considered to have had access to a tribunal with sufficient jurisdiction to examine all the factual and legal issues relevant to the determination of the dispute.[211]

Regarding the second of these questions, the ECHR had held that the expression "established by law" reflects a principle of the rule of law. "Law", for the purposes of article 6.1 comprises not only legislation in its technical sense, but also any other provision of domestic law which, if breached, would render the participation of one or more judges in the examination of a case irregular. Thus, the entire phrase covers not only the legal basis for the very existence of a "tribunal" but also compliance by the tribunal with the particular rules that govern it. In principle, therefore, a violation by a tribunal of domestic legal provisions relating to the establishment and competence of judicial organs gives rise to a violation of Article 6.1.[212]

In some cases, the ECHR has interpreted the requirement of having access to the case materials as a strict minimum requirement provided by article 6.1. For example, in *Schuler-Zgraggen v. Switzerland*, besides the allegation of a lack of a hearing, the

---

[209] ECHR, Case of Le Compte, Van Leuven, and De Meyere v. Belgium, no. 6878/75; 7238/75, Judgement of 23 June 1981, par. 55; ECHR, Case of Vasilescu v. Romania, 53/1997/837/1043, Judgment of 22 May 1998, par. 41; ECHR, Case of Chevrol v. France, no. 49636/99, Judgment of 13 February 2003, par. 76,77; ECHR, Case of Fedotova v. Russia, no. 73225/01, Judgment of 13 April 2006, par. 38, 43; ECHR, Case of Woś v. Poland, no. 22860/02, Judgment of 08 June 2006, par. 94; ECHR, Case of Savino and Other v. Italy, nos 17214/05, 20329/05, 42113/04, Judgment of 28 April 2009, par. 94.

[210] ECHR, Case of Chevrol v. France, no. 49636/99, Judgment of 13 February 2003, par. 10–19.

[211] ECHR, Case of Chevrol v. France, no. 49636/99, Judgment of 13 February 2003, par. 82, 83.

[212] ECHR, Case of DMD Group, a.s. v. Slovakia, no. 19334/03, Judgment of 5 October 2010, par. 58–61; ECHR, Case of Oleksandr Volkov v. Ukraine, no. 21722/11, Judgment of 9 January 2013, par. 150–156.

petitioner argued that he did not have access to the file at the Appeal Board that decided his cases concerning a medical social security benefit. The ECHR found that it was true that he did not have a detailed picture of the particulars supplied to the Board, but it did not find a violation to article 6 since this lack of access was remedied at the Federal Insurance Court.[213] Moreover, and in connection with the right to an adversarial proceeding, the ECHR had held that each party to a trial, no matter if it is a criminal or civil legal procedure, must have the opportunity to have knowledge of and comment on all evidence adduced or observations filed with a view to influencing the court's decision.[214]

I have applied much less the other codes I have used as identifiers of the checklist model (some of them not even in a single case in the ECHR case law). In this regard, I have identified that the ECHR decided on a procedural element based purely on considerations that the legal procedure as provided by regulation is the one that is due.

Most of these cases concerns admissibility and assessment of evidence. In *García Ruiz v. Spain*, a civil matter related to the enforcement of a contract of legal services, the petitioner contended that the appeals court dismissed his claim and upheld the first instance decision without giving proper consideration to his argument about the assessment of the evidence. The ECHR dismissed the claim and held that notwithstanding that article 6 guarantees the right to a fair hearing, "...it does not lay down any rules on the admissibility of evidence or the way it should be assessed, which are therefore primarily matters for regulation by national law and the national courts."[215] I found that this type of argument has a dual character. First, it may be considered part of the flexible approach since it recognizes that article 6.1. does not provide a strict catalog of procedural guarantees pertaining to the right to a fair hearing. Nevertheless, at the same time, it does conceive that this matter, which is closely connected to the right to a hearing and the right of defense, is a matter of legislation. That is why I coded this issue under this variable of the checklist approach. The domestic rules of evidence will be the legal procedure that is due under the right to a fair trial at least in terms of admissibility and assessment of evidence.

Similar reasoning may be found regarding domestic Legal Aid schemes. It is true that the case law on these matters refers to a less strict reading of the civil limb of article 6 on this particular procedural protection, by expressing that there is no obligation to provide legal aid on every civil case (which is why I have coded it as part of the flexible model). However, at the same time, the ECHR had expressed that as long as a domestic Legal Aid scheme provides enough protection from

---

[213] ECHR, Case of Schuler-Zgraggen v. Switzerland, no. 14518/89, Judgment of 24 June 1993, par. 47, 52.

[214] ECHR, Case of Pellegrini v. Italy, no. 30882/96, Judgment of 20 July 2001, par. 44; ECHR, Göç v. Turkey, no. 36590/97, Judgment of 11 July 2002, par. 55; ECHR, Case of Kök v. Turkey, no 1855/02, Judgment of 19 October 2006, par. 52–54; ECHR, Case of Augusto v. France, no 71665/01, Judgment of 11 January 2007, par. 50–52.

[215] ECHR, Case of García Ruiz v. Spain, no. 30544/96, Judgment of 21 January 1999, par. 11–15,28.

arbitrariness, then the provision of this procedural guarantee depends largely on the State's domestic regulation.[216] This is the reason why I think this is part of the checklist approach as well.

Finally, regarding procedural bars, such as time limits on the admissibility of appeals, the ECHR had held that these rules are designed to ensure the proper administration of justice, and legal certainty in particular. Therefore, litigants should normally expect those rules to be applied. How to apply such rules is a matter primarily for local courts. The ECHR will only verify whether the interpretation of such procedural rules is compatible with the Convention.[217]

To conclude this section, is important to note that in my set list there are no cases in which the ECHR applied the specific provisions of article 6.2 and 6.3 to civil cases. I think this is a consequence of the ECHR's continuous engagement in defining what is civil and what it is not in its case law, which has produced a clear division as well on the requirements of the general clause in comparison with the specific provisions on criminal matters of article 6.2 and 6.3. In other words, as long as the Court considers cases to be under the civil limb of article 6, the guarantees to be applied would be those of the general clause and not of the criminal provisions or, at least, not with the same normative justification. There is one case however, where the ECHR had the opportunity to do so (the only one in which I have applied this code). In *Albert and Le Compte v. Belgium*, a disciplinary procedure held by a professional association against the petitioner that the court exceptionally did not consider as criminal in nature since the right at issue was the right to continue to exercise the medical profession. The petitioner alleged a violation of his right to a fair trial under paragraph 2 and sub-paragraphs (a), (b) and (d) of paragraph 3, which are criminal in nature. However, the Court said that the principles enshrined therein were, for the purpose of this decision, already contained in the notion of a fair trial as embodied in paragraph 1 (since he alleged a lack of impartiality and publicity) and therefore took these principles into account to decide the case under article 6.1's civil limb.[218]

References

Alston P, Goodman R (2013) International human rights. The successor to international human rights in context: law, politics and morals. Oxford University Press, Oxford

---

[216] ECHR, Case of Del Sol v. France, no. 46800/99, Judgment of 26 February 2002, par. 20–26.

[217] ECHR, Case of Cañete de Goñi v. Spain, no. 55782/00, Judgment of 15 October 2002, par. 36; ECHR, Case of Běleš and Others v. The Czech Republic, no. 47273/99, Judgment of 12 November 2002, par. 60; ECHR, Case of Zvolský and Zvolská v. the Czech Republic, no. 46129/99, Judgment of 12 November 2002, par. 46.

[218] ECHR, Case of Albert and Le Compte v. Belgium, no. 7299/75; 7496/76, Judgement of 10 February 1983, par. 28, 30.

Council of Europe (2004) Explanatory report to protocol no. 14 to the Convention for the Protection of Human Rights and Fundamental Freedoms, amending the control system of the Convention. Available at: https://www.coe.int/en/web/conventions/full-list/-/conventions/treaty/194

Cross T (2010) Is there a "civil right" under article 6? Ten principles for public lawyers. Judicial Rev 15(4):366–376

Dworkin R (1967) The model of rules. Univ Chi Law Rev 35:14–46

Dworkin R (1977) Taking rights seriously. Harvard University Press, Cambridge

European Court of Human Rights (2013a) Filtering Section speeds up processing of cases from highest case-count countries. Available at: https://www.echr.coe.int/Documents/Filtering_Section_ENG.pdf

European Court of Human Rights (2013b) Guide on Article 6 of the European Convention on Human Rights. Right to a fair trial (Civil limb). Available at: https://www.echr.coe.int/documents/guide_art_6_eng.pdf

European Court of Human Rights (2019) The ECHR in facts & figures 2018. Available at: https://echr.coe.int/Pages/home.aspx?p=reports/factsfigures&c=

Francioni F (2017) The rights of access to justice under customary international law. In: Francioni F (ed) Access to justice as a human right. Oxford University Press, Oxford, pp 1–55

Galič A (2017) The inconsistency of case law and the right to a fair trial. In: Uzelac A, van Rhee C (eds) Revisiting procedural human rights. Fundamentals of civil procedure and the changing face of civil justice. Intersentia, Cambridge, pp 17–51

Goldman R (2009) History and action: the inter-American human rights system and the role of the inter-American commission on human rights. Human Rights Q 31(4):856–887

Hazelhorst M (2017) Free movement of civil judgments in the European Union and the right to a fair trial. The Hague, T.M.C. Asser Press

Scheinin M (2007) Access to justice before international human rights bodies: reflections on the practice of the UN human rights committee and the European court of human rights. In: Francioni F (ed) Access to justice as a human right. Oxford University Press, Oxford, pp 135–152

Chapter 8
A Brief Comparison Between Both Regional Systems

8.1 Identifying Some Commonalities and Differences Between Both Regional Systems

Prior to analyzing the differences I have found between the regional systems, it is good to notice that there also many similarities between them. In both tribunals, the main element of the right to a fair trial for non-criminal matters is the right to a court. This is relevant because it shows an important characteristic of the right to a fair trial in civil or non-criminal matters.[1]

If the focus is on the right to a court, both tribunals have established that what matters is that the access to a court should be not purely theoretical but effective in practice. In both systems, a limitation of this right may come from fact or through legislation. This criterion of effectiveness is central in both international courts although they have applied the same concept quite differently. As stated, in most cases I have studied of the Inter-American regional system, the IACHR confuses the right to an effective remedy with the right to a fair trial. By the application in conjunction of articles 8 and 25, in the IACHR case law, effectiveness is a component of the right to a fair trial, in the sense that a lack of effective remedy is a violation of article 8, and, at the same time, a violation of article 25.[2] On the contrary, in the ECHR, although there are a few cases where the right to an effective remedy has been analyzed under the right to a fair trial, in general terms, there is clear distinction between right to an effective remedy and the effectiveness approach in deciding on the right to a court. In this regard, in civil matters, the right to a fair trial under article 6.1 is *lex specialis* in relation to Article 13. What could be said is that while, in the ECHR, effectiveness is a more useful methodology to decide whether a

[1] This is a formula developed by the European Courts of Human Rights. See: ECHR, Case of Steel and Morris v. The United Kingdom, no. 68416/01, Judgment of 15 February 2005, par. 59.
[2] In this sense, see: Medina (2016), p. 355.

R. Lillo Lobos, *Understanding Due Process in Non-Criminal Matters*, Ius Gentium: Comparative Perspectives on Law and Justice 97,
https://doi.org/10.1007/978-3-030-95534-2_8

dimension of due process or a specific procedural element is required or not in a given case, in the IACHR it is a component by itself which is analyzed as a whole.

In terms of permissible restrictions on the right to a court, both systems use the proportionality test between the aims pursued and the means used. Recall the case of *Mémoli v. Argentina*, the only case between private individuals in my setlist for the IACHR. Here this court held that court fees or other types of monetary obligations imposed on litigants do not constitute per se an obstruction of access to justice. As said, it recognize that the right of access may be subject to limitations by the State as long as it keeps proportionality between means and objectives.[3] This is a similar approach to the one followed by the ECHR in cases like *Kreuz v. Poland*, where it held that the requirement to pay fees to civil courts could not be regarded as a restriction that is incompatible per se with article 6.1.[4]

The cases on the length of proceedings are similar in general terms. In both regional systems, the most frequent approach is a concrete analysis based on the circumstances of the cases under the same factors. Nevertheless, in both regional systems there are reasonable duration cases decided by a stricter approach that is identified with the checklist approach. Let me recall in this regard, the case of *Sawhoyamaxa Indigenous Community v. Paraguay*, where the IACHR found that the duration of the proceeding was considered "unreasonable" since it lasted two years more than the previous case of *Yakye Axa Indigenous Community v. Paraguay*, where it was found that the period exceeded the reasonable standard.[5] Similarly, the ECHR had applied similar reasoning in cases where there are systemic problems of delay in the respondent State. As in many cases against Italy, in *Di Mauro v. Italy*, the ECHR decided there was a violation of article 6.1 since delay in the Italian legal system was an ongoing situation, which by itself is a practice that is incompatible with the Convention.[6] While I classified these cases as an application of the variable of the checklist, at this point it is important to specify that in truth, in these cases the international courts do not interpret a requirement of due process but apply their own case law as a rule. Thus, even though I decided to keep them as such basically to explain that there are cases in which these courts use different approaches to decide

[3]I/A Court H.R., Case of Mémoli v Argentina, Preliminary Objections, Merits, Reparations and Costs. Judgment of August 22, 2013. Series C No. 265, par. 193.

[4]ECHR, Case of Kreuz v. Poland, no. 28249/95, 19 June 2001, par. 60, 61. See also: ECHR, Case of Weissman and Others v. Romania, no. 63945/00, Judgment of 24 May 2006, par. 34–37; ECHR, Case of Apostol v. Georgia, no. 40765/02, Judgment of 28 November 2006, par. 59; ECHR, Case of Bakan v. Turkey, no. 50939/99, Judgment of 12 June 2007, par. 67, 68; ECHR, Case of Stankov v. Bulgaria, no. 68490/01, Judgment of 12 July 2007, par. 51, 52; ECHR, Case of Anakomba Yula v. Belgium, no. 45413/07, Judgment of 10 March 2009, par. 32; ECHR, Georgel and Georgeta v. Stoicescu v. Romania, no. 9718/03, Judgment of 26 July 2011, par. 69.

[5]I/A Court H.R., Case of the Yakye Axa Indigenous Community v. Paraguay. Merits, Reparations and Costs. Judgment of June 17, 2005. Series C No. 125, par. 65; I/A Court H.R., Case of the Sawhoyamaxa Indigenous Community v. Paraguay. Merits, Reparations and Costs. Judgment of March 29, 2006. Series C No. 146, par. 95.

[6]ECHR, Di Mauro v. Italy, no. 34256/96, Judgment of 28 July 1999, par. 23.

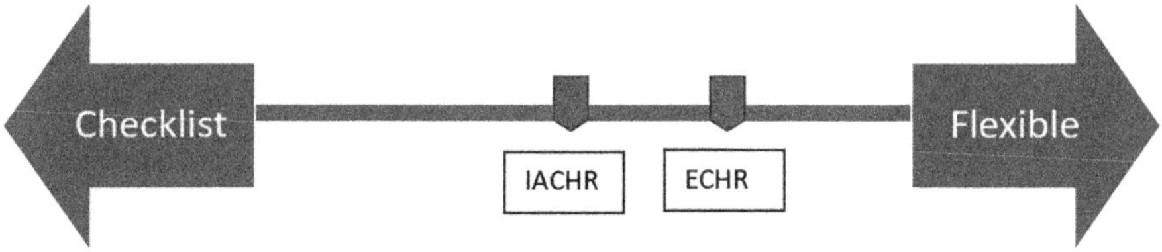

Fig. 8.1 IACHR and ECHR case law between both models

in these matters, it is good to notice they are not a "pure" checklist expression but what we might call a "second level" checklist.

Although both case laws comprise mostly what I have classified as administrative cases, in the ECHR there is a clear division between the civil and criminal limbs of the due process clause. On the other hand, in the IACHR case law the line between administrative or punitive or civil nature is often blurred, a variable that might explain the expansive approach to which I referred before. Provided that a right might be affected by a legal procedure, and not necessarily determined, article 8 applies. What is more, it not only applies but probably applies in full. Although there are some thematic reports calling for a degree of compatibility between article 8.2 guarantees over non-criminal matters, the IACHR case law just like other reports, applied expressly 8.2 guarantees (e.g. *Ivcher Bronstein v. Peru*). With a clear distinction between each field, on the other hand, the ECHR had expressly said that 6.1 gives more latitude on civil matters since many 6.2 or 6.3 guarantees are not mentioned in the general clause, they are not a strict minimum in civil matters.

The main difference is that in the IACHR case law the checklist approach is commonly used to decide over a right to a fair trial dimension or to decide whether a procedural element was or was not a requirement. In fact, in half of the cases the IACHR uses at least one of the checklist model variables. The Court may do so by expressly applying an 8.2 guarantee to non-criminal matters, or considering a requirement as a strict minimum, or interpreting the provision as a legal rule calling for a binary application. That is why I commented that the IACHR case law can be located between both models but probably closer to the checklist approach than the ECHR. By comparison, in the latter case, the flexible approach is much more frequent. As said, in most cases the ECHR decided if a procedural guarantee is required or a dimension of the right to a fair trial infringed by looking at the particular circumstance of the case, deciding if it was necessary to effectively pursue the case for the parties or according to the nature of the particular legal procedure. The checklist approach under ECHR case law is much more exceptional and circumscribed to specific topics. Some examples are cases with particular contexts (such as the context of systemic delay in the length of the proceeding), concerning particular elements such as the objective test on impartiality and independence, or regarding specific guarantees such as the right to a hearing (which is also frequently decided using the flexible approach variable of the nature of the proceeding). In sum, I have located the ECHR case law closer to the flexible ideal type (Fig. 8.1).

8.2 Possible Explanations and Future Research Questions

There may be several explanations of the differences described in the previous section. While it is not my main purpose in this book to find the right one, at least I may advance some possible explanations for future research.

A first plausible reason refers to the type of cases filed in the system. In this regard, as described by Alston, although normative provisions and structure might seem similar between both regional arrangements, the conditions under which they developed were radically different. For example, while in Europe authoritarian governments have been rare and short lived, in Latin America, they have been common, and in general, democracy is much more fragile.[7] Consequently, extra judicial killings, disappearances, torture, and other related gross human rights violations have been a constant feature in the Inter-American system, and especially during its first decades. This type of violation might occur also in the ECHR, but in general the type of case filed are much more diverse. Of course, this might be a result of the direct access that victims have to the ECHR in opposition to the Inter-American system where the Inter-American Commission serves as an important filter. While such differences in terms of diversity of cases are undeniable, with the consolidation and strengthening of democracy in Latin America and the incorporation of many former communist States to the Council of Europe, at least in terms of political regimes, both regional systems are more alike than before.[8]

The right to a fair trial is quite relevant in both case laws. Most decisions concern this right, but it might be true that in the Inter-American System there are still too few cases on non-criminal matters to develop a more robust conceptualization of its requirements. As already said, I have found only nineteen cases, and only one of these between private individuals concerning a civil claim for libel. All the others were administrative proceedings related to the right of access to information, asylum and electoral proceedings, or cases concerning the protection of property rights. Therefore, since most cases concern gross human violations, it might be natural that most of the development is in the criminal arena, with an expansion of such protections to other areas. The petitions filed to the ECHR on the article 6 civil limb, on the other hand, differ greatly from one another in terms of the main legal issues raised by the case (Fig. 8.2).

Another possible explanation, and of course closely connected to the first one, is the diversity of countries that are members States of each regional system. In the Inter-American regional system, most countries share the same legal traditions of Continental Law. While it is true that the ICHR has jurisdiction over some countries pertaining to the Common Law—such Barbados and Trinidad and Tobago—, they account for only a few cases on the entire list of its decisions[9] and none in my setlist

[7] Alston and Goodman (2013), p. 980.

[8] Alston and Goodman (2013), p. 986.

[9] See: I/A Court H.R., Case of Boyce et al. v. Barbados. Preliminary Objection, Merits, Reparations and Costs. Judgment of November 20, 2007. Series C No. 169; I/A Court H.R., Case of Da Costa

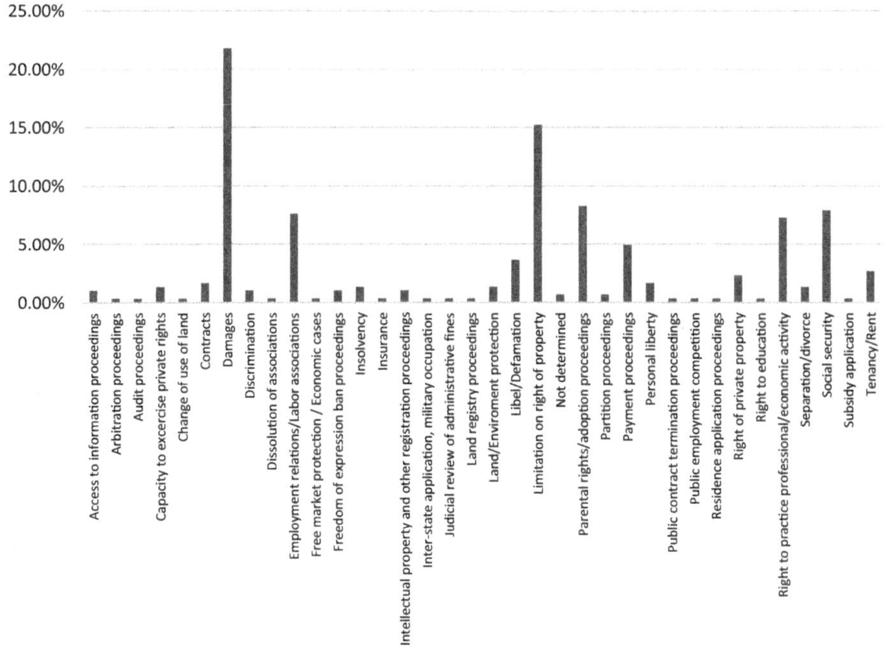

Fig. 8.2 Main legal issue of the article 6 civil limb petitions at the ECHR

according to my operational definition of civil or non-criminal cases. It would be interesting to analyze why these countries occupy such a minor place at the IACHR case law. By comparison, the European system is much more diverse in both regards. The ECHR have had to deal with strong and weak democracies and be flexible enough to encompass countries pertaining to different legal traditions, which might reflect different conceptions on how a civil procedure must be, the law should be interpreted, the judicial hierarchy organized, and many other relevant factors.[10] Although approximately 9% of the cases concern Common Law countries, which might seem low, it is important to note that most of these cases concern the United Kingdom. This country alone, as we recall section 3 occupies the third place in terms of the individual countries, so it has an important place at the ECHR case law on the article 6 civil limb. In fact, in this country, the case law of the ECHR has had an enormous impact on its judicial system in general and in its legal procedure in

Cadogan v. Barbados. Preliminary Objections, Merits, Reparations, and Costs. Judgment of September 24, 2009. Series C No. 204; I/A Court H.R., Case of Caesar v. Trinidad and Tobago. Merits, Reparations and Costs. Judgment of March 11, 2005. Series C No. 123; I/A Court H.R., Case of Hilaire, Constantine and Benjamin et al. v. Trinidad and Tobago. Merits, Reparations and Costs. Judgment of June 21, 2002. Series C No. 94.

[10]On the differences on the character of the governments involved in both systems: Alston and Goodman (2013), p. 986. Regarding the differences of the legal procedures between legal traditions, see: Millar (1952); Merryman and Pérez-Perdomo (2007).

particular.[11] In this regard the enactment of the Human Rights Act of 1998, which enhances the domestic enforceability of the European Convention,[12] was a key event, as well as the replacement of the House of Lords in 2009 by a new Supreme Court of the United Kingdom. Neil Andrews has described the latter as the most important contribution of the European Convention to the domestic law of Great Britain.[13]

If much of the concept of the right to a fair trial comes from the criminal law arena, and in general its development in civil matters grows in the shadow of criminal law concerns, it is possible that this influence is much higher in Latin America than Europe. Several factors might have caused this difference, but the type of cases and abuses that both courts have had to deal with, and the effort of the ECHR to provide content to the article 6 civil limb, are two explanations that would repay future research. I would include also the question of who the judges are in both courts. Factors such as their nationality, where they have studied their basic law and postgraduate degrees, which conceptions of the law and its role they have as judges, former political, judicial or legal careers, and why they were appointed, might also help to explain these differences.[14]

Related to diversity, another factor, which might explain the differences between the regional courts, is the explicit and broader use of the *margin of appreciation* doctrine by the ECHR. According to Legg, this doctrine is a judicial practice of assigning weight to the respondent State's reasoning in a case on the basis of one or more external factors.[15] In the context of the IACHR, margin of appreciation is used much less frequently and not explicitly, since deference applies prominently in cases where there is not an obvious violation of the relevant provision.[16] For this reason, some might think that this is why there are different approaches in how the regional courts have decided cases on these matters. However, as Legg himself recognizes, legal procedure and reasonable duration are areas where the court usually has more expertise because of its own judges' background and therefore, areas in which there is more scrutiny than deference.[17] That is why in such areas instead of margin of appreciation the court, in fact both regional courts, have decided on proportionality grounds. As a consequence, I think that the interplay between margin of appreciation and proportionality—understood heuristically to illustrate the assessment of different reasons and used to decide cases on rights' limitations[18]—is a factor that might

[11] See, e.g.: Andrews (2013).

[12] Hickman (2010), pp. 1–2.

[13] Andrews (2013), p. 4.

[14] The research of Erik Voeten is enlightening in this regard. See, especially: Voeten (2007), pp. 669–701; Voeten (2008), pp. 417–433.

[15] Legg (2012), p. 15.

[16] Legg (2012), p. 31.

[17] Legg (2012), pp. 167–174.

[18] Legg (2012), pp. 192–196.

explain better the similarities than the differences between them, at least regarding the right to a fair trial in non-criminal matters.

Finally, it is possible that in the future these differences between regional systems will diminish, as those between national countries. Indeed, some decades ago scholars in comparative law began to talk about the convergence of legal systems.[19] Globalization has led to a convergence even among countries or systems with different legal traditions, through the dissemination of the concept of rule of law and the requirements entailed by this basic principle. This is true in Latin America[20] and in Europe. For example, the British civil procedure was reformed by the Civil Procedure Rule of 1999, which was designed with article 6 of the European Convention and the jurisprudence of the European Court of Human Rights in mind.[21] At the same time, for Jacob, this reform led to its civil procedure approximating those of Continental Law countries and moving away from the legal proceedings of other Common Law countries like the United States. I fact, it was intended to take a significant step away from the so-called 'adversarial' model by curtailing the power of parties, strengthening the authority of courts to manage cases, and increasing the role of written materials. This was a process that, according to Jacob, came to complete a division path that began with the total obsolescence of juries from civil cases (which in turn started by the middle of the nineteenth century when they were made optional).[22]

We are left to reflect on the implications of the different conceptions on the right to a fair trial in civil matters and on the question of how to harmonize its requirements with those of the access to justice movement. According to the latter, it is important to keep proceedings simple and effective in order to enable people's access to justice. Therefore, whether to follow a stricter approach close to the checklist model, or one closer to the flexible ideal, is a critical question.

References

Alston P, Goodman R (2013) International human rights. The successor to international human rights in context: law, politics and morals. Oxford University Press, Oxford

Andrews N (2013) No longer an island: European influence on English civil procedure. University of Cambridge Faculty of Law Legal Studies Research Paper Series, Paper N° 40/2013

Hickman T (2010) Public law after the Human Rights Act. Hart Publishing, Oxford

Jacob J (2007) Civil justice in the age of human rights. Ashgate, England

Langer M (2007) Revolution in Latin American criminal procedure: diffusion of legal ideas from the periphery. Am J Comp Law 55:617–676

Legg A (2012) The margin of appreciation in international human rights law. Deference and proportionality. Oxford University Press, Oxford

---

[19] See: Merryman (1981).

[20] Langer (2007), pp. 631–632.

[21] Jacob (2007), p. 38.

[22] Jacob (2007), pp. 42, 43.

Medina C (2016) The American Convention on Human Rights. Crucial rights and their theory and practice, 2nd edn. Intersentia, Cambridge
Merryman J (1981) On the convergence (and divergence) of the Civil Law and the Common Law. Stan J Int Law 17:357–388
Merryman J, Pérez-Perdomo R (2007) The civil law tradition. An Introduction to the Legal Systems of Europe and Latin America, 3rd edn. Stanford University Press, California
Millar R (1952) Civil procedure of the trial court in historical perspective. The Lawbook Exchange, United States
Voeten E (2007) The politics of international judicial appointments: evidence from the European Court of Human Rights. Int Organ 61(4):669–701
Voeten E (2008) The impartiality of international judges: evidence from the European Court of Human Rights. Am Polit Sci Rev 102(4):417–433

Part IV
Procedural Due Process in the American Legal System

Chapter 9
Origins of the Due Process Clause. The Magna Carta Until Its Incorporation in the American Bill of Rights

The due process clause in the American legal system has a long tradition. From its British heritage founded on the Magna Carta, its migration to the colonies and its introduction into the American Bill of Rights, until in incorporation into the States by the 14th Amendment. Much has been written on the due process clause and the various legal institutions derived from it. Probably the most important issue is the distinction between substantive and procedural due process.[1]

While procedural fairness can be traced back to the ancient Greek philosophers, in this chapter I'll focus my analysis on the Magna Carta due process clause. First, because as stated by Sullivan and Massaro, it represents a historically significant codification of centuries of thinking and writing about the embedded idea of procedural justice.[2] But also, because it is an antecedent of the modern conception of the right to a fair trial generally speaking, and specifically in the context of the due process clause in the American Constitution, as indeed for many equivalent provisions in many other fundamental laws from a comparative perspective.[3]

In this chapter, my concern is in the procedural dimension of the due process clause, which by itself present a challenging task. In a famous article, Sanford H. Kadish, says that "It may well be wisdom to recognize that the definition of procedural due process is not susceptible of confinement within a formula."[4]

---

[1] Substantive due process has been defined as the "limitations on the powers of the state and federal legislatures, and of any other legal or administrative body, to deprive a person of life, liberty, or property." Galligan (1996), p. 191.

[2] Sullivan and Massaro (2013), pp. 6–7.

[3] In Latin America, see: Couture (1946), pp. 177–178. While the Magna Carta influenced the American Bill of Rights, in turn, this document influenced the French Declaration of the Rights of Man and Citizens of 1789. Regarding this connection, see: Johnson (1990), pp. 1–45; Sidhu (2017), p. 71. On its influence over the European Convention on Human Rights, see: Ristik (2015), pp. 145–146.

[4] Kadish (1957), pp. 319–363.

R. Lillo Lobos, *Understanding Due Process in Non-Criminal Matters*, Ius Gentium: Comparative Perspectives on Law and Justice 97,
https://doi.org/10.1007/978-3-030-95534-2_9

As I will argue in this chapter, the link between the legal procedure and due process is at the core of the provision. From its inception, the clause of Magna Carta incorporated the protection of fundamental liberties and rights against the arbitrariness of the Crown, as procedural safeguards concerned with the means used by the government in its relationship with their subjects.[5] Notwithstanding, it is important to keep in mind that its requirements over legal procedures, or fair trial, is one of those derivations from a more general clause. This fact adds more complexity to the analysis not just because the line between both dimensions is often blurred,[6] but also because deciding on what is the procedure that is due, the type of substantive right involved is another factor to take into account.

Here I explore the historical origins of procedural due process. While this chapter is not intended to provide a comprehensive and accurate historical account of the due process clause, I believe a basic description of its evolution is necessary because this is a legal institution that depends greatly on many cultural, socio-economic, and other context-related factors.[7] As stated by Schwartz, the significance of the Magna Carta lies in its potential for meaning different things to different ages.[8] This is particularly true with the due process clause. Thus, the idea is not to read the current clause from an originalist mode of interpretation, but rather to describe how the understanding of this clause evolved according to the context in which it was used. This might help to explain many of the ideas embedded in current legal institutions—such as impartiality, the right to counsel, etc.—, which can be identified as expressions of the due process clause. I argue that a study of the origins of this provision in the Magna Carta until its introduction into modern constitutions and other legal instruments will facilitate an understanding of what fair trial requires in non-criminal matters in general, and in civil proceedings in particular.

Although I will narrow the scope of my research to non-criminal matters as defined in the first chapter, part will refer to due process and its criminal justice origins. That is inevitable given that from the beginning the due process clause was an essential tool against the abuse of criminal prosecution and for that reason, most of its development was centered on guarantees for the accused. However, as I will explain, the implications for civil justice were there from the beginning. My intention is to show how it evolved in time until modern conceptions.

[5] Miller (1977), p. 4.

[6] According to Strauss, that occurs in cases related to state failures to provide relief in cases of private wrongdoings cause by impermissible personal interests of the decision maker. See: Strauss (1989), p. 60.

[7] Miller (1977), p. 3.

[8] Schwartz (1977), p. 7.

9.1 Origins of the Due Process Clause and the Link with the Legal Procedure. From the Thirteenth to the Sixteenth Centuries

Due process has its origins in the Magna Carta of 1215. Its clause 39 states in its English version: "No freeman shall be taken and imprisoned, or disseised, or outlawed, or exiled, or in any way destroyed, nor will we go upon him, nor will we send upon him, except by the lawful judgment of his peers and by the law of the land."[9] Its clause 40 adds: "To none will we sell, to none will we deny, to none will we delay right or justice."[10]

A modern interpretation of this clause could arguably be read as a safeguard of personal liberty, by ensuring to every individual that no person shall be punished for a crime except upon conviction before a jury, deprived of property except by due process of law, or denied access to a court. Notwithstanding, historical accounts of the social context in which the original provision was developed had found that its meaning in this initial phase could have been far from that interpretation.[11] In this regard, the original meaning of the due process clause at the initial stages is contested among authors.

According to Jenks, the rights and liberties to be protected under the original meaning of this clause were those of the feudal lords to oppress little men free of royal control.[12] The "equals" of the *judicium parium* in the clause may be only those barons who defeated King John and his progeny in arms, who were struggling later with Henry and Edward.[13] Thus, the idea of the judgment of peers most probably was linked to the right of a noble to be judged by his equals.[14] In this sense, the phrase "the law of the land", for McIlwain, would mean "...merely a protection of the immunity of the great lords from national control, and nothing more than a guarantee of their "liberties" of trying their own feudal dependents in their own courts by the customs of their of their own fiefs."[15]

However, the "law of the land" or *per legem terrae* also had a technical meaning referring to the old proof procedure. In this respect, it provided a sacred right to have court proceedings with judgment and proof (unless captured in the act, in which case

---

[9]Meyer (1977), p. 128.

[10]The Magna Carta versions of 1225 and merges both in a single clause numbered 29. Available at: http://www.nationalarchives.gov.uk/education/resources/magna-carta/magna-carta-1225-westminster/.

[11]Radin (1947), pp. 1060–1061.

[12]Radin (1947), p. 1061.

[13]Radin (1947), p. 1061; Schwartz (1977), p. 6. This is no to say that the Magna Carta was meant only for barons. As stated by Radin, the charter itself makes clear differentiation between the, and the simple freemen (liber homo). See: Radin (1947), p. 1090.

[14]Galligan (1996), p. 171.

[15]McIlwain (1914), p. 28.

conviction and execution came immediately after).[16] As consequence, this phrase in the clause was conceived in opposition to other forms of regulation, such as decrees of the King, and in a broad sense as the customary law of England, the Common Law.[17]

According to this interpretation, the due process clause at this point was a central admonition against arbitrariness from the Crown. In fact, some have argued that this was the primary usage of the provision during the first stage.[18] In particular, it was against King John and his methods of government which were seen among the barons as abusive and favoring who the subservient among them. This government approach ended by dividing them from the rest who were commonly denied the privileges that their social status demanded.[19] Thus the clause entailed the idea that if King John or one of his officers moved to take action against a person, certain procedures had to be followed.[20] That procedure is the proof procedure established for criminal proceedings.[21]

The phrase "process of law" by itself appears for the first time in 1354 in one of the so-called "six statutes," a collection of interpretations of the Magna Carta enacted under Edward III.[22] According to Miller, the reference came from the French phrase of "process de ley" which already appeared in legal documents by that time.[23] This statute stated: "That no man of what Estate or Condition that he be, shall be put out of land or Tenement, nor taken, nor imprisoned, nor disinherited, nor put to death, without being brought in answer by due process of law."[24] The modification, going from "the law of the land" to "due process of law," was made by the King to sanction the use of new forms of procedure in the King's Council. From now one, the charter would not provide a right to a particular process but to the regular given the type of the case according to the law for summoning people to trial and adjudicating their liability.[25] According to Thomson, in the fourteenth century interpretations of the six statutes, due process appears as a justification for petitions protesting the jurisdiction and procedure of special bodies, such as the council or the Court of the Constable and Marshal. These agencies were identified with the Crown and thus distrusted by the Parliament and the lawyers.[26]

---

[16] Meyer (1977), pp. 128–129.

[17] Miller (1977), pp. 5–6.

[18] Thompson (1948), p. 87.

[19] Holt (1985), pp. 129–134.

[20] Orth (2003), p. 9.

[21] Meyer (1977), p. 130.

[22] Thompson (1948), pp. 86–97.

[23] Miller (1977), pp. 3–68, p. 5; Meyer (1977), p. 135.

[24] Available at: http://www.legislation.gov.uk/cy/aep/Edw3/28/3?view=plain.

[25] Wasserman (2004), p. 3.

[26] Thompson (1948), pp. 87–88.

This step during the fourteenth century, going from the law of the land to the due process of law is critical for the future understanding of the clause.[27] According to Easterbrook, while the original clause was a limitation over the King when it came to criminal procedure only—because he could not declare the law without consulting his barons—, the six statues version broadened the scope of application over civil matters and implied a constraint now over the courts and not just over the King.[28] They could not proceed in any important civil or criminal case without service of a writ on the defendant giving him an opportunity to appear, forbidding ex parte procedures.[29]

Keith Jurow, based on a systematic method of interpretation of the several provisions on this statute (and from others without explicit but indirect references to due process), found that the clause required over trial "...that judgment and execution were not to be rendered against any man unless and until he was brought personally before the court by the appropriate writ. To put this somewhat differently, it insists that judgment was not to be given against a man in his absence."[30]

According to Thompson, the citations of the last part of the due process clause in its definitive version ("To none will we sell, to none will we deny, to none will we delay right or justice") was related mainly to some allegations against denial or delay of justice, and against the high rates for the sale of writs. Although it did not have the same level of practical applications as the ideas mentioned above of *per legem terrae* or *per judicium parium*,[31] it does have relevance in the American modern conception of the right to a access to justice, as I will explain in Chap. 10.

At this early stage, the connection between the due process clause and legal proceedings was fundamentally one of jurisdiction. Those who tried to enforce the clause claimed a right to be prosecuted under the Common Law courts and procedures instead of the machinery of the Crown. This led, by the end of the fifteenth century, to a rivalry between Common Law courts and the King's Council or other special courts such as the Court of Chancery (all of which used a procedure different form the common law) ending up with jurisdiction disputes between them.

As explained, it is believed that the original chapter 39 clause only dealt with criminal matters and it is only in the statutes of 1354 that the scope of application was broadened to other type of dispute. Notwithstanding, there are authors who argue that in fact the clause was applied to matters different from criminal prosecution, even before. According to Bebee, by the thirteenth century the line dividing administrative from judicial functions was blurred,[32] so in this context it is difficult to isolate the meaning of the due process clause over civil from criminal matters as from other government functions. However, the provision supported authorities'

[27] Thompson (1948), p. 69.

[28] Wasserman (2004), p. 2.

[29] Easterbrook (1982), pp. 95–96.

[30] Jurow (1975), p. 267.

[31] Thompson (1948), p. 97.

[32] Beebe (1933), p. 7.

interventions of different nature, such as in cases for the protection of properties against unlawful seizures or dispossession by the Crown or its officials. In this regard, the most important civil suit during those times concerned issues of the better right to freehold land or advowson.[33] By the late 1200's one of the most common complaints against officials was the disseizing of the claimants without the proper forms of common law procedures (e.g., the novel disseisin) or in general without a lawful judgment.[34] A case of 1236 exemplifies this type of dispute. When John the Scot, Earl of Chester, was summoned before the King Henry III to answer charges that he had deprived certain heirs of the inheritance, his primary defense was that this type of cases should be held not before the King but according to the common pleas proceedings and therefore it would be an infringement of the Magna Carta.[35]

9.2 The Petition of Rights of 1628. The Work of Sir Edward Coke and the Rise of the Modern Conception of Due Process

During the fifteenth and sixteenth centuries, in spite of being mentioned in statutes and other documents,[36] due process decays in British constitutional disputes.[37] It was not until the seventeenth century[38] when it blossoms again by the increasing role of the English Parliament in the context of its struggles with the Crown that ultimately led to a civil war.[39] In this regard, for the Parliamentary leaders, the due process clause was an instrument of resistance against the Stuart kings and, in the end, an essential tool to forge the structure of the English parliamentary monarchy.[40]

By the second decade of the seventeenth century, procedural due process arguments like the right to be heard under a fair procedure were heard regularly in courts and Parliament.[41] In this regard, the work done by Sir Edward Coke was influential.

[33]Beebe (1933), pp. 58–59.

[34]Thompson (1948), pp. 70–72.

[35]Holt (1985), p. 203.

[36]That's the case of the De Laudibus Legum Angliae of Sir John Fortescue, written during his exile in France between 1468 and 1471, where he refers to the British legal system, in comparison with those of civil law countries as one where its citizens "...are not brought to trial except before the ordinary judges, where they are treated justly according to the law of the land. Nor are they examined or impleaded in respect of their chattels, or possessions, nor arrested for crime of whatever magnitude and enormity, except according to the laws of that land and before the aforesaid judges." Lockwood (1997), pp. 52–53.

[37]Miller (1977), p. 6.

[38]Radin (1947), p. 1061; Thompson (1948), p. 295.

[39]Orth (2003), p. 25.

[40]Schwartz (1977), p. 7.

[41]Galligan (1996), p. 176.

After being discharged from his position as Chief Justice of King's Bench in 1616 (which might be a consequence of his role in Dr. Bonham's case[42]) he was elected to the House of Commons in 1620 and soon became a parliamentary leader. Together with other common lawyers, he was part of a movement pushing to subject the King to rule by law, first by guiding the elaboration of the 1621 Protestation against James I, and later by drafting the 1628 Petition of Rights against the abuses of Charles I.

The work by Coke in his Second Institutes influenced the Petition of Rights profoundly.[43] His account on the due process clause is of the highest importance because it was his understanding (or misunderstanding) of the provision that was later introduced in the American Legal system, and consequently the basis of modern conceptions of due process.[44]

First of all, regarding standing, or in other words those considered as entitled to its protection, Coke conceives due process as a source of liberties for all Englishmen, not just barons or feudal lords, and from this point on, much clearer. In this regard, Coke interprets the phrase *nullus liber homo* (no freeman shall) as applied to every free man and woman, and even for what he calls "villains."[45]

Notwithstanding that much of the modern development in the United States is based on the substantive approach, the due process conception of Coke is mainly procedural. Above all, it is focused primarily on criminal prosecution and in that regard comprises a set of basic guarantees:[46]

i) That no man be taken or imprisoned but by the law of the land (which is the Common Law, statute law or custom of England, and within the process of law stablished by it[47]);
ii) That no man shall be disseized, that is dispossessed of his freehold (which comprises his lands), or livelihood, or of his liberties, or free customs, unless by the lawful judgement of a verdict of his equals (that is, of men of his own condition) or by the law of the land, by the due course, and process of law;
iii) That no man shall be outlawed, that is, deprived of the benefit of the law, unless according to the law of the land);
iv) That no man shall be exiled or banished out of his country, unless according to the law of the land);
v) That no man shall be in any sort destroyed unless by the lawful judgment of a verdict of his equals or according to the law of the land (which might be

[42] Boudin (1929), pp. 229–230. See, also: Orth (1999), pp. 36–37; Easterbrook (1982), p. 96.

[43] Miller (1977), pp. 3–68, p. 6; Thompson (1948), pp. 354, 365.

[44] Meyer (1977), pp. 138, 140.

[45] Coke (1797), p. 45.

[46] Coke (1797), pp. 45–46.

[47] These sections refer specially to the process of indictment or by writ original of the Common Law. See, Coke (1797), p. 50.

interpreted as to be sentenced for life, or lose a limb, disinherited, tortured, or death[48]).

vi) No man shall be condemned at the kings' suite, either before himself on his bench, nor before any other commissioner or judge, but by the lawful judgment of his peers or according to the law of the land;

vii) That justice or right is no to be sell, denied or defer to no man.

The concept of "lawful judgment of his peers," according to Coke, comprises a requirement of trial by jury or by law—even before the charter (and then established by the Common Law)—, and second, that the verdict had to be legally given. This idea comprises that all the process of incorporation of evidence had to be in front of the prisoner and that during the deliberation process the jury could not ask the judges for any question or opinion on a point of law of the matter but in his presence.[49] According to Meyer, this point shows the main mistake on Coke's interpretation of the Magna Carta clause. In his account, judgment and verdict are pictured as being the same, although they never were. While judgement comes from the judge, verdict comes from the jury. Thus, the Magna Carta would require a judgment of equals "or" law of the land, which he equated to "process of the law." This move, while historically erroneous and with pernicious consequences, was directed to include Grand Jury and the procedural forms of the Common Law, as required by the Magna Carta clause.[50]

Although Coke's interpretation of the due process clause has been used in America as a limitation on the legislative arena, and as an ancient version of judicial review,[51] as described, Coke's work was focused on courts. During this time due process was used mainly as a claim of jurisdiction against the courts created by the Tudor and the Stuart monarchs that acted outside the constraints of Common law criminal procedures. Those courts were known for the use of inquisitorial tactics against opponents of the Crown, using secret proceedings and torture, both prohibited under the Common law, and imposing other mechanisms that undermined the role of the Grand Jury.[52] In this regard, during the debates of the Petition of Rights, the due process clause was linked with legal proceedings by serving as authoritative support to the incorporation of the Habeas Corpus as a safeguard of liberty in procedural terms.[53] In this regard, the best known is the case of the Five Knights, who were imprisoned without trial after refusing to a forced loan by King's order and backed up by the Court of the King's Bench. This document, then, was

[48]Coke (1797), p. 48.

[49]Coke (1797), pp. 48–49.

[50]Meyer (1977), pp. 137–140.

[51]See, on this regard: Boudin (1929); Orth (1999); Williams (2006); Helmholz (2009).

[52]Bodenhamer (1992), pp. 13–14.

[53]Habeas Corpus didn't had its origin in Magna Carta but in procedural writs used by courts of common law to extend its jurisdictions against rival courts. See: Thompson (1948), pp. 86–87.

meant directly to oppose and sought to restrict the arbitrary power of imprisonment of the King.[54]

In England, by the end of the seventieth century, the new constitutional order was in place. The supremacy of the Parliament was established and with it, the idea of due process intertwined with the concept of the Rule of Law. According to it, the King had to govern through the Parliament and the law of the land meant that public authorities, government, and administration, had to exercise their functions according to the framework provided by the Parliament and the Common law. Moreover, it meant the abolition of special administrative courts like the King's Council or the Star Chamber, and with it, the end of the inquisitorial type of proceedings used in them. In consequence, a significant element of this time was the role of the courts who had space not just to fill areas where Parliament did not regulate rights and liberties, solve disputes on scope and meaning, but also to settle questions of law authoritatively.[55]

9.3 The Migration of the Due Process Clause to America

By the end of the seventieth century, Coke's account of due process was predominant in America.[56] By contrast, after the Petition of Rights of 1628,[57] the due process clause disappears from further British provisions. As stated by Galligan, from that point the clause migrated to America and flourished there.[58] Currently, due process for English lawyers is no more than an American doctrine without practical relevance for them. Instead, in today's English legal system, the concepts of natural justice, as related to procedural fairness and the Rule of Law, embed due process principles and the core idea of limitation of arbitrariness in the exercise of power.[59] Moreover, in modern British law, procedural fairness is influenced profoundly in its current conception by the European human rights system especially by its incorporation of the Human Rights Act of 1998.[60]

The dissemination to America occurs in the context of the most dramatic effect of the Petition of Rights, the Stuarts being deposed from the monarchy,[61] and with the enactment of two other relevant legal documents. First, the 1649 Agreement of the People, which was meant to reestablish political order after the Civil War (which

[54] Schwartz (1977), pp. 7–13.

[55] Galligan (1996), p. 177.

[56] Galligan (1996), p. 177.

[57] Schwartz (1977), pp. 14–18.

[58] Galligan (1996), p. 170.

[59] Marshall (1977), p. 69.

[60] See, e.g.: Jacob (2006).

[61] Miller (1977), p. 6.

recognized several fundamental rights and procedural guarantees but in the end did not come into force as a written constitution) and the Bill of Rights of 1689.

In this political atmosphere, the first step for the colonies, founded by royal charter, was the recognition for the colonizers of the same rights that every British person had. The first document attempting this was the Virginia Charter of 1606, followed by the Charter of New England of 1620, and the Charter of Massachusetts Bay of 1629, among others. But these documents did not do much more than declare that the colonist possessed the same rights as Englishmen, but without specifying what these were.[62]

Although both versions of the due process clause—the Magna Carta language and the 1354 version—were known in the colonies, the earlier documents in the colonies used mostly the formula of the "law of the land."[63] Moreover, some of the constitutions that followed later and even some modern ones still follow this formula. On the contrary, other State constitutions and the modern federal clause of the Fifth and Fourteenth amendments use the terminology of due process of law or, at least, are a mixture of the two provisions.[64] Other colonial charters are examples of the transition from the usage of the law of the land to the concept of due process of law. In that sense, the New York Charter of 1683 provided: "Noe man of what Estate or Condition soever shall be putt out of his Lands or Tenements, nor taken, nor imprisoned, nor dishereited, nor banished nor any wayes distroyed without being brought to Answere by due Course of Law."[65,66] In spite of the language differences, both are commonly used with the same meaning.[67]

After the establishment of the colonies by the charters, the development of the properly local fundamental laws was the next natural step. These second-generation documents were more explicit than their English counterparts concerning the protections of specific individual rights.[68] The first proper American statute, or even as the first bill of rights,[69] incorporating the due process clause—but with the *per legem terrae* language—was the Maryland Act for the Liberties of the People, approved in 1639. In its Chapter 14 it declares: "...all the Inhabitants of this Province being Christians (Slaves excepted[)] Shall have and enjoy all such rights liberties immunities priviledges and free customs within this Province as any naturall born subject of England hath or ought to have or enjoy in the Realm of England by force or vertue of the common law or Statute Law of England...And Shall not be imprisoned nor disseissed or dispossessed of their freehold goods or Chattels or be out Lawed Exiled or otherwise destroyed fore judged or punished then according to the Laws of this

---

[62] Schwartz (1977), pp. 27–31.

[63] Easterbrook (1982), p. 96.

[64] Easterbrook (1982), p. 96.

[65] Schwartz (1977), p. 43.

[66] Available at: http://oll.libertyfund.org/pages/1683-charter-of-liberties-and-privileges-new-york.

[67] Orth (2003), p. 9.

[68] Schwartz (1977), p. 51.

[69] Schwartz (1977), p. 33.

province saveing to the Lord proprietarie and his heirs all his rights and prerogatives by reason of his domination and Seigniory over this Province and the people of the same. . ."[70] According to Schwartz, the relevance of this clause is not just that Magna Carta was a direct source but also that it entails the idea of colonist as part of the legal inheritance of the Common law. Moreover, it provides a direct link with the American Federal Constitution by providing that no colonist could be adversely affected in his persons or properties except "according to the Laws of this province."[71]

Notwithstanding, it is the Massachusetts Body of Liberties that is considered the first detailed American charter of liberties. Drafted by men fleeing the turmoil of the English Civil War[72] and enacted in 1641, it provides: "1. No mans life shall be taken away, no mans honour or good name shall be stayned, no mans person shall be arested, restrayned, banished, dismembred, nor any wayes punished, no man shall be deprived of his wife or children, no mans goods or estaite shall be taken away from him, nor any way indammaged under colour of law or Countenance of Authoritie, unlesse it be by vertue or equitie of some expresse law of the Country waranting the same, established by a generall Court and sufficiently published, or in case of the defect of a law in any parteculer case by the word of God. And in Capitall cases, or in cases concerning dismembring or banishment according to that word to be judged by the Generall Court. . .2. Every person within this Jurisdiction, whether Inhabitant or forreiner shall enjoy the same justice and law, that is generall for the plantation, which we constitute and execute one towards another without partialitie or delay."[73] The language in this provision comes from the intention of the colonist in charge of its drafting of framing a body of law ". . .in resemblance to a Magna Carta."[74] This document influenced other bills of rights like those in New Jersey and Pennsylvania,[75] and above all, was the most important forerunner of the Federal Bill of Rights.[76]

The incorporation of due process clause by this and other colonial documents was a response to the abuse of criminal prosecution made by English Parliament and the Crown. For example, according to Schwartz, many of the rights protected in colonial documents, and incorporated later in the Bill of Rights were influenced by the religious prosecution that Quakers suffered in the English Courts.[77]

As Chapter 39 of the Magna Carta itself (or its interpretation by Coke) influenced the first colonial documents, the incorporation of more specific procedural guarantees in subsequent ones came from the debates between the Parliament and the

[70] Available at: http://press-pubs.uchicago.edu/founders/documents/v1ch14s1.html.

[71] Schwartz (1977), p. 34.

[72] Miller (1977), p. 6.

[73] Available at: https://history.hanover.edu/texts/masslib.html.

[74] Bodenhamer (1992), pp. 15–16.

[75] Miller (1977), p. 6.

[76] Schwartz (1977), p. 45.

[77] Schwartz (1977), p. 45.

Crown that ended with the Petition of Rights and later with the Bill of Rights of 1689. Guarantees such as the right of a public trial, trial by juries in every type of cases, the right to appear and plead by their own, primary forms of legal representation, and the moderation on court fees and fines, that later became the foundation of the American system, find their origins in these debates.[78]

But like the charters, the first bill of rights did not have constitutional status. Both could be changed at will by the English government. Thus, it was the American Revolution declarations and constitutions which replaced those early documents in which due process and other individual rights came to be as binding fundamental rights.[79] By the lessons learned during the colonial period, by the time of the Declaration of Independence, according to Schwartz, most Americans firmly believed that governments should act under a constitutionally regulated framework and with a set of protected fundamental rights. Thus, the concept of a bill of rights had been fully developed in the American system and declared in the constitutions[80] made to replace British authority,[81] like the Maryland Declaration of Rights of 1776, the Massachusetts Constitution of 1780, and the Hampshire Constitution of 1783.[82]

As I will show later, in the Federal Bill of Rights it is possible to find the same guarantees as in these constitutions (and those of the colonial charters and declarations).[83] In view of the fact that such documents, which already provided for protections against many of the grievances that the original clause tried to avoid, related to abuse of criminal prosecution, it was not necessary to include the same entire phrase of the judgment of the peers and the specific trial procedure. That might explain why the Fifth and therefore the Fourteenth Amendments provides for a more general clause and not only related to criminal prosecutions. In fact, according to Meyer, even Madison also thought that a more general clause to guarantee access to the regular procedure might be desirable. As evidence, she argues that Madison offered in Congress a version expressly saying that no person shall be "...deprived of life, liberty, or property, without *due process of law...*" (Italics are mine).[84] I analyze the incorporation of the due process clause in the constitution and especially in both Amendments in the next section.

[78] Schwartz (1977), pp. 46–48; Bodenhamer (1992), p. 16.

[79] Schwartz (1977), p. 52.

[80] Schwartz (1977), p. 54.

[81] Schwartz (1977), p. 86.

[82] Wasserman (2004), p. 3.

[83] Schwartz (1977), pp. 85–86.

[84] Meyer (1977), pp. 147–148.

References

Beebe A (1933) Self-government at the King's command. A study in the beginnings of English democracy. The University of Minnesota Press, Minneapolis

Bodenhamer D (1992) Fair trial. Rights of the accused in American history. Oxford University Press, New York

Boudin L (1929) Lord Coke and the American doctrine of judicial power. N Y Univ Law Rev 6(3): 223–246

Coke E (1797) The second part of the institutes of the laws of England, vol 1. E. and R. BROOKE, London

Couture E (1946) Las garantías constitucionales del proceso civil. In: Estudios de derecho procesal en honor de hugo alsina. EDIAR, Buenos Aires, pp 153–213

Easterbrook F (1982) Substance and due process. Sup Ct Rev 1982:85–125

Galligan D (1996) Due process and fair procedures. A study of administrative procedures. Clarendon Press, Oxford

Helmholz R (2009) Bonham's case, judicial review, and the law of nature. J Leg Anal 1(1):325–354

Holt J (1985) Magna Carta and medieval government. Hambledon Press, London

Jacob J (2006) Civil justice in the age of human rights. Ashgate, Hampshire

Johnson V (1990) The French Declaration of the Rights of Man and of Citizens of 1789, the reign of terror, and the revolutionary tribunal of Paris. Boston Coll Int Comp Law Rev 13(1):1–45

Jurow K (1975) Untimely thoughts: a reconsideration of the origins of due process of law. Am J Leg Hist 19:265–279

Kadish S (1957) Methodology and criteria in due process adjudication. A survey and criticism. Yale Law J 66(3):319–363

Lockwood S (ed) (1997) Sir John Fortescue: on the laws and governance of England. Cambridge University Press, Cambridge

Marshall G (1977) Due process in England. In: Pennock R, Chapman J (eds) Due process, Nomos, vol XVIII. New York University Press, New York, pp 69–92

McIlwain C (1914) Due process of law in Magna Carta. Colum Law Rev 14(1):27–51

Meyer H (1977) The history and meaning of the fourteenth amendment. Judicial erosion of the constitution through the misuse of the fourteenth amendment. Vantage Press, New York

Miller C (1977) The forest of due process of law. In: Pennock R, Chapman J (eds) Due process, Nomos, vol XVIII. New York University Press, New York, pp 3–68

Orth J (1999) Did Sir Edward Coke mean what he said. Const Comment 16(1):33–38

Orth J (2003) Due process of law. A brief story. University Press of Kansas, Kansas

Radin M (1947) The myth of Magna Carta. Harv Law Rev 60(7):1060–1091

Ristik J (2015) Right to property: from Magna Carta to the European Convention on Human Rights. SEEU Rev 11(1):145–158

Schwartz B (1977) The great rights of mankind. Oxford University Press, New York

Sidhu O (2017) The concept of equality of arms in criminal proceedings under Article 6 of the European Convention on Human Rights. Intersentia, Cambridge

Strauss D (1989) Due process, government inaction, and private wrongs. Sup Ct Rev 1989:53–86

Sullivan T, Massaro T (2013) The arc of due process in American Constitutional Law. Oxford University Press, New York

Thompson F (1948) Magna Carta. Its role in the making of the English constitution, 1300-1629. The University of Minnesota Press, Minneapolis

Wasserman R (2004) Procedural due process. A reference guide to the United States Constitution. Praeger Publishers, Connecticut

Williams I (2006) Dr. Bonham's case and void statutes. J Leg Hist 27(11):111–128

Chapter 10
The Path of Procedural Due Process into the American Constitution. Scope of Application

The historical development of the due process clause and the political context by which it was incorporated in earlier American documents and further declarations and constitutions explains the general focus on criminal matters. As described, due process conceptions during the colonial and revolutionary period were much concerned with criminal prosecution and courts. As said, probably that is the reason why the general due process clause is accompanied with provisions to provide for specific procedural guarantees focused on those matters. That is especially true regarding the Fourth Amendment, which covers requirements for search and arrest warrants, and the Sixth Amendment, which provides a right to a fair trial applied to "all criminal prosecutions." As listed by Leubsdorf, the case law on criminal procedure and fair trial extends to specific subjects such as searches, warrants, arrests, police interrogation, witness identifications, presumptions and burdens of proof, death penalty procedures, double jeopardy, the right to counsel, trial by jury, undue delay, confrontation, exclusionary rule, standing requirements, consent and waiver doctrines, and obviously habeas corpus proceedings.[1]

This focus on criminal matters might explain why even early commentators such as Chancellor Kent, according to Easterbrook, saw the clause as limited to criminal cases.[2] However, as I will explain in this section, there is a connection between the due process clause in the American Constitution and civil procedure. Although there is not much literature on this subject,[3] I provide two approaches which might provide support to this argument. First, I will explore the debates over the amendments of the Constitution. In this regard, I explore the debates over the Fifth and Fourteenth Amendment, and the Seventh Amendment on civil jury trial. Second, I describe the

[1] Leubsdorf (1984), p. 600. See, also: Stuntz (1996), pp. 3–4.

[2] Easterbrook (1982), p. 99.

[3] See: Leubsdorf (1984); Rubenstein (2002); Little v. Streater, 452 U.S. 1, 101 S. Ct. 2202, 68 L. Ed. 2d 627 (1981); M.L.B. v. S.L.J., 519 U.S. 102, 117 S. Ct. 555, 136 L. Ed. 2d 473 (1996).

R. Lillo Lobos, *Understanding Due Process in Non-Criminal Matters*, Ius Gentium: Comparative Perspectives on Law and Justice 97,
https://doi.org/10.1007/978-3-030-95534-2_10

period from the early case law of the Supreme Court until the "Due Process Revolution". I will show how procedural due process were forged in the American Constitution while proving that at its origins it included non-criminal as well as criminal conceptions.

Today fair trial is an essential legal right and widely recognized as applicable to every type of legal proceeding. The question that remains is if the procedural due process clause applies in the same way for every type of legal proceeding. As I will argue, for several factors the specific requirements vary across subjects. Thus, the idea is not just to describe how its requirements differ but also explore some of the factors that explain these differences. Moreover, while much literature and case law have been devoted to the relation between the Constitution and the criminal procedure in detail, and up to some point to administrative agencies' adjudicatory and enforcement procedures as well, much less attention has been paid to other areas such as civil procedure.[4] Even though its application over civil procedure might be taken for granted,[5] there is a gap to fill from a scholarly point of view. This chapter is intended to fulfill in part that space too, at least from the perspective of procedural due process as a constitutional requirement.

10.1 The Fifth Amendment Clause and the Incorporation Clause in the Fourteenth Amendment

While, the Fourth and the Sixth Amendments texts are clearly reserved for criminal cases, the case of the Fifth Amendment is different. This clause includes three different provisions. In its first part,[6] it provides for fundamental criminal justice guarantees such the Grand Jury, the right against self-incrimination and double jeopardy. Undoubtedly, these are protections reserved only for criminal matters.[7] Moreover, many state constitutions that provided similar limitations expressly refer only to procedural safeguards related to criminal prosecution, such as the Virginia Declaration of Rights and the Constitution of Pennsylvania, both of 1776.[8] Its second provisions adds the language of the Magna Carta, and especially the language of the 1354 statutes, from which is derived substantive and procedural due

[4]Leubsdorf (1984), p. 579.

[5]Leubsdorf (1984), p. 588.

[6]"No person shall be held to answer for a capital, or otherwise infamous crime, unless on a presentment or indictment of a grand jury, except in cases arising in the land or naval forces, or in the militia, when in actual service in time of war or public danger; nor shall any person be subject for the same offense to be twice put in jeopardy of life or limb; nor shall be compelled in any criminal case to be a witness against himself. . ."

[7]Cogan (2015), p. 531.

[8]Cogan (2015), pp. 545–546.

process.[9] Finally, its third provision protects private property in what is known as the "just compensation clause."[10]

Especially by reading the Fifth Amendment within these divisions, and especially focusing on the second provision, it may be said that procedural due process under this clause—just like the 1354 statutes from which it was derived—goes further than criminal proceedings while it is clearly related to them. According to Meyer, "It meant that a person's life, liberty, or property may not be taken without his first having had a trial in accordance with procedural rules applicable to all alike."[11] More broadly, it is aimed to protect personal security and liberty, but also the right of private property against arbitrary state interventions as well.[12]

To reinforce the connection between the Fifth Amendment due process clause and civil procedure, it is useful to study its incorporation over states by the Fourteenth Amendment. Its section 1 reads "All persons born or naturalized in the United States, and subject to the jurisdiction thereof, are citizens of the United States and of the state wherein they reside. No state shall make or enforce any law which shall abridge the privileges or immunities of citizens of the United States; nor shall any state deprive any person of life, liberty, or property, without due process of law; nor deny to any person within its jurisdiction the equal protection of the laws." This Amendment was part of a significant departure from the first eleven, intended as checks or limitations on the Federal Government. From now on, the States' powers would be the focus of the constitutional limitations.[13]

From the text of this provision, several clauses are identified: the citizenship clause, privileges or immunities clause, the due process clause, and the equal protection clause. The connections of this Amendment with civil procedure derive mainly from its due process clause.[14]

[9]"...nor be deprived of life, liberty, or property, without due process of law."

[10]"...nor shall private property be taken for public use, without just compensation."

[11]Meyer (1977), p. 149.

[12]Blackstone (1861), pp. 100–103.

[13]Flack (1908), pp. 8–9.

[14]Notwithstanding, as argued by Rubinstein, there are cases were litigants have raised equal protection challenges against procedural rules and practices, these efforts have not had much impact on civil procedure. This author alleges that the nature of the equality under the Fourteenth Amendment is not the same as the one requested by the adversarial nature of the civil procedure. See: Rubenstein (2002), pp. 1869–1877. I agree with this author that the key for the constitutional requirements over civil procedure is not the equal protection clause. It is true that the right to a fair trial, which in America has been linked directly with the adversarial type of proceedings (as will describe below) requires a form of equality, which in some jurisdictions is known as equality of arms. See: Sidhu (2017). Notwithstanding this might result an alien concept in the American jurisprudence, there is at least some literature calling for its recognition as enshrined in the Constitution but as part of the adversarial legal procedure and a requirement of fairness and the due process clause but not in the equal protection clause. See: Silver (1990), pp. 1032–1038. On the contrary, in the criminal justice arena have received much more attention. Mashaw (1976), p. 47, fn. 61.

The Fourteenth Amendment had the purpose of providing the same protections given by the Freedmen's Bureau and Civil Rights Bills after the Civil War, now in the Constitution.[15] In this regard, it was meant to protect the freedmen within the territory previously controlled by the Union forces, and later to stop discrimination against black population in the laws of the southern states.[16] According to Flack, this section was enacted to give Congress the power to enact affirmative legislation and make the first eight Amendments binding upon the States as well as on the Federal Government. The idea was that the Congress would be empowered to see that they were enforced in the States to secure citizens their privileges and immunities.[17] As a third goal, and with Senate contribution, this Amendment also was meant to declare who were citizens of the United States.[18]

Regarding the due process clause in the Fourteenth Amendment, its introduction came without discussion in 1866.[19] That is why the first legislative interpretations of the clause came only in 1871, when the House discussed the Ku Klux Klan bill. In that debate, it was said that the congressional intent was to copy the due process clause of the Fifth Amendment but now as a direct restraint upon States, in a context where many of them had different procedural rules for black people or from other minorities.[20] It seems that at least in the initial stage the congressional understanding of the provision was that the Fourteenth Amendment did not add anything new but the idea that States can provide any legal proceedings as long as being the same for every person. Using other terms, the concept of a right to a pre-established regular procedure. For this reason, this section of the amendment passed without much debate as there was agreement on the protections provided already by the Fifth Amendment, since the originated from the States' constitutions.[21] In conclusion, this clause would mean that the States could legislate their own procedural rules as long as they were the same for every person.[22]

As stated, both provisions rely on the language of the 1354 statutes, which, as explained before, apply to criminal and civil matters. However, at this point is possible to find an essential difference on how the Supreme Court has interpreted the due process clause in criminal versus non-criminal matters. While many criminal procedural guarantees have been incorporated through the Fourteenth Amendment to the States,[23] to other types of procedural guarantees that may not happen yet. The

[15]Flack (1908), pp. 76–78.

[16]Flack (1908), pp. 20–21; 95.

[17]Flack (1908), p. 82.

[18]Flack (1908), p. 94; Dripps (2018), p. 52.

[19]Meyer (1977), p. 125.

[20]Meyer (1977), pp. 125–126.

[21]Meyer (1977), pp. 126–127.

[22]Meyer (1977), p. 127.

[23]Regarding the exclusion of unconstitutional searches, see: Mapp v. Ohio, 367 U.S. 643, 655 (1961). The Court held that "Since the Fourth Amendment's right of privacy has been declared enforceable against the States through the Due Process Clause of the Fourteenth, it is enforceable

best example is the right to a jury trial in civil cases, which notwithstanding some struggles in some States,[24] traditionally have been denied in its application through the Fourteenth Amendment.[25]

10.2 Fair Trial Conceptions in the Seventh Amendment Right to Jury Trial in Civil Cases

The Seventh Amendment reads: "In suits at common law, where the value in controversy shall exceed twenty dollars, the right of trial by jury shall be preserved, and no fact tried by a jury, shall be otherwise reexamined in any court of the United States, than according to the rules of the common law."

This Amendment was a response to the powers given to the Supreme Court of deciding on matters of law and fact in the proposed Federal Constitution, and especially taking into consideration that criminal trials by jury were expressly guaranteed in the Constitution but not for civil cases. Just as was recognized later by the judiciary in *United States v. Wonson*, this provision (or its omission) suffered one of the most robust objections in the debates because of the appellate jurisdiction of the Supreme Court. Being able to pronounce on matters both as to law and fact, now the Court would be able to re-examine the whole facts previously settled by a jury.[26] The danger with such provision for those arguing for the proposal was that trial by jury in civil cases would be in practice abolished.[27]

Trial by jury was fiercely defended as a part of the common distrust for authorities at the origin of the United States legal system. The jury was a restraint against the government but also to the judiciary, since through experiences in England and in the colonies, they also learned what could happen without juries. Even before the Constitution, the desire of the founders for juries both in civil and criminal matters was expressed in several debates in state assemblies.[28]

During the debates of the Amendment it was clear how the original alternative of an appeal to the Supreme Court in federal matters, with the power to decide on issues of facts, was an attempt to introduce the civil law method of trial, that was linked

---

against them by the same sanction of exclusion as is used against the Federal Government." Regarding the right to counsel of the Sixth Amendment, see: Gideon v. Wainwright, 372 U.S. 335 (1963).

[24] Gonzalez-Oyarzun v. Caribbean City Builders, Inc., 27 F. Supp. 3d 265 (2014). But this decision was reversed on appeal. See: González-Oyarzun v. Caribbean City Builders, Inc., 798 F.3d 26 (2015).

[25] See: McDonald v. City of Chicago, 561 U.S. 742 (2010), pp. 867–868; City of Monterey v. Del Monte Dunes, 526 U.S. 687 (1999), pp. 718–719; Gasperini v. Ctr. for Humanities, Inc., 518 U.S. 415 (1996). See, also: Balboni v. Ranger Am. of the V.I., Inc., 70 V.I. 1048 (2019).

[26] United States v. Wonson, 28 F. Cas. 745, 750 (1812).

[27] Cogan (2015), pp. 849, 853.

[28] Thomas (2016), p. 11.

politically with more authoritarian forms of government.[29] In the case of North Carolina, in the state's convention of 1788, Mr. J. McDowall expressed the right to a jury in this way: "We know that the trial by jury of the vicinage is one of the greatest securities for property. If causes are to be decided at such a great distance, the poor will be oppressed; in land affairs, particularly, the wealthy suitor will prevail. A poor man, who has just claim on a piece of land, has not substance to stand it. Can it be supposed that any man, of common circumstances, can stand the expense and trouble of going from Georgia to Philadelphia, there to have a suit tried? And can it be justly determined without the benefit of a trial by jury? What made the people revolt from Great Britain? The trial by jury, that great safeguard of liberty, was taken away, a stamp duty was laid upon them. This alarmed them and led them to fear that great oppressions would take place. . ."[30] In this sense, trial by jury was a device allowing the participation of common people in the judicial system. Like with the case of the representatives, this provision would give them the tools ". . .to acquire information and knowledge in the affairs and government of the society; and to come forward, in turn, as the centinels(sic) and guardians of each other."[31] With the participation of ordinary people, trial by jury was defended as a mechanism against corruption.[32]

The civil trial by jury was known long before the migration of the due process clause to the United States. In fact, it was used during the thirteen century and even before the Magna Carta. For example, according to Beebe, disputes over cattle and horses by that epoch were sometimes turned over to a jury.[33] Of course, the form and procedure of the trial by jury differ from modern conceptions. For example, in civil matters the work done by the juries was often out of the courts, functioning more as an expert decision panel, not just for the determination of facts but also regarding damages and other remedies.[34] By the eighteenth and nineteenth centuries, in English civil and criminal jury were in many ways similar, commonly used as well to decide over monetary damages.[35]

In the United States, since the colonial epoch trial by jury was seen as a part of the Common law procedure inherited both in civil and criminal matters, and in consequence, the one the colonists were entitled to as a right of the people. In this regard, the General Laws of New-Plimouth (1671) declares: "That all Trials, whether Capital, Criminal, or between Man and Man, be tried by Jury of Twelve good and lawful Men, according to the commendable custome of England. . ."[36] This idea appears later too during the documents enacted during the Revolution, for example

---

[29] See, e.g. A Farmer, No 4, March 21, 1788. Cited in: Cogan (2015), pp. 871–873.

[30] Cogan (2015), p. 821.

[31] Cogan (2015), p. 848.

[32] The Federalist, No 83, May 28, 1788. Cited in: Cogan (2015), pp. 875–877.

[33] Beebe (1933), pp. 44, 58–59.

[34] Beebe (1933), pp. 68–72.

[35] Thomas (2016), pp. 19, 20.

[36] Cogan (2015), p. 808.

in the Declaration of Rights of 1776 of Maryland.[37] Moreover, constitutional propositions made in states like New York, North Carolina, Pennsylvania, Rhode Island, and Virginia (all between 1788 and 1790), expressly recognize the jury trial in civil cases as a right of the American people inherited from the English common law.[38]

With recognition of the relevance of trial by juries in civil cases, the debates were focused on a provision able to accommodate the particularities that each State had in the specific regulations. For example, in Massachusetts, it was discussed that many States constitutions differed regarding the jury trial in civil matters while in criminal cases it was mandatory.[39] In North Carolina, Mr. Bloodworth asked: "It has said that the trial should be by jury in criminal cases; and yet this trial is different in its manner in criminal cases in the different states. If it has been possible to secure it in criminal cases, notwithstanding the diversity concerning it, why has it not been possible to secure it in civil cases? I wish this to be cleared up..."[40] For Mr. Iredell, the answer was that while in criminal cases there were a unique source or arbitrary exercise of power, the criminal prosecution, and in this regard, there was no safer mode to control that danger than the trial by jury. On the contrary, civil cases are more diverse.[41] In this context, in many State Conventions was recognized that in several civil suits the courts in practice decide without the intervention of a jury, for example in cases of recovery of sums paid as securities by one joint obligor against another.[42] Still, others argued that oppression of government does not come just from criminal prosecution. In fact, they said that there were many civil cases where the government is a party and might act with whole weight thrown, such as in cases of forfeitures and demands of public debts. In some opportunities, civil cases might serve as a form of harassment to the subject perhaps even more effective than direct criminal prosecution.[43]

Still, other more procedurally oriented arguments were held to defend the jury trial in civil cases. In this regard, the trial by neighbors was a part of the adversarial model of witness examination, especially by cross-examination and the introduction of oral instead of written evidence. On the contrary, if the triers of fact are removed from vicinity then oral testimony becomes too expensive and would lead the parties

[37] Cogan (2015), p. 807.

[38] Cogan (2015), pp. 806–807.

[39] Cogan (2015), p. 820.

[40] Cogan (2015), p. 825.

[41] Cogan (2015), p. 826. In the same sense: The Federalist, No 83, May 28, 1788. Cited in: Cogan (2015), pp. 875–877.

[42] See the comment of Mr. John Marshall at the State Convention of South Carolina in 1788. See also, the Address to the Citizens of Philadelphia on October 6, 1787 at the Pennsylvania Herald. Cogan (2015), pp. 840–841; 845.

[43] Cogan (2015), p. 850.

to use more written evidence, commonly taken ex-parte and not very efficient for the proper discovery of truth.[44]

Currently, while it is true that most State constitutions provide the right to a civil jury trial,[45] they differ in their regulation. Some constitutions provide a general clause of the right to a jury without distinguishing between criminal and civil matters,[46] others have exclusive provisions for this type of proceedings.[47] Even between them, they differ in issues such as waiver requirements, composition and majorities.[48] These differences among States might explain why the right to a jury trial in civil matters has not been incorporated yet through the Fourteenth Amendment.[49]

Although most States provides for this right, in modern American jurisprudence Civil juries have diminished in importance. For example, while in the late eighteenth-century English jury—the source of the American counterpart—monetary remedies were often decided by juries, in modern times in many circumstances this type of decisions had shifted to other tribunals or agencies.[50] Other procedural limitations includes the determination of facts by the judge in many stages of the civil procedure, the power to reduce damages decided by juries, and even to limit the maximum amounts in certain matters through legislation.[51] But more importantly, this lack of relevance is clear by the decisions of the Supreme Court to not incorporate this institution though the Fourteenth Amendment as a requirement to the States legal systems, as explained before.[52]

Notwithstanding the right to a jury trial in civil matters in modern times is diminished and might not be considered a minimum requirement, this section has

---

[44]The Federal Farmer, No 4, October 12, 1787. In: Cogan (2015), p. 848.

[45]A quick analysis of the Constitutions of the Fifty States, at least forty-nine of them provides a right to a jury in civil matters. The Constitution of Louisiana provides civil juries only in expropriation proceeding and to determine compensation only. See: Louisiana Constitution, Article I. Section 4.B.

[46]See, e.g.: Alabama Constitution, Section 11.

[47]For example, the Indiana Constitution provides: "In all civil cases, the right of trial by jury shall remain inviolate." Indiana Constitution, Article 1. Section 20.

[48]For example, in Alaska, the Constitution provides civil juries for cases where the amount in controversy exceeds two hundred fifty dollars. It provides also that the legislature may make provision for a verdict by not less than three-fourths of the jury and, in courts not of record, may provide for a jury of not less than six or more than twelve. See: Alaska Constitution, Article 1, Section 16. On the contrary, in California, while there is no limit amount for civil juries, there are different requirements regarding waiver and verdict between civil and criminal matters. See: California Constitution, Article 1, Section 16. In other, such as Rhode Island, while there is general right to a jury, in civil cases the legislative body might reduce the size of the jury at less than twelve but not less than six. See: Constitution of the State of Rhode Island and Providence Plantations, Article 1, Section, 15.

[49]Thomas (2012), p. 174.

[50]Thomas (2012), p. 33.

[51]Thomas (2012), p. 33.

[52]Thomas (2012), pp. 33–37.

shown that the connection between the Seventh Amendment and the due process clause in the Magna Carta is clear. Therefore, if trial by jury in civil cases was a part of the procedure guaranteed by chapter 39 that would mean that this clause did not concern criminal matters only. The American early case law interpreting the Fifth and Fourteenth Amendments reaffirm this interpretation, as I will explain in the next section.

10.3 From the Early Case Law on Procedural Due Process Until the Due Process Revolution

After the incorporation of the due process clause in the American Constitution through the Fifth Amendment in 1791, it fell dormant for nearly sixty-five years. While the Supreme Court decided cases interpreting many other constitutional provisions, it only refers to due process clause of in 1856.[53] To Easterbrook, the Court neglected the clause because as a constraint over the executive and the judiciary, it stated an uncontroversial principle thought to be trivial. Even in the early days, tyranny from any of those branches was not seen as something to worry about.[54] From that point on, the understanding of this clause by the Supreme Court has been characterized as a "continuous search",[55] influenced by many social, political, and legal factors occurring at the end of the Nineteen and the first half of the Twentieth centuries which lead to what has been called the "Due Process Revolution". On this section I try to describe this evolution before embarking on the modern debates on the meaning and content of procedural due process in non-criminal matters.

As said, the first case decided by the Supreme Court providing an interpretation of the meaning and content of the clause was *Den Ex Dem. Murray v. Hoboken Land & Improv. Co.* This case arose from an action of ejectment, in which both parties claimed title to certain property. Defendants claimed title under a sale by virtue of what was referred to as a distress warrant, issued by the solicitor of the treasury under an act of Congress. The legal issue in was whether the statutory basis for the distress warrant at issue was in conflict with the constitutional guarantee of due process.[56] In other words, it was whether "...the effect of the proceedings authorized by the act in question is to deprive the party, against whom the warrant issues, of his liberty and property, 'without due process of law;' and, therefore, is in conflict with the fifth article of the amendments of the constitution."[57]

---

[53] But it was mentioned earlier as a clause in State constitutions. See: Trs. of Dartmouth College v. Woodward, 17 U.S. 518, 624 (1819).

[54] Easterbrook (1982), p. 99.

[55] Mashaw (1976), p. 47, fn. 61.

[56] Den Ex Dem. Murray v. Hoboken Land & Improv. Co., 59 U.S. 272 (1855), p. 274.

[57] Den Ex Dem. Murray v. Hoboken Land & Improv. Co., 59 U.S. 272 (1855), p. 275.

According to the Supreme Court, the phrase "due process of law" had the same meaning as "the law of the land" in the Magna Carta (something which, as explained in the previous section, authors disagree on). It follows the general formula of the clause but excluding the trial by jury because it was already in the Sixth Amendment for criminal cases, and in the Seventh Amendment for civil matters.[58] In this regard, it says that "[T]o have followed. . .the words of Magna Charta, and declared that no person shall be deprived of his life, liberty or property but by the judgement of his peers of the law of the land, would have been in part superfluous and inappropriate."[59]

So, it held that while the Constitution contains no description of those processes which it was intended to allow or forbid, "the law of the land" means that it is not left to the legislative power to enact any process which might be devised either. In this regard, the clause is a restraint on the legislative as well as on the executive and judicial powers of the government.[60] According to the Court, in cases like this where there was an executive order without judicial cognizance, to determine what is the procedure that is due the answer was twofold. First, the constitution itself must be analyzed to see whether this process conflicts with any of its provisions. If not found to be so, the second step is to look to those settled usages and modes of proceeding existing in England before the emigration of the colonist, and which are shown not to have been unsuited to their civil and political condition by having been acted on by them after their settlement.[61]

After the enactment in 1866 of the incorporation clause, as a requirement over States in the Fourteenth Amendment, two cases are relevant to understanding the meaning of the due process clause. In *Davidson v. New Orleans*, the Court held that when the Fourteenth Amendment says that a State may not deprive a person of property without due process of law, it meant that ". . .whenever by the laws of a State, or by State authority, a tax, assessment, servitude, or other burden is imposed upon property. . ., and those laws provide for a made of confirming or contesting the charge thus imposed, *in the ordinary courts of justice, with such notice to the person, or such proceeding in regard to the property as is appropriate to the nature of the case*, the judgment in such proceedings cannot be said to deprive the owner of his property without due process of law, however obnoxious it may be to other objections" (Italics are mine).[62] It adds, ". . .that it is not possible to hold that a party has, without due process of law, been deprived of his property, when, as *regards the issues affecting it, he has, by the laws of the State, a fair trial in a court of justice, according to the modes of proceeding applicable* to such a case" (Italics are mine).[63]

[58] Den Ex Dem. Murray v. Hoboken Land & Improv. Co., 59 U.S. 272 (1855), p. 276.

[59] Den Ex Dem. Murray v. Hoboken Land & Improv. Co., 59 U.S. 272 (1855), p. 276.

[60] Den Ex Dem. Murray v. Hoboken Land & Improv. Co., 59 U.S. 272 (1855), p. 276.

[61] Den Ex Dem. Murray v. Hoboken Land & Improv. Co., 59 U.S. 272 (1855), p. 276.

[62] Davidson v. New Orleans, 96 U.S. 97, 104–105 (1877).

[63] Davidson v. New Orleans, 96 U.S. 97, 105 (1877). Similarly, see: Kennard v. La., 92 U.S. 480, 483 (1876).

Regarding the relation between the due process clause in the Fourteenth and the Fifth Amendments, in *Hurtado v. California* (1884), a criminal case concerning the right to a Grand Jury in capital offenses, the Supreme Court held that this clause meant the same than the one in the Fifth.[64] In his dissent, Justice Harlan refers to the same *Den Ex Dem. Murray v. Hoboken Land & Improv. Co.*, as a general statement of what the Fifth, and in consequence, the Fourteenth Amendment required now to states: "The constitution contains no description of those processes which it was intended to allow or forbid. It does not even declare what principles are to be applied to ascertain whether it be due process. It is manifest that it was not left to the legislative power to enact any process which might be devised. The article is a restraint on the legislative as well as on the executive and judicial powers of the government, and cannot be so construed as to leave congress free to make any process 'due process of law,' by its mere will."[65] According to Dripps, in none of the formulations of the clause does "process" consist of whatever the government decrees. The process must be what is, in some vague sense, "due."[66] According to Kadish, *Hurtado* flexibilized the test under *In Den Ex Dem. Murray v. Hoboken Land & Improv. Co.*, since now a procedure as sanctioned by immemorial usage necessarily is due process, but not necessarily that a procedure beyond those could not be respectful of the clause.[67]

According to Justice Harlan, the similarity between the provision of the Fourteenth Amendment and the one in the Fifth was not accidental. On the contrary, it "...evinces a purpose to impose upon the states the same restrictions, in respect of proceedings involving life, liberty and property, which had been imposed upon the general government."[68] During the discussion of the amendments, people were not content just with the provision in the Constitution establishing the right to jury trial only in criminal cases. Moreover, they desired "...a fuller and broader enunciation of the fundamental principles of freedom, and therefore demanded that the guarantees of the rights of life, liberty, and property...should be placed beyond all danger of impairment or destruction by the general government through legislation by congress."[69] In consequence, in both Amendments according to Justice Harlan, the words due process of law should be interpreted with the same meaning given at the Common Law from which they were derived.[70] This definition, for Harlan, was broader than criminal matters. It was to be applied to every proceeding involving life, liberty, or property, no matter if they are civil or criminal cases, *in rem* or *in personam*.[71]

[64]Hurtado v. California, 110 U.S. 516 (1884), pp. 534–535.

[65]Den Ex Dem. Murray v. Hoboken Land & Improv. Co., 59 U.S. 272, (1855), p. 276.

[66]Dripps (2018), p. 48.

[67]Kadish (1957), p. 322.

[68]Hurtado v. California, 110 U.S. 516, 4 S. Ct. 111, 28 L. Ed. 232, 1884 U.S., (1884), p. 541.

[69]Hurtado v. California, 110 U.S. 516, 4 S. Ct. 111, 28 L. Ed. 232, 1884 U.S., (1884), p. 541.

[70]Hurtado v. California, 110 U.S. 516, 4 S. Ct. 111, 28 L. Ed. 232, 1884 U.S., (1884), p. 542.

[71]Hurtado v. California, 110 U.S. 516, 4 S. Ct. 111, 28 L. Ed. 232, 1884 U.S., (1884), pp. 552–553.

Following *Hurtado v. California*, the Supreme Court in *Hagar v. Reclamation Dist. No. 108*, held that by due process of law is meant one, which, following the forms of law, is appropriate to the case and just to the parties to be affected. In other words, while respecting the prescribed legal procedure, it must be adapted to the end to be attained.[72] Moreover, while the court recognizes that a strict minimum is that the party to be affected shall have notice and an opportunity to be heard,[73] the particular way of provide both requirements, may be more or less formal. In this particular case, concerning tax determination and further actions to sell a land to satisfy unpaid taxes by the competent agency, the Court held that due process is satisfied by giving notice and an opportunity to be heard in the ordinary courts of justice after complaining of the administrative decision.[74]

Two decades later, in *Ballard v. Hunter*, another tax case concerning nonresident landowners who claimed in foreclosure proceedings that they were not personally served, the Supreme Court held that there is no precise definition of due process. While an opportunity for a hearing and defense is a minimum, there is no a fixed procedure as demanded. On the contrary, the procedure may be adapted to the nature of the case and even, as added in this case, it does not always mean proceedings in court.[75] Similarly, in *Londoner v. Denver*, the plaintiffs filed a claim to relieve lands owned by them from an assessment of a tax for the cost of paving a street upon which the lands abutted.[76] According to the Supreme Court, when the legislature commits to some subordinate body the duty of determining such assessment, due process of law requires that at some stage of the proceedings before the tax becomes irrevocably fixed, the taxpayer shall have an opportunity to be heard.[77] While the Supreme Court held that in in this type of cases many requirements essential in strictly judicial proceedings might be dispensed, it does not suffice this requirement a chance to submit in writing all the objections. The right to a hearing demands an opportunity to "…support his allegations by argument however brief, and, if need be, by proof, however informal."[78]

At this early stage at least in terms of the public administration as explained by Rubin, the main question was whether the administrative agency decision was rulemaking -alike legislative function- or adjudicative and as such closer to the judicial function. Procedural due process would be applicable only to the latter,[79] and if so, the exigencies where basically the same than those applied to civil matters, notice and opportunity to be heard. In this regard, in the already cited *Londoner*

[72] Hagar v. Reclamation Dist. No. 108, 111 U.S. 701 (1884), pp. 707–708.

[73] A conception, that according to Kadish comes from the case law on the Fifth Amendment such as Trs. of Dartmouth College v. Woodward, 17 U.S. 518 (1819). See: Kadish (1957), p. 323.

[74] Hagar v. Reclamation Dist. No. 108, 111 U.S. 701 (1884), p. 710.

[75] Ballard v. Hunter, 204 U.S. 241 (1907), p. 255.

[76] Londoner v. Denver, 210 U.S. 373 (1908), p. 374.

[77] Londoner v. Denver, 210 U.S. 373 (1908), p. 385.

[78] Londoner v. Denver, 210 U.S. 373 (1908), p. 386.

[79] Rubin (1984), p. 1050.

v. Denver, the Court held that in the assessment, apportionment and collection of taxes upon property, the Constitution imposes few restrictions upon the States, and such limitation are of substance but not form. Something completely different is the assessment of the cost to individual property owners by the administrative agency empowered by legislature.[80] As such, it goes under the umbrella of adjudication since it is particularized or individualized justice and, therefore, triggers the due process requirements. Beyond such basic requirements, the pre-established legal procedure is the due process afforded and in cases where there is none, tradition sets the standard.

According to Redish and Marshall, the approach followed by the Supreme Court during this early case law is the beginning of a long-standing position that the Constitution does not provide for a specific procedure to be followed once a protected interest has triggered the due process analysis.[81] This early stage of the case law has been described as the continuity between the due process clause of the Constitution and the principles of English law, which only required to be "accommodated" to the American context.[82] Flexibility, during this time, meant that procedural due process applies according to the nature of the case, while there is no single procedure to be followed but it must be adapted to the to be attained.[83] Regarding many public decisions triggering the clause, only strict minimum of notice and an opportunity to be heard might apply, which in turn, might be provided in more or less formal ways.[84]

The holding on *Twining v. New Jersey* -a criminal case- provides a good summary of this approach. While this flexibility does not mean that legislature may enact any procedural regulation, beyond basic requirements applicable to both civil and criminal cases such as jurisdiction, notice and opportunity to be heard, "...which seem to be universally prescribed in all systems of law established by civilized countries, this court has up to this time sustained all state laws, statutory or judicially declared, regulating procedure, evidence and methods of trial, and held them to be consistent with due process of law."[85] This transformation process has been a slow and gradual movement which found its roots in this case in which the Supreme Court held that the legislature could omit any historical procedural step unless it embeds a "fundamental principle."[86]

In support of the jurisdiction requirement, the Court in *Twining* cites a case from 1878, *Pennoyer v. Neff,* a possession recovery proceeding between two private individuals who asserted title. Here, the defendant alleged that he was not personally

[80]Rubin (1984), pp. 385–386.

[81]Redish and Marshall (1986), p. 456.

[82]Galligan (1996), p. 199.

[83]Hagar v. Reclamation Dist. No. 108, 111 U.S. 701, 707–708 (1884).

[84]Hagar v. Reclamation Dist. No. 108, 111 U.S. 701, 710 (1884); Ballard v. Hunter, 204 U.S. 241, 255(1907).

[85]Twining v. N.J., 211 U.S. 78 (1908), p. 111.

[86]Twining v. N.J., 211 U.S. 78 (1908), pp. 106–111.

served but only by summons of publications, as established in the Code of Oregon for cases of non-residents and defendants but with property within the State.[87] The Supreme Court said that due process of law on the Fourteenth Amendment when applied to judicial proceedings "...mean course of legal proceedings according to those rules and principles which have been established in our systems of jurisprudence for the protection and enforcement of private rights."[88] In this regard, "...there must be a competent tribunal to pass upon their subject-matter; and, if that involves merely a determination of the personal liability of the defendant, he must be brought within its jurisdiction by service of process within the State, or by his voluntary appearance."[89]

In *Iowa C. R. Co. v. Iowa* from 1896, the State of Iowa sought a mandatory injunction to compel the defendant -a railroad company- to obey an order from a prior decree as the successor, assignee, and grantee of the prior owner. The defendant claimed that it was not a party in those proceedings, and filed a demand for a jury trial, which was refused. In front of the Supreme Court, it was alleged that jury trial was required under the Fourteenth Amendment.[90] But following the described doctrine, the Court held that the due process clause does not control the power of a State to determine by what process legal rights may be asserted or legal obligations be enforced, provided that the method of procedure adopted for these purposes gives reasonable notice and affords fair opportunity to be heard before the issues are decided. Therefore, there is no constitutional right to have a controversy in the State court prosecuted or determined by one form of action instead of another. Moreover, it decided that mere errors or irregularities in the procedure are matters of State regulation and not for the Supreme Court.[91]

Another case regarding the basic minimum requirement of prior notice is *Roller v. Holly*. Here, the issue in dispute was whether a notice served upon the defendant in another State (Virginia) five days prior the date to appear in Texas to answer a foreclosure suit was considered as due process of law within the meaning of the Fourteenth Amendment.[92] The Court recognizes that the requirement of notice before liberty or property deprivation "...is an axiom of the law to which no citation of authority would give additional weight," but on the contrary, at that point there was little case law on the question of the length of such notice. Notwithstanding, it says that it is manifest that the requirement of notice would be of no value whatever, unless such notice were reasonable and adequate for the purpose (citing the already mentioned cases of *Hagar v. Reclamation Dist. No. 108* and *Davidson v. New Orleans*).[93] Following the traditional method, to decide that five days of prior notice

[87]Pennoyer v. Neff, 95 U.S. 714 (1878), pp. 719–720.

[88]Pennoyer v. Neff, 95 U.S. 714 (1879), p. 733.

[89]Pennoyer v. Neff, 95 U.S. 714 (1879), p. 719.

[90]Iowa C. R. Co. v. Iowa, 160 U.S. 389 (1896), p. 392.

[91]Iowa C. R. Co. v. Iowa, 160 U.S. 389 (1896), p. 393.

[92]Roller v. Holly, 176 U.S. 398 (1900), p. 402.

[93]Roller v. Holly, 176 U.S. 398 (1900), p. 409.

was not reasonable, the Court follows British practical guides on Justices of the Peace (citing Chitty's General Practice) but also the practice and regulations of several states.[94] Moreover, in *Louisville & N. R. Co. v. Schmidt*—a civil case regarding the enforcement of a prior judgement on a lease against an a assignee who was not a party the first set of proceedings—the Court held that with the exception of the fundamental requirements of notice and adequate opportunity to defend, the due process clause of the Fourteenth Amendment does not control mere forms of procedure in State courts or regulate practice therein.[95]

According to Easterbrook, an author associated with positivism and historical methods of interpretation of due process, the traditional approach of the early case law began to change at the beginning of the twentieth century. First, cases were traditionally associated with substantive due process, such as *Lochner v. New York,*[96] while the procedural due process transformation began a couple of decades later.[97] In this regard, this doctrine of not providing for a specific procedure beyond the basic requirements of notice and opportunity to defend, well established in cases such as *Pennoyer v. Neff* or *Twining v. New Jersey*, controlled the case law on procedural due process until the 1920s.

For example, in *Grannis v. Ordean,* from 1914, the Supreme Court held, citing the precedent of *Pennoyer v. Neff*, that constructive notice to the parties concerned in proceedings of titles to lands but who reside beyond the reach of regular service process suffice due process of law. But in this case, it was alleged that a mistake in the name of the defendant was fatal. The answer of the Court was that the due process clause does not impose an unattainable standard of accuracy in this regard, and that the rule was clear especially for defendants within the jurisdiction but also applies to non-residents. What seems to be the important test here was a practical one, which is whether the letter with the summons probably would have reached the right person, as in fact happened in this case.[98]

Pennoyer v. Neff is an important case regarding one the basic requirements of due process in civil matters. As I described before, from the origins of the due process clause it was used as a matter of jurisdiction. The idea is well captured in this case where the Supreme Court held that while the authority of every tribunal is necessarily restricted by the territorial limits of the State in which it is established, the State through its tribunals, may subject property situated within its limits owned by non-residents for the payment of the demand of its own citizens against them.[99] On the contrary, where the case involves the determination of the personal liability of a defendant, he or she must be brought within its jurisdiction by service of process

[94] Roller v. Holly, 176 U.S. 398 (1900), pp. 409–412.

[95] Louisville & N. R. Co. v. Schmidt, 177 U.S. 230 (1900), p. 236. Similarly, Simon v. Craft, 182 U.S. 427 (1901), p. 437.

[96] Lochner v. New York, 198 U.S. 45 (1905).

[97] Easterbrook (1982), p. 104.

[98] Grannis v. Ordean, 58 L. Ed. 1363 (1914), pp. 1369–1370.

[99] Pennoyer v. Neff, 95 U.S. 714 (1877), pp. 720–724.

within the State, or his voluntary appearance. With this case, personal jurisdiction as a requirement which is more a matter of the inherited common law or "general law" as Sachs calls it, became a subcategory or it is enforced through the due process clause.[100] From now on, a court lacking in personal jurisdiction has not the power to issue a lawful judgment, and therefore a deprivation on the property of the defendant is an infringement of the due process clause.[101]

In *Ownbey v. Morgan*, a case regarding a proceeding brought by plaintiff executors by foreign attachment against the property of the debtor -the plaintiff in error-, who in practice complained that the state courts declined to exercise equity jurisdiction, resulting in excessive hardship.[102] Since the State legislation did nothing more than to avail to an inherited ancient practice, under *Den Ex Dem. Murray v. Hoboken Land & Improv. Co.* and *Pennoyer v. Neff,* the State could not be held responsible for applying the procedure provided by the statutes of Delaware long before the case arose.[103] The court held that the due process clause "…does not impose upon the States a duty to establish ideal systems for the administration of justice, with every modern improvement and with provision against every possible hardship that may befall. It restrains state action, whether legislative, executive, or judicial, within bounds that are consistent with the fundamentals of individual liberty and private property, including the right to be heard where liberty or property is at stake in judicial proceedings…A procedure customarily employed, long before the Revolution…and generally adopted by the States as suited to their circumstances and needs, cannot be deemed inconsistent with due process of law, even if it be taken with its ancient incident of requiring security from a defendant who after seizure of his property comes within the jurisdiction and seeks to interpose a defense."[104]

As explained before, in terms of procedural due process, the early case law is a flexible one in the sense that the Constitution does not provide for a specific procedure to be followed once a protected interest has triggered the due process analysis.[105] Yet, reliance on the inherited mode of proceedings as a standard to compare the procedure followed by the decision under questioning against—inaugurated as said by *Den ex Dem. Murray v. Hoboken Land & Imp*—has been equated with the so-called "historical method", criticized since, as described by Mashaw, as part of a tradition characterized by a conservative, precedent-oriented, historical approach,[106] closely linked with legal positivism and its reliance in originalism as a method of interpretation. As such, I identify this early case law with to the checklist model I have presented in Chap. 1, if not in its "pure form" at least closer than it

[100] Stephen (2017), pp. 1253–1255.

[101] Stephen (2017), p. 1288.

[102] Ownbey v. Morgan, 256 U.S. 94 (1921), p. 110.

[103] Ownbey v. Morgan, 256 U.S. 94 (1921), pp. 108–110.

[104] Ownbey v. Morgan, 256 U.S. 94 (1921), pp. 110–111.

[105] Redish and Marshall (1986), p. 456.

[106] Mashaw (1976), p. 47, fn. 61.

would be from this point forward under a new methodology based on dignitary values.[107]

Several factors might lead to an important change from the flexible but historically oriented method to a new one where the emphasis was on flexibility but for the protection of individual rights and dignitary-based considerations. According to Mashaw, while used occasionally before 1900 in the search for a procedural due process in this context, these arguments were the most frequently used mode of analysis in the next period until the 1950s.[108]

Easterbrook, describes a gradual progression of this new approach applied over procedural due process cases, and it seems to be particularly intense in the criminal field. First, *Moore v. Dempsey*, a criminal case concerning "kangaroo courts" or mob-dominated trials, where the Court held that they were unconstitutional as a violation of due process of law but without any reference to statutes or historically recognized procedures but decided under "purely natural law conceptions." According to this author, this was the first time the Supreme Court went beyond the already mentioned doctrine of *Twining* of upholding State procedural regulations, except for ex-parte proceedings.[109]

Later, in *Tumey v. Ohio*,[110] the Supreme Court declared for the first time a state law unconstitutional over the requirements of an adequate procedure beyond the traditional case law. The case concerned a convicted defendant who contended that he was denied due process of law by the lack of impartiality of the mayor who convicted him, since he could only be paid for his services as a judge if he convicted those who were brought before him.[111] According to the Court, while many aspects of judicial qualification are matters of legislative discretion, it violates the Fourteenth Amendment, and deprives a defendant in a criminal case of due process of law, if his liberty or property is decided by a judge who has a direct, personal, substantial, pecuniary interest in reaching a conclusion against him in his case.[112] To reach this conclusion, and responding to an argument of the State counsel who brought it, the Supreme Court analyzed the embedded practices of the common law using the *Den ex Dem. Murray v. Hoboken Land & Imp.* historical method, and finally rejected this rule as an exception to general disqualifications.[113]

Then came the famous case of *Powell v. Alabama*, regarding the right to counsel of a group of young and -according to the Court- illiterate defendants sentenced to capital punishment in a very hostile context.[114] The Supreme Court, expressly recognized that the historical method test was not met in this case, since such rights

[107] Mashaw (1976), p. 47, fn. 61.

[108] Mashaw (1976), p. 47, fn. 61.

[109] Easterbrook (1982), p. 105.

[110] Tumey v. Ohio, 273 U.S. 510 (1927).

[111] Tumey v. Ohio, 273 U.S. 510 (1927), p. 514.

[112] Tumey v. Ohio, 273 U.S. 510 (1927), p. 523.

[113] Tumey v. Ohio, 273 U.S. 510 (1927), pp. 523–531.

[114] Powell v. Ala., 287 U.S. 45 (1932), pp. 51–52.

were not part of the "settled usages and modes of proceeding under the common and statute law of England" as inherited and adjusted to the political and social conditions of the Colonies.[115] Notwithstanding, it found that the right to a counsel has a fundamental character as part of the right to a hearing, in the sense that in many circumstances it would have little avail without it. It adds that arbitrarily denying a party to be assisted by a counsel in any civil or criminal case "...it reasonably may not be doubted that such a refusal would be a denial of a hearing, and, therefore, of due process in the constitutional sense."[116] Given its fundamental character, and the specific circumstances of the defendants and the trial in which they were convicted, the Court should not just provide the opportunity to secure a counsel, but make an effective -and not a mere formal- appointment of one,[117] even in the absence of a statute providing for it.[118]

This "fundamental fairness" approach that emerged according to Sullivan and Massaro, based on the concept of fairness embedded in the due process clause,[119] is present too in the well-known case of *Brown v. Mississippi*.[120] Here the Supreme Court clearly says that while a State is free to regulate the procedure, it may do so unless it offends some principle of justice ranked as fundamental.[121] And it adds, that "It would be difficult to conceive of methods more revolting to the sense of justice than those taken to procure the confessions of these petitioners, and the use of the confessions thus obtained as the basis for conviction and sentence was a clear denial of due process."[122] By using the precedents of *Moore v. Dempsey* and *Powell v. Alabama*, it says just like a trial dominated by a mob or without the aid of a counsel, a trial would equally be mere pretense where the state authorities have contrived a conviction resting solely upon confessions obtained by violence.[123] At this point, and as criticized by Easterbrook, the test used in *Murray v. Hoboken Land & Imp.* and *Hurtado*, does not appear in the decision.[124]

In *Rochin v. California* (1952), the Supreme Court recognized that the vagueness of due process does not leave judges full discretion. Its limits are derived from considerations fused in the nature of the judicial process, deeply rooted in reason and in the compelling traditions of the legal profession.[125] A due process claim requires an evaluation balancing the conflicting interest, "...on a judgment not ad hoc and episodic but duly mindful of reconciling the needs both of continuity and of change

[115]Powell v. Ala., 287 U.S. 45 (1932), p. 65.
[116]Powell v. Ala., 287 U.S. 45 (1932), pp. 68–69.
[117]Powell v. Ala., 287 U.S. 45 (1932), pp. 71–72.
[118]Powell v. Ala., 287 U.S. 45 (1932), p. 73.
[119]Sullivan and Massaro (2013), pp. 83–85.
[120]Brown v. Mississippi, 297 U.S. 278 (1936).
[121]Brown v. Mississippi, 297 U.S. 278 (1936), p. 285.
[122]Brown v. Mississippi, 297 U.S. 278 (1936), p. 286.
[123]Brown v. Mississippi, 297 U.S. 278 (1936), p. 286.
[124]Easterbrook (1982), p. 106.
[125]Rochin v. California, 342 U.S. 165 (1952), pp. 170–172.

in a progressive society."[126] In this specific case, the Court concluded that the way in which the evidence (a confession) that led to the conviction was obtained by means "that shocks the conscience."[127] Finally, the Court states that "Due process of law, as a historic and generative principle, precludes defining, and thereby confining, these standards of conduct more precisely than to say that convictions cannot be brought about by methods that offend 'a sense of justice.'"[128]

In the non-criminal field, the literature coming from the doctrine on Administrative law, which is quite relevant on the understanding of due process in non-criminal matters, this approach has been characterized as a reaction against the proliferation of new government functions and the emergence of the administrative state associated with the Depression, New Deal legislation and, later, with emergency war measures.[129]

Now that administrative agencies were empowered to make decisions in areas previously governed by the common law, an important question was how to provide a clear line between the power of such agencies and the courts. An interesting case in this regard is *Brinkerhoff-Faris Trust & Sav. Co. v. Hill*, where a taxpayer, acting as trustee for its shareholders, filed an action against the tax collector to enjoin him from collecting or attempting to collect taxes that were allegedly discriminatorily assessed. The State courts denied the action since it did not first seek an administrative remedy which, in fact, was never available and which was not subsequently open to the plaintiff.[130] The Court held that the judgment denying its action deprive the plaintiff of the only remedy ever available for the enforcement of its right to prevent the seizure of its property, and therefore to its property. It added that even though this decision came from the judiciary, the due process clause applies to the judicial as well as the legislative, executive or administrative branch of government.[131]

Where the decision making process comes from administrative agencies, the problem was at this point to establish the minimum requirements in such proceedings. In these cases, as expressed by Mashaw, at this point, if the Court was not to be

[126] Rochin v. California, 342 U.S. 165 (1952), p. 172.

[127] The Court said: "Illegally breaking into the privacy of the petitioner, the struggle to open his mouth and remove what was there, the forcible extraction of his stomach's contents by agents of government, to obtain evidence is bound to offend even hardened sensibilities." Rochin v. California, 342 U.S. 165 (1952), pp. 172–173. An older case in the Second Circuit Court of Appeals had applied before the "shock the conscience" standard to Sixth Amendment right to counsel: "A lack of effective assistance of counsel must be of such a kind as to *shock the conscience* of the Court and make the proceedings a farce and mockery of justice." United States v. Wight, 176 F.2d 376 (2d Cir. 1949), p. 379. The expression, on the contrary, is present even in even older cases but not applied to due process. See: Graffam v. Burgess, 117 U.S. 180 (1886), p. 191.

[128] Rochin v. California, 342 U.S. 165 (1952), pp. 172–173.

[129] Mashaw (1976), p. 47, fn. 61; Rubin (1984), p. 1049.

[130] Brinkerhoff-Faris Trust & Sav. Co. v. Hill, 281 U.S. 673 (1930), p. 674.

[131] Brinkerhoff-Faris Trust & Sav. Co. v. Hill, 281 U.S. 673 (1930), pp. 679–680.

a continual barrier in the progressive emergence of the administrative state, it was clear that a more flexible approach still was needed.[132]

As governmental functions increased, the Court was faced with due process problems that had no compelling historical analogies to determine what the required minimum was. Some cases arose during the 1930s against agencies' authority to fix different types of fixed rates such as in goods shipped by the carriers,[133] services of stock yards,[134] or telephone service rates.[135] For example, in *Ohio Bell Tel. Co. v. Public Utilities Com.*, a case concerning the determination of telephone service rates by a public agency, the Supreme Court held that in the decision making process, these agencies should meet the procedural standards of a civil trial.[136] It held that while broad deference has been extended to these agencies, their decisions are exempt of revision only as long as their decision is reached within the safeguard of a fair and open hearing, which must be "maintained in its integrity."[137] It adds that "[T]here can be no compromise on the footing of convenience or expediency, or because of a natural desire to be rid of harassing delay, when that minimal requirement has been neglected or ignored."[138] Moreover, this standard was applied too in *Opp Cotton Mills, Inc. v. Administrator of Wage & Hour Div.*, a case challenging an order from the Circuit Court of Appeals for the Fifth Circuit that sustained an order made by the respondent, an administrator of the Wage and Hour Division of the Department of Labor. That order fixed a uniform minimum wage for the textile industry under the Fair Labor Standards Act of 1938.[139] Here the Court held that no hearing is required at the initial stage or at any particular point in an administrative proceeding, so long it is held before the final order becomes effective.[140]

Changing circumstances of the first half of the Nineteen century, and the rapid growing of corporation's presence in different states,[141] also made that the new approach followed by the Court also reflected in the requirement of jurisdiction. In this regard, in *International Shoe Co. v. Washington*, the Court made the *Pennoyer v. Neff* rule on personal jurisdiction a more flexible one by holding that due process requires only that in order to subject a defendant to a judgment, if he is not present within the territory of the forum, he must have at least certain *minimum contacts* with

---

[132] Mashaw (1976), p. 47, fn. 61.

[133] Atchison, T. & S. F. R. Co. v. United States, 284 U.S. 248 (1932).

[134] St. Joseph Stock Yards Co. v. United States, 298 U.S. 38 (1936).

[135] Ohio Bell Tel. Co. v. Public Utilities Com., 301 U.S. 292 (1937).

[136] Rubin (1984), p. 1049.

[137] Ohio Bell Tel. Co. v. Public Utilities Com., 301 U.S. 292 (1937), p. 304.

[138] Ohio Bell Tel. Co. v. Public Utilities Com., 301 U.S. 292 (1937), p. 304.

[139] Opp Cotton Mills, Inc. v. Administrator of Wage & Hour Div., 312 U.S. 126 (1941), p. 133.

[140] Opp Cotton Mills, Inc. v. Administrator of Wage & Hour Div., 312 U.S. 126 (1941), pp. 152–153.

[141] Yeazell and Schwartz (2016), p. 76.

it such that the maintenance of the suit does not offend "traditional notions of fair play and substantial justice."[142]

One of the most relevant cases during this epoch, at least for non-criminal matters is *Mullane v. Cent. Hanover Bank & Trust Co.*, where the Supreme Court established basic standards on the minimum requirements of notice and opportunity to be heard. In particular, it decided whether the notice method to the beneficiaries of a judicial settlement of accounts by a trustee of a common trust fund established under the New York Banking Law was in conformity with the due process clause. While such a decree in each judicial settlement of accounts is made binding and conclusive on everyone having any interest in the common fund, the only notice given to them was a publication in a local newspaper in accord with the statute.[143] The court, abandoning the traditional distinction between actions *in rem* and in *personam,* held that the clause does not depend upon a classification, for which the standards are so elusive and confused. A definition of the chosen procedure in such matters is dependent on the State, provided that its procedure accords full opportunity to appear and be heard. In this regard, the interest of the State in bringing any issues as to its fiduciaries to a final settlement can be served only if the interests or claims of individuals who are outside the State can somehow be determined. A balance must be sought between the interest of the State and the individual interest sought to be protected by the Fourteenth Amendment; the right to be heard has little reality or worth unless one is informed that the matter is pending and can choose for himself whether to appear or default, acquiesce or contest.[144] According to it, the Court declared incompatible the statute allowing this notice by publication, since "[I]t would be idle to pretend that publication alone, as prescribed here, is a reliable means of acquainting interested parties of the fact that their rights are before the courts. It is not an accident that the greater number of cases reaching this Court on the question of adequacy of notice have been concerned with actions founded on process constructively served through local newspapers. Chance alone brings to the attention of even a local resident an advertisement in small type inserted in the back pages of a newspaper, and if he makes his home outside the area of the newspaper's normal circulation the odds that the information will never reach him are large indeed. The chance of actual notice is further reduced when, as here, the notice required does not even name those whose attention it is supposed to attract, and does not inform acquaintances who might call it to attention. In weighing its sufficiency on the basis of equivalence with actual notice, we are unable to regard this as more than a feint."[145]

A quite clear use of this approach in the non-criminal field is the concurring opinion of Justice Frankfurter in *Joint Anti-Fascist Refugee Committee v. McGrath.* In this case, the Attorney General included three organizations in a list of groups

[142]International Shoe Co. v. Washington, 326 U.S. 310 (1945), p. 316.

[143]Mullane v. Cent. Hanover Bank & Trust Co., 339 U.S. 306 (1950), pp. 307–309.

[144]Mullane v. Cent. Hanover Bank & Trust Co., 339 U.S. 306 (1950), pp. 312–314.

[145]Mullane v. Cent. Hanover Bank & Trust Co., 339 U.S. 306 (1950), p. 315.

designated by him as communist without notice or hearing. As required by the President's Executive Order No. 9835, the list was transmitted to all government departments and agencies, for use in administrative proceedings for the discharge of disloyal government employees. The plaintiff sued the Attorney General for declaratory and injunctive relief, seeking the deletion of their names from the list because of the resulting harm to their activities. According to him, "[F]airness of procedure is 'due process in the primary sense.'" It adds: "...'due process', unlike some legal rules, is not a technical conception with a fixed content unrelated to time, place and circumstances...cannot be imprisoned within the treacherous limits of any formula." Moreover, it recognizes that behind the clause there is a value "...of fairness between man and man, and more particularly between the individual and government, 'due process' is compounded of history, reason, the past course of decisions, and stout confidence in the strength of the democratic faith which we profess. Due process is not a mechanical instrument. It is not a yardstick. It is a process. It is a delicate process of adjustment inescapably involving the exercise of judgment by those whom the Constitution entrusted with the unfolding of the process."[146]

This evolution reached a climax in what has been called the "Due Process Revolution" by the hand of the Warren Court, beginning in the second half of the twentieth century. While an important part of the "revolution" concerns the criminal justice system,[147] in the non-criminal there was an outburst of relevant decisions which shaped the way the Supreme Court understood procedural due process.[148] In fact, the procedural due process revolution was forged in a series of decisions issued between 1970 and 1972, which has been described by Pierce as a dramatic expansion of the scope of the interests that are protected and the procedural safeguards that apply to those interests.[149] In the next chapter, I will describe this process, before embarking on some modern debates in the area of procedural due process.

References

Beebe A (1933) Self-government at the King's command. A study in the beginnings of English democracy. The University of Minnesota Press, Minneapolis

Blackstone W (1861) Commentaries on the laws of England: in four books; with an analysis of the work, vol 1. JB. Lippincott & Co., Philadelphia

Cogan N (ed) (2015) The complete bill of rights. The drafts, debates, sources, and origins, 2nd edn. Oxford University Press, New York

[146]Joint Anti-Fascist Refugee Committee v. McGrath, 341 U.S. 123(1951), pp. 162–163.

[147]Famous in this regard are the cases of Mapp v. Ohio, 367 U.S. 643 (1961), Gideon v. Wainwright, 372 U.S. 335 (1963), Miranda v. Ariz., 384 U.S. 436 (1966), Katz v. United States, 389 U.S. 347 (1967), and Terry v. Ohio, 392 U.S. 1. (1968).

[148]Parkin (2012), p. 1319.

[149]Pierce (1996), p. 1973.

Dripps D (2018) Due process: a unified understanding. In: Orren K, Compton J (eds) The Cambridge Companion to the United States Constitution. Cambridge University Press, Cambridge, pp 45–71

Easterbrook F (1982) Substance and due process. Sup Ct Rev 1982:85–125

Flack H (1908) The adoption of the fourteenth amendment. The Johns Hopkins Press, Baltimore

Galligan D (1996) Due process and fair procedures. A study of administrative procedures. Clarendon Press, Oxford

Kadish S (1957) Methodology and criteria in due process adjudication. A survey and criticism. Yale Law J 66(3):319–363

Leubsdorf J (1984) Constitutional civil procedure. Tex Law Rev 63(4):579–637

Mashaw J (1976) The Supreme Court's due process calculus for administrative adjudication in Mathews v. Eldridge: three factors in search of a theory of value. Univ Chic Law Rev 44(1): 28–59

Meyer H (1977) The history and meaning of the fourteenth amendment. Judicial erosion of the Constitution through the misuse of the fourteenth amendment. Vantage Press, New York

Parkin J (2012) Adaptable due process. Univ Pa Law Rev 160(5):1309–1378

Pierce R (1996) The due process counterrevolution of the 1990s? Colum Law Rev 96:1973–2000

Redish M, Marshall L (1986) Adjudicatory independence and the values of procedural due process. Yale Law J 95(3):455–503

Rubenstein W (2002) The concept of equality in civil procedure. Cardozo Law Rev 23:1865–1915

Rubin E (1984) Due process and the administrative state. Cal Law Rev 72(6):1044–1179

Sidhu O (2017) The concept of equality of arms in criminal proceedings under Article 6 of the European Convention on Human Rights. Intersentia, Cambridge

Silver J (1990) Equality of arms and the adversarial process: a new constitutional right. Wis Law Rev 4:1007–1042

Stephen S (2017) Pennoyer was right. Tenn Law Rev 95(6):1249–1328

Stuntz W (1996) Substance, process, and the civil-criminal line. J Contemp Leg Issues 7(1):1–41

Sullivan T, Massaro T (2013) The arc of due process in American Constitutional Law. Oxford University Press, New York

Thomas S (2012) Nonincorporation: the bill of rights after McDonald v. Chicago. Notre Dame Law Rev 88:159–204

Thomas S (2016) The missing American jury: restoring the fundamental constitutional role of the criminal, civil, and grand juries. Cambridge University Press, Cambridge

Yeazell S, Schwartz J (2016) Civil procedure, 9th edn. Aspen Casebook Series, Wolters Kluwer, United States

Chapter 11
Modern Conceptions of Procedural Due Process and the Right to a Fair Trial in Civil Matters

The Constitution does not expressly mention a clear scheme of procedural protections in civil matters—with the exception of right to a jury—, and neither there is a fruitful case law that supply for it, nor at least in comparison with criminal justice. Notwithstanding, that does not mean that the Constitution does not provide a basic framework that applies in such matters. As explained in the previous chapter, from the early case law the due process requirements over civil matters are jurisdiction, prior notice, and the right to a hearing.

As described, during the first half of the Nineteen century the governmental functions increased greatly. Theses changing circumstances made that the minimum requirements as applicable to civil matters did not fit properly to the necessities required to allow the expansion of the administrative state. In this regard, the main approach used by the Supreme Court during that time, based on dignitary values or "natural law", has been described as an "chaotic array."[1] Therefore, the next period, in the late 1950s and early 1960s the Supreme Court began to try another structure of analysis to provide a workable framework, which resulted in *Mathews v. Elridge* and the current method of analysis.[2]

In this regard, in *Cafeteria & Restaurant Workers Union v. McElroy*, it held that the due process clause of the Fifth Amendment does not require a trial-type hearing in every conceivable case of government impairment of private interest. As expressed in the traditional approach, due process does not provide for inflexible procedures universally applicable to every imaginable situation. Before embarking on the question of what is the procedure that is due, first must it be determined what the precise nature of the government function is involved, as well as that of the private interest that has been affected by governmental action. If such private interest

[1] Kadish (1957), p. 319.

[2] Mashaw (1976), p. 47, fn. 61.

R. Lillo Lobos, *Understanding Due Process in Non-Criminal Matters*, Ius Gentium: Comparative Perspectives on Law and Justice 97,
https://doi.org/10.1007/978-3-030-95534-2_11

is a mere privilege notice and hearing are not constitutionally required.[3] Under this approach, the due process clause applies to any proceeding where a person could be affected in his life, liberty or property by a legal or administrative decision or action. Only when this condition is met, the second question is what the minimum requirements are to be considered as a procedure that is "due."[4]

Regarding the nature of the government function, it was required to determine whether the administrative agency decision was rulemaking—akin to a legislative function—or adjudicative and as such closer to a judicial function. Procedural due process would be applicable only to the latter.[5] As such, it goes under the umbrella of adjudication since it is particularized or individualized justice and, therefore, triggers the due process requirements.

A good example is *Hannah v. Larche*, a case filed against the Federal Commission on Civil Rights because its procedural rules do not disclose the identity of the persons filing the charges, and the right to cross-examine witnesses, which the appellant found unconstitutional.[6] The Supreme Court held that requirements of due process frequently vary with the type of proceeding involved. In this regard, first it was necessary at the outset to ascertain both the nature and function of this Commission, which was found to be purely investigative and fact-finding. On the contrary, it was not adjudicative since it does not hold trials or determine anyone's civil or criminal liability, nor impose any legal sanctions. Under such circumstances, such procedural features were not constitutionally required in the proceedings of the Commission.[7] It adds that "...when governmental agencies adjudicate or make binding determinations which directly affect the legal rights of individuals, it is imperative that those agencies use the procedures which have traditionally been associated with the judicial process. On the other hand, when governmental action does not partake of an adjudication, as for example, when a general fact-finding investigation is being conducted, it is not necessary that the full panoply of judicial procedures be used."[8] Finally, it develops a test to determine whether the Constitution requires a particular procedural right. Basically, it says that it will depend on a complexity of factors such as the nature of the alleged right involved, the nature of the proceeding, and the possible burden on that proceeding.[9]

As an application of this doctrine, in *Willner v. Committee on Character & Fitness*, the Supreme Court decided what procedural due process requires if the license to practice law is to be withheld.[10] Basically, the Court held since the Committee in charge was more than an investigator, confrontation and

[3]Cafeteria & Restaurant Workers Union v. McElroy, 367 U.S. 886 (1961), pp. 894–895.

[4]Galligan (1996), p. 190.

[5]Rubin (1984), p. 1050.

[6]Hannah v. Larche, 363 U.S. 420 (1960), p. 421.

[7]Hannah v. Larche, 363 U.S. 420 (1960), pp. 440–442.

[8]Hannah v. Larche, 363 U.S. 420 (1960), p. 442.

[9]Hannah v. Larche, 363 U.S. 420 (1960), p. 442.

[10]Willner v. Committee on Character & Fitness, 373 U.S. 96 (1963), p. 103.

cross-examination of those whose word deprives a person of his livelihood were required by procedural due process.[11]

Still, it is not an easy task to define what is adjudication, beyond the scope of rulemaking versus individualized justice, especially to differentiate administrative from judicial adjudication. For example, in the administrative law literature, the standard conception of adjudication has the following features: i) an issue to be resolved, which might include or not a dispute between parties but also may concern the affair of only one person; ii) the issue will be determined according to settled standards; iii) by itself it requires impartiality on the part of a decision-maker; iv) an inquiry must be made into the relevant facts; v) the parties will usually be able to present their cases.[12]

Thus, where procedural due process applies, doctrine seems to describe an historical predominance of, and faith in, the adversarial type of legal proceedings as the one respectful of fair trial ideals. As argued by Sklansky, the adversarial system is seen as a type of legal procedure respectful of fundamental rights such as fair trial, praised over the inquisitorial criminal procedure of civil law countries.[13] While this author refers especially to criminal procedure, where much of the case law in this regard the Supreme Court had developed, it could be applied to civil matters as well. Although they have their particular properties, its adversarial features characterize both criminal and civil systems.[14] Nevertheless, and because very different procedural settings might be covered under the adversarial ideal umbrella, the concrete procedure that is due depends largely on what protected interest triggers the due process clause. Thus, the process that is due varies according to the context and the interest at stake.[15]

In non-criminal settings, the focus has been on what procedural safeguards are due when a State action affects property as a protected interest. Early cases distinguished between rights and privileges, and only the former were under due process protection. This distinction was considered problematic and gradually abandoned for a test of significant interest. Under this test, it is necessary to show the existence of a precise liberty or property interest and, then, a legal entitlement to it.[16] In non-criminal cases, in particular, it emerged within the realm of administrative law by the denial of due process protections to the recipients of government benefits created by statute and then expanding the concept of property as a protected interest.[17] In this regard, the procedural due process revolution was forged in a series of decisions issued between 1970 and 1972, which has been described by Pierce as a dramatically expansion of the scope of the interests that are protected and

[11] Willner v. Committee on Character & Fitness, 373 U.S. 96 (1963), pp. 103–104.

[12] Galligan (1996), p. 247.

[13] Regarding both categories from an historical and comparative perspective, see: Langer (2016).

[14] Kagan (2003), pp. 99–125.

[15] Galligan (1996), p. 198.

[16] Galligan (1996), p. 193.

[17] Sullivan and Massaro (2013), pp. 42–44.

the procedural safeguards that apply to those interest.[18] I devote the first part of this section to describing how the case law during the Due Process Revolution made an attempt to broaden this protection of procedural due process and to search for a test to determine what is the procedure that is due once the clause is triggered, at least in the non-criminal arena. Then, I will describe how this case law led to the *Mathews v. Eldridge* test,[19] the current approach used by the Court, and the debates that have arisen in the last decades.

11.1 The Due Process Revolution in Non-criminal Matters. The *Mathews v. Eldridge* Test

The Due Process Revolution in non-criminal arena began with the case *Goldberg v. Kelly*,[20] which started a string of cases recognizing government benefits such as welfare payments or public employment as "property" for purposes of the due process clause.[21] Before this decision, rights were narrowly defined to include only traditional forms of individual property and forms of liberty recognized in the Bill of Rights.[22] Pierce argues that the Court, highly influenced by an article of Charles Reich calling for judicial recognition of what he called the "new property," broadened the scope of protection by recognizing such entitlements as protected property rights.[23] Accordingly, the Supreme Court held that a welfare pre-termination hearing had to provide minimum procedural guarantees adapted to the characteristics of the recipients and the nature of the controversy. By doing so, to determine what procedure is due, the Court applied a balancing test weighing the competing interest of the state and the individual in the particular context.[24] In this specific case, and perhaps honoring the flexible character of the clause, the Court held that in many circumstances due process requires only "some kind of hearing." In that regard, before public assistance payments could be terminated on a finding of ineligibility a relatively informal hearing might suffice, one that a welfare agency is constitutionally required to provide, a form of hearing functionally indistinguishable from a judicial trial.[25]

Following *Goldberg v. Kelly*, in *Board of Regents v. Roth* a university professor argued he was denied his right to due process because the university never gave him a reason for their decision not to re-hire him and further he had no opportunity to

---

[18] Pierce (1996), p. 1973.

[19] Mathews v. Eldridge, 424 U.S. 319 (1976).

[20] Goldberg v. Kelly, 397 U.S. 254 (1970).

[21] Dripps (2018), p. 30.

[22] Pierce (1996), p. 1974.

[23] Pierce (1996), p. 1974.

[24] Sullivan and Massaro (2013), p. 87.

[25] Pierce (1996), p. 1977.

challenge their decision at a hearing.[26] First, the Court recognized a broad conception of property interest and expressly rejects the distinction between "rights" and "privileges" that once seemed to govern the applicability of procedural due process rights.[27] Notwithstanding, it rejected the application since a "property interest," to be protected by due process, must go beyond a mere unilateral expectation. There must be a legitimate claim of entitlement, in the sense that people could rely on in their daily lives, a reliance that must not be arbitrarily undermined. This property interest is not created by the Constitution but under existing rules or understandings that stem from an independent source such as the state. Only in such cases there is a right to a hearing to provide an opportunity for a person to vindicate those claims.[28] In a similar case concerning a teaching contract termination (or non-renewal), *Perry v. Sindermann*, the Court applied that approach to recognize that the respondent in this case should have been given an opportunity to prove the legitimacy of his claim of such entitlement in light of "the policies and practices of the institution."[29] Basically, the Court considers that the "property" protected by the clause covers a broad range of interests that are secured by "existing rules or understandings." That legitimacy might be provided by regulation through mutually explicit understandings that support his claim of entitlement to the benefit and that he may invoke at a hearing.[30]

Pierce characterizes the next period between 1973 and 1978 as a partial retreat and consolidation of the expansion of the procedural due process revolution initiated with *Goldberg v. Kelly.* The idea was to limit the scope of the new rights with a flexibilization of the minimum procedural safeguards required based on the nature of the protected interest.[31] Since a trial-type hearing could create a high burden for many public agencies taking countless decisions, case law of this period aimed to leave *Goldberg* as a high water mark and to send a message that in many other contexts due process could be satisfied by the use of procedures far less demanding.[32] No matter whether legislative or adjudicative, in many areas—such as prison or public school disciplinary procedures, or public employment discharge—this meant there was a "willingness" to accept much less than the full judicial model for the determination of facts.[33]

The most important case from this period is *Mathews v. Eldridge* (1976),[34] in which the Court developed a new test for determining the minimum procedural

---

[26] Board of Regents v. Roth, 408 U.S. 564 (1972), p. 566.

[27] Board of Regents v. Roth, 408 U.S. 564 (1972), p. 571.

[28] Board of Regents v. Roth, 408 U.S. 564 (1972), p. 577.

[29] Perry v. Sindermann, 408 U.S. 593 (1972), p. 603.

[30] Perry v. Sindermann, 408 U.S. 593 (1972), p. 601.

[31] Pierce (1996), p. 1981.

[32] Pierce (1996), p. 1983.

[33] Friendly (1975), p. 1274.

[34] Mathews v. Eldridge, 424 U.S. 319, 96 S. Ct. 893, 47 L. Ed. 2d 18, (1976).

safeguards required by the due process clause.[35] Unlike Goldberg, where the protected interest concerned welfare benefits, in *Mathews v. Eldridge* the main legal issue was social security disability benefits termination. In such proceedings, the government provided a two-tier decision-making process. Before terminating the benefits, the proceedings were written and only if the decision was challenged by the person affected was there a post-deprivation trial-type hearing.[36] The Court established that the specific procedure to be followed has to be determined by a balancing or "cost-benefit" test. This test is a three-prong analysis of several factors: "First, the private interest that will be affected by the official action; second, the risk of an erroneous deprivation of such interest through the procedures used, and the probable value, if any, of additional or substitute procedural safeguards; and finally, the Government's interest, including the function involved and the fiscal and administrative burdens that the additional or substitute procedural requirement would entail."[37]

The Supreme Court in this case held that the judicial model is neither required, nor the most effective method of decision making in all circumstances. What due process requires is that a person in jeopardy of a serious loss be given the meaningful opportunity to present his or her case and to be considered in the decision making. Deciding what specific process should be met, there must be some deference to those individuals charged by Congress with such a task. This is especially so where the prescribed procedures not only provide the claimant with an effective process for asserting his claim prior to any administrative action, but also assure a right to an evidentiary hearing, as well as to subsequent judicial review, before the denial of his claim becomes final.[38] Another reading of this holding is that where a decision might affect a private interest, the due process clause applies, but if there is no risk of a serious loss, something less than an evidentiary hearing is sufficient prior to adverse administrative action.[39]

Subsequent decisions relaxed even more the requirement established in *Goldberg v. Kelly* by upholding procedures far less demanding than a trial-type hearing in many contexts.[40] An example, in this regard, is the decision of the Supreme Court in *Arnett v. Kennedy*. Here, a federal civil service employee was removed from federal service under a statute allowing such decision after he was found to have recklessly made statements that an officer of the agency had been involved in bribes.[41] The Court held that, in this case, liberty as the protected interest was not offended by dismissal from employment itself, but instead by a dismissal which might damage the reputation of the employee. Since the purpose of the hearing in such a case is to

[35] Pierce (1996), p. 1981.

[36] Pierce (1996), p. 1982.

[37] Dripps (2018), p. 67.

[38] Mathews v. Eldridge, 424 U.S. 319 (1977), pp. 348–349.

[39] Dixon v. Love, 431 U.S. 105 (1977), p. 113.

[40] Pierce (1996), p. 1983.

[41] Arnett v. Kennedy, 416 U.S. 134 (1974), p. 136.

provide an opportunity to clear his name, a hearing afforded by administrative appeal procedures after the actual dismissal was sufficient compliance with the requirements of the due process clause.[42]

The period between this decision and the 1990s has been described by Pierce as an uneasy equilibrium, with failed and more successful attempts at a counterrevolution This counterrevolution was fought on several matters such as prisoner rights and public employment discharges, where the issue has been how to limit the scope of the concept of protected interest and not much on procedural grounds. In the field of public benefit programs, more discretion has been given to government agencies by statute to decide on the availability of the benefits under economic constraints, which in other words means to deny the status of "entitlement" to such benefits.[43]

11.2 Some Modern Debates on Procedural Due Process in Non-criminal Matters

After *Mathews v. Eldridge,* a debate arose regarding the application of the three-prong test as a general approach to decide in procedural due process cases or, in other words, whether it is applicable beyond welfare and public benefit cases. As such, *Mathews v. Eldridge* has been quite relevant in the administrative law arena in a very broad range of applications. In this regard, in *Smith v. Organization of Foster Families for Equality & Reform*, a case regarding parenthood rights against government agencies in charge of child protection, and *Parham v. J.R.*, concerning voluntary commitment procedures for children under the age of 18, the *Mathews v. Eldridge* test has been considered also as a general approach for testing challenged state procedures under a due process claim.[44] More recently, in *City of Los Angeles v. David*, the Supreme Court used the three prong test to decide whether the due process clause require an earlier payment-recovery hearing in a parking ticket proceeding. The problem according to the owner of a car which was towed away and fined for being parked on a spot which was forbidden, was that only 27 days after the vehicle was towed the city held a hearing only to deny his claim.[45] The Court decided first stating that the three factors of *Mathews v. Eldridge* "...normally determine whether an individual has received the 'process' that the Constitution finds 'due'".[46] Accordingly, the Court considered that such delay in holding a hearing in this case reflects no more than a routine delay substantially required by

---

[42] Arnett v. Kennedy, 416 U.S. 134 (1974), p. 157.

[43] Pierce (1996), pp. 1984–1995.

[44] Smith v. Organization of Foster Families for Equality & Reform, 431 U.S. 816 (1977), pp. 848–849; Parham v. J.R., 442 U.S. 584 (1979), p. 599.

[45] City of Los Angeles v. David, 538 U.S. 715 (2003), p. 716.

[46] City of Los Angeles v. David, 538 U.S. 715, 716 (2003).

administrative needs, and agencies are not forbidden under the due process clause from imposing such delay in claims of this nature.[47]

Less clear is the answer on the question whether this test applies in other non-criminal subjects. In this regard, has been applied in civil proceedings where the State have a relevant interest in litigation. For example, in *Little v. Streater,* it was applied by the Supreme Court to decide whether a Connecticut statute, which provides that in paternity actions the cost of blood grouping tests is to be borne by the party requesting them, violated the due process clause when applied to deny such tests to indigent defendants.[48] Under the three prong test, the Supreme Court took into consideration the unique quality of blood grouping tests as a source of exculpatory evidence, the State's prominent role in the litigation of this particular case,[49] and the character of paternity actions under Connecticut law.[50] So, analyzing the private interest in this case, which is apparent since at issue was the creation of a parent-child relationship, the probative value of the blood grouping tests, and the interest of the State, the Court concluded that the requirement of "fundamental fairness" expressed by the Due Process Clause was not satisfied.[51] It held that "[W]ithout aid in obtaining blood test evidence in a paternity case, an indigent defendant, who faces the State as an adversary when the child is a recipient of public assistance and who must overcome the evidentiary burden Connecticut imposes, lacks a meaningful opportunity to be heard."[52]

Similarly, in *Santosky v. Kramer*, the three factors test was used also regarding the required burden of proof on a parental rights termination proceeding to be compatible with the Fourteenth Amendment due process clause. In this regard, the Supreme Court held that in parental rights termination proceedings "...the private interest affected is commanding; the risk of error from using a preponderance standard is substantial; and the countervailing governmental interest favoring that standard is comparatively slight. Evaluation of the three Eldridge factors compels the conclusion that use of a 'fair preponderance of the evidence' standard in such proceedings is inconsistent with due process."[53]

---

[47] City of Los Angeles v. David, 538 U.S. 715, 719 (2003).

[48] Little v. Streater, 452 U.S. 1 (1981), pp. 3–4.

[49] The mother was compelled by Connecticut law to disclose the name of the putative father under oath and to institute an action to establish the paternity of said child because appellee's child was a recipient of public assistance. In addition, the State's Attorney General automatically became a party to the action, and any settlement agreement required his approval or that of the Commissioner of Human Resources or Commissioner of Income Maintenance. Little v. Streater, 452 U.S. 1 (1981), p. 9.

[50] In general under Connecticut law a defendant in a paternity suit is placed at a distinct disadvantage in that his testimony alone is insufficient to overcome the plaintiff's prima facie case. Even though it is considered a civil proceeding, in Connecticut this type of proceeding have "quasicriminal" tones. Little v. Streater, 452 U.S. (1981), pp. 10, 12.

[51] Little v. Streater, 452 U.S. 1, (1981), pp. 13–16.

[52] Little v. Streater, 452 U.S. 1 (1981), p. 16.

[53] Santosky v. Kramer, 455 U.S. 745 (1982), p. 758.

Regarding the application of this test over other more "traditional" civil cases, such as those arising from a dispute between two private parties, the answer is more complicated. For example, scholars have used this test to analyze procedural guarantees such as the right to a lawyer or rights for pro se litigants in civil matters. Scherer, in this regard, has said that from the perspective of the fairness of the procedure, by applying the three factors, the right to counsel would be warranted in many civil matters such as tenants facing evictions.[54]

Nevertheless, as described above, the Constitution does provide a minimum framework that applies in civil matters, whose basic requirements are developed in cases like *Mullane v. Central Hanover Trust.* Beyond such a minimum, in recent years through *Mathews v. Eldridge* and its progeny the Supreme Court has provided a workable method from which lower courts can determine the form of procedural due process to which a person is entitled when the state deprives him or her of liberty or property even in a civil context.[55]

Of course, a more robust theory on due process as applied over civil matters in general may provide guidance to design or interpret legislative and court decisions related to procedural fairness. There are authors, such as Robert Bone, who call for such a theory,[56] which could, for example, provide some clarity regarding many modern alternatives to the traditional judicial process which have emerged in recent decades. Class actions or statistical adjudication provide good examples in this regard.

As described by Garth, "[C]lass actions rest on a relatively simple proposition: self-selected class representatives and their lawyers, properly supervised by the court, can represent class members as a group sufficiently well to overcome members' individual rights to be heard."[57] Class actions were established in the Rule 23 of the Federal Rules of Civil Procedure, allowing some of the persons constituting a class to represent the others, where other forms of joinder are otherwise inadequate.[58] As expressed in its modern version, after the amendments of 1966 and 2017, it applies as long as the class is so numerous that a joinder of all members is impracticable; there are questions of law or fact common to the class; the claims or defenses of the representative parties are typical of the claims or defenses of the class; and the representative parties will fairly and adequately protect the interests of the class.[59] The idea behind class actions, ". . .is to provide a pragmatic method of dispute resolution that is fair to the individual and responsive to the needs of the community and the challenges generated by widely spread and shared harms."[60]

---

[54] Scherer (2006), p. 677. See also: Bradlow (1988).

[55] Brett (2016), p. 358.

[56] See: Bone (1993), pp. 594–617.

[57] Garth (1987), pp. 497–505.

[58] Grossi and Allan (2020), p. 60.

[59] Federal Rules of Civil Procedure, Rule 23.

[60] Grossi and Allan (2020), p. 98.

According to Yeazell and Schwartz, the due process clause imposes two main questions on class actions. First, whether a party can be bound by litigation to which he is not a party, and second, whether due process requires certain procedures within the class action in order for it to be a valid adjudication of the absentees' rights.[61] The basic answer is provided by the Supreme Court in *Hansberry v. Lee,* in which, while recognizing the basic rule that a person is not bound by a judgment in a litigation in which he is not designated as a party, class action proceedings are an exception as long as the procedure fairly ensures the protection of the interests of absent parties who are to be bound by it.[62] For Grossi, in this decision, the Court did not impose any stringent dogma of due process beyond a constitutional requirement of adequate representation. From another perspective, that the "...demands of justice supersede the goal of efficiency when the purported representatives of the class do not share a common interest and goal with the class."[63]

In *Phillips Petroleum Co. v. Shutts*, it established further requirements especially for out-of-state plaintiffs. The Court held that since the Fourteenth Amendment protects "persons," not "defendants," absent plaintiffs are entitled to some protection too. These minimal procedural due process guarantees are notice, plus an opportunity to be heard and participate in the litigation, whether in person or through counsel. In this regard, the notice should describe the action and the plaintiffs' rights, and the chosen method must be the best practicable, requiring only to be reasonably calculated, under all the circumstances, to appraise interested parties of the pendency of the action and afford them an opportunity to present their objections. Due process requires at a minimum that an absent plaintiff be provided with an opportunity to remove himself from the class and, finally, following *Hansberry*, the named plaintiff must always adequately represent the interests of the absent class members.[64]

From the point of view of the due process clause, the dissenting opinion of Justice Breyer in *Ortiz v. Fibreboard Corp.*, is quite interesting. In this case, a litigation settlement in the context of the massive claims due to asbestos contamination in the United States, the Supreme Court rejected a class certification basically because the rules were not designed for such massive individual claims, since it did not fit into Rule 23(b)(1)(B), while calling for national legislation to solve the problem. Justice Breyer dissented since in the context of this mass litigation—the case involved a settlement of an estimated 186,000 potential future asbestos claims against Fibreboard—for approximately $ 1.535 billion—the alternative to a class action settlement was not going to be a fair opportunity for each plaintiff but probably no justice at all. Therefore, besides a claim for a regulatory solution, judges "...should

[61] Yeazell and Schwartz (2016), p. 545.

[62] Hansberry v. Lee, 311 U.S. 32 (1940), pp. 40–42.

[63] Grossi and Allan (2020), p. 64.

[64] Phillips Petroleum Co. v. Shutts, 472 U.S. 797 (1985), pp. 811–812.

search aggressively for ways, within the framework of existing law, to avoid delay and expense so great as to bring about a massive denial of justice."[65]

Other debates arise regarding the requirements of due process over Alternative Dispute Resolution mechanisms, which since the well-known Pound Conference of 1976 have expanded greatly, and even further with the Alternative Dispute Resolution Act of 1998.[66] More recently, Galanter described the decline of confidence in adjudication and courts while judicial, political and business actors have embraced other "alternative" processes such as mediation, arbitration, and others.[67] Especially, arbitration has been a focus in many of the debates, one of them regarding its compatibility with the due process clause. Arbitration, in broad general terms, is a dispute resolution mechanism that resembles adjudication but where a private arbitrator decides a dispute after having heard from both sides. Both sides may agree in many aspects of the arbitration, beginning with the arbitrator itself, its selection method, the substantive rules to apply, and procedural rules. These apparent advantages may produce imbalances between the parties, especially in areas where the arbitration agreement terms are dictated by one party only.[68]

Particularly problematic is the use of mandatory arbitration clauses to block access to the courts[69] in contracts of adhesion, more so considering that they are widely used, as in cellphone contracts, credit cards, employment, including by government agencies to resolve disputes over eligibility for government benefits.[70] The most significant problem from this point of view, according to Golann, is that many civil justice issues could be deprived by mandatory ADR mechanisms which might be significant enough to require compliance with the due process clause, and if so, what due process principles are required to be satisfied under such alternative procedures.[71]

Enacted in 1925, the purpose of the Federal Arbitration Act (FAA) was to counter judicial hostility to pre-dispute arbitration agreements.[72] In this regard, the Court used to read the FAA as neither favoring arbitration over other federal regulatory goals nor applying it in contexts where parties had significantly different bargaining power.[73] Moreover, according to Hensler and Khatam, in the early case law interpreting the FAA the Court recognized many of its limitations, such as the curtailment of the right to a jury and public courts, lack of reasoned opinions, relaxed evidentiary standards, no formal right to discovery, and limited appellate

[65] Grossi and Allan (2020), pp. 77–81; Ortiz v. Fibreboard Corp., 527 U.S. 815 (1999), pp. 866–867.

[66] Reuben (2000), p. 954.

[67] Galanter (2007), p. 17.

[68] Yeazell and Schwartz (2016), p. 373.

[69] Galanter (2007), p. 29.

[70] Golann (1989), p. 498; Resnik (2014), pp. 1809–1811; Yeazell and Schwartz (2016), p. 374.

[71] Golann (1989), p. 532.

[72] Yeazell and Schwartz (2016), p. 374.

[73] Resnik (2014), p. 1812.

review.[74] Beginning in the 1980's it began to interpret the act as favoring a policy for the enforcement of *knowing and voluntary* arbitration agreements.[75] More recently, according to Resnik, the Court has expressed that arbitration is to be preferred against adjudication. In this regard, she refers to *AT&T Mobility LLC v. Concepcion*,[76] where the Court enforced waivers of class actions in arbitration based on the idea that the FAA not only mandated "bilateral" arbitration but also did so to avoid the "costliness and delays of litigation."[77]

Of course, the requirements of a valid waiver present complex questions, such as those concerning adhesion contracts or class-action waivers in arbitration agreements. As expressed by Reuben, while a valid waiver may operate to renounce substantive and procedural rights, in order to conform with the Constitution this cannot mean that the individual waives all procedural rights, especially those that meet the most basic requirements of fundamental fairness.[78]

One of such rights could be the right to access to justice which, as I will describe in the next section, according to some doctrine is embedded in the due process clause as a requirement of fairness. Under the FAA, private parties, especially in the context of mandatory arbitration agreements and adhesion contracts, would be empowered to bar access to the public courts and the public law that would apply therein for many individuals.[79] And arbitration in the American Legal system has been widening its scope dramatically. From commercial disputes it has gone further into subjects characterized by an imbalance between parties, such as employment relations, consumer and service providers, and patients and health care providers.[80]

The expansion of the scope of arbitration in areas such as employment agreements has been criticized amongst worker advocates and legal scholars. As argued by Stone, arbitration clauses are so widely used that today, more employees are covered by such clauses than by collective bargaining agreements. As such, the perception is that there is a judicial roll back on labor rights and a severe curtailment of access to the courts. According to this author, the FAA has become a central pillar of national policy by the hand of several decisions by Justice Scalia. His reasonings, she argues, have created a wall between federal courts and most lawsuits brought by ordinary individuals, while arbitration has become the exclusive forum for most of these claims.[81]

Beside access to a court, it is a matter of debate that as long as an arbitration might affect life, liberty, or property, the bare minimum of due process requirements—such as notice and hearing—should be afforded even if their particularities vary according

---

[74] Hensler and Khatam (2018), p. 389.

[75] Regarding these requirements, see: Reuben (2000), pp. 1020–1030.

[76] See: AT&T Mobility LLC v. Concepcion, 563 U.S. 333 (2011).

[77] Resnik (2014), p. 1813.

[78] Resnik (2014), pp. 1018–1019.

[79] Reuben (2000), p. 1036.

[80] Hensler and Khatam (2018), p. 393.

[81] Stone (2017), pp. 190–192.

to the nature of the case. As described by Reuben, while a waiver under the FAA may limit substantive and many procedural rights—especially those of a full-blown trial—constitutional due process would still require this bare minimum to ensure that arbitration, especially when administered by state actors, complies with the Constitution.[82] In this regard, another basic procedural guarantee which has been upheld by the Supreme Court, at least in the case of arbitrations made by government agencies, is the impartiality requirement. In *Concrete Pipe & Prods. v. Constr. Laborers Pension Trust*, concerning a due process claim against an arbitration proceeding regarding pension funds withdrawal liability,[83] the Supreme Court held that no matter the criminal or civil setting, one is entitled to an adjudicator who is not in a situation "'...which would offer a possible temptation to the average man as a judge...which might lead him not to hold the balance nice, clear and true...". It adds that adjudication procedures need to satisfy the appearance of justice, and this stringent rule may sometimes bar trials even by judges who have no actual bias and who would do their very best to weigh the scales of justice equally between contending parties. This is true even in cases like this one where the decision maker is a private party acting by its given authority to adjudicate by statute.[84]

Another example is the debate on federal court delay, which might be framed as a constitutional claim under the due process clause. In *Logan v. Zimmerman Brush Co.*, the Supreme Court held that although minimum procedural requirements are a matter of federal law, and the legislature may elect not to confer a property interest, it may not constitutionally authorize the deprivation of such an interest, once conferred, without appropriate procedural safeguards. The adequacy of statutory procedures for deprivation of a statutorily created property interest must be analyzed in constitutional terms.[85] According to Hittner and Weisz, such analysis calls for a decision under the *Mathews v. Eldridge* test.[86]

Notwithstanding the relevance of *Mathews v. Eldridge* as a general understanding of the concept of flexibility of the due process clause,[87] the Court has refused to apply the *Eldridge* test to criminal cases,[88] at least at federal level. According to Dripps, while in civil cases a fair hearing means a procedure that satisfies the balancing test of *Mathews v. Eldridge*, in criminal cases it means the fair trial provisions in the Bill of Rights, supplemented by any other procedures required as a matter of "fundamental fairness."[89] In *Medina v. California*, the Supreme Court

[82] Reuben (2000), p. 1040.

[83] Concrete Pipe & Prods. v. Constr. Laborers Pension Trust, 508 U.S. 602 (1993), p. 605.

[84] Concrete Pipe & Prods. v. Constr. Laborers Pension Trust, 508 U.S. 602 (1993), pp. 617–618.

[85] Logan v. Zimmerman Brush Co., 455 U.S. 422 (1982), p. 424.

[86] See: Hittner and Weisz (1990), pp. 352–354.

[87] Sullivan and Massaro (2013), pp. 87–88. See: Parham v. J.R., 442 U.S. 584, 599, 99 S.Ct. 2493, 2502, 61 L.Ed.2d 101 (1979).

[88] Cited only in two criminal cases but not applying its balancing test to the due process analysis: United States v. Raddatz, 447 U.S. 667 (1980); Ake v. Oklahoma, 470 U.S. 68 (1985).

[89] Dripps (2018), p. 69.

gave a rationale not to apply the *Mathews v. Elridge* balancing test to criminal justice. It said it does not provide the appropriate framework for assessing the validity of state procedural criminal regulation. Where the Bill of Rights speaks in explicit terms to many aspects of criminal procedure, the Court prefers to define the category of infractions that violate fundamental fairness very narrowly. The idea is that beyond the specific guarantees enumerated in the Bill of Rights, the Due Process Clause has limited operation in the criminal justice arena.[90]

Finally, the *Mathews v. Eldridge* test has been criticized for many reasons, especially in the literature from the field of administrative law. The main criticism is that it is not informed by any theory on the values underlying procedural due process. This test seems a utilitarian calculus but, according to Mashaw, it is incomplete even in this regard.[91] The problem is that without such determination it is impossible to fix the floor of procedural safeguards, and as Redish and Marshall point out, a house without a floor is not a house at all.[92] But also, for example, because the test inherently tilts in favor of the government's position, since procedural safeguards impose administrative costs and burdens on the government that would not otherwise exist, and thus are apparent, while the benefits of such safeguards are not always immediately recognizable.[93]

11.3 The Right of Access to the Courts and the Due Process Clause. A Brief Look at States' Legal Systems

To provide a complete picture of the conception of a fair trial in civil matters, access to justice is fundamental. For this purpose, and to finish this chapter, we will briefly address the question of the right of access to a court and its relationship with the right to a due process.

As described in chapter 8, the original Magna Carta of 1215 provided in two different clauses, the traditional law of the land formula in its clause 39, and in clause 40 it added "To none will we sell, to none will we deny, to none will we delay right or justice." A subsequent and more successful version of 1225 enacted during the reign of Henry III,[94] merged both in a single provision, the Chapter 29.[95]

---

[90] Medina v. California, 505 U.S. 437 (1992). More recently, by applying the Mathews v. Elridge test to a post-and-forfeit procedure, the Court of Appeal of the District of Columbia Circuit, gave the same rationale to not apply this test to criminal procedure. Kincaid v. Gov't of D.C., 854 F.3d 721 (D.C. Cir. 2017), p. 726.

[91] Mashaw (1976), p. 46.

[92] Redish and Marshall (1986), pp. 472–474.

[93] Redish and Marshall (1986), p. 473.

[94] Holt (2015), pp. 325–327.

[95] Available at: http://www.nationalarchives.gov.uk/education/resources/magna-carta/magna-carta-1225-westminster/.

Chapter 29 was a one of Coke's favorites provisions[96] which he interpreted as conferring a right to have a remedy for any injury suffered (whether to its person or its property) freely without sale, denial or delay.[97] This provision that have been equated in modern American law to the right to a court or of access to justice,[98] unlike many other Coke's interpretations of the Magna Carta did not ended up expressly in the Constitution.

Accordingly, the complexity of studying the right of access to justice in the American legal system, and in its constitutional history in particular, is that without such recognition its nature as a constitutional right is debated. In this regard, there are authors arguing that this right at least insofar as civil litigants are concerned, is not a fundamental right protected by the Constitution by itself.[99] But this is not to deny that access to justice might be imbedded in the same due process clause, as we saw, for example, regarding other international jurisdictions such as in the case of the European and the Inter-American regional systems for human rights protection, or even in the case of Chile. In this regard, according to other literature, the Fourteenth Amendment incorporated the due process clause of the Fifth, that embedded the value of fair procedure already which gave citizens a right to access to the courts as a stronger conviction that the judicial system should be usable by all citizens.[100]

Notwithstanding, and because of the lack of an express recognition, access to justice has not been equated only to procedural due process, but also to other constitutional provisions. In this regard, access to justice has been identified with the equal protection clause under the Fourteenth Amendment. In this regard, Deborah Rhodes, a leading scholar on this subject links access to justice with the concept of "Equal justice", which is usually taken to mean "equal access to justice," which in turn is taken to mean access to law.[101] As described by Leubsdorf, this Amendment was proposed to "constitutionalize" the Civil Rights Act of 1866, which at its hart was meant to assurance equal access to the courts in the context of civil litigation. In this regard, its Section I states that: That all persons...shall have the same right, in every State and Territory in the United States, to make and enforce contracts, to sue, be parties, and give evidence, inherit, purchase, lease, sell, hold, and convey real and personal property, and to full and equal benefit of all laws and proceedings for the security of person and property..."[102] As an application of this doctrine over access to appellate review, the Supreme Court had held that while the due process does not require a State to provide appellate review, when it is afforded, it cannot be granted

[96]Thompson (1948), p. 97.
[97]Coke (1797), pp. 55–56.
[98]Pankratz (1992), p. 1099.
[99]Hittner and Weisz (1990), p. 350. See also: Hart (1953), pp. 1362–1402.
[100]Pankratz (1992), pp. 1099–1102.
[101]Rhode (2001), p. 1786.
[102]14 Stat. 27, 39 Cong. Ch. 31, Sec. 1.

to some litigants and capriciously or arbitrarily denied to others without violating the Equal Protection Clause.[103]

Others have considered that access to justice is under Constitutional protection through the Petition Clause of the First Amendment. Regarding the latter, as pointed out by Leubsdorf, the Supreme Court in in *NAACP v. Button*, upheld under the protection of this right to organize in bringing constitutional and non-constitutional grievances to the courts.[104] This right would be an specification of the ancient right to present grievances to the government, and recognized in the last section in the First Amendment of the Constitution. According to Rice, the Supreme Court in 1972 recognized for the first time an individual's right of access to court under the Petition Clause in the case of *California Motor Transport Co. v. Trucking Unlimited*,[105] where it held: "Petitioners, of course, have the right of access to the agencies and courts to be heard on applications sought by competitive highway carriers. That right, as indicated, is part of the right of petition protected by the First Amendment.[106] For Rice, this avenue has the most potential in the context of curtailment of access to justice under the due process clause during the 1970s.[107]

Those who support the right of access under the due process clause consider that civil litigants have an analytically distinct protected interest in a meaningful opportunity to be heard from any other substantive claim supporting the legal action.[108] If the basic notion of due process is that people are entitled to meaningful opportunities in court when they face losses of important interest,[109] this embeds the idea of access to a court at least regarding claims on protected interest. Anything to the contrary would deprive the opportunity of any meaningful character. This is the connection between the concept of access to justice with procedural due process, since the latter would be at stake whenever the state denies a fair hearing to a person alleging a 'good' cause of action. For Michelman, the access to such a hearing is, therefore, if not a part of procedural due process itself, a "preferred freedom" or "fundamental interest" contained within substantive due process liberty.[110]

The question under the due process clause, is whether access to justice is a right only whenever a protected interest is deprived, or if it is a right by itself to be protected under the clause. This first approach has been recognized by the Supreme Court in *Boddie v. Connecticut*, where at least recognized that this right must be protected when access is sought to pursue a fundamental right and there exists no manner to vindicate that right other than through the courts.[111] In other words, there

---

[103] Lindsey v. Normet, 405 U.S. 56 (1972), p. 77.

[104] Leubsdorf (1984), p. 590.

[105] Rice (1999), p. 559.

[106] California Motor Transport Co. v. Trucking Unlimited, 404 U.S. 508 (1972), p. 513.

[107] Rice (1999), p. 562.

[108] Bradlow (1988), p. 677.

[109] Scherer (2006), p. 677.

[110] Michelman (1974), pp. 556–557.

[111] Hittner and Weisz (1990), p. 350.

is no constitutional recognition of a general right to pursue a legal action, but only in cases where a protected interest is pursued through it. Specifically, the Court held that while not deciding that access for all individuals to the courts is a right that is, in all circumstances, guaranteed by the clause, it was for the purpose of a protected interest in this case. Since the requirement for the appellants to enforce the right to dissolve this legal relationship through judicial process was an entirely a state-created matter, therefore the same State may not pre-empt it without affording all citizens access to the means it has prescribed for doing so.[112] In this regard, in *Logan v. Zimmerman*, the Supreme Court of the United States declared: "The Court traditionally has held that the Due Process Clauses protect civil litigants who seek recourse in the courts, either as defendants hoping to protect their property or as plaintiffs attempting to redress grievances."[113]

In cases such as *Boddie v. Connecticut*, the Supreme Court had linked the right of access with the right to an opportunity to be heard. In this regard, it has considered whether cost and fees might involve a due process violation, if in practice they foreclose a particular party's opportunity to be heard.[114] In this case, the main legal issue was whether the imposition of fees and cost of service as a requirement for indigent litigants, prior to the filing of a claim over a protected interest, is against the due process clause. In this regard, although it supports the establishment of such requirements as a matter of State's interest, e.g. in the prevention of frivolous litigation and to allocate scarce resources, none of these considerations is sufficient to override the interest of the plaintiffs in having access to the only avenue open for dissolving their allegedly untenable marriages.[115] In the specific circumstance of the case, the Supreme Court held, "...the State's refusal to admit the appellants to its courts, the sole means in Connecticut for obtaining a divorce, must be regarded as the equivalent of denying them an opportunity to be heard upon their claimed right to a dissolution of their marriages."[116]

Under the same rationale, the Supreme Court in *United States v. Kras* this time held that access to the bankruptcy courts could be denied to those unable to pay a fifty-dollar filing fee.[117] Unlike *Boddie*, where the parties' main legal issue concerned the status of the heir's marital relationship, which is a fundamental interest under the Constitution, in Kras the alleged interest was the elimination of debt burden, which although important (and so recognized by the enactment of the Bankruptcy Act), it is not a constitutionally protected interest. Moreover, in contrast with divorce, bankruptcy is not the only method available to a debtor for the

[112] Boddie v. Connecticut, 401 U.S. 371 (1971), pp. 382–383.
[113] Logan v. Zimmerman Brush Co., 455 U.S. 422 (1982), p. 429.
[114] Boddie v. Connecticut, 401 U.S. 371, (1971), p. 379.
[115] Boddie v. Connecticut, 401 U.S. 371, (1971), p. 381.
[116] Boddie v. Connecticut, 401 U.S. 371, (1971), pp. 380–381.
[117] Hittner and Weisz (1990), p. 351.

adjustment of his legal relationship with his creditors, as he could have entered into an agreement with them.[118]

The connection between access to justice and the due process clause would explain why chapter 40 of the original clause, one of the Sir Edward Coke's favorites, had an important recognition in many colonial charters and in States' constitutions. By briefly looking into the current States' constitutions, it is clear that the due process clause and the right to access to justice are well ingrained in the American system.

As described before, in many ways the path of due process and its requirements over legal procedures were profoundly influenced by the conception that colonies first and States later had of it. Surely, after the enactment of the Bill of Rights and later of the Fourteenth Amendment, it might be said that the influence goes in both directions. This is especially true of those Constitutions adopted after 1866 (38 of the 50 States), but even of older ones since all of them currently in force were adopted after the Bill of Rights (the oldest in force being the Constitution of Wisconsin, adopted in 1848). Notwithstanding the chronological order, to complete the picture provided in the previous chapters, it is necessary to take a brief look at the current State Constitutions.

From the fifty current State Constitutions, in thirty-nine it is possible to find a general due process clause such as the one in the Fifth and Fourteenth Amendments.[119] In the other eight, it is more debatable because the clause is part of a provision related to criminal justice. Notwithstanding, in such instances, the State constitution provided for a general clause on the language of the "law of the land",[120] or more importantly for this section, provided a clause in a language similar to that the clause 40 as a general right to a fair trial provision.[121] For example, the Constitution of Idaho provides in its Art. 1 Section 13 entitled "Guarantees in Criminal Actions and Due Process of Law," a sentence with the phrase of "... nor be deprived of life, liberty or property without due process of law," and in its section 18, entitled "Justice to be Freely and Speedily" reads: "Courts of justice shall be open to every person, and a speedy remedy afforded for every injury of person, property or character, and right and justice shall be administered without sale, denial, delay, or prejudice."[122]

---

[118]United States v. Kras, 409 U.S. 434 (1973), pp. 444–445.

[119]I did not find the language of clause in its 1354 version only in the current constitutions of three States: Maryland (1867), New Jersey (1947), Vermont (1793). Only the Constitution of New Jersey does not provide for a clause with the language of "due process" or neither with the "law of the land".

[120]This is the case, for example, with the constitutions of Arkansas (1874) and New York (1938).

[121]Arkansas (1874), Idaho (1890), Minnesota (1857), New Hampshire (1784), North Dakota (1889). The Constitution of Michigan (1963) provides in its article 1 section 17 a due process clause inside a provision that reads: Art. 1. Section 17. Sec. 17. "No person shall be compelled in any criminal case to be a witness against himself, nor be deprived of life, liberty or property, without due process of law."

[122]Information available at: https://sos.idaho.gov/ELECT/stcon/article_I.html.

In total, thirty-nine out of the fifty State constitutions provide a clause providing for a right of access to justice (Table 11.1). Many of them use the language of clause 40 of the Magna Carta. For example, in the Florida Constitution (1968), art. 1 section 21 provide: "Access to courts.-The courts shall be open to every person for redress of any injury, and justice shall be administered without sale, denial or delay."[123] Moreover, others such as article 1 section 9 of the Constitution of North Dakota (1889), provide a formula comprising both the language of "due process of law" and of clause 40, already mentioned: "All courts shall be open, and every man for any injury done him in his lands, goods, person or reputation shall have remedy by due process of law, and right and justice administered without sale, denial or delay..."[124]

11.4 Two Possible Explanations and Lines for Future Research

As explained throughout this chapter, there is a long tradition in the American legal system on procedural due process. From its origins in the Magna Carta to the American Constitution and especially since its incorporation in the Fourteenth Amendment, the understanding of what is the procedure that is due as a constitutional right has evolved greatly. In this process, the decisions of the Supreme Court have shaped its content and scope until the modern framework on the constitutional requirements over legal procedures.

Procedure was at the core of the due process clause even in its inception in the Magna Carta. As explained, many authors had interpreted it as a right to a specific mode of proceedings and in opposition to other forms of regulations, such as the decrees of the King and against the arbitrariness from the Crown and its justice machinery. That is why there are authors who believe that the original clause only dealt with criminal matters.

In the seventeenth century, when the clause blossoms again, it was used as an instrument of resistance against the Stuart kings, and therefore its importance in criminal prosecution was fundamental. In this regard, the work done by Sir Edward Coke interpreting the original clause and deriving from it a set of basic judicial guarantees provided guidance for the understanding of due process in the American colonies.

---

[123] Similar clauses might be found in: Arizona (1910), Arkansas (1874), Colorado (1876), Florida (1968), Georgia (1982), Idaho (1890), Illinois (1970), Maryland (1867), Massachusetts (1780), Minnesota (1857), Missouri (1945), Montana (1972), Nebraska (1875), New Hampshire (1784), Rhode Island (1986), South Carolina (1895), Vermont (1793), Washington (1889), Wisconsin (1848), Wyoming (1889).

[124] In the same situation might be: Alabama (1901), Connecticut (1965), Delaware (1897), Indiana (1851), Kansas (1861), Kentucky (1891), Louisiana (1974), Mississippi (1890), North Carolina (1971), North Dakota (1889), Oklahoma (1907), Oregon (1857), Pennsylvania (1968), South Dakota (1889), Tennessee (1870), Texas (1876), Utah (1895), West Virginia (1872).

Table 11.1 Summary of due process and right to a court clauses in state constitutions

State (date of adoption)	Access to civil justice related provision?	Due of process of law formula?	Law of the land formula?
Alabama (1901)	Yes (Section 13)	Yes (Section 13)	No
Alaska (1956)	No	Yes (Section 7)	No
Arizona (1910)	Yes (Art. 2. Section 11)	Yes (Art. 2. Section 4)	No
Arkansas (1874)	Yes (Art. 2. Section 13)	Yes (Art. 2. Section 8)	Yes (Art. 2. Section 21)
California (1849)	No	Yes (Art. 1. Section 7)	No
Colorado (1876)	Yes (Art. 2. Section 6)	Yes (Art. 2. Section 25)	No
Connecticut (1965)	Yes (Section 10)	Yes (Section 10)	No
Delaware (1897)	Yes (Section 9)	Yes (Section 9)	Yes (Section 7)
Florida (1968)	Yes (Art. 1. Section 21)	Yes (Art. 1. Section 9)	No
Georgia (1982)	Yes (Art. 1. Section 1. Par. XII)	Yes (Art. 1. Section 1. Par.I)	No
Hawaii (1950)	No	Yes (Art. 1. Section 5)	Yes (Art. 1. Section 8)
Idaho (1890)	Yes (Art. 1. Section 18)	Yes (Art. 1. Section 13)	No
Illinois (1970)	Yes (Art. 1. Section 12)	Yes (Art. 1. Section 2)	No
Indiana (1851)	Yes (Art. 1. Section 12)	Yes (Art. 1. Section 12)	No
Iowa (1857)	No	Yes (Art. 1. Section 1.9)	No
Kansas (1861)	Yes (Section 18)	Yes (Section 18)	No
Kentucky (1891)	Yes (Section 14)	Yes (Section 14)	Yes (Section 11)
Louisiana (1974)	Yes (Art. 1. Section 22)	Yes (Art. 1. Section 2)	0
Maine (1820)	No	Yes (Section 6-A)	Yes (Art. 1 Section 6)
Maryland (1867)	Yes (Art. 19)	No	Yes (Art. 24)
Massachusetts (1780)	Yes (Art. XI)	Yes (Art. X)	Yes (Art. XII)
Michigan (1963)	No	Yes (Art. 1. Section 17)	No
Minnesota (1857)	Yes (Section 8)	Yes (Section 7)	No
Mississippi (1890)	Yes (Art. 3. Section 24)	Yes (Art. 3. Section 14)	No
Missouri (1945)	Yes (Art. 1. Section 14)	Yes (Art. 1. Section 10)	No
Montana (1972)	Yes (Art. 2. Section 16)		No

(continued)

Table 11.1 (continued)

State (date of adoption)	Access to civil justice related provision?	Due of process of law formula?	Law of the land formula?
		Yes (Art. 2. Section 17)	
Nebraska (1875)	Yes (Section 1-13)	Yes (Section 1-3)	No
Nevada (1864)	No	Yes (Art. 8.5)	No
New Hampshire (1784)	Yes (Art. 14)	Yes (Art. 15)	Yes (Art. 15)
New Jersey (1947)	No	No	No
New Mexico (1911)	No	Yes (Art. 2. Section 18)	No
New York (1938)	No	Yes (Art. 1. Section 6)	Yes (Art. 1. Section 1)
North Carolina (1971)	Yes (Art. 1. Section 18)	Yes (Art. 1. Section 18)	Yes (Yes (Art. 1. Section 19)
North Dakota (1889)	Yes (Section 9)	Yes (Art. 1. Section 12)	No
Ohio (1912)	Yes (Section 16)	Yes (Section 16)	No
Oklahoma (1907)	Yes (Section II-6)	Yes (Section II-7)	No
Oregon (1857)	Yes (Art. 1. Section 10)	Yes (Art. 1. Section 10)	No
Pennsylvania (1968)	Yes (Art. 1. Section 11)	Yes (Art. 1. Section 11)	Yes (Art. 1. Section 9)
Rhode Island (1986)	Yes (Art. 1. Section 5)	Yes (Art. 1. Section 2)	Yes (Art. 1. Section 10)
South Carolina (1895)	Yes (Art. 1. Section 9)	Yes (Art. 1 Section 3)	No
South Dakota (1889)	Yes (Art. 6 Section 20)	Yes (Art. 6. Section 2)	No
Tennessee (1870)	Yes (Art. 1. Section 17)	Yes (Art. 1. Section 17)	Yes (Art. 1. Section 8)
Texas (1876)	Yes (Art. 1 Section 13)	Yes (Art. 1. Section 19)	Yes (Art. 1 Section 19)
Utah (1895)	Yes (Art. 1 Section 11)	Yes (Art. 1. Section 7)	No
Vermont (1793)	Yes (Art. 4)	No	Yes (Art. 10)
Virginia (1971)	No	Yes (Section 11)	Yes (Section 8)
Washington (1889)	Yes (Section 10)	Yes (Section 3)	No
West Virginia (1872)	Yes (Art. 3-17)	Yes (Art. 3-10)	No
Wisconsin (1848)	Yes (Art. 1. Section 9)	Yes (Art. 1. Section 9)	No
Wyoming (1889)	Yes (Section 8)	Yes (Section 6)	No

From the first Charters, during the colonial and revolutionary period, until its incorporation in the Bill of Rights, the relevance of the clause for criminal prosecution was clear. As explained, that may be a reason why the general clause was accompanied with other specific provisions related to such matters, such as the Fourth and Six Amendments. Notwithstanding this focus on criminal prosecution, I have explained during the last chapters how the debates on the Seventh Amendment and the incorporation clause of the Fourteenth Amendment included conceptions of procedural due process applicable to non-criminal matters as well.

During the debates on the incorporation clause, the congressional understanding was that the amendment did not add anything new but the idea of a right to a pre-established regular procedure. That would explain why the amendment passed without much debate in Congress, but it also explains the early approach followed by the Supreme Court in cases such as *In Den Ex Dem. Murray v. Hoboken Land & Improv. Co.* or *Davidson v. New Orleans*. As such, the focus was on tradition, the procedures inherited from England, and it was respectful of regular proceedings as established by States. This conception of the early case law, as such, could be considered closer to the checklist approach that it would ever be. Procedural due process was reduced to the minimum requirements set forth in the pre-Fourteenth Amendment case law, as inherited from England and part of the common law, and, as said, to those established and "fixed" by legislation.[125] In other words, what was "fair treatment" was decided ex ante by a rule-making authority or defined by tradition.

Notwithstanding, the understanding of procedural due process in the Constitution has been described as a continuous search for meaning and adaptation to the times, and such a search could be characterized as a process more or less close to the flexible ideal type, as described in the first part. As early as 1884, with *Hurtado v. California* the flexible approach began a slow process of evolution. Cases such as *Hagar v. Reclamation Dist. No. 108*, *Ballard v. Hunter, Londoner v. Denver*, or *Twining v. New Jersey*, are good examples in this regard. The peak was reached during the first half of the nineteen Century by the hand of a "dignitary" approach that marked the substantive due process law in cases such as *Lochner v. New York*, and soon after, procedural due process as well by the 1920s. After that, and especially during the Due Process Revolution, the search has been to provide a workable framework to administer the flexible content of due process beyond the basic minimum requirements that were inherited from the initial period and further developed and adapted to the requirements of modern times in cases like *Mullane v. Central Hanover Trust*. This workable framework has been *Mathew v. Elridge* which, as seen, has been criticized and there are calls for a new test based not only in utilitarian considerations but on value-oriented considerations.

---

[125] Kadish, distinguishes between "fixity" and "flexibility" as the two dominant motifs in the Supreme Court approaches to provide meaning to the due process clause. According to it, this to cases are expressions of this intent. Kadish (1957), p. 322.

As explained, many legal scholars described an uneven development and focus of attention by the Supreme Court case law. The focus on criminal matters has been continuous in this evolution. On the contrary, the constitutional doctrine development in non-criminal matters has been much more recent and thinner in non-criminal matters, especially in civil matters, where most of the procedural due process standards come from sub-constitutional regulation such as the Federal Rules of Civil Procedure.

How to explain that such development differs in different matters? While in this section I do not try to attempt definite answers, I would like to explore some possible explanations and suggest further future research questions.

11.4.1 Historical Developments Leading to the Modern Understanding of Due Process

History and tradition of course play an important role. As explained, criminal prosecution has been a concern since the origins of the due process clause, but also during the first half of the twentieth century and later during the Due Process Revolution. Fear of the abuse of criminal prosecution has been a recurrent topic, as explained in the previous part not only in regard to the American legal system but also at an international level. In this regard, this is a commonality between both international systems of rights protection described above, and the American legal system in particular.

There is some literature that shades light on the evolution of the meaning of the due process clause for non-criminal matters. Gary Debele, in an article explaining the historical and jurisprudential developments of the first half of the twentieth century in the field of juvenile justice, describes many of the surrounding social, economic, and political circumstances that accompanied this transformation process. Since his study centers on juvenile justice, his focus on the issue of race and the movement leading to *Brown v. Board of Education* and later to *In Re Gault*.[126] In this regard, he points as a crucial step towards the due process revolution in the civil rights movement and the NAACP's struggle against racial discrimination during the 1920s. The 1930s were marked by the Great Depression and the New Deal, which led to the strengthening of the national government by centralizing power in the executive branch. According to this author, incrementally individuals, cities, and States looked to Washington for guidance—but also to apportion blame when things went wrong—not just in terms of economic help but also in terms of advocacy for the civil rights cause.[127] World War II furthered the concentration of power in the executive, strengthening agencies in several matters not just of an economic nature but also those relevant for the civil rights movement. In this regard, while there was a

[126] Debele (1987), pp. 515–519.

[127] Debele (1987), pp. 524–525.

discourse of national unity during those times, race remained a source of enormous division in American life. Although fighting a war in which race issues were at the core made many Americans reconsider the underlying basis for racial segregation, still there was not enough political support to reverse Jim Crow laws and discriminatory government policies. Post-war decades and the Cold War saw an increase of the tension between the civil rights movement and the government over the latter's compliance with standards that its foreign policy vociferously espoused abroad in its new position of power. In this regard, while the executive—during the presidency of Truman and Eisenhower—attempted to move in previously uncharted directions in dealing with the social problems of the era, other forces defeated its efforts. Many egalitarian proposals were defeated during those times by the Congress, in which Southern Democrats held enough power to block them. Afro-Americans continued to experience discrimination in the 1950s, and the NAACP continued its legal struggle during these post-war years, in a trend that led to *Brown v. Board of Education*.[128]

According to Debele, this half of the century also led to a crucial change in American jurisprudence. Judicial realism emerged moved up to the Supreme Court in 1937 with Roosevelt appointees, a Court, which while allowing the expansion of federal and state legislative attempts to regulate economic matters, focused on a new constitutional doctrine on civil rights and liberties. This new trend, for Debele, was in part a response to the expansion and growth of government power and reflected a preoccupation for social crisis over the strict application of precedent and syllogistic application of the law.[129]

According to Kadish, this first half of the century saw the growth of the Supreme Court appeal to principles of natural law, "...neither articulated in any document nor capable of being confined in words, but which the Court has a duty nonetheless to discover."[130] For this author, the due process clause was the "trojan horse" for its incorporation in substantive law areas as to regulate legal procedure. While in economic matters it diminished rapidly since the New Deal, the procedural spectrum saw its most important articulation and application.[131] To discover such principles, the Court recurred to what Kadish calls the "opinions of the progenitors and architects of American institutions," the "implicit opinion of the policy making organs of state government," the "opinion of other American courts," or the "opinions of other countries in the Anglo-Saxon tradition."[132] Formulas like those expressed in *Twining v. New Jersey*, requiring basic guarantees "...which seem to be *universally prescribed in all systems of law established by civilized countries*,"

[128] Debele (1987), pp. 527–536.

[129] Debele (1987), pp. 536–542.

[130] Kadish (1957), p. 325.

[131] Kadish (1957), p. 325.

[132] Kadish (1957), p. 325.

(Italics are mine),[133] or in *Brown v. Mississippi* when the Courts referred to "methods more revolting to the *sense of justice,*"[134] are examples in this regard.

The methodology used by the Court, which has been called the "intuitive approach,"[135] began to receive criticism for its lack of systematization and ad hoc character. Justice Black, in his dissent in *Adamson v. California*, says that the "natural law" theory of the Constitution upon which *Twining* relies "...appropriates for this Court a broad power which we are not authorized by the Constitution to exercise."[136] And while, as shown by Kadish, the promotors of such doctrine tried to avoid to let their personal notions of fairness reflect in their decisions with the kind of justifications just summarized, this soon led to inconsistency or what this author calls a "chaotic array."[137] As described before, during the period after the late 1950s and early 1960s the Supreme Court began to try another structure of analysis to provide a workable framework, which resulted in *Mathews v. Elridge* and the current method of analysis.

This context may explain why there is a welter of decisions in the field of administrative law, but more profound reasons may be needed to explain why there has not been a similar growth in the civil justice arena, beyond the minimum protections afforded. One possible explanation is the State action doctrine and the lack of a horizontal rights conception theory in the American legal system.

11.4.2 The State Action Doctrine and a Brief Critique of Its Application to Civil Matters

As explained earlier, the due process clause evolved greatly in those areas where there are government direct interventions. That might be a result of a doctrine that goes further than due process but concerns constitutional rights in general. According to Gardbaum, the traditional understanding in the United States is that constitutional rights bind only the state and may be invoked only against actions of the State.[138] This traditional idea comes from the liberal constitutionalism ideal of limiting the States in its relationship with individuals subject to its authority.[139] While debated among legal scholars,[140] that seems to be an understanding at the foundation of the Constitution. In this regard, Chemerinsky argues that "...at the

---

[133] Twining v. N.J., 211 U.S. 78 (1908), p. 111.

[134] Brown v. Mississippi, 297 U.S. 278 (1936), p. 286.

[135] Redish and Marshall (1986), p. 470.

[136] Adamson v. California, 332 U.S. 46 (1947), p. 70. Cited in: Redish and Marshall (1986), pp. 455–503, fn.71.

[137] Kadish (1957), p. 319. Cite in: Mashaw (1976), p. 47, fn. 61.

[138] Gardbaum (2003), p. 411.

[139] Horan (1976), pp. 848–849.

[140] See, e.g.: McAffe (2007).

time the Constitution was written, since it was thought that the common law completely safeguarded personal liberties from private infringements, it was unnecessary for the Constitution to discuss that which already was thoroughly protected. The primary concern in creating a national government was that it would be unconstrained by common-law principles and could infringe liberties in ways that private entities could not. It was feared that the federal government could invoke sovereign immunity and thereby violate individual rights."[141]

The State action doctrine comes from a "vertical" approach to constitutional rights, and according to it, a public-private division is desirable to limit its scope, leaving the private sphere free from constitutional regulation.[142] I believe these ideas are expressed in cases concerning substantive due process such as *Lochner v. New York*, where the Supreme Court held that the general right to make a contract in relation to one's business, and the right to purchase or to sell labor, was part of the liberty protected by the Fourteenth Amendment. Unless a statute limits such rights by reason of public health or the health of the individuals who labored, the State has no power to interfere with such a right.[143]

If the focus of the Supreme Court has been on direct government or State actions, that might explain why its case law has developed the constitutional requirements of due process less in the civil context, at least in such cases where there is no clear government interest. Civil cases between private individuals are quite different from the administrative arena since there is no direct government action threatening deprivation of life, liberty, or property. Civil courts, in contrast to criminal courts, are established by the government to afford citizens the opportunity of a neutral government agency to adjust their differences with their neighbors.[144]

Therefore, the question that remains is whether such a test applies to judicial proceedings between private individuals. The problem is that it has traditionally been understood that no matter the protected interest, it is a State action that triggers the clause.[145] That is why after criminal procedure the second most relevant subject in terms of case law on procedural due process is administrative law, which is concerned mainly with legal issues arising from cases where the government is a party. That might explain why the case law is far less developed in civil matters where only a portion of cases are related to governmental interference, and many of them are disputes initiated by and between private actors.[146] Moreover, that might explain why most specific due process standards are sub-constitutional in the

[141] Chemerinsky (1986), p. 513.

[142] Gardbaum (2003), p. 394.

[143] Lochner v. New York, 198 U.S. 45 (1905), pp. 52–58.

[144] Hittner and Weisz (1990), p. 349.

[145] On the contrary, inaction or omission from public agencies (e.g., providing protection against private wrongdoings) is a much more debatable trigger of the clause. Regarding this debate, see: See: Strauss (1989), pp. 53–86.

[146] For a critic on this rationale, see: Leubsdorf (1984), pp. 602–603.

American legal system.[147] According to Grossi, the Federal Rules of Civil Procedure enacted in 1938 had that exact purpose, to advance ideas of procedural due process[148] as expressed in its Rule 1 "...to secure the just, speedy, and inexpensive determination of every action and proceeding."[149]

For some part of the doctrine, in traditional civil matters between private individuals the outcome of the judicial proceeding or a court decision during the legal procedure might be considered the "State action" resulting in the deprivation of a protected interest. According to Leubsdorf, a victory for a civil plaintiff always deprives the defendant of liberty or property, while the defendant's victory deprives the plaintiff of her property right in her claim.[150] In this regard, procedural due process is considered by itself as an entitlement established by the Constitution.[151] This entitlement implies an obligation of the State—not private defendants—to ensure that anyone claiming to have suffered a legally cognizable injury to have recourse to a court to protect their rights.

This interpretation may encompass Gardbaum's idea of an "indirect" horizontal effect of constitutional rights, whereby although constitutional rights apply directly only to the government, they are nonetheless permitted to have some degree of indirect application to private actors.[152] For this author, the United States does not in fact adhere to the vertical position, at least in full. His argument is that no matter the source of law, "...whether public or private, whether statutory or judge-made, whether relied on in litigation between and individual and the state or between individuals," are equally subject to the Constitution.[153] So the question is not about a State action, but whether the applicable law is contrary or not to the Constitution. And this is a question not for the Fourteenth Amendment, which is the vehicle to help to resolve the substantive issue of which laws violate the Constitution but is a matter of scope under the Supremacy Clause. While he refers mainly to substantive laws, I see no reason not to apply the same rationale to procedural laws.[154]

References

Bone R (1993) Statistical adjudication: rights, justice, and utility in a world of process scarcity. Vand Law Rev 46:561–663

Bone R (2010) Procedure, participation, rights. Boston Univ Law Rev 90:1011–1028

[147] Bone (2010), p. 1011.

[148] Grossi and Allan (2020), pp. 59–60.

[149] USCS Fed Rules Civ Proc R 1.

[150] Leubsdorf (1984), p. 588.

[151] Michelman (1974), p. 548.

[152] Gardbaum (2003), p. 398.

[153] Gardbaum (2003), p. 415.

[154] Gardbaum (2003), pp. 418, 421.

Bradlow J (1988) Procedural due process rights of pro se civil litigants. Univ Chic Law Rev 55(2): 659–683
Brett B (2016) A matter of balance: Mathews v. Eldridge provides the procedural fairness Rhode Island's judiciary desperately needs. Roger Williams Univ Law Rev 21:355–369
Chemerinsky E (1986) Rethinking state action. Northwest Univ Law Rev 80(3):503–557
Coke E (1797) The second part of the institutes of the laws of England, vol 1. E. and R. BROOKE, London
Debele G (1987) The due process revolution and the juvenile court: the matter of race in the historical evolution of doctrine. Law Ineq 5:513–548
Dripps D (2018) Due process: a unified understanding. In: Orren K, Compton J (eds) The Cambridge Companion to the United States Constitution. Cambridge University Press, Cambridge, pp 45–71
Friendly H (1975) Some kind of hearing. Univ Pa Law Rev 123:1267–1317
Galanter M (2007) A world without trials? 2006(1):1–33
Galligan D (1996) Due process and fair procedures. A study of administrative procedures. Clarendon Press, Oxford
Gardbaum S (2003) The "horizontal effect" of constitutional rights. Mich Law Rev 102(3):387–459
Garth B (1987) Studying civil litigation through the class action. Ind Law J 62(3):497–505
Golann D (1989) Making alternative dispute resolution mandatory: the constitutional issues. Or Law Rev 68(2):487–568
Grossi S, Allan I (2020) The modern law of class actions and due process. Or Law Rev 98(1):53–98
Hart H (1953) The power of congress to limit the jurisdiction of federal courts: an exercise in dialectic. Harv Law Rev 66(8):1362–1402
Hensler D, Khatam D (2018) Re-inventing arbitration: how expanding the scope of arbitration is re-shaping its form and blurring the line between private and public adjudication. Nev Law J 18(2):381–426
Hittner D, Weisz K (1990) Federal civil trials delays: a constitutional dilemma? S Tex Law Rev 31: 341–360
Holt J (2015) Magna carta, 3rd edn. Cambridge University Press, Cambridge
Horan M (1976) Contemporary constitutionalism and legal relationships between individuals. Int Comp Law Q 25(4):848–867
Kadish S (1957) Methodology and criteria in due process adjudication. A survey and criticism. Yale Law J 66(3):319–363
Kagan R (2003) Adversarial legalism. The American way of law. Harvard University Press, Cambridge
Langer M (2016) In the beginning was Fortescue: on the intellectual origins of the adversarial and inquisitorial systems and common and civil law in comparative criminal procedure. In: Ackerman B, Ambos K, Sikirić H (eds) Visions of justice. Liber amicorum in honor of professor Damaška. Duncker & Humblot, Berlin, pp 273–299
Leubsdorf J (1984) Constitutional civil procedure. Tex Law Rev 63(4):579–637
Mashaw J (1976) The Supreme Court's due process calculus for administrative adjudication in Mathews v. Eldridge: three factors in search of a theory of value. Univ Chic Law Rev 44(1): 28–59
McAffe T (2007) Restoring the lost world of classical legal thought: the presumption in favor of liberty over law and the court over the Constitution. Univ Cin Law Rev 75(4):1499–1594
Michelman F (1974) Supreme court and litigation access fees: the right to protect one's rights, Part II. Duke Law J 1974(3):527–570
Pankratz J (1992) Neutral principles and the right to neutral access to the courts. Ind Law J 67(4): 1091–1112
Pierce R (1996) The due process counterrevolution of the 1990s? Colum Law Rev 96:1973–2000
Redish M, Marshall L (1986) Adjudicatory independence and the values of procedural due process. Yale Law J 95(3):455–503

Resnik J (2014) The privatization of process: requiem for and celebration of the Federal Rules of Civil Procedure at 75. Univ Pa Law Rev 162(7):1793–1838

Reuben R (2000) Constitutional gravity: a unitary theory of alternative dispute resolution and public civil justice. UCLA Law Rev 47:949–1104

Rhode D (2001) Access to justice. Fordham Law Rev 69:1785–1820

Rice C (1999) A right of access to court under the petition clause of the first amendment: defining the right. Ohio St Law J 60(2):557–692

Rubin E (1984) Due process and the administrative state. Cal Law Rev 72(6):1044–1179

Scherer A (2006) Securing a civil right to counsel: the importance of collaborating. N Y Univ Rev Law Soc Change 30(4):675–688

Stone K (2017) The bold ambition of Justice Scalia's arbitration jurisprudence: keep workers and consumers out of court. Empl Rights Employ Policy J 21:189–220

Strauss D (1989) Due process, government inaction, and private wrongs. Sup Ct Rev 1989:53–86

Sullivan T, Massaro T (2013) The arc of due process in American Constitutional Law. Oxford University Press, New York

Thompson F (1948) Magna Carta. Its role in the making of the English constitution, 1300-1629. The University of Minnesota Press, Minneapolis

Yeazell S, Schwartz J (2016) Civil procedure, 9th edn. Aspen Casebook Series, Wolters Kluwer, United States

Part V
Escaping from the Shadow. A Due Process Theory in Non-criminal Matters to Harmonize with Access to Justice Demands

Chapter 12
Why Civil and Criminal Procedures Require Different Theories on Procedural Due Process

Most developments on due process standards comes from criminal justice. That is true of both regional systems of rights protection studied and the American legal system. Civil justice, on the contrary, has received much less attention. By reviewing these experiences, it might be said that the due process requirements over civil matters have grown "under the shadow" of such developments in the criminal justice arena.

As explained in Part III, from the long journey of procedural due process until its recognition in the American Constitution, historical accounts marked by prosecution abuse led to express criminal justice related provisions that enhanced the individual's protections against the State. Englishmen first, and later colonists who wanted the same protections they had had against abuse of prosecution by the Crown and Parliament. We saw as well how in the context of the Inter-American Human Rights system, the IACHR and the Commission have developed an expansive doctrine in the sense that guarantees afforded expressly for criminal matters are applied in other type of procedures. The type of human rights violation that the court has had to deal with might explain this expansive doctrine. At national level, in Latin America, while the judicial reform movement in many countries of the region was broader than criminal justice alone, it was in this area that most of the efforts were focused. In this regard, Langer has said that a key element for the success of the movement was the existence of a movement led by a group of lawyers or experts who served as a catalyst for the idea that the criminal systems in Latin America were in crisis and a main cause for human rights violations.[1]

Still, perhaps civil justice due process requirements have grown under the shadow of criminal justice, purely as a natural consequence of the enormous expansion that this area of the administration of justice has had globally. According to Genn, one of the external threats to civil justice comes today from the outgrowth of criminal

[1] Langer (2007), p. 632.

R. Lillo Lobos, *Understanding Due Process in Non-Criminal Matters*, Ius Gentium: Comparative Perspectives on Law and Justice 97,
https://doi.org/10.1007/978-3-030-95534-2_12

justice in a context of resource constraint. The criminalization of many social and economic activities, and other factors, have led to a substantial increase in public spending on criminal justice. Currently, in many corners, a measure of success of a government refers to this growing criminalization and focus on criminal justice.[2]

If the only reasons for differences between what due process requires in criminal and non-criminal matters are context-dependent, there is no reason why we could not in our modern conception change such a situation. If members of a society think they deserve the same consideration, why not provide them with the same requirements? In fact, nothing forbids legislatures to do just that. However, as I will argue in this chapter, although due process, both in criminal and non-criminal matters, shares a common theoretical core based on the concept of procedural fairness, they differ in important respects. In one type of proceeding, the focus is on the protection of the right of defense due to the imbalance between the individual and the machinery of state.[3] In contrast, in other types of judicial proceedings, especially in those between private parties, the procedural protections must be those required for both sides to be *effectively* heard under conditions that ensure a relative balance between parties.

In the first part of this chapter, I argue that in civil matters, unlike criminal justice, fairness not only requires procedural rights in order to ensure accurate determination of fact as proxy for a quality outcome, but also to ensure a legal need has been satisfied, a dispute solved, a right has been protected. Procedural due process, in this regard, and as an inherent element of it, requires also access to the legal procedure and the capacity to maintain it until the end. In this sense, a procedure would also be unfair if no matter how accurate it might be or protective of procedural guarantees, it is too costly or ineffective to be useful. In this regard, the social cost of providing a legal procedure is not an exogenous element of a theory of procedural fairness, but must be an inherent part of it.[4]

To integrate social cost as an inherent element of procedural due process requires, first, to comprehend the goals of civil justice. By distinguishing the proper functions of civil adjudication, it must be understood that due process, notwithstanding the common theoretical core it shares, has different goals which call for different due process requirements.

---

[2]Professor Genn makes this claim for England, but it may be applied to many other places as well. Genn (2010), pp. 24–25. In the U.S. for example, between 1982 and 2007, the cost of the nation's police protection, corrections, and judicial and legal services increased by 171%. The largest proportion of public expenditure in justice were police protection and correctional services, which increased for the same period in 125.6% and 255.3%, respectively. See: U.S. Department of Justice, Justice Expenditures and Employment, FY 1982-2007 - Statistical Tables, pp. 2, 5. Available at: https://www.bjs.gov/index.cfm?ty=pbdetail&iid=2192. Based on the UN Crime Survey of Crime and Criminal Justice, Spencer in 1993 found that during the 1980's at least there was increase in all areas of criminal justice of the 93 countries which make up the data. While he did not found a correlation between expenditure increase and the rate of total crime—or with any outcome in particular—, he infer that the aim of expenditure is to achieve short-term goals, and that these goals are politically driven to meet momentary concerns. Spencer (1993), pp. 1, 4, 10.

[3]This is somewhat the original understanding of Due Process, see e.g.: Eberle (1987).

[4]Bone (2003), p. 515.

12.1 From the State v. Individual to the Individual v. Individual Paradigm

The requirements of due process, notwithstanding the common theoretical core they share based on the concept of procedural fairness, differ in important respects between criminal and non-criminal matters. Here I argue that such differences between legal procedures of a punitive nature and those that are not, require a different conception of procedural due process. In particular, a procedural due process theory for civil matters must take into account the proper functions of civil adjudication.

Some might think that the differences between criminal and civil procedure result from a different level of seriousness of the deprivation that each party risks with a decision contrary to their interests. In other words, that a criminal punishment might produce more serious consequences of a physical, psychological, economic, or of any other nature, than civil justice. While civil matters usually involve property, obligations enforcement, or monetary compensation, criminal sanctions might entail jail time or other severe limitations on personal liberty. This route has been taken, for example, by the Inter-American Commission on Human Rights, which recognizes that in non-criminal proceedings against a migrant worker, the "quantum" of procedural guarantees of article 8.2. of the Convention applies to the expected outcomes in terms of liberty restrictions.[5] However, this is not the best way to explain such differences of treatment, at least not if a general solution to the problem is sought. As Leubsdorf has pointed out regarding the American context:

> Most constitutional safeguards apply even to a prosecution that leads only to a fine or a symbolic punishment, but a civil suit may lead to bankruptcy, to a decision blighting a party's future, or to relief affecting thousands of people. Moreover, the Supreme Court has required procedural safeguards in administrative proceedings that could lead to sanctions no more severe than the loss of a driver's license, of the right to buy liquor, or of a few days of school. Although these are not trivial deprivations, they are no more grave than those at stake in most civil suits.[6]

Ronald Dworkin's definition of procedural fairness, in *A Matter of Principle*, distinguishes between two types of harm resulting from an erroneous decision. Bare harm is the one a person might suffer resulting from adjudication no matter the decision is just or unjust, just like the one Leubsdorf criticizes as a difference between criminal and civil procedures. For example, bare harm might count as suffering, frustration, pain, or dissatisfaction of desires that the individual suffers because he loses his liberty or is beaten or killed. Besides such harm, the individual might suffer harm whenever a decision is unjust, just in virtue of that injustice. Dworkin calls this a moral harm or the "injustice factor".[7]

---

[5] ICHR, Second progress report of the special rapporteurship on migrants workers and their families in the hemisphere, par. 95. Available at: https://www.cidh.oas.org/annualrep/2000eng/chap.6a.htm.

[6] Leubsdorf (1984), p. 602.

[7] Dworkin (1985), p. 80.

Dworkin's theory is outcome-based, and according to it, both legal procedures are similar in the sense that both have the basic purpose of enforcing law to a given set of facts. He says that even though in complex civil cases where the law is not settled it might be difficult to see it, at the end of the day the judge will apply the version of the law he finds to be correct to a given set of facts.[8] If both legal procedures serve the same function, then, individuals should have the same two basic rights based on procedural fairness: first, a right to a procedure that attaches the correct importance to the risk of moral harm (not to a general level of accuracy in adjudication). Second, a right to a consistent application of the weighting of the importance of moral harm associated to a given procedure. According to Dworkin, while procedural fairness does not provide a right to a procedure that ensures perfect accuracy, at least these two rights provide a minimum protection in the sense that they can be used to trump utilitarian considerations.[9] To identify the acceptable risk of moral harm, under Dworkin's theory, the social consequences of different rules and practices must be assessed.[10] Regarding the consistency requirement, one most look at the rules and practices of the legal system and it is constructed by interpreting the features of that system treated as a coherent whole.[11]

However, the acceptable risk of moral harm resulting from error is not necessarily the same if unjust criminal convictions are compared with a civil adjudication. It is possible, under this theory, that what society considers as an acceptable risk of moral harm differs from one type of legal procedure to another. Therefore, under this theory, perhaps a particular society may perceive a greater injustice when a factually innocent person is convicted in a crooked criminal procedure than when a civil party loses because a judge made a wrong decision. For example, a reflection of such coherent whole might explain why the American Constitution establishes many more protections in criminal justice or why substantive law might entertain differences in regard to burden of proof, standard of proof, or considerations such as the presumption of innocence. In fact, according to Dworkin's theory, the design of criminal and civil procedures is an expression of communities' convictions about the relative weight of different forms of moral harm, compared to each other and against other forms of injuries or sacrifices.[12]

Summarizing, according to Dworkin, basic procedural fairness requirements are the same in civil and criminal procedures. They provides the same two minimum rights (a procedure that attaches the correct importance to the risk of moral harm, and a right to a consistent application of such an acceptable level of risk). What changes, in this regard, may be the acceptable level of risk of moral harm that a particular society is willing to accept and distributed between criminal and civil procedures,

[8]Dworkin (1985), p. 75.

[9]Dworkin (1985), pp. 89–90.

[10]Dworkin (1985), p. 95.

[11]Dworkin (1985), pp. 80–88.

[12]Dworkin (1985), p. 86.

and the settled practices of the system as a whole by which the consistent application is assessed.

Robert Bone finds potential flaws on Dworkin's theory. One is that in civil adjudication moral harm resulting from an unjust decision is not as clear as in criminal arena. For example, because in civil matters, moral harm is not suffered necessarily by one of the parties as in criminal justice, but by either of them and might even greater for one or the other.[13] Moreover, civil adjudication does not necessarily convey a punishment to punish moral transgressions or convey a message of moral blame, or it is not always so easy to distinguish the moral wrong resulting from an unjust decision from the moral wrong that the substantive law is trying to prevent.[14] Another possible flaw is in the assessment of the importance of the error risk associated with the moral harm that a given society would find acceptable. The problem is that Dworkin assumes that the willingness to invest of the society has a moral significance, while it is perfectly possible that such assessment depends on other types of consideration.[15]

I agree with Dworkin's theory that in both legal procedures the outcomes are a matter of principle rather than policy, that is, an argument about whether an individual is entitled to a right but not on a decision made to promote some conception of the general welfare or public interest.[16] In other words, when a judge decides on a legal issue concerning a procedural right, the question is whether the individual is entitled to such a procedural right and not if providing it is better for the society. I think the problem of his theory is that it relies entirely on the moral harm resulting from a lack of accuracy. While this make sense in criminal justice, in civil matters, at least under some circumstances, his interpretation of procedural fairness does not fit the practice entirely.

As an outcome-based theory, Dworkin's account of procedural fairness relies on accuracy or reliability in how the adjudication process determines facts to apply law. But while he recognizes the complexity that might arise in civil matters,[17] not taking into consideration the different characteristics of parties' disposition and the purpose of legal procedure, by measuring effectiveness in terms of accuracy alone, it commits the same error of applying the same categories of criminal justice over non-punitive legal procedures.

Therefore, based on the nature of outcome of the legal procedure, and the parties' relative position between them, I provide a simple characterization which allows the differences between criminal and non-criminal matters, or more specifically, between punitive and non-punitive legal procedures, to be understood.

[13] Bayles (1986), p. 46.

[14] Bone (2010), pp. 1020–1022.

[15] Bone (2010), p. 1023.

[16] Dworkin (1977), pp. 22–31; Dworkin (1985), p. 74.

[17] Dworkin (1985), p. 74.

12.1.1 The Paradigm of the State v. Individual

Legal procedures where State prosecutes an individual represent the highest degree of imbalance between both sides of the dispute, especially under a legal procedure whose outcome is the imposition—or not—of punishment upon conviction. This imbalance comes from one side, the machinery of the State acting as prosecutor, and in the other, an individual accused of having committed a crime. State is enforcing the law created by the legislature, as an expression of public power. I shall call this the State v. Individual paradigm, in which the obvious practical expression is criminal justice.

Hebert Packer's conceptualization of the criminal justice system is illustrative in this regard. He conceives criminal justice as a system of competing values under a potential contest between—if not equals—two independent actors.[18] One side of the equation is the model of crime control whose fundamental value is law enforcement. The purpose of the system in this regard, is to apprehend, try, convict, and dispose of the highest proportion of criminal offenders as possible. Efficiency under this model is referred to the capacity of the system to comply with such objectives as expediently as possible. In this regard, the machinery of the State works under a presumption of guilt requiring a routinized administrative process of fact finding with as few restrictions as possible.[19] The opposed model is due process, which is conceived more as an obstacle course confronted by the enormous pressure of the State machinery under the crime control model. Procedural guarantees, during the entire proceeding but whose paradigmatic core is the trial, provides the controls on abuse of power. This model sees maximum efficiency as maximum tyranny. The model of due process relies heavily on the Constitution because in that regard tensions are decided authoritatively by the courts. This is why most procedural guarantees under this model are directed to provide defense,[20] if not in equal capacity, at least to provide an outcome as reliable as possible through its faith in the adversarial fact-finding process.[21] This is the reason why access to justice issues in the criminal arena are focused on access to legal assistance rather than on access to the courts.[22] The state is compelling the individual to attend court, and the defendant is particularly vulnerable.[23] Therefore, due process under such model has the objective to ensure a

---

[18]Packer (1964), p. 9.

[19]Packer (1964), pp. 9–13.

[20]This is somewhat the original understanding of Due Process, see e.g.: Eberle (1987), pp. 339–362.

[21]Packer (1964), pp. 13–23.

[22]See, e.g.: Rhode (2004), pp. 122–144.

[23]Medina (2016), p. 260. According to Sarah Summers, at the core of the development of the modern criminal justice systems were the idea of stopping the injustices of the procedures of the Inquisition. And, based on the nineteenth-century liberal ethos of the Enlightenment, to begin to treat the accused not as a mere object subject to investigation first as a citizen, and later as a relevant part of the criminal proceedings. See: Summers (2007), pp. 22–23.

reliable fact-finding process but not at any price since it must be respectful of individuals' dignity.[24]

This tension between the crime control model and the due process model under Packer, allows us to understand why Dworkin is correct in assessing the outcome of criminal procedure as based on the reliability of the fact-finding process. Here, the individual is not voluntarily going to a court but he or she is forced or compelled to attend. On the opposite side the State, with all its machinery, is the one willing to present the case, while basic procedural fairness rights allow the defendant, who is in an inherently unequal position, to at least check on that version. Procedural fairness—or due process requirements—serve as obstacles intended to ensure that if he or she is going to be convicted, at least, it will be done with a low margin of error risk (even though not based on perfect accuracy). The classic adversarial procedural guarantees to be afforded, such as cross examination, and an independent decision maker, and others, are those that ensure the minimum protection appropriate to the risk of moral harm resulting from an "unjust" outcome.

12.1.2 *The Paradigm of Individual v. Individual*

To define what civil justice is might be complex in comparison with criminal procedure, given the broad range of potential actors, and especially taking into consideration the differences between legal systems in this regard.[25] For the purposes of this section, I rely on Genn's conception (already described), according to which civil justice is a forum in which citizens and business can exercise their right of action to set in motion the machinery to make good their rights.[26] This conception covers the conflict-solving dimension that is one common side of civil justice across jurisdictions.[27] In this regard, Bayles argues that legal procedure, especially in civil matters, tries to diminish the error risk from inaccuracy, but it also serves an important function of dispute resolution. As such, other features of legal procedure are valuable independently of the decision, but they might flow from the procedure itself, since they are valuable for other purposes such as I explained before.[28]

Individuals use civil justice as a forum, not like criminal justice to enforce substantive criminal law enacted by legislation, but to disagree regarding rights of quite different legal natures. Many disputes are related to contract rights which were designed by the parties, others regarding the contours of legal rights entitled by substantive legal rights. In such cases, and especially in cases between private individuals, imbalance is not an inherent but a contingent element. I shall call this

[24]Kadish (1957), pp. 346–347.

[25]See: Uzelac (2014), pp. 3–34.

[26]Genn (2010), p. 11.

[27]Uzelac (2014), pp. 6, 7.

[28]Bayles (1986), pp. 50–53.

the Individual v. Individual paradigm. What is characteristic of such legal procedures is that, here, at least one of the parties is not forced to attend the court. The plaintiff, normally, will voluntarily decide to make use of a basic right—which might have a different nature—normally called a right of action, to enforce another legal right.

In short, I argue that procedural fairness in disputes between private individuals requires more than minimum protection against an appropriate level of risk of moral harm. It entails a basic right to be able to use the legal procedure. As unjust as a wrong assessment of risk of a moral harm resulting from a mistakenly decided case, is the impossibility of having any such decision at all.

This not to say that accuracy is not relevant in civil justice. Nevertheless, civil procedure is not designed to place obstacles and checks against the fact-finding procedure followed by the State, but to have the opportunity to disagree on the contours of legal rights between equals. That is the main feature of a procedure that has the purpose of providing a peaceful manner to disagree. Therefore, in this paradigm based on the adjudication of rights in a conflict between private individuals, the procedural protections must be those required for both sides to be effectively heard under conditions that ensure both parties to be heard meaningfully.[29] This means that the State must ensure the proper conditions in that regard. As I will explain later, this does not mean a right to a procedure of perfect accuracy, just as Dworkin says. The adversarial features will still be afforded to ensure the appropriate level of accuracy or distribution of risk of moral harm, but which procedural guarantees will be afforded will be those required for both parties to participate effectively. Therefore, such conditions must be those required for the individual to have the capability of going to court to pursue a legal claim until the end. This change of prism makes the procedural decisions quite different between punitive legal procedures and those that are not.

12.2 Different Configurations Between Purpose and Party Disposition

In the previous section I have argued that between the State v. Individual and the Individual v. Individual paradigms there are differences of purpose and parties' relative position of power in the legal procedure, in terms of the imbalance between them. Using both variables, purpose and party-relative position, I believe is an easier way to understand the application of due process between different legal procedures, at least in comparison with other possible explanations, such as the seriousness of the consequences. I agree with Leubsdorf that such an explanation seems an

[29] This is a formula developed by the European Courts of Human Rights, see: ECHR, Case of Steel Morris v. The United Kingdom, Judgment of 15 February 2005, par. 59.

over-simplification.[30] While the gravity of the consequences may be a factor, it does not explain the differences in practice.

To understand what I mean by purpose, I think it is important to differentiate between purpose and outcome. The latter refers to the expected result of the legal procedure that is measured in accuracy. In other words, how good is a specific procedure to determine the facts over that in which the decision-maker applies the legal rule. Let us recall at this point the two minimum rights provided by procedural due process according to Dworkin (a procedure that attaches the correct importance to the risk of moral harm, and a right to a consistent application of such an acceptable level of risk). Purpose is somewhat different. It answers the question why a specific legal procedure was designed and provided by the legal system.

While every legal procedure basically has the same expected outcome, it does not necessarily convey the same purpose. I distinguish between two, the imposition of a punishment and those procedures whose fact determination and law application has the inherent purpose of settling a dispute (especially, but not necessarily, through adjudication). Uzelac, in a comparative study, shows that in many legal systems around the world, civil justice has the goal of providing resolution of individual disputes by the system of State courts. Still, others mention the implementation of social goals and policies, which might cover a different array of things. While this purpose may be somewhere on the continuum between solving conflicts and imposing sanctions, it is good to notice that a civil procedure might serve beyond an individualistic conception of solving private conflicts and also include, by solving them, the enhancement of social goals.[31] In other words, I do not refer to the conflict-solving function as a purely private function of civil justice. As I argued in the first part of the book, I believe that by resolving disputes the courts serve an inherently public function. But this is not to say, of course, that every civil justice system is in practice fulfilling such a public goal. For example, as explained, in Chile the main users of the civil justice system are big corporations as part as their collection strategies, that is for the enforcement of debts or, according to tax regulation, to deduct their unrecoverable credits from their payable taxes. In this respect, Chilean legal scholars has characterized, the civil system as serving a private good.[32] In the United States, while the Federal Rules of Civil Procedure acknowledge that the purpose of the rules is "...to secure the just, speedy, and inexpensive determination of every action and proceeding,"[33] Richard Marcus has described how in practice American civil justice functions as the private enforcement of public norms, that is, private litigation serving as an effective substitute for having government seek to enforce the law.[34]

[30] Leubsdorf (1984), p. 602.

[31] Uzelac (2014), pp. 7–12.

[32] Correa et al. (2000), pp. 391–392.

[33] USCS Fed Rules Civ Proc R 1.

[34] Marcus (2014), pp. 129–133.

The other axis is represented by what I have called the relative position of the party in the legal procedure. By that I refer not to the position in the procedure as a relation between claimant/defendant/decision-maker but to the differences of power between them. There are different types of parties who might possess a greater advantage to persist in a legal procedure. For example, Galanter, in its article "Why the 'Haves' Come out Ahead: Speculations on the Limits of Legal Change", distinguish between one-shooters and repeat players. Repeat players, for many reasons like their size, resources, and other structural reasons such as State laws, have many occasions to utilize the courts (in the broad sense), and usually the stakes in a legal procedure tend to be lower than those of the one-shooters. The system provides several advantages to repeat players such as the expertise they acquire in time, relationships they form with court personnel, the economies of scale they enjoy, and the low start- up costs for any case, among others. For Galanter, the issues is that there are parties, those with the "haves," who enjoy a position of advantage in the configuration of contending parties and how the structure of the legal procedure tend to perpetuate such differences in relation to those who "have not."[35] Similarly, Cappelletti and Garth, describe the same phenomenon regarding "party capability", and how they enjoy different advantages such as financial resources to enjoy better legal assistance or to endure the length of the proceedings.[36] This is what I call the relative position of the parties. While in strict consideration both occupy equally relevant position as parties, in reality several factors might produce that one party—those with the "haves"—enjoys a critical advantage over the others.

Using both elements, purpose and imbalance, I explore how different configurations place different challenges on procedural due process. Of course, and just to be clear, I am not saying that procedural due process does not apply depending on the party-relative position and purpose of the proceedings, but that the focus of the protection might vary across such different configurations (Fig. 12.1).

The State v. Individual paradigm, characteristic from criminal justice as explained in the last section, represents one extreme position in this diagram, a legal procedure whose outcome is to ascertain facts to apply the law with the purpose of imposing a penal sanction. On one side the State, which enjoys all its machinery to enforce its criminal law without regard to the finality of the criminal sanction, to guide conducts of the entire society or as a pure retributive goal. In the other side, there is an individual who is facing such apparatus. High imbalance and legal procedures whose purpose is to impose a sanction might be present as well in other types of cases, even though not necessarily to the same degree. In modern administrative law there are many agencies that decide on the imposition of penalties for non-compliance with administrative regulation. Imagine an administrative agency enforcing a regulation whose punishment is a fine against a small enterprise or even an individual. In such cases, of course enhanced due process protections, with focus on the right to defense

[35] Galanter (1974), pp. 97–104.

[36] Cappelletti and Garth (1978), pp. 190–195.

Fig. 12.1 Purpose and Party position of power

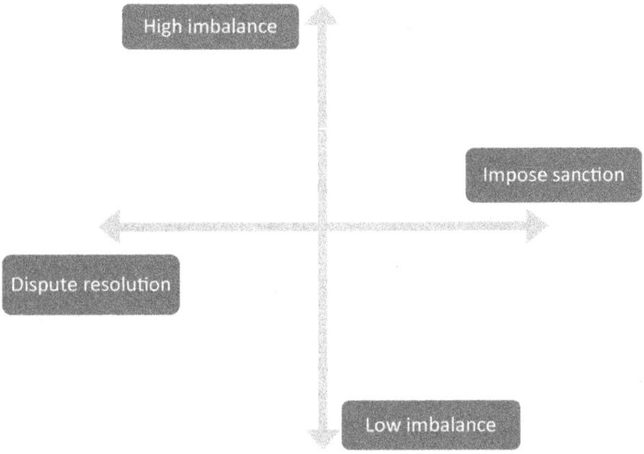

in its several dimensions, might allow the citizen to confront the machinery of the State effectively.

Of course, there could be legal procedures whose main function is to impose sanctions but the imbalance between parties is not as critical as in the State v. Individual paradigm. Perhaps we could think of a corporation's criminal liability. And by that, I mean the corporation itself and not the individuals who comprise it. ¿Are the due process guarantees afforded to an individual accused the same as those enjoyed by a big corporation such as a transnational company? At an international level there seem to be different answers. While the International Covenant on Civil and Political Rights and the American Convention on Human Rights does not provide protection for legal persons as victims, in the European System the ECHR has expressly applied fair trial guarantees without distinction between individuals and legal persons.[37] ¿If so, should they be applied equally or with the same intensity? Might the difference between the criminal liability of a big and a small corporation, be relevant for example? In the case of *OAO Neftyanaya Kompaniya Yukos v. Russia*, a complex series of proceedings of different natures for the tax liability of this company, a publicly-traded private open joint-stock company, the Court held that in the criminal proceedings against the company it was protected by the right to have sufficient time for preparation of its defense.[38] In other cases the Court has applied article 6 in its criminal limb on cases regarding multinational companies, such as in *Fortum Corporation v. Finland*. The problem is that the ECHR when deciding on fair trial requirements does not appear to take into consideration whether the petitioner is an individual or a legal person.[39] Therefore, it is quite difficult to analyze whether there are different focuses of protection between them. Of course,

[37] van Kempen (2010), pp. 3–6, 14.

[38] ECHR, Case of OAO Neftyanaya Kompaniya Yukos v. Russia, Judgment of 20 September 2011, par. 536–551.

[39] ECHR, Case of the Fortum Corporation v. Finland, Judgment of 15 July 2003, p. 373.

this is not the main purpose of this chapter, but I believe it is an interesting future research question and application of this diagram.

On the other side, there may be procedures with a conflict-solving purpose in which there may be high imbalance between parties as well. A clear example are those civil cases concerning faulty service or goods damages against big corporations, or even against governmental agencies. In the international arena it is interesting to recall the debate over the application of article 6.1. civil limb in the European regional system, and how civil litigation includes claims against the State acting as a party, or there are cases where governing legislation on the matters comes from public and private law. In the United States, I have described how in *Little v. Streater,* the Supreme Court held—using the *Mathew v. Elridge* test—that since the cost of blood group tests was relevant evidence, taking into consideration the evidentiary burden and having to face the State as an adversary, an indigent defendant without aid in obtaining such evidence lacked a meaningful opportunity to be heard.[40] Similarly, in *Santosky v. Kramer*, the court held that before a State may sever completely and irrevocably the rights of parents in their natural child, due process requires that the State support its allegations by at least clear and convincing evidence. Since the interest at stake were no less than the dissolution of a family by a government-initiated proceeding, the Court held that the standard of proof required by procedural due process is an intermediate standard between the preponderance of the evidence but less than beyond reasonable doubt.[41]

On the other extreme side of the diagram, if we imagine a well-functioning civil justice system where citizens as equals debate, settle their disputes, and which shapes the contours of the law in a public forum—as authors such as Genn has proposed for civil justice[42]—the requirements of procedural process are not the same.

The point is that where the imbalance is as high as it is in punitive legal proceedings, fair treatment protections focus on defense against the fact-finding process followed by the State. The problem is when the same answers to the question of how to treat someone fairly in the State Vs. Individual paradigm are transferred *en bloc* to other types of judicial proceedings.[43] On the contrary, as imbalance diminishes and the purpose goes further toward provide a forum for dispute resolution, procedural fairness requires something different. As I argue in the next chapter, from a normative point of view due process for non-punitive legal procedures requires us to consider the right to a court as its core issue.

[40] Little v. Streater, 452 U.S. 1, 16 (1981).

[41] Santosky v. Kramer, 455 U.S. 745, 747–748, 755–757 (1982).

[42] Genn (2010), p. 3; Resnik (2014), p. 10.

[43] A good example on this regard is the movement for a Civil Gideon in the United States. On this regard, see: Gardner (2008). For a critical appraisal of this claim, see: Barton (2010).

References

Barton B (2010) Against civil *gideon* (and for pro se litigation reform). Fla Law Rev 62:1227–1274
Bayles M (1986) Principles for legal procedure. Law Philos 5(1):33–57
Bone R (2003) Agreeing to fair process: the problem with contractarian theories of procedural fairness. Boston Univ Law Rev 83:485–552
Bone R (2010) Procedure, participation, rights. Boston Univ Law Rev 90:1011–1028
Cappelletti M, Garth B (1978) Access to justice: the newest wave in the worldwide movement to make rights effective. Buff Law Rev 27:181–292
Correa J, Peña C, Vargas J (2000) ¿Es la Justicia un Bien Público? Rev Perspectivas 3(2):389–409
Dworkin R (1977) Taking rights seriously. Harvard University Press, Cambridge
Dworkin R (1985) A matter of principle. Harvard University Press, Cambridge
Eberle E (1987) Procedural due process: the original understanding. Const Comment 4:339–362
Galanter M (1974) Why the "haves" come out ahead: speculations on the limits of legal change. Law Soc Rev 9(1):95–160
Gardner D (2008) Justice delayed is, once again, justice denied: the overdue right to counsel in civil cases. Univ Balt Law Rev 37(1):59–77
Genn H (2010) Judging civil justice. Cambridge University Press, Cambridge
Kadish S (1957) Methodology and criteria in due process adjudication. A survey and criticism. Yale Law J 66(3):319–363
Langer M (2007) Revolution in Latin American criminal procedure: diffusion of legal ideas from the periphery. Am J Comp Law 55:617–676
Leubsdorf J (1984) Constitutional civil procedure. Tex Law Rev 63(4):579–637
Marcus R (2014) 'American exceptionalism' in goals for civil litigation. In: Uzelac A (ed) Goals of civil justice and civil procedure in contemporary judicial systems. Springer, Switzerland, pp 123–141
Medina C (2016) The American Convention on Human Rights. Crucial rights and their theory and practice, 2nd edn. Intersentia, Cambridge
Packer H (1964) Two models of the criminal process. Univ Pa Law Rev 113(1):1–68
Resnik J (2014) Reinventing courts as democratic institutions. Daedalus 143(3):9–27
Rhode D (2004) Access to justice. Oxford University Press, Oxford
Spencer J (1993) Criminal justice expenditure. A global perspective. Howard J Crim Justice 32(1): 1–11
Summers S (2007) Fair trials. The European criminal procedural tradition and the European Court of Human Rights. Hart Publishing, Oxford
Uzelac A (ed) (2014) Goals of civil justice and civil procedure in contemporary judicial systems. Springer, Switzerland
van Kempen P (2010) Human rights and criminal justice applied to legal persons. Protection and liability of private and public juristic entities under the ICCPR, ECHR, ACHR and AfChHPR. EJCL 14(3)

Chapter 13
The Right to Access to Justice as a Key to Understand the Right to a Fair Trial in Civil Matters

As said in the previous chapter, while in criminal matters, or punitive legal procedures, basic requirement of fairness are meant to protect the individual faced by the machinery of the State, in non-criminal matters the individuals put in motion the same machinery but this time to enforce and make their rights effective,[1] which legal scholars calls the right of action or simply civil action.[2]

Here, and based on the findings of my research on how due process is applied in practice in non-criminal matters, I shall argue that access to justice or the right to a court is a basic right which procedural fairness entails.[3] Either a process-based or an outcome-based theory on procedural fairness presuppose access to a court in a meaningful way. This is the answer that allows to harmonize due process as a right by refusing to consider social costs as an extraneous element. Moreover, if the right to a court is an inherent part of due process in civil matters, this idea allows the requirements of the civil justice movement to be harmonized with those of the right to a fair trial.

With this purpose, in the first section I argued that the right to access to justice is a basic requirement of procedural due process both under process-based theories and outcome-based theories. In the next section, I explained why I believe that such an understanding of procedural due process is consistent with the use of due process common in both the international and national jurisdictions studied in the previous chapters. Finally, in this chapter I describe the role played by the flexible and the checklist models under this conception based on the right to a court.

---

[1] See: Genn (2010), p. 11.

[2] See, e.g.: Couture (1950).

[3] As in previous chapters, I use both concepts, access to justice and right to a court as synonymous. While they are not the same, for these purposes I understand that both implies not just the possibility of filing a claim but also effectively pursing a case until the end.

R. Lillo Lobos, *Understanding Due Process in Non-Criminal Matters*, Ius Gentium: Comparative Perspectives on Law and Justice 97,
https://doi.org/10.1007/978-3-030-95534-2_13

13.1 The Right to Access to Justice as a Requirement Under Process-based and Outcome-based Theories of Procedural Fairness

A process-based theory of procedural fairness requires identifying the value of participation in the legal procedure independently of its influence on the outcome. Some have put their focus on the legitimacy that participation gives to the decision and in the long run to the legal system.[4] Others have valued how participation in the decision-making process respects the dignity of the individuals potentially affected.[5] According to Waldron, legal procedure is one of the forms by which a legal system protects dignity. It does so by providing a forum where parties will counter each other's arguments in a very specific way and the decision maker will be bound by their arguments and proof and at the end provide reasons for its decision. These features capture the idea that a legal system is a mode of governing people that acknowledges that they have a view or perspective of their own to present on the application of the norm to their conduct and situation.[6] As Yeazell and Schwartz say, procedure reflects our most basic notions of fairness of justice. If the only thing that matters were a quick decision, we could flip a coin to solve cases. However, we do not do so since solving a dispute without taking into consideration the merits of the arguments brought by the parties, strikes us as unjust.[7] That might be true even if the party who won the toss of the coin was factually right on his or her claim. That is why access to justice has been conceptualized as a right not only to enter a court of law, but as a right of an individual "...to have his or her case heard and adjudicated in accordance with substantive standards of fairness and justice".[8] As such, here I do not argue that access to justice is a synonymous with the right to a fair trial but that there is an inherent two-way relation between them. While authors such as Palombella argues that the right to a fair trial has become essential to access to justice—just like the right to an effective remedy—since without a proper protection it might end up making this right an "empty ritual",[9] I shall argue that access to justice is a requirement of procedural fairness as well.

From an outcome-based conception of procedural fairness, it must be taken into account that in a dispute-resolution type of legal procedure, the decision—the outcome—whether the claimant had an entitlement or not is a decision on principle—that is, a standard that is to be observed because it is a requirement of

[4]For an explanation on legitimacy as a process value, see: Summers (1974), pp. 21–22.

[5]In the field of administrative law, see: Mashaw (1981), pp. 885–931. In civil matters, Bayles provides an interesting account of process values independent from accuracy. See: Bayles (1986), pp. 53–57. See also, Saphire (1978), pp. 119–125.

[6]Waldron (2011), pp. 12–16.

[7]Yeazell and Schwartz (2016), p. 25.

[8]Francioni (2017), p. 1.

[9]Palombella (2021), p. 122.

fairness.[10] As pointed out by Dworkin, although the plaintiff has a claim of a legal right, that is not to say that he or she has a right to a perfectly reliable procedure, nor to the most accurate procedure that society can provide.[11] What the plaintiff—and the defendant—has a right to, as a trump against pure utilitarian considerations, is a procedure that assesses the correct weight of risk of moral harm decided by the community, and to a consistent evaluation of such risk. This assessment must show equal concern and respect for the importance of the moral harm at risk. This is Dworkin's answer to the puzzle of how to make room for arguments of social cost without stripping due process of its character of a right under an outcome-based theory of procedural fairness.[12]

The procedural rights as presented by Dworkin, are rights against the authority in charge of the design of a civil procedure or the judges when deciding on procedure in its adjudicative capacity. Both must show they have taken into consideration such an assessment. But I believe both types of decisions must take into account a risk of moral harm beyond accuracy. If the individual has a right to a procedure that correctly assesses the distribution of moral harm risk, that means that as a previous step the individual must first have the capability of using such procedure. Not being able to use a procedure is no less morally wrong than having a bad outcome.

Here I argue that access to justice is not just a matter of policy. In Dworkin's terms, it is not a goal to be reached for the whole community. On the contrary, access to justice is a matter of principle. As a requirement of fairness, it entails that the individual cannot be obstructed from claiming a legal right in a civil court for utilitarian considerations. As Dworkin says:

> When a person goes to law in a civil matter he calls on the court to enforce his rights, and the argument, that the community would be better off if that right were not enforced, is not counted a good argument against him.[13]

However, this argument does not mean that there are not valid considerations based on the common good in deciding what legal procedure and specific procedural guarantees should be afforded. The point is that such considerations are not exogenous to the question of what is the procedure that is due, and that such a decision should not be made purely based on a criterion of accuracy. As explained in chapter I, every civil justice system should be measured not only by its capacity to determinate facts, but also regarding other factors related to its "usability," such as time and cost.[14]

To integrate this idea with the basic procedural rights of Dworkin's procedural fairness theory, the right to a court or access to justice must be incorporated in the concept of procedural fairness as one of its inherent elements. In other words,

---

[10] Dworkin (1977), pp. 22–31.

[11] Dworkin (1985), p. 90.

[12] Bone (2010), pp. 1018–1020.

[13] Dworkin (1985), p. 95.

[14] Zuckerman (1999), p. 48.

procedural fairness in this area is meant to ensure not just accuracy but also to meet the basic conditions required to access the machinery enabled to enforce rights under the established legal procedure that distributes the risk of a moral harm. A legal procedure fails this test if is too costly or ineffective as a mechanism to enforce legal rights, no matter if the risk of moral harm is correctly assessed and consistently applied.

How important moral harm is may be better left to democratic institutions to decide, as in many other moral issues about which people disagree. This way may be easier as well to check on whether such a political decision treats individuals as equals and not as an arbitrary act against one single person.[15] If the allocation of risk of moral ham is distributed in different legal procedures by ex-ante democratic legislation, as an expression of societies' conviction of its importance, it allows social considerations of accessibility to be included as an inherent part of the right to a legal procedure and not as an exogenous element. A sacrifice of procedural guarantees is justified under a policy decision that allows distribution of scarce resources to all potential litigants, just as in any other public budget decision. It will still comply with basic fair play requirements since it will treat individuals with equal consideration.[16] Whenever a court under its adjudicative function must decide whether to afford a particular procedural guarantee, such decision must be based on similar considerations. That is, it has to decide based on an assessment of the risk of moral harm resulting from such a decision,[17] not just from the point of view of accuracy, but also of the conditions necessary to enforce rights under the established legal procedure that distributed the risk of a moral harm.

13.2 How This Theory Fits Practice

I believe that this conception on what procedural fairness requires in non-punitive legal procedures is consistent with the common use of due process, both in the American legal system and at international level. In every jurisdiction analyzed, access to justice has been understood in a similar way, even in cases where this right is not expressly provided.

In the American legal system, the adversarial system is the model of legal procedure that provides the most reliable results both in civil and criminal matters. As explained in the previous chapter, constitutional criminal procedure, history, and practice explains why the specific procedural guarantees to be provided are meant to protect the individual against prosecution, on what is required to a proper defense or to check on the fact-finding process followed by the State. All these sources show the existence of the right to a consistent application of the distribution of risk to a moral

[15] Dworkin (1985), p. 87.
[16] Dworkin (1985), p. 85.
[17] Dworkin (1985), p. 96.

harm. Civil procedure design, on the contrary is less bound by those constraints beyond the minimum requirements of the right to a hearing, notice, and an independent decision maker, as described in Chap. 10. The focus in this regard, as decided in *Boddie v. Connecticut*, is that both parties—defendant and plaintiff—as long they are forced to settle their claims of right or duty through judicial procedure, must be given a *meaningful* opportunity to be heard.

As described in Chap. 10, access to justice while not expressly provided in the American Constitution,[18] has been identified with the equal protection clause, the right to petition, or as a requirement of procedural due process (even though limited to protected interests). This is the case in *Boddie v. Connecticut*, where the Supreme Court held that if a State establishes a legal procedure to solve a dispute, the same State may not pre-empt it without affording access to the means it has prescribed for doing so.[19] In this case, the Supreme Court—at least in cases where there is a protected interest—connected access with the right to an opportunity to be heard, a characteristic feature of the adversarial type of legal procedures that the American legal system praises for reliable outcomes.

This justification explains also, why in the American legal system Small Claims procedures are present in the fifty States even though many basic features of the adversarial system are limited or waived. For example, the Small Claims Court Act of California, established expressly that "…individual minor civil disputes are of special importance to the parties and of significant social and economic consequence collectively." And, therefore, that "…[I]n order to resolve minor civil disputes expeditiously, inexpensively, and fairly, it is essential to provide a judicial forum accessible to all parties directly involved in resolving these disputes."[20]

Regarding the access to justice role in due process, the case law of the ECHR is quite important. As explained before, most decisions of the ECHR on article 6.1. in its civil limb concern legal issues related with access to justice (45% in the sample I collected). Especially, the decisions in *Golder v. United Kingdom* and *Airey v. Ireland*, already described in Chap. 6, show how access to justice relates to the right to a fair trial, and how in civil matters this right is centered around which other procedural guarantees are required or not.

In *Golder v. United Kingdom*, the ECHR says that access to justice is embedded in the right to a fair trial, since it would be inconceivable to have detailed procedural guarantees afforded to parties in a pending lawsuit and not first protect what alone makes it possible to benefit from such guarantees. Other guarantees are of no value at all if there are no judicial proceedings. Moreover, from the point of the rule of law, which is the basic principle behind article 6, one can scarcely conceive of complying

---

[18] Notwithstanding, many States constitutions follow such path and incorporates provisions in this regard by using the formula of the Magna Carta of Chapter 40.

[19] Boddie v. Connecticut, 401 U.S. 371, (1971), pp. 382–383.

[20] West's Ann. Cal. C.C.P. § 116.120.

with it if there is no possibility of having access to the courts.[21] In this regard, the capability of filing a civil claim must ranks as one of the universally recognized fundamental principles of law, such as the forbidding of denial of justice as a principle of international law.[22] Therefore, according to the Court, article 6.1. *must be read* in the light of these principles. Such guarantees, if they were related only to an action that had already been initiated, would be a source of arbitrary power and would have serious consequences that are repugnant to such basic principles.[23]

The case of *Airey v., Ireland*, for its part, provides a good example on how access to justice is the center around which other procedural guarantees may be afforded, not for accuracy—or not only for that purpose which neither is the most important—, but to ensure access. As explained in Chap. 6, in this case, the petitioner alleged that her right to a court was denied since she could not afford the cost of litigation and legal aid was not at the time available in Ireland for seeking a judicial separation.[24] While deciding for the petitioner, the ECHR said that the fact that Ms. Airey in particular required legal aid to have effective right of access, does not hold good for all cases concerning civil matters. On the contrary, under certain eventualities, the possibility of appearing before a court in person, even without a lawyer's assistance, will meet the requirements of article 6.1. As said, the connection between the right to a lawyer and to access to a court arise in cases where the impossibility of obtaining legal aid impairs the real chance of effectively pursuing and sustaining a legal procedure. The issue in question was whether Mrs. Airey's appearance without the assistance of a lawyer would be effective, in the sense of whether she would be able to present her case properly and satisfactorily.[25] Accordingly, to provide an effective right of access to the courts in civil matters the State must have a free choice of the means to be used towards this end. The institution of a legal aid scheme is one of those means but there are others, such as, for example, a simplification of procedure. The conclusion appearing at the end of paragraph 24 above does not therefore imply that the State must provide free legal aid for every dispute relating to a civil right.[26]

At the Inter-American regional system, while access is not guaranteed expressly in the Convention either, the IACHR has said that is upheld by articles 8, providing the right to a fair trial, and 25, which guarantees an effective remedy. IACHR case law on the main dimensions of due process decided by the court—besides reasonable duration and effective remedy—was access to justice. By deciding these cases under article 8 and 25 of the Convention, an obstruction of the right of access to a court—beyond what is reasonably needed for the administration of justice—implies

[21] ECHR, Case of Golder v. United Kingdom, no. 4451/70, Judgment of 21 February 1975, par. 33, 34.

[22] Regarding access to justice as customary international law, see: Francioni (2017).

[23] ECHR, Case of Golder v. United Kingdom, no. 4451/70, Judgment of 21 February 1975, par. 35.

[24] ECHR, Case of Airey v. Ireland, no. 6289/73, Judgment of 9 October 1979, par. 11, 20.

[25] ECHR, Case of Airey v. Ireland, no. 6289/73, Judgment of 9 October 1979, par. 24.

[26] ECHR, Case of Airey v. Ireland, no. 6289/73, Judgment of 9 October 1979, par. 24.

a violation of both provisions, since the formal existence of such proceeding is not enough, they also need to be effective.[27]

A good example of how procedural guarantees depend on access to justice under this regional system, is the case of *Furlán and Family v. Argentina.* As described, this case concerns a claim for damages against the State of Argentina stemming from the disability of Sebastián Furlan.[28] The Court found that in this civil procedure there was several violations. Among them, a violation of the right to be heard, since the judge did not consider his opinions on the matter personally, nor through the Juvenile Defender's Office which was not notified of the proceedings, even though this was required by law. According to the IACHR, taking the especial situation of inequality of Sebastian Furlán and his family, compensatory measures were required to help reduce or eliminate the obstacles he faced to an effective defense, and their absence amounted to a lack of access to justice.[29]

13.3 The Role of the Flexible and Checklist Models in a Balance Based on Effectiveness

In this section, I will argue that to make the right to a court part and parcel of a procedural due process theory for non-criminal matters, the basis to be followed is the flexible model presented in Chap. 1. From a legislative or judicial perspective, due process must be flexible enough to weigh different factors such as the complexity of the rights involved, the need for accuracy, the necessary conditions to be effectively heard, the resulting burden on the state for adopting such a procedure, as well as other functions that those legal proceedings may serve. But such theory does also require a floor to ensure respect for dignity and legitimacy, as well as a basic level of reliability.

The central question to answer, as described at the beginning of this book was how to provide a simple, fast, and low-cost mechanism to provide access to justice, but in a way that does not sacrifice the other goals of a fair procedure and ascertaining the truth while respecting fundamental guarantees. In this chapter, I have argued that procedural due process in civil matters entails encompassing a right to a legal procedure that attach the correct importance to the risk of moral harm, a consistent application of such a level of risk, and the conditions to effectively pursue such a procedure. This is a right both to the rule-making authority when designing civil procedure, as it is to the judge when deciding on procedure in its adjudicative

[27] I/A Court H.R., Case of Cantos v. Argentina. Merits, Reparations and Costs. Judgment of November 28, 2002. Series C No. 97, par. 50–52.

[28] I/A Court H.R., Case of Furlan and family v. Argentina. Preliminary Objections, Merits, Reparations and Costs. Judgment of August 31, 2012. Series C No. 246, par. 78, 99.

[29] I/A Court H.R., Case of Furlan and family v. Argentina. Preliminary Objections, Merits, Reparations and Costs. Judgment of August 31, 2012. Series C No. 246, par. 268, 269.

capacity. This section suggest answers to the question how specific procedural guarantees should be allocated so that they satisfy these basic requirements.

There might be different strategies on this regard. Under utilitarian considerations, to provide a more accessible civil procedure as demanded by the access to justice movement, would be preferable only when such a procedure would so substantially increase social welfare that its rejection seems irrational.[30] In other words, it might allow trading as many procedural guarantees of the adversarial legal procedural as are necessary to further social welfare. That might even include curtailing some potential litigants in order to improve the situation of a majority or others whose legal claims are seen as more valuable in the long run, for example, because society expect an increase in the inflow of cases and therefore in the costs of the administration of justice. In the United States, for example, one of the most influential civil reform movements claim that civil litigation—especially in areas such as torts litigation—is too accessible for those who initiate litigation while too costly and unreliable against defendants. These critics has been especially successful in many States, limiting the maxim amount to be awarded in damages for pain and suffering, establishing caps on punitive damages, or enacting "frivolous litigation statutes". According to Croley, this reform movement relies on a doubtful empirical basis and mostly on "high profile" or blockbuster cases, while the real threat to civil justice in America is not excessive accessibility but, on the contrary, its frequent inaccessibility.[31]

One of the criticisms that the *Mathews v. Elridge* test in the American system has received is that focusing on accuracy from a utilitarian analysis, it might fail to provide at least a basic minimum protection. Let us recall that this balancing test implies a consideration of the private interest that will be affected by the official action, the risk of an erroneous deprivation of such interest and the probable value of the additional procedural safeguard, and finally, the government's interest, including the function involved and the fiscal and administrative burden.

At least, in civil cases where the State has a relevant interest at stake, such as in *Little v. Streater,* the Supreme Court has used the test in connection with the requirement of a meaningful opportunity to be heard. As explained in Chap. 10, this test was applied to decide whether the cost of blood grouping tests was to be borne by indigent defendants under a procedure where the State had a prominent interest.[32] Since this evidence was relevant, taking into consideration the evidentiary burden and having to face the State as an adversary, an indigent defendant without aid in obtaining blood test evidence in a paternity case lacks a meaningful opportunity to be heard.[33]

Notwithstanding, in civil procedures between private individuals, where the State has no direct interest, the application seems more problematic. Since under this test

[30] Mashaw (1976), p. 48.

[31] Croley (2017), pp. 93–130.

[32] Little v. Streater, 452 U.S. 1, (1981), p. 9.

[33] Little v. Streater, 452 U.S. 1, (1981), p. 16.

the focus is on accuracy, and, as argued by Dworkin, in terms of risk of bare harm but not moral harm, the problem is that such balancing test does not allow to take into consideration other values underlying procedural due process. Without such a determination it is impossible to fix the floor of procedural safeguards.[34] Therefore, the balancing test under *Mathews v. Elridge* may give rise to a situation in which an individual possesses an undisputed property interest—and thus, a clear right to due process—but has no right to any procedures at all.[35]

So, while flexible balancing is required, a purely utilitarian calculation is not respectful of the right to a court as in inherent part of procedural fairness in civil matters. In this section, I provide a flexibility approach that take this right into account. Next, I develop the role of the checklist approach as an instrument to provide such a floor.

13.3.1 The Balance on Effectiveness Under the Flexible Approach

As described in Chap. 1, the flexible ideal model entails a conception on due process whose content is not rigid, and in its application dependent on the particular circumstances of the case under a case-by-case balancing on what it is required to be considered as "fair." As said, the maxim under this ideal model is that those differently situated required to be treated differently to be equal.[36]

To provide protection of procedural fairness using a flexible content to be determined case-by-base, normative provisions providing for basic requirements tend to be written in a broad language. While any of the jurisdictions I have studied provide for a "pure" flexible ideal in the sense that the entire content must be determined under a case-by-case approach, they are closer to it in civil than in criminal matters. From the text of both regional human rights protections system, this is quite clear. Both basic normative provisions applicable to civil matters are general clauses providing only for basic rights, which are construed in turn in broad terms as well. In this regard, article 8.1 of the American Convention on Human Rights provides for a "...right to a hearing, with due guarantees and within a reasonable time, by a competent, independent, and impartial tribunal, previously established by law". Similarly, article 6.1. of the European counterpart says that "...everyone is entitled to a fair and public hearing within a reasonable time by an independent and impartial tribunal established by law..." Both normative provisions

[34] Redish and Marshall (1986), pp. 472–474.

[35] Redish and Marshall (1986), p. 472.

[36] Sunstein (2006), p. 633.

reserve more specific provisions only for criminal matters.[37] In the American legal system, the requirements over civil matters goes even closer to the flexible ideal. As explained in part III, due process requirements over civil matters are derived from the Fifth, Fourteenth Amendments which derives I turn from the general clause of the Chapter 39 of the Magna Carta. On the contrary, with the exception of the Seventh Amendment right to a jury, the constitutional express provisions establish specific safeguards only for criminal matters. In the States, even in those who provides for a clause that include the right to a court follows a general clause, many times incorporating the language of the original chapter 40 clause.

The determination of the specific content—beyond the "minimum floor" as I will explain in the next section—requires a specific methodology. From the practice of the international and national jurisdictions I have studied, the key to encompass the required balance with the rest of the minimum requirements is the concept of *effectiveness*. Most case law on procedural due process in civil matters tries to analyze whether the individual was capable to access and then to participate in a *meaningful* or *effective* way. While both concepts might not be synonymous, I think both points to the fact that the parties, beyond formal recognition, must be able to use and influence the outcome in the legal procedure for the purpose that was designed, which is to enforce a claim of legal right and settle a dispute. Therefore, in this section I use both concepts indistinctly.

Of course, this is a broad concept constructed more as a legal principle that requires a purposive interpretation. Therefore, under this flexible approach, to decide what is the procedure that is due entails taking a consideration of the specific circumstances of a case, which I have said, in this matters it relates to how necessary a procedural guarantee is to effectively pursue a legal claim. In the next section, I describe how this is used in the jurisdictions analyzed in the previous chapter.

13.3.1.1 Particular Circumstances Are Analyzed to Ensure Effectiveness

In both regional jurisdictions, this approach was the frequent methodology to decide *ex post facto* on cases of reasonable duration. This analysis is made based on several factors such as the complexity of the case, the conduct of the parties and the relevant authorities, and what was at stake for the applicant in the dispute.[38] In the case of the

[37] Notwithstanding, beyond the text as explained in Chap. 5, in the Inter-American regional system procedural rights of the paragraphs 2, 3, 4, and 5 has been applied in cases involving non-punitive legal procedures.

[38] ECHR, Case of König v. Germany, no. 6232/73, Judgment of 28 June 1978, par. 99, 111; ECHR, Case of Buchholz v. Germany, no. 7759/77, Judgment of 6 May 1981, par. 49; ECHR, Case of Zimmermann and Steiner v. Switzerland, no. 8737/79, Judgment of 13 July 1983, par. 24; ECHR, Case of Deumeland v. Germany, no. 9384/81, Judgment of 29 May 1986, par. 78. In the case of the IACHR, see: I/A Court H.R., Case of the Sawhoyamaxa Indigenous Community v. Paraguay. Merits, Reparations and Costs. Judgment of March 29, 2006. Series C No. 146, par. 88–89; I/A

American legal system, undue delay of civil justice maybe framed as an infraction of the due process clause, according to which the *Matthews v. Eldridge* test would apply. While this is a case-by-case approach, according to Hittner and Weisz the claim to obtain an efficient vindication of legal rights will depend upon showing a relatively extensive delay and a resultant deprivation of justice that is considerably pervasive.[39]

As shown in the context of the European system, most cases on the article 6 right to a fair trial civil limb were decided analyzing if under the specific circumstances of the individual or regarding the case, a specific element or specific procedural guarantee were required by the right to a fair trial. As explained in Chap. 6, this approach has been used in cases on the right to a court and as well regarding the right to an independent and impartial judicial body, but also to decide on the admissibility of appeal to higher courts, judicial decision enforcements, legal aid, the right to a public hearing, among others.

The right to a lawyer is a good example of the specific circumstances' analysis under the case law of the ECHR. For example, under current case law to decide whether legal assistance is required, entails a determination on whether the individual would be able to participate in order to support his or her claims effectively. In this regard, must be taken into consideration whether representation is compulsory by national legislation under the specific legal procedure, the complexity of the procedure including on points of law or facts, the seriousness of what is at stake and emotional involvement, and whether the individual is on substantial disadvantage vis a vis his or her adversary.

In the Inter-American regional system, we saw how in *Barbani Duarte et. al. v. Uruguay,* the IACHR analyzed the right to be heard both from the point of view of access to the competent body to determine the legal right, and, second, as a guarantee that the decision produced by the proceedings satisfies the end for which it was conceived.[40] In this particular case, this element failed since the administrative body acting as decision maker did not considered a key element of the legal claim presented, and that had a direct impact on the decision on whether accept or not the petitions of the alleged victims.[41]

In other cases, the lack of effectiveness—and as such a violation of the right to a fair trial—came from an unjustified delay in reaching or enforcing a decision. In the case of *The Mayagna (Sumo) Awas Tingni Community v. Nicaragua* the delay came

---

Court H.R., Case of Fornerón and daughter v. Argentina. Merits, Reparations and Costs. Judgment of April 27, 2012. Series C No. 242, par. 66–77.

[39] Hittner and Weisz (1990), pp. 353–354.

[40] I/A Court H.R., Case of Barbani Duarte et al. v. Uruguay. Merits, Reparations and Costs. Judgment of October 13, 2011. Series C No. 234, par. 122.

[41] The requirements of article 31 of Law 17,613 were: (1) to be a "depositor" of the Banco de Montevideo or the Banco La Caja Obrera; (2) whose savings had been transferred to other institutions, and (3) without his consent. I/A Court H.R., Case of Barbani Duarte et al. v. Uruguay. Merits, Reparations and Costs. Judgment of October 13, 2011. Series C No. 234, par. 141, 142, 153.

from a constitutional claim presented by the indigenous community since the applicable legal procedure proved to be ineffective to protect their lands. All this cases implied the idea that an effective protection must takes into account the specificities, economic and social characteristics, customs and values, and their special situation of vulnerability of indigenous population.[42] In the case of *Colindres Schonenberg v. El Salvador*, the undue delay was on a civil claim which notwithstanding it was decided for the claimant on first instance, since filing to enforcement the proceeding lasted more than fifteen years.[43] Similar solution are found in the effective remedy cases of the ECHR against Italy in the so-called "Pinto Proceedings", where it held that the delay on the implementation of the decisions on damages resulting from unreasonable duration of civil proceedings, implied article 6 guarantees had any *effet utile*.[44]

13.3.1.2 The Nature of the Legal Procedure to Decide What Serves Better Its Purpose

As said, the flexible approach, to provide a more focused protection, entails a value-oriented interpretation of what due process require in a specific legal procedure. Besides taking into consideration the specific circumstances of the individual, that means to consider the nature of the legal procedure. This criterion has been used quite similarly in the case of the ECHR and in the SCOTUS regarding the right to a hearing. While both case law recognizes that such requirement is a minimum protection, something about which I will further develop in the next section, the specific form of the hearing and whether additional procedural safeguards are to be afforded, varies according to the nature of the proceeding.

In the America legal system has been considered that while the traditional judicial hearing is the paramount against which other are compared, other procedural rights such as personal and oral participation, the right to confront and cross-examine adverse witnesses, the character of the witnesses, or mandatary legal representation, depends on several factors.[45] For example, in *Memphis Light, Gas & Water Div. v. Craft*, the Supreme Court held—relying on *Mathews v. Eldridge* test—, that notwithstanding this requirement, where the potential deprivation does not indicate a likelihood of serious loss, and where the procedures are sufficiently reliable to minimize the risk of erroneous determination, government may act

---

[42] I/A Court H.R., Case of the Yakye Axa Indigenous Community v. Paraguay. Merits, Reparations and Costs. Judgment of June 17, 2005. Series C No. 125, par. 62; Case of the Sawhoyamaxa Indigenous Community v. Paraguay. Merits, Reparations and Costs. Judgment of March 29, 2006. Series C No. 146, par. 83.

[43] I/A Court H.R., Case of Colindres Schonenberg v. El Salvador. Merits, Reparations and Costs. Judgment of February 4, 2019. Series C No. 373, par. 53–55, 114–119.

[44] ECHR, Case of Simaldone v. Italy, no 22644/03, Judgment of 31 March 2009, par. 55.

[45] Saphire (1978), pp. 161–166.

without providing additional "advance procedural safeguards."[46] Moreover, in the United States, depending on the susceptibility of the particular subject—and often in the administrative law arena—the right to a hearing might be respected through written presentations, as long that does not curtail the ability of the counterpart to understand the case against him and to present his arguments effectively, and depending on the administrative costs involved.[47] Therefore, as argued in *Boddie v. Connecticut*, the key element, especially in the context of a judicial process, is that the persons who are forced to settle their claims through such means must be given a *meaningful* opportunity to be heard.[48]

In the European system, the right to a hearing is a minimum protection but there are exceptions where a public hearing might be dispensed. For example the ECHR had established the nature of the issues to be decided must be taken into account since procedures devoted exclusively to points of law or highly technical can fulfill the conditions of Article 6 even in the absence of public debates.[49] It has decided also that where a public hearing has been held at first instance, a less strict standard applies to the appellate level in general. In the interests of the proper administration of justice, it is normally more expedient that a hearing be held at first instance rather than only before the appellate court.[50] In *Kennedy v. The United Kingdom*, as explained in Chap. 2, the ECHR held that the obligation to hold a hearing is not absolute, and in certain cases a judge may fairly and reasonably decide the case on the basis of the parties' submissions and other written materials. That depends on the nature of the issues to be decided by the competent national court.[51] For example, if there are no issues of credibility or contested facts and dispensing a public hearing might serve other functions such as the expeditious handling of the courts' caseload.[52]

13.3.1.3 Procedural Guarantees May Be Limited Under a Criterion of Proportionality

Another expression of flexibility is the use of a balance on proportionality on the limitations that might be imposed to this right. As decided in the case of *Mémoli*

[46] Memphis Light, Gas & Water Div. v. Craft, 436 U.S. 1 (1978), p. 19.

[47] Friendly (1975), p. 1281.

[48] Boddie v. Connecticut, 401 U.S. 371, (1971), p. 377.

[49] ECHR, Case of Ernst and Other v. Belgium, no 33400/96, Judgment of 15 July 2003, par. 66. More recently: ECHR, Case of Nikolova and Vandova v. Bulgaria, no. 20688/04, Judgment of 17 December 2013, par.70.

[50] ECHR, Case of Miller v. Sweden, no. 55853/00, Judgment of 8 February 2005, par. 30.

[51] ECHR, Kennedy v. The United Kingdom, no. 26839/05, Judgment of 18 May 2010, par. 188. See, also: ECHR, Case of Tommaso v. Italy, no. 43395/09, Judgment of 23 February 2017, par. 163.

[52] ECHR, Case of Mutu and Pechstein v. Switzerland, nos. 40575/10 and 67474/10, Judgment of 2 October 2018, par. 177.

v. Argentina, where the petitioners claimed a violation of their right to access to justice by the imposition of court fees. The IACHR held access to justice is not absolute and therefore it can be limited by the State as along as the measure imposed ensure correspondence between the means used and the objective pursued. Moreover, it held that court fees are not an obstruction per se but only if the charge was unreasonable or represented a serious prejudice to their financial capacity.[53]

In the case of *Cantos v. Argentina*, the IACHR held that disproportionate or excessive filing fees court fees to enforce a judicial decision might entail a problem from the point of view of effectiveness. The court said it is not enough that a proceeding exist, those participating in the proceeding must be able to do so without fear of being forced to pay an amount that attach the debtor's property or deny him the opportunity to do business, only because they decided to claim a legal right in courts.[54] Similar rationale may be found in cases such as *Boddie v. Connecticut*. Here, the Supreme Court decided that while the establishment of court fees or related cost is a legitimate interest from the State—e.g., for the prevention of frivolous litigation and to allocate scarce resources—, none of these considerations are sufficient to override a protected interest where under States law the sole means for enforcing such rights are the courts. For indigent litigants, that might be regarded as the equivalent of denying them an opportunity to be heard.[55] Under this rationale, whether people are entitled to meaningful opportunities in court when they face losses of important interest as a matter of due process,[56] this embed the idea of access to a court at least regarding claims on protected interest.

Similarly, in the ECHR case law, it is clear that restrictions cannot impair the very essence of this right. Between the measures imposed and the goals pursued—which must be a legitimate aim—must be a relation of proportionality. Regarding litigation cost and fees, as described in Chap. 6, the case law of the ECHR is clear in the sense that the right to a fair trial in civil matters does not include an unqualified right to obtain free legal aid from the State in a civil dispute, nor a right to free proceedings in civil matters. Therefore, court fees in civil courts cannot be regarded, as a restriction that is incompatible *per se* with the Convention. On the contrary, according to the particular circumstances of the case must be analyzed if the imposed fee impaired the very essence of the right to a court. According to it, factors such as the applicant's ability to pay them, and the stage of the proceedings are material in this regard.[57] As

[53] I/A Court H.R., Case of Mémoli v Argentina, Preliminary Objections, Merits, Reparations and Costs. Judgment of August 22, 2013. Series C No. 265, par. 193.

[54] I/A Court H.R., Case of Cantos v. Argentina. Merits, Reparations and Costs. Judgment of November 28, 2002. Series C No. 97, par. 55.

[55] Boddie v. Connecticut, 401 U.S. 371, (1971), pp. 380–381.

[56] Scherer (2006), p. 677.

[57] ECHR, Case of Kreuz v. Poland, no. 28249/95, 19 June 2001, par. 60, 61. See also: ECHR, Case of Weissman and Others v. Romania, no. 63945/00, Judgment of 24 May 2006, par. 34–37; ECHR, Case of Apostol v. Georgia, no. 40765/02, Judgment of 28 November 2006, par. 59; ECHR, Case of Bakan v. Turkey, no. 50939/99, Judgment of 12 June 2007, par. 67, 68; ECHR, Case of Stankov v. Bulgaria, no. 68490/01, Judgment of 12 July 2007, par. 51, 52; ECHR, Case of Anakomba Yula

described in Chapter II, similar approach has been used in cases concerning the admissibility of appeals by the applicants on civil proceedings but denied by local courts.

13.3.1.4 More Latitude in Civil Matters and Deference to the Decision-Maker

Another way to understand the flexibility as the desired approach in civil matters is the specific recognition that on civil matters there is a broad space for discretion for the rule-making authority or the judge deciding under its adjudicative capacity. While in the IACHR that is not that clear, since in many cases the line between administrative of punitive or civil nature is blurred and an expansive approach is frequently used there are least some thematic reports calling for a degree of compatibility. On the contrary, in the European system there is a clear distinction between both fields and the ECHR has expressly said that 6.1 gives more latitude on civil matters, for example regarding how evidence is to be incorporated at trial, such as witnesses examination and cross-examination.[58] The SCOTUS has expressly refused to apply *Mathews v. Eldridge* in criminal matters. In civil matters the key is the concept of flexibility of the due process clause,[59] and the minimum requirements has settled in notice, hearing—with various degrees between administrative and judicial settings—, and an impartial decision maker.[60] On the contrary, in criminal cases it means the fair-trial provisions of the Bill of Rights, supplemented by any other procedures required as a matter of "fundamental fairness."[61] In *Medina v. California*, the Supreme Court held that the *Mathews v. Elridge* does not provide the appropriate framework for due process in criminal justice, where the court prefers to define the category of infractions that violate fundamental fairness very narrowly.[62]

Both national and international jurisdictions show that civil matters require a flexible conception of the right to a fair trial. This flexible approach tries to take into consideration the particular circumstances of the parties and the nature of the legal procedure to ensure that the legal claims are *effectively* pursued, from the filing to the enforcement of the decision. From the rulemaking and design of civil procedure until

---

v. Belgium, no. 45413/07, Judgment of 10 March 2009, par. 32; ECHR, Georgel and Georgeta v. Stoicescu v. Romania, no. 9718/03, Judgment of 26 July 2011, par. 69.

[58] ECHR, Case of Jokela v. Finland, no. 28856/95, Judgment of 21 May 2002, par. 66.

[59] Sullivan and Massaro (2013), pp. 87–88. See: Parham v. J.R., 442 U.S. 584, 599, 99 S.Ct. 2493, 2502, 61 L.Ed.2d 101 (1979).

[60] Rubin (1984), p. 1109.

[61] Dripps (2018), p. 67.

[62] Medina v. California, 505 U.S. 437, 443, 112 S. Ct. 2572, 2576, 120 L. Ed. 2d 353. More recently, by applying the Mathews v. Elridge test to a post-and-forfeit procedure, the Court of Appeal of the District of Columbia Circuit, gave the same rationale to not apply this test to criminal procedure. Kincaid v. Gov't of D.C., 854 F.3d 721, 726 (D.C. Cir. 2017).

the court decision on procedural guarantees, that entails a great latitude in this field. But that is not to say that any kind of legal procedure would be acceptable. The flexibility that procedural fairness gives in this matter has the purpose of providing an effective right to a legal procedure that correctly asses the risk of moral ham under a right balance with costs and time, and in that regard, accessible for all the potential litigants. How to do it in concrete terms will depend much in the inherent values of each legal system, reflected in history or settled practices.[63]

As said in Chap. 1, in many situations it is necessary to differentiate to treat someone equally. And procedural guarantees in the form of clear-cut legal rules in many situations might result in unjust situations for one side more than the other. For example, in civil matters where there is an imbalance between the sporadic litigant against the repeat player, an strict conception of impartiality resulting in an passive judge, might imply that for pro se litigants a meaningful opportunity to be heard might end only as a formal recognition without practical effects. On the contrary, for those repeat players in positions of power, the passiveness of the judge provides an advantage beyond the merits of the claim.

The flexible approach in civil matters allows to further improve the dispute resolution function of the courts, beyond mere law enforcement. By taking the particularities of the individuals, also might improve perception of overall fairness of a given legal procedure, and in that regard promote responsiveness of the outcomes.[64]

But in the name of flexibility, in order to provide speed dispute resolution, we may end up by flipping a coin. In other words, we might end up by sacrificing features of the legal procedure that we consider as valuable for several functions, as related to the existence of the forum to solve such disputes but also in terms of accuracy. To provide a basic floor over which the flexible balance of effectiveness will serve, the checklist approach I have described in Chap. 1 has an important role to play, not only theoretically, but as reflected in the practice on how different legal system understand the requirements of due process in civil matters.

13.3.2 The Floor Provided by the Checklist Approach

From the analysis on how due process has been applied in non-punitive legal procedures, although none of the national or international jurisdictions described in the previous section follows a pure version of the checklist model, at least some of its features are used for special purposes. Mainly, practice reveals that such approach serves in the rule-making dimension to provide special protection for specific vulnerable groups, establish especial legal procedures with procedural guarantees established ex ante, but mainly to provide what we may call the "floor" of the

[63] Redish and Marshall (1986), pp. 474–475. See also: Dworkin (1985), p. 90.

[64] Sunstein (2006), p. 634.

requirements of procedural fairness in civil matters. These are the types of minimum protections which cannot be discarded without compromising the fairness of the procedure.

13.3.2.1 Checklist Approach to Enhance Protection in Vulnerable Conditions

The Inter-American system use of the checklist approach in civil matters is an example of how sometimes it is necessary to use clear and strict rules providing minimum protections in situations where the risk of abuse might be higher than regular civil matters. For example, in the case of *the Pacheco Tineo family v. Bolivia,* the IACHR decided a series of minimum guarantees that must be afforded to asylum seekers as they risk serious consequences for the basic rights.[65] Moreover, this approach has been used in cases where the dividing line, or the purpose of the legal procedure between dispute resolution and imposition of a punishment, is not clear, or where a party is facing the State which has a direct interest in the case. For example, in *Ivcher Bronstein v. Peru*, the IACHR held that in the administrative procedure, which ended with the termination of citizenship by resolution of the Director General of Migration and Naturalization,[66] the petitioner required in full the guarantees of article 8 to defend himself adequately against the State.[67] According to petitioner, his rights to intervene, fully informed, in all the stages were violated, despite being the person whose rights were being determined.[68]

13.3.2.2 Final Judicial Decision and Its Enforcement as Strictly Required

The checklist model has been used to decide on particular procedural guarantees such as the duty to state reasons and the enforcement of judicial decisions, interpreting them as a strict minimum that is applicable in all-or-nothing fashion.[69] Regarding the enforcement of judicial decisions, in the case of *The Kichwa*

[65] I/A Court H.R., Case of the Pacheco Tineo family v. Bolivia. Preliminary Objections, Merits, Reparations and Costs. Judgment of November 25, 2013. Series C No. 272, par. 159.

[66] I/A Court H.R., Case of Ivcher Bronstein v. Peru. Merits, Reparations and Costs. Judgment of February 6, 2001. Series C No. 74, par. 76.e).

[67] I/A Court H.R., Case of Ivcher Bronstein v. Peru. Merits, Reparations and Costs. Judgment of February 6, 2001. Series C No. 74, par. 102.

[68] I/A Court H.R., Case of Ivcher Bronstein v. Peru. Merits, Reparations and Costs. Judgment of February 6, 2001. Series C No. 74, par. 107.

[69] I/A Court H.R., Case of Kichwa Indigenous People of Sarayaku v. Ecuador. Merits and Reparations. Judgment of June 27, 2012. Series C No. 245, par. 263. Similar strict approach might be seen in: I/A Court H.R., Case of the "Five Pensioners" v. Peru. Merits, Reparations and Costs. Judgment of February 28, 2003. Series C No. 98, par. 138; I/A Court H.R., Case of Furlan and

Indigenous People of Sarayaku v. Ecuador, the Court held that to execute the decisions or judgments issued by judicial authorities is a strict minimum to provide effectiveness.[70] Similar reasoning is found in the ECHR for cases concerning *res iudicata* and the judicial determination of a case, and the enforcement of such decisions. For example, in *Driza v. Albania*, it held that a after a final and enforceable judicial decision, a Supreme Court should not examine an entire case afresh but only correct miscarriage of justice.[71] Regarding the enforcement of judicial decisions, in *Immobiliarie Saffi v. Italy*, the ECHR held that even though States may, in exceptional circumstances, intervene in enforcement proceedings, the consequence of such intervention should not be that execution is prevented, invalidated or unduly delayed or, still less, that the substance of the decision is undermined.[72]

13.3.2.3 Right to an Impartial and Independent Tribunal

The study of the ECHR case law and the American legal system procedural due process tradition shows how the requirement of an independent and impartial tribunal is one basic right that deserves an enhanced protection.

As explained in Part III, while many of these cases in the ECHR are decided by an analysis of the circumstances of the case, there are others where the normative provision has been interpreted as a clear-cut rule. These cases are usually associated with cases in which there is a clear situation that fails an objective test, that is, that any individual would fear for the lack of independence or impartiality of the decision maker. For example, in *Sramek v. Austria*, the ECHR held that in cases where a tribunal's members include a person who is in a subordinate position, vis-à-vis one of the parties, litigants may entertain a legitimate doubt about that person's independence and in that regard trigger a violation of this right.[73] Quite clear as well is the case of *Brudnicka and Others v. Poland*, where the ECHR held that since the decision-makers, the members of the maritime chambers, were appointed and removed from office by political officers with relevant interest in the case, the

---

family v. Argentina. Preliminary Objections, Merits, Reparations and Costs. Judgment of August 31, 2012. Series C No. 246, par. 209.

[70] I/A Court H.R., Case of Kichwa Indigenous People of Sarayaku v. Ecuador. Merits and Reparations. Judgment of June 27, 2012. Series C No. 245, par. 263. Similar strict approach might be seen in: I/A Court H.R., Case of the "Five Pensioners" v. Peru. Merits, Reparations and Costs. Judgment of February 28, 2003. Series C No. 98, par. 138; I/A Court H.R., Case of Furlan and family v. Argentina. Preliminary Objections, Merits, Reparations and Costs. Judgment of August 31, 2012. Series C No. 246, par. 209.

[71] ECHR, Case of Driza v. Albania, no. 33771/02, Judgment of 13 November 2007, par. 63–70. See, also: ECHR, Case of Brumărescu v. Romania, no. 28342/95, Judgment of 28 October 1999, par. 62.

[72] ECHR, Case of Immobiliare Saffi v. Italy, no. 22774/93, Judgment of 28 July 1999, par. 74. Similar reasoning may be found in: ECHR, Case of Okyay and Others v. Turkey, no. 36220/97, Judgment of 12 July 2005, par. 72–74.

[73] ECHR, Case of Sramek v. Austria, no. 8790/79, Judgment of 22 October 1984.

applicants were justified in having doubts as to their independence and impartiality.[74] Additionally, there are been cases in which the close family ties between the opposing party's advocate and the judges, or the presidency of the court by a person with whom the petitioner had an argument in the press, are gross violations which objectively justify the applicant's fears as to the court's impartiality.[75] These cases apply a doctrine of appearances and the question is if the conditions of the case calls for a legitimate doubt of impartiality or independence. If this objective test is fulfilled, petitioners are not required to provide concrete evidence on the judges' behavior in the case or regarding his or her state of mind.

In the American system, the protection of the independent and impartial adjudicators is a basic right that applies to non-punitive legal procedures as a part of a long Anglo-American tradition expressed in the Article III of the Constitution.[76] In this regard, this constitutional provision basically says that judges will hold their offices during good behavior and be compensated,[77] had the purpose of protect the judiciary from being overpowered by the other branches of government.[78] But this constitutional provision also protect against bias by establishing a personal jurisdiction requirement.[79]

This procedural guarantee points to having—at least—one hearing on the merits before a judicial—or quasi-judicial—body, with a decision maker characterized by their independence and impartiality under the umbrella of adversary procedures.[80] In the legal procedure, that means the judge or the jury should not be biased.[81] In this regard, in *Marshall v. Jerrico*, a case concerning civil penalties imposed for child

[74] ECHR, Case of Brudnicka and Others v. Poland, no. 54723/00, Judgment of 03 March 2005, par. 41. See, also: ECHR, Case of Langborger v. Sweden, no. 11179/84, Judgment of 22 June 1989, par. 32–35; ECHR, Case of McGonell v. The United Kingdom, no. 28488/95, Judgment of 8 February 2000, par. 52–57.

[75] ECHR, Case of Buscemi v. Italy, no. 29569/95, Judgment of 16 September 1999, par. 64, 67–68.

[76] This was the basic argument of Sir Edward Coke in the famous Dr. Bonham case. See: Williams (2006), pp. 111–128.

[77] Article III. Section 1. "The judicial Power of the United States, shall be vested in one supreme Court, and in such inferior Courts as the Congress may from time to time ordain and establish. The Judges, both of the supreme and inferior Courts, shall hold their Offices during good Behaviour, and shall, at stated Times, receive for their Services, a Compensation, which shall not be diminished during their Continuance in Office."

[78] Redish and Marshall (1986), p. 480.

[79] Article III. Section 2. The judicial Power shall extend to all Cases, in Law and Equity, arising under this Constitution, the Laws of the United States, and Treaties made, or which shall be made, under their Authority;--to all Cases affecting Ambassadors, other public Ministers and Consuls;--to all Cases of admiralty and maritime Jurisdiction;--to Controversies to which the United States shall be a Party;--to Controversies between two or more States;--between a State and Citizens of another State;--between Citizens of different States;--between Citizens of the same State claiming Lands under Grants of different States, and between a State, or the Citizens thereof, and foreign States, Citizens or Subjects.

[80] Michelman (1974), p. 557.

[81] Bayles (1986), p. 55.

labor regulation, the Supreme Court held that the due process clause entitles a person to an impartial and disinterested tribunal in both civil and criminal cases. Therefore, it is not just the idea of impartiality under adjudication but in the form of the adversarial type of legal proceeding.[82]

This requirement of neutrality in adjudicative proceedings safeguards the two central concerns of procedural due process. First, is the prevention of unjustified or mistaken deprivations, which is be considered an accuracy purpose. In this regard, the neutrality requirement helps to guarantee that life, liberty, or property will not be affected by an erroneous or distorted conception of the facts or the law. And, second, neutrality fosters the promotion of participation and dialogue by affected individuals in the decision making process—a fairness purpose.[83] In this regard, according to the Court in *Marshall v. Jerrico*, such a guarantee preserves both the appearance and reality of fairness, by ensuring that no person will be deprived of his interests in the absence of a proceeding in which he may present his case with the assurance that the arbiter is not predisposed to find against him."[84]

According to authors such as Redish and Marshall, even though the Supreme Court insist on identifying notice and hearing as the basic floor, the independence of the adjudicator is such an essential safeguard that it may be the only one. The argument is that none of the strict minimums can be fulfilled without the participation of an independent adjudicator. First, from an instrumental conception, as the clause is to ensure accuracy of the decision, which following an adversarial conception of the procedure can only be ensured through the effective participation of the parties and their opportunity to influence the decision maker. Of course, that would assume, as a necessary condition, that the decision maker is an impartial one. From the point of view of the underlying value of fairness, it furthers the subjective perception that justice is "fair," which of course, would be diminished if the decision maker is perceived to be biased.[85] In this regard, Lon Fuller, in his famous "the forms and limits of adjudication," says "...that the integrity of adjudication is impaired if the arbiter not only initiates the proceedings but also, in advance of the public hearing, forms theories about what happened and conducts his own factual inquiries. In such a case the arbiter cannot bring to the public hearing an uncommitted mind; the effectiveness of participation through proofs and reasoned arguments is accordingly reduced."[86]

In *Schweiker v. McClure,* claimants on a Part B Medicare claim challenged the hearing afforded to them because the hearing officers who heard their case were

---

[82] There might be different conceptions of impartiality. For example, while in adversarial type of proceeding, which has been characterized as party driven impartiality means neutrality and even passivity. On the contrary, in inquisitorial model impartiality may have be disinterested in relation with the parties but active in terms of attitude towards establishing facts and gathering evidence. See: Langer (2014).

[83] Marshall v. Jerrico, Inc., 446 U.S. 238 (1980), p. 242.

[84] Marshall v. Jerrico, Inc., 446 U.S. 238 (1980), p. 242.

[85] Redish and Marshall (1986), pp. 475–476.

[86] Fuller (1978), pp. 385–386.

biased. Beside recognizing impartiality as a requirement for officers of judicial or quasi-judicial capacities, it held that such status is presumed unless rebutted by the parties who are charged with the burden of providing enough evidence of a conflict of interest or reason for disqualification.[87] As we saw in the previous chapter with *Concrete Pipe & Prods. v. Constr. Laborers Pension Trust*, this requirement applies even in cases like this one where the decision maker is a government agency acting as an arbiter by its given authority to adjudicate by statute.[88]

According to Redish and Marshall, there are three categories of bias which threatens this guarantee. First, the decision maker may have a financial stake in the outcome, may have some personal bias toward a party, or may be predisposed toward a certain position. While they may differ in degree, they do not in kind. Any of them might be threatening and might be enough to disqualify a judge. Notwithstanding, some degree of risk is tolerated mainly for practical reasons, for example, in the so-called Rule of Necessity.[89] According to this rule, the disqualification of a member of a court of last resort will not excuse such member from performing his official duty if failure to do so would result in a denial of a litigant's constitutional right to have a question adjudicated.[90]

As decided in *Schweiker v. McClure,* such requirements apply over officers of judicial or quasi-judicial capacities.[91] Similarly, the strict minimum variable in the ECHR has been used as well to establish that notwithstanding a public agency might serve different functions—administrative, regulatory, adjudicative, advisory and disciplinary—, under its adjudicative capacity, if considered as a tribunal it must satisfy the requirements of article 6.1. including independence of the executive and of the parties to the case.[92]

Under the ECHR this approach has been used as well for the right to a tribunal established by law. In this regard, as explained in Chap. 7, by identifying an organ as a tribunal with full jurisdiction to decide over all matters of facts and law, it must satisfy the requirements of the right to a fair trial such as independence of the executive and of the parties to the case, duration of its members' term of office, and others. As such, the Court has held that a violation by a tribunal of domestic

---

[87] Schweiker v. McClure, 456 U.S. 188 (1982), pp. 195–196.

[88] Concrete Pipe & Prods. v. Constr. Laborers Pension Trust, 508 U.S. 602 (1993), pp. 617–618.

[89] Redish and Marshall (1986), p. 492.

[90] United States v. Will, 449 U.S. 200 (1980), p. 214.

[91] Schweiker v. McClure, 456 U.S. 188, (1982), pp. 195–196.

[92] ECHR, Case of Le Compte, Van Leuven, and De Meyere v. Belgium, no. 6878/75; 7238/75, Judgement of 23 June 1981, par. 55; ECHR, Case of Vasilescu v. Romania, 53/1997/837/1043, Judgment of 22 May 1998, par. 41; ECHR, Case of Chevrol v. France, no. 49636/99, Judgment of 13 February 2003, par. 76, 77; ECHR, Case of Fedotova v. Russia, no. 73225/01, Judgment of 13 April 2006, par. 38, 43; ECHR, Case of Woś v. Poland, no. 22860/02, Judgment of 08 June 2006, par. 94; ECHR, Case of Savino and Other v. Italy, nos 17214/05, 20329/05, 42113/04, Judgment of 28 April 2009, par. 94.

legal provisions relating to the establishment and competence of judicial organs gives rise to a violation of Article 6.1.[93]

13.3.2.4 Prior Notice and Hearing as a Minimum Requirement

One of the most important grounds for the use of the checklist approach is to consider the right to a hearing as a strict minimum that must be afforded to the parties. As described before, even though in many cases the characteristics of the hearing are decided, as a general rule, by the nature of the proceeding, there must at least be a hearing. In the section on the ECHR, we saw that since its early case law the ECHR has established that this right is a basic requirement in civil proceedings where article 6.1 applies. The lack of a hearing can only be cured if a subsequent procedure of full review provides such opportunity.[94] The strict exceptions on publicity are mentioned in the second sentence of the clause,[95] but also, it's a right that may be waived.[96] The ECHR has found an exception to the hearing requirement on proceedings concerning exclusively legal or highly technical questions, which may be better decided in private or over purely written material.[97] For example, in *Schuler-Zgraggen v. Switzerland*, the ECHR held that legal proceeding where the legal issue is highly technical and of medical nature, a public proceeding may deter future applicants and as such, it might be processed in written form.[98]

While in the American legal system, the requirements over civil procedure of the due process clause are a contested issue, at least a bare minimum has settled on the

[93]ECHR, Case of DMD Group, a.s. v. Slovakia, no. 19334/03, Judgment of 5 October 2010, par. 58–61; ECHR, Case of Oleksandr Volkov v. Ukraine, no. 21722/11, Judgment of 9 January 2013, par. 150–156.

[94]ECHR, Case of Malhous v. the Czech Republic, no. 33071/96, Judgment of 12 July 2001, par. 62.

[95]Article 6.1.: Judgment shall be pronounced publicly but the press and public may be excluded from all or part of the trial in the interests of morals, public order or national security in a democratic society, where the interests of juveniles or the protection of the private life of the parties so require, or to the extent strictly necessary in the opinion of the court in special circumstances where publicity would prejudice the interests of justice.

[96]ECHR, Case of Le Compte, Van Leuven and De Meyere v. Belgium, no. 6878/75; 7238/75, Judgment of 23 June 1981, par. 59, 60; ECHR, Case of Albert and Le Compte v. Belgium, no. 7299/75; 7496/76, Judgment of 10 February 1983, par. 34, 35; ECHR, Case of H. v. Belgium, no. 8950/80, Judgment of 30 November 1987, par. 54; ECHR, Case De Moor v. Belgium, no. 16997/90, Judgment of 23 June 1994, par. 55, 56.

[97]ECHR, Case of Eisenstecken v. Austria, no. 29477/95, Judgment of 3 October 2000, par. 31–36. See also: ECHR, Case of Miller v. Sweden, no. 55853/00, Judgment of 8 February 2005, par. 29; ECHR, Case of Jurisic and Collegium Mehrerau v. Austria, no. 62539/00, Judgment of 27 July 2006, par. 65–67; ECHR, Case of Koottummel v. Austria, no. 49616/06, Judgment of 10 December 2009, par. 19, 20; ECHR, Case of Nikolova and Vandova v. Bulgaria, no. 20688/04, Judgment of 17 December 2013, par. 69, 70.

[98]ECHR, Case of Schuler-Zgraggen v. Switzerland, no. 14518/89, Judgment of 24 June 1993, par. 58, 59.

requirement of notice and hearing.[99] Regarding the right to a hearing, since early case law it has been established that such a hearing might not be the same in every legal procedure.

As explained, from early on in cases such as *Ballard v. Hunter*, the Supreme Court held that while an opportunity for a hearing and defense is a minimum, there is not a specific or fixed procedure required to comply with such procedural guarantees. On the contrary, the procedure may be adapted to the nature of the case.[100] Sometimes, as in *Londoner v. Denver*, the right to a hearing demands an opportunity to "...support his allegations by argument however brief, and, if need be, by proof, however informal."[101] In many cases, "some kind of hearing" would be the minimum requirement.[102] For example, in *Memphis Light, Gas & Water Div. v. Craft*, the Supreme Court held—relying on the *Mathews v. Eldridge* test—, that notwithstanding this requirement, where the potential deprivation does not indicate a likelihood of serious loss, and where the procedures are sufficiently reliable to minimize the risk of erroneous determination, government may act without providing additional "advance procedural safeguards."[103]

As said, and similarly to what we saw in the ECHR, the specific form and additional procedural safeguards to be provided in the hearing depend much on the nature of the subject at issue. Of course, the traditional judicial hearing is the paradigm against which other procedures are compared. In this regard, other procedural rights such as personal and oral participation, the right to confront and cross-examine adverse witnesses, the character of the witnesses, or mandatary legal representation, depend on several factors.[104]

When it is said that this right is an essential minimum, it means that when in conflict with other procedural safeguards it might, as a matter of collision between legal principles,[105] weigh against others. For example, in *Richards v. Jefferson County,* the Court said that since the opportunity to be heard is an essential requisite of due process of law in judicial proceedings, a State may not enforce a judgment against a party named in the proceedings without a hearing or an opportunity to be heard.[106] In this regard, the limits of *res iudicata* rest on the basic principle that one

[99]Grannis v. Ordean, 234 U.S. 385 (1914), p. 394. See, also: See, e.g.: Roller v. Holly, 176 U.S. 398 (1900).

[100]Ballard v. Hunter, 204 U.S. 241 (1907), p. 255.

[101]Londoner v. Denver, 210 U.S. 373, (1908), p. 386.

[102]Bd. of Regents v. Roth, 408 U.S. 564 (1972), pp. 569–570.

[103]Memphis Light, Gas & Water Div. v. Craft, 436 U.S. 1 (1978), p. 19. But see: Goss v. Lopez, 419 U.S. 565 (1975), pp. 575–576. Holding that "...the length and consequent severity of a deprivation, while another factor to weigh in determining the appropriate form of hearing, 'is not decisive of the basic right' to a hearing of some kind. The Court's view has been that as long as a property deprivation is not de minimis, its gravity is irrelevant to the question whether account must be taken of the Due Process Clause."

[104]Saphire (1978), pp. 161–166.

[105]Dworkin (1967), p. 27.

[106]Richards v. Jefferson County, 517 U.S. 793 (1996), p. 797.

is not bound by a judgment in a litigation in which he is not designated as a party or to which he has not been made a party by service of process."[107] This ability to trump other procedural safeguards, does not mean, at least for the defendant, that due process requires that in every civil case the parties actually have a hearing on the merits. As recognized in *Boddie v. Connecticut*, a State can, for example, enter a default judgment against a defendant who, after adequate notice, fails to make a timely appearance, or who, without justifiable excuse, violates a procedural rule requiring the production of evidence necessary for orderly adjudication.[108]

Under the constitutional requirement, such a hearing in general must be held prior to the deprivation of the protected interest.[109] In this regard, in *Boddie v. Connecticut*, the Supreme Court held that formality and procedural requisites can vary depending upon the importance of the interests involved and the nature of the subsequent proceedings, or even be waived. Notwithstanding, that does not affect the essential requirement that "...an individual be given an opportunity for a hearing *before* he is deprived of any significant property interest, except for extraordinary situations where some valid governmental interest is at stake that justifies postponing the hearing until after the event."[110] Moreover, as said, in some circumstances, the right to a hearing is complied with by providing only the opportunity to allege *ex post facto* against the decision, even in the administrative law arena, as explained in the discussion of *Arnett v. Kennedy* in Chap. 10.[111]

Still, in *U.S. v. James Daniel Good Real Property*, the Supreme Court held that in civil forfeiture cases in the absence of exigent circumstances, the Fifth Amendment prohibits the Government in a civil forfeiture case from seizing real property (but not necessarily personal property[112]) without first affording the owner notice and an opportunity to be heard.[113] Moreover, it held that whether there are extraordinary situations to serve as an exception to the general rule requiring pre-deprivation notice and whether the hearing requires an examination of the competing interests at stake, along with the promptness and adequacy of later proceedings, such an inquiry requires the three-part test we saw in Chap. 10 under *Mathews v. Eldridge*.[114]

A similar strict minimum approach has been argued regarding the notice requirement. As we saw in the previous chapter, the basic doctrine already existed in early Supreme Court cases. In *Pennoyer v. Neff,* the Court held, in cases with out-of-state defendants, that they must be brought within its jurisdiction by service of process

---

[107] Richards v. Jefferson County, 517 U.S. 793 (1996), p. 798. More recently but providing some exception to this general principle: Taylor v. Sturgell, 553 U.S. 880 (2008), pp. 893–895.

[108] Boddie v. Connecticut, 401 U.S. 371 (1971), p. 378.

[109] Cleveland Bd. of Educ. v. Loudermill, 470 U.S. 532 (1985), p. 542.

[110] Boddie v. Connecticut, 401 U.S. 371, (1971), pp. 378–379.

[111] Arnett v. Kennedy, 416 U.S. 134, (1974), 157.

[112] Calero–Toledo v. Pearson Yacht Leasing Co., 416 U.S. 663 (1974).

[113] United States v. James Daniel Good Real Prop., 510 U.S. 43 (1993), p. 46.

[114] United States v. James Daniel Good Real Prop., 510 U.S. 43 (1993), p. 53.

within the State, or by their voluntary appearance.[115] The other relevant case in this regard is n *Mullane v. Cent. Hanover Bank & Trust Co.*, where the Court recognized that the right to be heard has little reality or worth unless the individual is informed that the matter is pending and can choose for himself whether to appear or default, acquiesce or contest.[116]

The notice requirement is linked with the long-standing tradition of forbidding ex parte proceedings, since there are circumstances where a judicial procedure might affect persons who were not present at the litigation. In *Richards v. Jefferson County,* the Court held that to have a hearing or an opportunity to be heard, means a requirement of previous notice to have such an opportunity.[117] In the American legal system, the basic requirements in this regard to conform with the due process clause is that the chosen method is of such nature as to reasonably convey the required information, and it must afford a reasonable time for those interested to make their appearance.[118]

The requirement over states' civil procedures, as established in *Greene v. Lindsey* concerning a tenant eviction proceeding, is that personal service is the general requirement. This method presents the ideal circumstance and has traditionally been deemed necessary in actions styled *in personam.* Nevertheless, the Court recognizes that in many circumstances, in light of history and the practical obstacles to providing personal service in every instance, it has allowed judicial proceedings initiated on the basis of procedures that do not carry with them the same certainty level of personal service. Notwithstanding, the due process clause puts a limit over the chosen method provided, which must be "*reasonably calculated, under all the circumstances, to apprise interested parties of the pendency of the action* and afford them an opportunity to present their objections."[119]

For example, in class actions, members of a class not present as parties to the litigation may be bound by the judgment where parties who are present are entitled to stand in judgment for the latter in fact adequately represent them.[120] In these circumstances, notice as well as adequacy of representation are required.[121] In this regard, the Court decided that before an absent class member's right of action was extinguished, due process requires notice plus an opportunity to be heard and participate in the litigation, and at minimum, an absent plaintiff must be provided with an opportunity to remove himself from the class.[122]

---

[115]Pennoyer v. Neff, 95 U.S. 714, 719 (1879).

[116]Mullane v. Cent. Hanover Bank & Trust Co., 339 U.S. 306 (1950), p. 314.

[117]Richards v. Jefferson County, 517 U.S. 793 (1996), p. 797.

[118]Mullane v. Cent. Hanover Bank & Trust Co., 339 U.S. 306 (1950), pp. 314–315.

[119]Greene v. Lindsey, 456 U.S. 444 (1982), pp. 449–450.

[120]Richards v. Jefferson County, 517 U.S. 793 (1996), pp. 800–801.

[121]Eisen v. Carlisle & Jacquelin, 417 U.S. 156 (1974), p. 176.

[122]Ortiz v. Fibreboard Corp., 527 U.S. 815, (1999), p. 848. Similarly, see: Taylor v. Sturgell, 553 U.S. 880, (2008), p. 900.

In *Armstrong v. Manzo*, the Supreme Court set aside an adoption decree because of the failure of the mother and her successor husband to notify the divorced father of pendency of adoption proceedings, depriving the father of due process of law.[123] By deciding the case, the Supreme Court held: "It is clear that failure to give the petitioner notice of the pending adoption proceedings violated the most rudimentary demands of due process of law. Many controversies have raged about the cryptic and abstract words of the Due Process Clause but there can be no doubt that at a minimum they require that deprivation of life, liberty or property by adjudication be preceded by notice and opportunity for hearing appropriate to the nature of the case."[124]

13.3.2.5 Some Issues Are Best Left to Legislation

Under the checklist model, there is a preference for ex ante regulation of what will be considered as fair treatment via rule-making authority. The most important part is legal design, trying to provide a regulation that is as general and clear as possible. As explained, there is space for flexibility but only if the legislator has provided ex ante for broad categories of cases. The maxim in this regard, is that similar situations demands similar treatment.[125] Therefore, a procedural regulation—let us say a code of civil procedure providing for different procedures, affording different procedural guarantees—is perfectly possible under the checklist approach. The idea is to make the legal certainty it provides available to private actors. By following this model, citizens may know in advance what to expect in a legal procedure and act and plan their activities accordingly.[126] This, in turn, might reduce decision costs on those potential litigants,[127] but also at the end might impact in duration, accuracy, and economic costs of the legal procedure and therefore be attractive for both private and public budgets.

As an expression of these features, both the ECHR and SCOTUS has recognized that in civil matters there is a great deference to civil procedure design by the rule-making authority. In ECHR case law, one of such fields, the regulation of admissibility and assessment of the evidence, is a matter for regulation by the proper authorities.[128] The domestic rules of evidence will be the legal procedure that is due under the right to a fair trial at least in terms of admissibility and assessment of evidence. Similar reasoning may be found regarding domestic Legal Aid schemes. While the right to a fair trial in civil matters in some cases might imply a right to a

[123] Armstrong v. Manzo, 380 U.S. 545 (1965), p. 550.

[124] Armstrong v. Manzo, 380 U.S. 545 (1965), p. 550.

[125] Sunstein (2006), p. 619.

[126] Kennedy (1976), p. 1688.

[127] Sunstein (2006), p. 629.

[128] ECHR, Case of García Ruiz v. Spain, no. 30544/96, Judgment of 21 January 1999, par. 11–15, 28.

lawyer, as explained before, and the ECHR has held that there is no obligation to provide legal aid on every civil case, it is a matter of domestic legislation how to provide for Legal Aid, and any method would suffice as long as it provides enough protection from arbitrariness.[129] Finally, regarding procedural bars such as time limits on the admissibility of appeals, the ECHR had held that these rules are designed to ensure the proper administration of justice and, in particular, legal certainty. The ECHR will only verify whether the interpretation of such procedural rules is compatible with the Convention.[130]

13.4 Final Remarks and Future Lines of Research

After reviewing the data on the national and international jurisdictions, it is clear that civil justice requires its own theory of procedural due process, distinct especially from criminal matters—which today weigh heavily on other subjects—but also probably from administrative law. This theory should tell us what the basic requirements of the right to a fair trial on civil matters are, what we can and cannot sacrifice in designing a civil procedure that correctly distributes the risk of moral harm while remaining accessible to people with complex and simple legal needs. The key of this proposal was to answer that question based on a process-based or on an outcome-based theory. Procedural fairness requires finding the balance between access to justice and due process. No matter if it is perceived as more respectful treatment befitting the dignity of the individual, or as a right to a procedure that correctly distributes the risk of a moral harm, both concepts of a fair procedure presuppose first having access to it.

Access to justice—or the right to a court, I have taken the two concepts as synonymous—[131] entails negative, but also positive obligations on the State, as is recognized in both international jurisdictions. As such, the theory as described in the last chapters might have implications for policy questions from the perspective of the distribution of resources, and social justice, while protecting due process by not stripping it of its character as a right. As such, considerations on access to justice not only have a social value—which they surely have—but ensuring that a judicial procedure is accessible and useful should also be a requirement of procedural

[129] ECHR, Case of Del Sol v. France, no. 46800/99, Judgment of 26 February 2002, par. 20–26.

[130] ECHR, Case of Cañete de Goñi v. Spain, no. 55782/00, Judgment of 15 October 2002, par. 36; ECHR, Case of Běleš and Others v. The Czech Republic, no. 47273/99, Judgment of 12 November 2002, par. 60; ECHR, Case of Zvolský and Zvolská v. the Czech Republic, no. 46129/99, Judgment of 12 November 2002, par. 46.

[131] I have argued as well that while access to justice and the right to a court might be conceptually different in strict sense, for practical reasons they might be treated as the same. It does not make any sense to have only a right to file a claim or to "knock at the door of the court" but not been able to sustain and endure the whole proceeding until a final decision and its enforcement. That is why I take both as synonymous and I have argued that the ECHR follow a similar approach.

fairness. For example, this justification explains why in the American legal system small claims procedures are present in the fifty States even though many basic features of the adversarial system are limited or waived. In this regard, the Small Claims Court Act of California, established expressly that "...individual minor civil disputes are of special importance to the parties and of significant social and economic consequence collectively." And, therefore, that "...[I]n order to resolve minor civil disputes expeditiously, inexpensively, and fairly, it is essential to provide a judicial forum accessible to all parties directly involved in resolving these disputes."[132]

To develop this theoretical framework, I showed how profoundly criminal and civil legal procedures differ, differences that I explained by using the State v. Individual and the Individual v. Individual paradigms. As has been recognized by the IACHR and in the American legal system, the seriousness of the loss in an important factor, but I believe using that factor alone does not explain many of the differences between criminal and non-criminal processes that are present even in those jurisdictions. Therefore, the model I described in the previous chapter, using purpose and relative position of the parties as two axes, explains how in different contexts procedural due process requires different things.

After studying these specific jurisdictions, it was clear that none of them represent a pure version of both ideal types described in the first chapter. I explained how the two international courts, and the United States differ on how they understand due process and on its application to criminal and non-criminal matters. Moreover, they differ not only among themselves, but their own understanding of due process varies across different epochs. In criminal matters, the understanding of due process, if not a pure type, is at least evidently closer to the checklist approach compared to the notions of due process in civil matters. Not only from the wording of the express provisions, but as in one way or another the IACHR, the ECHR, and the United States Supreme Court have all recognized more laxity on civil matters.

As such, any of the studied jurisdictions are characteristic of one model nor the other. That is caused by the complexity of due process as I explained in Chap. 1. In that regard, I conclude that at the end of the day due process is a legal principle in Dworkin's sense. While it might be understood to be closer to the checklist approach for some situations or contexts, and in that regard, use strict legal rules to provide a fixed content, originalism as method of interpretation, and other elements pertaining to this model, the fact that it varies across subjects and time proves that it is a legal principle.

Notwithstanding this complexity and the different conception on how to understand procedural due process, all jurisdictions in civil matters—the ECHR and the United States, which I have characterized closer to the flexible ideal, at least in comparison with Chile and the IACHR—all have important similarities. They tend to recognize almost the same minimum protections that I have characterized as the floor provided in the checklist approach: impartiality and independence, prior notice

[132]West's Ann. Cal. C.C.P. § 116.120.

(and protections against *ex parte* proceedings), and the right to a hearing. Moreover, they recognize access to justice—if they do not recognize it expressly, they do so as an inherent element or previous requirement of the other guarantees of due process—and the importance of a *meaningful or effectiveness* criterion that such a right should entail. This is the test I believe should prevail in civil matters. The question is whether beyond the protected minimums a specific procedural guarantee should be afforded; such a decision should take into account whether providing it might effectively deny a party's right to a court. Of course, such a test would require a purposive interpretation by a concrete analysis of the nature and particular circumstances of the case, providing deference for the legislator to express the correct distribution of the moral risk associated to it, and to a possible limitation of a right under a criterion of proportionality.

Barriers of access to justice might arise from circumstances of fact or by legal regulation, and as said, putting the right to a court at the center implies that other procedural guarantees might recede. For example, a broad right to appeal or a mandatory legal representation in practice might impair this right, as analyzed in the context of the ECHR case law but also in the context of the United States where such a requirement does not exist. That is a good example of the flexibility needed, which might require different answers in different contexts, and sometimes simplification of the procedure might be an answer. Looked at from the other side, court fees are usually not a violation *per se* of the guarantee; that depends on the circumstances of the case. In the final analysis, what matters is that such legislative decisions should be based on a concern for the *practical effectiveness* of the right to the court. Particularly relevant in this regard is the case law of the ECHR, which by dividing the application of article 6 into a civil and criminal prong, has been forced to develop a more refined theory on what the right to a court entails and how it interplays with those elements I have considered as the core minimum protections and with other dimensions of the right to a court.

One future research question for an empirical study is whether countries closer to the flexible ideal show better results on access to justice. That would require classifying them according to a set of variables by which they were "ranked" and comparing such results against an access to justice metric such as the one provided by the World Justice Project.[133] By sufficiently identifying such variables and those results, it would even be possible to estimate probabilities of what kind of policy measures would help improve on those rankings.

Another research question—connected to another factor that might explain these differences—is whether judges and/or legislators actually think of access to justice when deciding cases on procedural due process in non-criminal matters. One possible approach to answer this question, is to compare jurisdictions, national or international that have a higher development of theories on horizontal rights, which might lead their courts and legislator in stronger developments of procedural due process on civil matters.

---

[133] Available at: http://data.worldjusticeproject.org/accesstojustice/#/.

At this point, it might seem obvious that I developed this theoretical framework to support a legislative design of procedural regulation in the context of adjudication in a broad sense. That is, where there is a legal dispute between parties who assert a claim of right and participate by reasoned arguments and proof and which require an authoritative solution by an impartial decision-taker.[134]

Notwithstanding, I believe it might be useful in other areas where decisions might affect civil rights such as in the context of ADR. In this regard, since the right to a court is not an absolute right but might be subject to limitations according to a proportionality criterion and also might be renounceable, such mechanisms that might affect a civil right do not necessarily convey the same due process requirements. A main focus of protections, both in the ECHR and in the United States, has been the volition by which parties waive its rights. Moreover, since arbitration might not be clearly distinguishable from adjudication, that might explain why in the United States, for example, protocols have been enacted providing for basic procedural rights in areas such as employment or consumer law where private dispute resolution has displaced public trial greatly.[135]

A proper theory on procedural due process for civil matters should be useful also in administrative law arena. For example, a further elaboration of the scheme based on purpose and imbalance might lead to a clear distinction between decision-making processes that are adjudication from those that are not, clarifying what the requirements are and avoiding confusion with those of a civil trial. As such, if there is no legal procedure in an adjudicative context beyond protection against arbitrariness, the requirements of procedural fairness are not the same as in civil matters, prior to any type of decision by a government agent that might affect a right. But when there is such a context, this framework would allow us to take into consideration the values of the legal process, as many critics of the *Mathews v. Elridge* test have pointed out.

The contribution intended with this project was to provide a normative theory based on empirical grounds. As such, this book is aimed to a broad audience, those interested in theoretical questions in jurisprudence but also those familiar with empirical legal studies and other socio-legal studies. I hope this will trigger debates and research questions on both aspects.

References

Bayles M (1986) Principles for legal procedure. Law Philos 5(1):33–57
Bone R (2010) Procedure, participation, rights. Boston Univ Law Rev 90:1011–1028
Couture (1950) The nature of the judicial process. Tul Law Rev 25(1):1–28
Croley S (2017) Civil justice reconsidered. Toward a less costly, more accessible litigation system. New York University Press, New York

[134] Bayles (1986), pp. 36–39; Fuller (1978), pp. 363–372.
[135] Hensler and Khatam (2018), pp. 395–397.

Dripps D (2018) Due process: a unified understanding. In: Orren K, Compton J (eds) The Cambridge Companion to the United States Constitution. Cambridge University Press, Cambridge, pp 45–71
Dworkin R (1967) The model of rules. Univ Chic Law Rev 35:14–46
Dworkin R (1977) Taking rights seriously. Harvard University Press, Cambridge
Dworkin R (1985) A matter of principle. Harvard University Press, Cambridge
Francioni F (2017) The rights of access to justice under customary international law. In: Francioni F (ed) Access to justice as a human right. Oxford University Press, Oxford, pp 1–55
Friendly H (1975) Some kind of hearing. Univ Pa Law Rev 123:1267–1317
Fuller L (1978) The forms and limits of adjudication. Harv Law Rev 92(2):353–409
Genn H (2010) Judging civil justice. Cambridge University Press, Cambridge
Hensler D, Khatam D (2018) Re-inventing arbitration: how expanding the scope of arbitration is re-shaping its form and blurring the line between private and public adjudication. Nev Law J 18(2):381–426
Hittner D, Weisz K (1990) Federal civil trials delays: a constitutional dilemma? S Tex Law Rev 31: 341–360
Kennedy D (1976) Form and substance in private law adjudication. Harv Law Rev 89(8): 1685–1778
Langer M (2014) The long shadow of the adversarial and inquisitorial categories. In: Dubber M, Hörnle T (eds) The Oxford handbook of criminal law. Oxford University Press, Oxford, pp 887–912
Mashaw J (1976) The Supreme Court's due process calculus for administrative adjudication in Mathews v. Eldridge: three factors in search of a theory of value. Univ Chic Law Rev 44(1): 28–59
Mashaw J (1981) Administrative due process: the quest for a dignitary theory. Boston Univ Law Rev 61(4):885–931
Michelman F (1974) Supreme court and litigation access fees: the right to protect one's rights, Part II. Duke Law J 1974(3):527–570
Palombella G (2021) Access to justice: dynamic, foundational, and generative. Ratio Juris 34(2): 121–138
Redish M, Marshall L (1986) Adjudicatory independence and the values of procedural due process. Yale Law J 95(3):455–503
Rubin E (1984) Due process and the administrative state. Cal Law Rev 72(6):1044–1179
Saphire R (1978) Specifying due process values: toward a more responsive approach to procedural protection. Univ Pa Law Rev 127(1):111–195
Scherer A (2006) Securing a civil right to counsel: the importance of collaborating. N Y Univ Rev Law Soc Change 30(4):675–688
Sullivan T, Massaro T (2013) The arc of due process in American Constitutional Law. Oxford University Press, New York
Summers R (1974) Evaluating and improving legal processes. A plea for "process values". Cornell Law Rev 60(1):1–52
Sunstein C (2006) Two conceptions of procedural fairness. Soc Res 73(2):619–646
Waldron J (2011) The rule of law and the importance of procedure. Nomos 50:3–31
Williams I (2006) Dr. Bonham's case and void statutes. J Leg Hist 27(11):111–128
Yeazell S, Schwartz J (2016) Civil procedure, 9th edn. Aspen Casebook Series, Wolters Kluwer, United States
Zuckerman A (1999) Justice in crisis: comparative dimensions of civil procedure. In: Zuckerman A (ed) Civil justice in crisis. Comparative perspectives of civil procedure. Oxford University Press, Oxford, pp 3–52